CONSUMER REPORTS

BEST TRAVEL DEALS 1997 EDITION

How to Get Big Discounts on Airfares, Hotels, Car Rentals, and More

Ed Perkins with Walt Leonard
and the Editors of
Consumer Reports Travel Letter

Consumer Reports
A Division of Consumers Union
Yonkers, New York

  ISBN: 0-89043-862-5
  ISSN: 1091-6288

Design by Suzette Ruys
Page composition by Jennifer Dixon
First printing, January 1997
This book is printed on recycled paper. ✺
Manufactured in the United States of America

CONTENTS

INTRODUCTION
The travel-buying challenge 1
The 10 best travel deals for 1997 2
The five worst travel deals 5
How to use this book 5
About Consumer Reports
    Travel Letter 6

SOME NUTS AND BOLTS

1. YOUR TRAVEL ABCS
Picking a travel agent 7
Rebating travel agencies 8
Travel clubs 12
Travel off-season? 15
Resources for seniors 16
Singles take a hit 17

2. BUYING PACKAGE TOURS AND CRUISES
A package-tour primer 21
Cruising for discounts 25

3. SPEND YOUR WAY TO FREEBIES?
What's out there 31
Charting your course 34
The dining option 40
Which for you? 42

WINGS AND WHEELS

4. STRATEGIES FOR CUTTING AIRFARES
Recognizing bargains 43

Sale fares: hard to beat 43
Low-fare airlines 45
Check out charters 46
Hubbing reductions 47
Discount tickets 47
Discount coupons 47
Twofers 48
Rebates 48
Status fares 48
Other cost cutters 49
Premium seats at a better price 50
Roomy seats in coach 51
Premium coach/economy 51
Cheap premium class 52
Discounted premium seats 53
Posh frequent-flier seats 53
Mileage upgrades 54
Purchased upgrades 54
Become a VFF member 55
Try a premium charter 56
Watch for twofers 56

5. CONSOLIDATORS FOR DISCOUNT AIRFARES
Who's who 59
What you can save 59
Front-cabin discounts 60
A few annoyances 60
Making your deal 61
Discount ticket directory 62
For travel agents only 70

6. CHARTERS: SOMETIMES GOOD BETS
Any drawbacks? 73
Buying your ticket 74

7. THE SEAT SQUEEZE ALOFT

Yardsticks of comfort 76
Flying in coach/economy 77
Some good news 79
. . . but mostly bad 83
Seat strategy 83
How about Business Class? 85
Figures of merit 85
How they measured up 86

8. FOR SENIORS, YOUTH, AND THE BEREAVED

A bargain for seniors 90
Fares for youngsters 93
Compassionate fares 94
Getting your ticket 95

9. FREE TRIPS FOR FREQUENT FLIERS

How the basic plans compare 98
Figuring your payoff 98
How you earn credit 99
Where you can go 100
How well credit ages 101
Blackouts and limits 102
Upgrades to better seats 104
Finding a seat 106
What's best for you 106

10. LOUNGE CLUBS: AIRPORT OASES

What members get 113
What price tranquillity? 115
Some special features 115
Value for money? 117
A hubber's survival guide 122

11. AIRPORT SHUTTLES: CHEAP AND FAST

How shuttles work 127
Some cautions 128
The price you pay 128
Arranging your trip 129

12. THE CAR-RENTAL GAME

Scouting out bargains 146
Hidden extras 147
Pitfalls and potholes 150

13. RAIL PASSSES: US AND CANADA

Canadian offerings 155
Passes for the US 156

BEST BUYS IN LODGINGS

14. SCOPING OUT HOTEL DEALS

Where the buys are 159
Finding preferred rates 160
Picking a hotel 161

15. HALF-PRICE HOTELS: SAVINGS COAST TO COAST

A closer look 167
The program to pick 168

16. HOTEL BROKERS FOR EASY DISCOUNTS

Arranging the discount 174
Multicity specialists 175
Local brokers 177
Overseas options 178

17. REWARDS FOR FREQUENT HOTEL STAYS

What you spend 180
. . . and what you get 184
Figuring your payoff 185
Just for signing up 190
Which program to join? 190

18. HOTEL DISCOUNTS FOR SENIORS

Come and get it 193
Members only 193
Hotel-chain "clubs" 196

Making your deal. 198

THE SAVVY TRAVELER ABROAD

19. FLYING OVERSEAS

Low-fare airlines. 202
   Icelandair. 202
   LTU 203
   Martinair 205
   Tower. 206
Alternatives 206
Deals on local air trips overseas 207
The fine print 207
Flying around Europe. 208
Excursions in Latin America 209
Australia and the Pacific. 209
Winging it in Asia 209
Deals on one-way flights abroad. 209
Getting tickets abroad. 210

20. FOREIGN LODGINGS FOR LESS

Foreign hotels at half price. 212
How they stacked up 212
A tale of 10 cities. 214
Half of what? 215
Wholesale deals at Asian hotels 216
Any other discounts to be had? 217
List-price bargains 218
Your personal best buy 220
Budget motels. 220

21. SEEING EUROPE: ROAD OR RAIL?

Overseas renters and their deals. 226
Figuring costs. 226
Trying 'em for size. 228
Save with a French lease? 229
Nuisances and extras. 229
Booking and pickup 240
Trains: your best bet for intercity travel. . . 244

Types of pass 246
Large and small. 248
Seniors, couples, youth. 252

22. RAIL PASSES: ASIA AND THE SOUTH PACIFIC

The mechanics of passes. 256
India. 257
Japan 257
Malaysia. 258
Thailand. 259
Australia 259
New Zealand 260

23. THE TRAVEL STRATEGIST

Avoiding trouble abroad 262
Money matters 263
VAT refunds—maybe. 266
Baggage liability 267
When duty calls. 268
Phoning home. 269

24. SHOULD YOU INSURE YOUR TRIP?

Policy types 275
Decoding the coverage 277
How TCI pays off. 281
Which policy for you? 282

25. KEEPING HEALTHY ABROAD

Steps to take before you go. 284
Doctor visits 284
Immunizations 285
Once you arrive. 290
Returning home 296
Packing your medical kit 299

DIRECTORY OF TOLL-FREE RESERVATION NUMBERS

DIRECTORY OF TOLL-FREE RESERVATION
NUMBERS 300

INDEX 305

INTRODUCTION

The 1997 edition of *Consumer Reports Best Travel Deals* is a matchless handbook of down-to-earth information about buying travel services. It names the suppliers that offer the best services and prices, outlines strategies for getting the best deals on just about any travel service, and tells how to avoid ripoffs and scams. Most chapters are based on *Consumer Reports Travel Letter (CRTL)* articles.

This book is about buying travel, not the travel experience itself. It assumes you've already answered the questions ordinary guidebooks address—where to go and what to do when you get there. Here, the focus is on buying the arrangements you'll need, avoiding services you don't need, and recognizing the frauds and deceptions you'll face.

THE TRAVEL-BUYING CHALLENGE

Many of the sales gimmicks in travel differ from those in other markets. Most travel services are perishable: Unsold seats and cabins become worthless as soon as the plane or boat leaves. Inventory can't be carried over and sold later, even at a discount. Any promotional markdowns must somehow be taken before departure—often at the same time that the suppliers are still trying to sell their services at full price.

Various parts of the travel industry deal with perishability in various ways, so no one buying strategy works best in all circumstances. Think of this handbook as a kit of buying tools, each specialized for different situations.

•**Airlines** split their market into two segments. They figure that *business* travel isn't much affected by price changes, so they set fares aimed at businesspeople very high. *Leisure* travel, however, is seen as price-sensitive, so the airlines offer low, promotional fares for vacationers—with restrictions (advance purchase, Saturday-night stayovers, blackout dates) that make them difficult for business travelers to use.

If you can live with the restrictions, promotional airfares are often good deals, especially during a fare war. If not, this book will help you sort out your other options—among them, discount tickets from consolidators, other back-door deals, and trips on low-fare airlines. It also examines the implications of frequent-flier programs on your choices.

- **Hotels** follow the airlines' pattern, with separate deals for business and leisure travelers and relatively high list prices that are often selectively discounted. The hotels' own promotional deals aren't always your best choice; this book will guide you to some low-profile sources of bigger discounts.
- **Car-rental companies,** too, offer lower rates to leisure travelers than to business travelers. As their main ploy, they offer vacationers savings on weekend rentals or longer rentals that encompass a weekend, times when business travelers want to be home.

But the car-rental companies have a unique pricing quirk. They often advertise attractive daily or weekly rates, then try to squeeze you for more money when you show up at the counter—sometimes by adding mandatory extras, sometimes by trying to con you into buying add-ons that you don't really need. This book alerts you to those extra charges and tells how to avoid or minimize them.

- **Other travel services,** too, have their own peculiar pricing and promotional approaches. This handbook also sets forth strategies for buying services as diverse as cruises, tours, restaurant meals, phone calls, and currency exchange.

THE 10 BEST TRAVEL DEALS FOR 1997

To make the overall Top 10 list, a travel service must be available broadly to just about anyone who wants to travel, not to just a segment of the market, such as seniors or students.

1. **Sale-priced air tickets.** For several years, the big US airlines have periodically cut the prices of their cheapest Coach excursion tickets by as much as 50%. Typically, the purchase "window" for such sales is only a week or so, but sales cover travel for as long as three months. During those sales, the airlines' asking prices are lower than any discount fare you're likely to find.

As recently as late 1996, a sale price for a transcontinental round-trip was available for about $400. If you can accept the restrictions—typically, a Saturday-night stay and up to 21-day advance purchase—you'd be hard-pressed to find a better travel deal anywhere. We look for continued airfare sales through 1997.

2. **Low-fare airlines.** Wherever they fly, Southwest and its smaller imitators bring fares down. The US Dept of Transportation estimates that, in 1995, low-fare lines saved consumers nearly $6 billion, compared to what they'd have paid in the absence of low-fare competition. In general, if a low-fare line flies where you're going, its fares will be attractive throughout the year, not just during sales. Moreover, you'll usually face fewer restrictions: Most low-fare lines don't require that you buy a round trip to

get the lowest rate, so there's no minimum stay, and some don't impose an advance-purchase requirement, either.

Unfortunately, the ValuJet crash temporarily slowed the dramatic growth of many low-fare lines, due mainly to the indiscriminate and largely unwarranted bashing of their safety. We expect that most of those lines will recover and continue to grow in 1997.

3. **Consolidator airfares.** Discount tickets from consolidators will continue to be among the best air-travel buys. According to survey data, *CRTL* readers frequently save as much as $200 per ticket, compared with the cheapest advertised fares on the major airlines. The best deals have traditionally been to Europe in the summer, when published fares are high, and to Asia or South America any time of the year.

A minority of travelers continues to report problems with consolidators—especially slow delivery of tickets and failure to make timely reservations. We recommend that you deal only with discount agencies in or near your home city, so that you can visit the office personally if a problem arises. Also, buy with a charge card so that you can request a chargeback if you don't get your tickets.

4. **Very-Frequent-Flier status.** Some of the most substantial benefits of a frequent-flier plan don't kick in until you've reached at least the first very-frequent-flier plateau in a major airline's program. Typically, you have to log 25,000 miles each year to attain and maintain that status—bonus miles, charge-card miles, and partner miles don't count. Once you get there, you receive additional bonus miles for each flight. More importantly (to many travelers), you can use the inexpensive purchased upgrade coupons with a Coach excursion ticket, not just a full-fare ticket (as is the case for other frequent fliers). See chapter 9 for more information.

5. **Rail passes in Europe and Japan.** Trains are an efficient and comfortable way to travel around within Europe, and rail passes are a good way to cut the costs of that rail travel. The best pass deals are for those that cover individual countries or small national groups such as Benelux and Scandinavia. Although a Eurailpass covers far more territory, it has become quite expensive over the last few years. You needn't choose between taking the train and driving, either. Several countries offer passes that combine a few days of rail travel with a few additional days of a rented car.

Japan's rail pass is also attractive. A one-week pass costs about the same as one round-trip ticket between Tokyo and Kyoto. Since that's a trip you're likely to take, in any case, the extra travel is pure gravy. See chapter 22 for more information.

6. **Weekly car rental.** Despite all the talk about big rate increases, you can still rent a compact car in most of the US for less than $150 a week. Similar rental fares are also applicable in at least some European countries, including Germany, Switzerland, and the

UK. As long as you don't fall for the overpriced extras the rental companies try to foist on you, a rental car can be a very inexpensive way to tour once you've arrived in your destination area. See chapter 12 for more information.

7. **Hotel brokers.** By far the easiest way to get a big discount on a hotel room is to call a hotel broker. They're the "outlet stores" of the hotel business, often cutting prices by as much as 50%. You needn't join any program, carry any special ID, or call around to find which hotel (if any) will give you a break on some sort of program. Instead, just call one office, which will give you a rundown of all the deals it has for the time when you'll need a room.

The biggest problem with brokers is that most of them cover only a few of the biggest US cities and some cover only one or two. Even the biggest include deals in only a few dozen cities, and even with those you may not find anything outside the central business district. Still, for a downtown hotel, they're hard to beat. See chapter 16 for more information.

8. **US budget motels.** As we've said for several years now, the US budget motel is the world's best accommodations buy. For $30–50 a night, depending on location, you get a good-size room, usually with two double or queen-size beds, good heating/air-conditioning, a modern bath, and color TV. Usually, you'll also find a swimming pool and other amenities.

The only discount you're likely to find is a modest (10% or so) reduction for seniors and for members of AAA or a few other touring clubs. But with regular rates as low as they are, who needs discounts? See chapter 18 for more information.

9. **Promotional hotel rates in Europe.** Over the past few years, several big European hotel chains have offered special rates that help American travelers beat the weak dollar. At different times of the year—typically including the peak summer travel season—such chains as Inter-Continental, Holiday Inn, Mount Charlotte–Thistle, and Sofitel have cut rates as much as 50% for travelers from the US and Canada. Typically, you must reserve in advance, and you may have to prepay in US dollars. The deals may also be tied into some other organization (such as AARP) or to one of the big charge cards.

Obviously, at press time, we can't promise that those promotions will be repeated this summer. However, given what happened in 1995 and 1996, we recommend you keep an eye out for similar promotions this year. See chapter 20 for more information.

10. **Discount-rate cruises.** While hotel and resort rates have been in a steady climb, the average daily cost of cruising has remained fairly steady. Moreover, over the past few years, a continued excess of supply over demand has led to extensive discounting. Last year, mass-market lines were routinely selling cabin space for less than $200 a day, per couple, with a few sale rates actually dipping under the $100 mark. Given that cabin rates include accom-

modations, meals, entertainment, and local transportation, cruising has become a real bargain.

For 1997, the big cruise lines will continue to add new ships—and new cabins—at rates that will probably outstrip growth. As a result, we expect that discounting will continue —and cruising will therefore remain a good value. As in the past, the best rates will be for either very early or very late bookings. See chapter 2 for more information.

THE FIVE WORST TRAVEL DEALS

(As usual, the worst travel buys you'll find this year are services at inflated list prices but also are widely sold at substantial reductions—or those that you don't need at all.)

1. **Full-fare Coach/Economy air tickets.** Nothing is a worse buy than paying top dollar for a very bad product.
2. **Rack rate at an expensive hotel.** When daily ("rack") rates get into the $300 range, it's time to ask for a big discount—or to go somewhere else.
3. **Rental-car collision insurance.** Not only is it priced at three to four times its real value, but also you probably don't need it. Rely on your auto insurance or a charge card that provides that coverage.
4. **A new timeshare.** Why pay an up-front developer's markup as high as 50% when you can buy a resale unit for a fraction of the cost?
5. **Designer luggage.** Overpaying is bad enough; why also, in effect, put a "steal me" sign on your personal belongings?

HOW TO USE THIS BOOK

Best Travel Deals is organized for use by readers ranging from beginners to seasoned travelers:

- •For a grounding in the travel industry and how to shop it, consider reading the whole book first, then returning to descriptions of travel services you use the most.
- •For experienced travel shoppers, this book will serve as a good reference source.
- •If you prefer to turn all planning over to a travel agent, you can still benefit by reading selected portions. You'll work more efficiently and effectively with your agent if you know as much as possible about the travel services in which you are most interested.
- •For now-and-again travelers, there are many money-saving trip strategies.

DIVISIONS BY SUBJECT. This book is arranged in four parts, most of them describing a *type* of travel service. Most chapters deal mainly with the intricacies of those services in the United States and Canada: Travelers going overseas will find similar information in *The Savvy Traveler Abroad* section.

Best Travel Deals begins with a range of discount ideas and information sources—everything from travel agencies that rebate part of their commissions to deals for senior citizens and single travelers. Other sections are devoted to the specifics of saving money on air and land travel and on lodgings. Also included is a *Directory of Toll-Free Reservation Numbers* for major travel-service providers.

If you can't find what you're looking

for by scanning the names of the parts and chapters in the contents, check the index.

CHAPTER CONTENTS. Phone numbers and addresses for companies and resources mentioned in the text or in tables are provided in each chapter or in *Where to Find It* at the end of the chapter, along with information on the credit cards or charge cards each provider accepts:

AE = American Express
CB = Carte Blanche
DC = Diners Club
Disc = Discover Card
MC= MasterCard
V = Visa

HOW UP-TO-DATE? All addresses and phone numbers of the travel-service providers have been checked and rechecked. Chapters are marked to show the source of the material, and all tables show when the data were collected.

At press time, the 10% tax on domestic airline tickets was scheduled to expire at the end of 1996. In all probability, Congress will again extend the tax for 1997, but the exact form hasn't yet been determined. Several of the giant airlines have suggested a new formula that would effectively reduce the percentage tax on the expensive tickets used by business travelers and increase the percentage tax on the cheaper tickets most consumers use—those on low-fare lines and on big lines at Coach-excursion fares. Industry experts expect that the old 10% formula will simply be extended. But if the giant lines get their way, travelers on low-fare tickets will face a bigger hike.

ABOUT CONSUMER REPORTS TRAVEL LETTER

Consumer Reports Travel Letter (CRTL) is a monthly newsletter designed to help you track down the best travel values. It presents strategies for finding the best airfares, hotel rates, and car-rental rates and offers inside travel information with specific recommendations, warnings about frauds and scams, ways to avoid hassles, and lots of other timely guidance for travelers. Ed Perkins has been the editor of *CRTL* since its launching in May 1985. Subscriptions are $39 for one year and $59 for two years. To subscribe, call 800-234-1970 or write to *Consumer Reports Travel Letter* Subscription Department, P.O. Box 53629, Boulder, CO 80322-3629.

SOME NUTS AND BOLTS

YOUR TRAVEL ABCs

Why pay list price? In this book, we'll introduce you to important discount sources—consolidators, travel clubs, half-price and preferred-rate hotel programs, and cruise discounters.

But first, let's look at how you can find a good travel agent and whether bargain-conscious shoppers should use off-season and bartered-travel trip strategies. We'll also take a look at senior and single travelers and give you some tips on tipping. (*Where to Find It*, pages 18–20, lists detailed information about the companies mentioned in the chapter.)

PICKING A TRAVEL AGENT
To help loyal customers cut costs, a good travel agent will be willing and able to find or arrange for:
- **Discount airline tickets,** secured from wholesale brokers—known as consolidators—and sold to travelers at substantially lower prices than the airlines ask. (See chapter 5.)
- **Discount hotel accommodations,**

obtained through consolidators, tour operators, travel-agency consortiums, and other sources. (See the section later in this book called *Best Buys in Lodgings*—chapters 14–18—and chapter 20.)
- **Discount cruises and package tours,** obtained either directly from the tour and cruise operators or from discount clearinghouses. (See chapter 2.)
- **Reallocation of airline seats** from expensive to inexpensive categories and selective waiver of restrictions on ticket purchase. Those rule-bending adjustments are offered in various ways by some airlines to some travel agencies.

Not every agency can take advantage of all those tools. Large agencies in major metropolitan centers generally have the broadest access. Some discounts are more readily available to agencies that specialize in business travel. Some—especially airline seat reallocation and waiver of restrictions—are often limited to certain markets or applied only in limited circumstances.

WHAT CREDENTIALS MATTER?
Many of the certificates on an agency's wall may merely indicate membership in trade organizations. But one credential has real meaning: a certificate recognizing a certified travel counselor, awarded by the Institute of Certified Travel Agents (ICTA). It attests to five years of professional experience as well as to the completion of a five-part course covering sources of information beyond those found in the computer-reservation systems used by travel agencies.

PAY BY THE HOUR? You may be better off when the agent acts as your consultant. You pay the agent a per-hour fee for services; the agent arranges all services at the lowest available net price and rebates all commissions. That system removes the inherent agency conflict between maximum income and client service. But very few agencies work that way.

PAY A FEE? Two years ago, the main US domestic airlines imposed a cap on commissions paid to travel agencies. To offset the loss of revenue, many agencies started adding a modest fee—up to $25 or so—to issue an airline ticket.

REBATING TRAVEL AGENCIES

These agencies refund about half (or a bit more) of their commission: Your discount is typically 4–5% of the list price (but it can run higher on some purchases). On many travel purchases, that doesn't add up to much. You're often better off paying full commission to an agency, especially one that's adept at finding the best discounts that suppliers offer. But on some services—especially those that aren't usually discounted—a small rebate is the best you're likely to do.

Rebating agencies are no-frills operations. They expect you to do your own homework—checking for the best airfare, cruise, or tour deal and deciding exactly what you want to buy. Then they'll make reservations and (where required) issue tickets or vouchers.

Here are six rebaters that serve consumers throughout the country; they typify what's available.

- **All-American Travel Club (AATC),** Naples FL. Membership club, annual dues $29.95 (deducted from first rebate) includes bimonthly newsletter.

  On airline tickets, cruises, and package tours costing $500 or more the rebate is 10%, less a fee of $24.95 per ticket. On cheaper tickets, the rebate is a flat 5%, with no fee. Travelers pay list price; a rebate check is sent along with the travel documents. Rebates are not offered on hotel or car-rental bookings, but the agency can arrange discounted hotel rates through a large preferred-rate program. Hotel and car-rental bookings also earn points toward travel awards arranged by the club. Members can make their own reservations or have AATC make them.

- **Pennsylvania Travel,** Paoli PA. Stand-alone agency; no membership fee.

  Clients receive a rebate of the full commission, less a fee of $35 (for transactions under $700), $50 ($700–$1499), $100 ($1500–$3999), $150

($4000–$5999), $200 ($6000–$7999), $250 ($8000–$9999), $300 ($10,000–$12,499), or $350 ($12,500–$14,999); fees on transactions larger than $15,000 are $50 for each $2500. The fee is based on the total transaction, not the price of a single ticket. Up to four people traveling together would pay just one $35 fee for their tickets, as long as they totaled less than $700.

Clients usually make their own airline reservations. The agency will do that for you if you call in with your specific requirements: travel dates and times, and the airline, cruise line, hotel, or other supplier you prefer.

On most purchases, if you pay by check you pay just the net cost, deducting the rebate from your initial payment. But you initially pay full price for car rentals and hotel accommodations; rebate checks are mailed after the agency receives the supplier's commission. If you use a charge card, the full price is billed to your card; you receive a rebate check four to six weeks after completion of your trip. There's usually a fee of $25 per person for cancellations; ticket reissue fees vary.

- **PriceCostco Extra Travel,** San Diego. Rebates currently offered to Price Club or Costco members. No fee beyond membership in the warehouse-discount chain.

The rebate is 5–10% off select cruises. The rebate is taken off the price of the cruise at time of purchase. PriceCostco Travel also offers members substantial savings on car rentals, hotels, and vacation packages. For these services, members call the toll-free number for the company of their choice and make a reservation using the PriceCostco ID number with Dollar, Alamo, Avis, Red Lion Hotels, Days Inn, Howard Johnson, Ramada, La Quinta, and Runaway Vacations for packages to Hawaii and Mexico.

- **Sam's Travel Club,** Rogers AR. Program information is available at 450 Sam's Club locations, nationwide. No fee beyond membership in the warehouse-discount chain.

For cruises and package tours, members receive a merchandise gift certificate rebate of 10% on cruises and 5% on tours on the first booking and 12% on subsequent cruise bookings only. Members receive discounted rates (through a directory) rather than rebates on hotel accommodations and rental cars; hotels are discounted up to 50%. At this writing, Sam's Travel Club does not sell air tickets.

Travelers reserve cruises by a toll-free call through one central travel office. Hotels and rental cars are reserved directly with the supplier. Clients pay full cruise price. Charge-card acceptance depends on the cruise line. Rebates are in the form of merchandise certificates for future purchases at Sam's Club. Travelers pay the net (discounted) price directly to hotels and car-rental companies; charge card acceptance depends on the supplier.

- **The Smart Traveller,** Coconut Grove

FL. Stand-alone agency; no membership fee.

The basic rebate on international airline tickets, scheduled and charter, is 4–25% (a bit more on some airlines). The agency also sells consolidator tickets at a net price that represents a reduction of up to 25% of the advertised fare.

On cruises and package tours, the rebate is about 6–7%, even on bookings made at a cruise line's own discounted early-bird rate. (See chapter 2.) Smart Traveller provides brochures and mentions any known specials for your travel period.

Hotel rooms are often arranged through wholesalers and a preferred-

SIZING UP YOUR AGENT

Pick a travel agency as carefully as you would an investment firm: Do you need a travel adviser or merely an efficient order-processor? Identify 5 to 10 services that you consider critical. Get recommendations from friends and associates. Set up appointments with agency managers to assess how well each agency measures up on the services you require. Consider the following areas:

KNOW-HOW
- Does the staff have recent personal experience with the destinations and carriers you're considering in the price range and class you usually use?
- Is the agency knowledgeable about no-fee and two-signature traveler's checks, currency exchange, visa service, insurance, and so on, and does it know where you can conveniently get those services?
- Does the agency have frequent-flier program brochures from all major airlines and current copies of at least one independent frequent-flier newsletter?

TRIP PLANNING
- Does the agency have an adequate guidebook and video library and a wide selection of brochures available for loan? It should at least have books from one of these annual series: the *Birnbaum Travel Guides,* the *Michelin Red* or *Green Guides,* either *Frommer's Budget Travel Guides* or the *Let's Go Budget Guides,* *Fodor's Travel Guides,* and good US and world atlases.
- Does the agency have good industry resources for its own use and for browsing by clients? (It should have print copies of both the domestic and international *Official Airline Guide* editions; the *Thomas Cook* worldwide rail and shipping guides; *Star Service,* the leading trade source for evaluating hotels and cruises; and *Specialty Travel Index,* the semiannual directory of special-interest tours.)
- Do all (or at least most) agents in the office have an Apollo, Worldspan, Sabre, or System One terminal at their desks and are they being used?
- Can agents cite recent experiences of their clients with destinations, carriers, and tours?

rate program; the rebate is about 4%, in addition to the wholesale or preferred-rate reduction. The rebate on car rentals is about 4–5%.

Clients generally make their own airline reservations (other than for complicated itineraries), but the agency makes reservations for cruises, tours, and air trips on consolidator tickets. You pay just the net cost if you pay by check, deducting the discount from your initial payment. Rebates on charge-card purchases are by check, mailed after you finish your trip. You initially pay full price for car rentals, cruises, tour packages, and lodgings; rebate checks are mailed when the agency receives the

PERSISTENCE
- How effectively do the agents work with their clients? Probably the best test is to ask for—and check—a few client references.
- Will the agency (or individual agent) shop for the best deal? Or does it have a financial incentive to book clients with a specific airline, hotel chain, cruise line, tour company, or car-rental company?
- Does the agency routinely go beyond the first answer served up by the computer —or even go outside the computer system to find the lowest airfare?
- Is the agency willing to book hotels that aren't in the computer-reservation system?
- Does the agency belong to a consortium or hotel-booking service offering preferred corporate hotel rates in major US and foreign cities?
- Does the agency have an arrangement with a consolidator to supply discount tickets?
- Does the agency regularly follow up on clients' problems?
- Does the agency maintain client files, and are they conveniently available through a computer?
- Does the agency accept the charge cards you prefer to use for airline tickets, hotel accommodations, cruises, tours, and other travel services?

AMENITIES
- How convenient is the agency's location? Are there arrangements for parking?
- Does the agency offer 24-hour, 7-day-a-week phone service?
- Do the agents put incoming calls on hold when meeting an in-office client?
- How does the agency normally deliver tickets ordered by phone—and how fast can it do so in an emergency?
- Does the agency offer record-keeping services?
- Does the agency have branch or affiliated offices in other cities that can assist you with trip changes?

supplier's commission check. There's usually no fee for changes or refunds beyond any penalties charged by an airline or cruise company.

• **Travel Avenue,** Chicago. Stand-alone agency; no membership fee.

Rebates are offered only on transactions totaling $300 or more. The rebate on domestic air tickets is 7% or more (depending on airline). For transactions over $500, there is a $20 fee for one traveler (domestic flights only); $25 for two travelers on the same itinerary; or $35 for three or four travelers on the same itinerary. The rebate on international air tickets is 5–18% (depending on airline), less $25 for one traveler, $35 for two, or $45 for three. Charter and consolidator tickets are sold at a net price. The rebate on cruises is 7–20%, less $25 per passenger. Rebates on hotels and car rentals are 5%; the agency offers special rates in addition to rebates.

You needn't make your own reservations before calling Travel Avenue. But if you don't, you should know precisely when, how, and where you're going. A *Resfax* service lets you make reservations or request the best available fare by fax while avoiding the complex voice-mail trappings of the agency's regular reservations lines. You use a form provided by the agency or your own.

On most purchases, you pay the list price (by certified check, money order, or charge card) and receive a rebate check along with your tickets. Rebates for hotel rooms and car rentals are sent after you complete your trip. The agency charges no cancellation fees beyond those established by suppliers.

OTHER REBATERS. Some full-service travel agencies rebate part of their commission (usually well under 5%) to large business clients. Employees of those clients may be able to take advantage of those rebates for personal travel.

Hundreds of banks package travel-agency services (including rebates) with their *MasterCard* and *Visa* cards or other customer services. Some include that service with their ordinary cards or service packages; others limit it to *Gold* versions.

Several rebating agencies now maintain sites on the Internet, where travelers can check on the specific discounts offered and buy tickets either by E-mail or by phone.

TRAVEL CLUBS

Clubs were once just about the only way to save on travel. No longer: You can usually match or beat their best deals by finding a discount cruise agency for cruises, a consolidator for air tickets, a preferred-rate or half-price hotel program (see chapters 2, 5, 14, and 16, respectively), and a rebating agency for when you have to pay list price (see pages 8–12). But you have to pay, in any case, for a half-price hotel program, a discount condo-rental program, dining discounts, and roadside service. So despite its dues, a club that offers those services can be a good deal.

• Five oil-company clubs—Amoco, BP, Chevron (*Gold*), Gulf, and Shell—plus Road America and TravelAlert offered all four of those key services, we found when we checked for a report in 1995.

• If you prefer to use the American Automobile Assn for roadside services, note that Allstate, Encore, National, and Texaco give you the other three key services.

• For features you can't easily get through regular discount agencies, we liked Hideaways (for its condo/villa program), Travel World Leisure (for its barter deals), and American Golf, Golf Access, and Hale Irwin's (for golfing deals).

At the time of our report, club dues ranged from just under $22 a year to a stiff $144 (for Players Club, slanted to high-rollers). Clubs noted as *national* in *Where to Find It*, at the end of this chapter, cater to a broad audience; they offer the features that most readers probably want. But if your vacations center on golf, gambling, or shopping, check out the players that target your market niche. If you usually travel by car, a club that's slanted to drivers could turn out to be a good bet.

Among the deals the clubs offer:

• **Hotel discounts.** Most clubs provide access to a large half-price hotel program, through which you can get 50% off the regular price at participating hotels whenever they expect to be less than about 80% full. ITC-50 runs many of the clubs, so many feature the ITC-50 hotel program.

You can sometimes buy into a half-price program more cheaply through a club than directly from the program's sponsor. Quest's stand-alone retail price is $99 a year, for example, but it was included in the $21.97 annual cost of the National Travel Club (and in the higher dues of a few others).

A few clubs offer preferred hotel rates, either in addition to or in place of a half-price program. Typically, preferred rates are 10–40% off rack (regular) rates; you book your room through the club or an affiliated travel agency. The advantage over half-price discounts is that preferred rates usually remain available until a hotel is fully booked, rather than just until the occupancy hits 80%.

The hotel discounts that several clubs claim to provide turn out to amount to only a trivial 10% or so. Just about any organization can arrange 10% hotel discounts, just by requiring participants to bypass travel agencies and deal directly with each hotel. In effect, the hotels rebate the 10% agency commission to the customer.

Anyone serious about keeping travel costs down should have access to a half-price program, a preferred-rate program, or both. Most of the clubs provide that access. Of course, there are other ways to go. For instance, you can buy one of the several Entertainment Publications directories; those offer half-price discounts at a large number of hotels in the US, Canada, and Europe (see chapters 15 and 20). You needn't join a club to get access to preferred rates. Any competent travel agency can arrange those at no fee to you.

• **Condo/villa rentals.** Several clubs feature vacation rentals, condos, "villas," and resorts in addition to or in place of regular hotels and motels. If you're interested, look first at Hideaways, which publishes an especially attractive catalog of options.

• **Car-rental discounts.** Almost all the clubs claimed to provide modest car-rental discounts, but most give you certificates with so many conditions that they're not worth much. Moreover, such discounts are readily available elsewhere.

• **Roadside services.** Clubs oriented to motorists offer roadside assistance or automobile-towing if members break down on the highway. Anyone who drives extensively should belong to a program offering roadside service. If it offers additional benefits, so much the better.

• **Commission rebates.** Several clubs share with you some of the standard agency commission on travel services bought through the club or an affiliated travel agency. Typically, you'll save about 5% of the total price (see *Rebating Travel Agencies* on page 8). But again, you needn't belong to a club to get a modest rebate. Any number of agencies are happy to share part of their commission with you without your having to pay club dues.

• **Package-tour and cruise discounts.** More than half the clubs offer dis-

counts on package tours and cruises (a few offer last-minute deals, too). But so do thousands of full-service, discount, and cruise-only travel agencies. Our spot-checks indicate that the clubs don't do any better than other discounters.

• **Airfare discounts.** Several clubs claimed to offer discount airfares. But we found only three that had either negotiated reduced airfares for their members or sold discount (consolidator) tickets: Moment's Notice, Players Club, and The Travel Club. The others' "discount" claims were based on their rebating operations, described above.

• **Dining discounts.** A dining program is a built-in feature of the ITC-50 hotel program that many clubs offer, and a few others provide a comparable program. The discounts are usually a mix of percent-off (25% off a total check, up to 50% off a single item) and two-for-one deals.

• **Golf.** Three clubs target golfers with programs centered on nationwide golfing deals—typically reductions on greens fees, cart fees, and pro-shop prices at participating courses. Over the course of a year, traveling golfers will probably save far more than the annual club fee.

• **Other services.** Some clubs promote a laundry list of additional benefits, from merchandise discounts to reduced-rate car washes, movie admissions, or film processing. Many also include minor insurance features. Those extras aren't worth much. And local discount retailers are often competitive with club discount prices. The extras aren't a reason to join a club, but if you join for a more important reason, you may find them useful occasionally.

TRAVEL OFF-SEASON?

Many of the world's vacationers want to travel in the same few months. As a result, airfares and hotel rates tend to rise and fall with the seasons. If you can schedule your travel at times when most visitors are at home, you can often enjoy substantially lower prices and less crowding than in peak touring season.

BY AIR. Intercontinental routes linking the United States with Asia, Europe, South America, and the South Pacific have at least two seasonal price levels, usually called High and Low. On all those routes, seasonal changes are limited to Economy Excursion fares. Some routes have only one seasonal fluctuation each year. Others may have several.

Several US–Europe and US–South Pacific fares have an intermediate, "shoulder" level. Shoulder fares usually cover a period of several weeks between the other two seasons.

In most instances, the round-trip fare you pay is determined by the date on which you start your trip. The return can be at any time permitted by the ticket's length-of-stay restrictions. In a few cases, however, the price of the round-trip varies by the date of your return flight as well.

Fares within North America are generally not called seasonal, but they do often vary through seasonal promotions. Airlines also adjust the number of seats assigned to various price categories to change their yield without changing advertised fare levels. And some low fares can be blacked out during periods of highest demand. (On many routes, fares vary by hour, day, or week.)

BY RAIL. Amtrak, the private US intercity rail passenger system, uses multiple rates for each route in its system; some of them vary seasonally. VIA Rail, Canada's passenger rail system, also offers off-peak rates on many of its routes.

BY RENTED CAR. In some countries, several of the major car-rental companies adjust rates seasonally. They also offer special US promotions during slow seasons.

ROOMS. Hotel prices are seasonally adjusted in most resort areas and in some major cities. Seasonal price changes are common in the Caribbean, the main European beach destinations (French and Italian rivieras, Greek islands, Spanish coasts), Hong Kong (most big tourist hotels), the major South American vacation areas (Bariloche, Rio), the prime US winter vacation areas (Arizona, Florida and adjacent states, and Hawaii), and in many US summer-vacation areas (lakes, mountains, seacoasts). Low-season rates may be less than half the peak rates.

Seasonal adjustments in hotel rates vary greatly according to destination. Some areas have only one high and one low season a year, while others have several. (But special local festivals or conventions always push up rates.)

Hotels in major cities rarely adjust their prices by season, but some manage to make seasonal adjustments by promoting special rates or airline packages. Tour operators often offer reduced-rate promotions at major European city hotels in July and August, when most business activity grinds to a halt.

Seasonal variations can be found through discount sources, but there are no hard-and-fast rules. Some half-price coupon and club rates are available only during off-season. Preferred rates, on the other hand, are apt to remain constant throughout the year (see chapter 14).

HIGH-VALUE SEASONS. In many destinations, spring and fall shoulder seasons provide the best mix of weather and cost. Those seasons can be relatively short (Quebec) or quite long (Greek islands). In Ft Lauderdale, moderate weather and low rates overlap for only a few weeks in early December. The low costs and mild climate make Australia's winter (our summer) a good time to visit.

Low-season travel provides benefits that often go beyond lower prices and good weather. Major tourist areas that may be mobbed in high season are uncrowded and far more accessible. You can even enjoy weather-dependent activities, with reasonable luck, in the shoulder season. But check guidebooks or call tourist offices before you schedule a trip. In some places, there are so few off-season visitors that key attractions and visitor services may be closed or may operate only on reduced hours.

RESOURCES FOR SENIORS

Travelers who reach their fiftieth birthday can join the American Assn of Retired Persons (AARP). It costs only $8 per year (including free membership for a spouse) and brings many benefits, including some discounts on hotel and car rentals.

Currently, a number of big hotel chains participate, giving discounts of 10–50% to AARP members. (See chapter 18.) Several car-rental companies and one bus-tour firm participate as well. Other firms also give discounts to AARP members, even though they have no contractual arrangement with AARP.

Other seniors' organizations also offer travel benefits, including discounts, to their members. Examples include Catholic Golden Age, Mature Outlook (a travel club—see page 17), Natl Alliance of Senior Citizens, National Assn of Retired Federal Employees, and United Airlines' Silver Wings Club. The smart policy is to list the organizations you belong to when you make your airline, hotel, or car-rental reservation, and ask if you're eligible for any deals.

Consumer Reports Travel Letter (CRTL) regularly covers senior discounts and travel tips. Other resources include specialized travel agencies and clubs. Here are five that *CRTL* has examined:

- **Golden Age Travellers Club.** For an annual fee of $10 per person, $15 per couple, travelers over age 50 get a quarterly newsletter. The club also arranges discount cruises and tours, including last-minute offerings and same-sex roommate matching.

- **Grand Circle Travel.** This agency has served the over-50 age group for nearly 40 years with land tours, cruises, and roommate matching.
- **Grandtravel.** A tour company specializing in escorted tours for grandparents traveling with their grandchildren.
- **Mature Outlook.** A Sears travel and discount club for the over-50 crowd. An annual $19.95 fee enrolls member and spouse. Benefits include merchandise discounts, half-price hotel discounts up to 50%, and restaurant and car-rental discounts.
- **Saga Holidays.** Packages for travelers over 50. Also offers same-sex matching and guaranteed single shared programs.

SINGLES TAKE A HIT

Traveling solo can be expensive. Anyone who's read a travel brochure knows about the high extra charge a single traveler on a package tour or cruise must pay for sole occupancy of a double hotel room or cabin. The single supplement typically runs some 25–75% of the "land" portion of a tour or cruise —sometimes almost 100%. Such outrageous surcharges are tough, but not impossible, to beat.

The travel industry aggressively courts singles. But when you take a closer look, you find that most tours and cruises promoted for singles really aren't aimed at people who want to travel alone for reasons of privacy or flexibility. Instead, the tour operators are usually offering a matching service: They'll find some other single to share accommodations and costs with you. (See *Where to Find It*, pages 18–20, for some examples.)

If you really want a room or cabin to yourself, not a traveler's blind date, you do have some choices:

- **Cruises.** Solo cruisers are a bit better off than solo package-tour travelers. Most cruise ships have some single-berth cabins (though they often cost as much as a bottom-of-the-line double cabin with the single supplement added). Cruise lines sometimes offer promotional rates for single occupancy.

  Some cruise lines reduce or eliminate the single supplement for last-minute single-occupancy bookings on cruises that aren't filled. Many are sold through travel clubs and discount cruise brokers (see chapter 2).

- **Package tours.** Conventional sightseeing or resort tours that target travelers who don't want to share are few and far between. Your best bet if you're up to the physical demands is an adventure tour.

Those meager options aside, your best bet is to travel independently, not on a package tour. Arrange your own single-rate hotel accommodations. Several of the business-oriented preferred-rate hotel programs specialize in single-rate hotel discounts (see chapter 16). In many parts of the world, older hotels often have some small single rooms at rates well below the double rate. And solo travelers can save by traveling by train rather than renting a car.

If you're really interested in solo travel, we suggest you subscribe to *Going Solo*, a newsletter for people traveling alone (see *Where to Find It* below).

WHERE TO FIND IT

REBATING TRAVEL AGENCIES

All-American Travel Club (AATC): 2950 Tamiami Trail North, Suite 5, Naples FL 34103; 800-451-8747; fax 941-261-8746.

Pennsylvania Travel: 15 Maple Ave, Paoli PA 19301; 800-331-0947, 610-251-9944; fax 610-644-2150.

PriceCostco Extra Travel: 4649 Morena Blvd, San Diego, CA 92117; 619-581-3600.

Sam's Travel Club: 812 Walnut Plaza, Rogers AR 72756-3538; 800-955-7267. Program information is available at 450 Sam's Club locations, nationwide.

Smart Traveller: 3111 SW 27th Ave, Box 330010, Coconut Grove FL 33133; 800-448-3338; fax 305-443-3544.

Travel Avenue: 10 S Riverside Plaza, Suite 1404, Chicago 60606; 800-333-3335, 312-876-6866; fax 312-876-1254.

TRAVEL CLUBS

AAA: 1000 AAA Dr, Mailstop 75, Heathrow FL 32746; 800-926-4222; local office or CAA in Canada. Membership focus: drivers; members also receive discounts on cruises, tours, airfares, hotels, restaurants, and more.

Allstate Travel Club: 6001 N Clark St, Chicago 60660; 800-992-3841. Membership focus: national. *Disc, MC, V.*

All-American Travel Club: 2950 Tamiami Trail North, Suite 5, Naples FL 34103; 800-451-8747, 941-261-3279. Membership focus: national. Dues deducted from first rebate.

American Golf Travel Club: 3443 N Central Ave, Suite 819, Phoenix 85012; 800-847-4653. Membership focus: golfers. *AE, MC, V.*

America Direct: 8000 Towers Crescent Dr, Suite 1350, Vienna VA 22182; 703-847-3609. Membership focus: national. *MC, V.*

Amoco Motor Club: Box 9049, Des Moines 50368; 800-782-7887. Membership focus: drivers. *Amoco, MC, V.*

Amoco Traveler: 6001 N Clark St, Chicago 60660; 800-628-3735. Membership focus: drivers. *Amoco.*

BP Motor Club: 6001 N Clark St, Chicago 60660; 800-633-3224. Membership focus: drivers. Call for application. *Gulf Motor Club.*

Chevron Travel Club: P.O. Box P, Concord CA 94524; 800-222-0585. Membership focus: drivers. *Chevron.*

CitiTravel and Travelers Advantage: Box 1015, Trumbull CT 06611-9938; 800-548-1116. Membership focus: global and national. *MC, V.*

Driver's OneCard: 4040 Mystic Valley Pkwy, Boston 02155; 800-846-4000. Membership focus: drivers. *AE, Disc, MC, V.*

Encore: 4501 Forbes Blvd, Lanham MD 20706; 800-444-9800. Membership focus: national. *AE, Disc, MC, V.*

Exxon Travel Club: P.O. Box 3633, Houston 77253; 800-833-9966. Membership focus: drivers. *Exxon, MC, V.*

Golf Access: Box 27965, Salt Lake City 84127; 800-359-4653. Membership focus: golfers. *AE, Disc, MC, V.*

Gulf Motor Club: 6001 N Clark St, Chicago 60660; 800-633-3224. Membership focus: drivers. Call for application. *Gulf.*

Hale Irwin's Golfers Passport: Box 220067, St Louis 63122; 800-334-3140, 618-939-4011. Membership focus: golfers. *MC, V.*

Hideaways Intl: 767 Islington St, Portsmouth NH 03801; 800-843-4433, 603-430-4433. Membership focus: International. *AE, Disc, MC, V.*

Intl Airline Passengers Assn (IAPA): 4125 Keller Springs Rd, Suite 108, Dallas 75244; 800-821-4272, 214-404-9980. Membership focus: national. *AE, MC, V, DC.*

Moment's Notice: 7301 New Utrecht Ave, Brooklyn, NY 11204; 718-234-6295. Membership focus: national. Checks only for members, or any credit card.

National Travel Club: Box 5235, Harlan IA 51593; 800-234-4901. Membership focus: national. *MC, V.*

One Travel Place/Montgomery Ward: 200 N Martingale Rd, Schaumburg IL 60173; 800-843-4681. Membership focus: national. *AE, Disc, MC, Montgomery Ward, V.*

Players Club Intl: Box 190120, Atlanta 31119; 800-275-6600. Membership focus: gamblers. *AE, MC, V.*

Road America Motor Club: 225 Alcazar Ave, Coral Gables FL 33134; 800-443-4187. Membership focus: national. *Disc, MC, V.*

Sam's Club: 812 Walnut Plaza, Rogers AR 72756-3538; 800-955-7267. Membership focus: national. *Disc.*

Sears Discount Travel Club: Box 1015, Trumbull CT 06611; 800-548-1116 (travelers); 800-526-4848 (Shoppers Advantage). Membership focus: travelers and shoppers. *Disc, MC, Sears, V.*

Shell Motorist Club: 6001 N Clark St, Chicago 60660; 800-852-0555. Membership focus: drivers. *AE, MC, Shell, V.*

Sun Travel Club: 6001 N Clark St, Chicago 60660; 800-562-2238. Membership focus: drivers. *Sunoco.*

Texaco Travel Club: 6001 N Clark St, Chicago 60660; 800-526-6786. Membership focus: drivers. *Texaco.*

The Travel Club: Box 705, Plymouth Meeting PA 19462; 800-292-9892. Membership focus: national. *Disc, MC, V.*

Travel World Leisure Club: 225 W 34th St, 9th Floor, NYC 10122; 800-444-8952, 212-239-4855. Membership focus: national. *MC, V, Disc.*

TravelAlert: 100 Executive Way, Suite 110, Ponte Vedra Beach FL 32082; 800-822-2300, 904-285-5757. Membership focus: national. *MC, V.*

Travelers Advantage: Box 1015, Trumbull CT 06611; 800-367-4443. Membership focus: national. *AE, Disc, MC, V.*

Worldwide Discount Travel Club: 1674 Meridian Ave, Suite 206, Miami Beach 33139; 305-534-2082. *AE, MC, V, DC.*

SENIOR CLUBS AND ORGANIZATIONS

American Assn of Retired Persons (AARP): 601 E St, NW, Washington DC 20049; 202-434-2277. Annual dues $8 per household, $10 per household out of the District of Columbia (DC).

Catholic Golden Age: P.O. Box 3658, Scranton PA 18540; 800-836-5699, 717-342-3294. $8 per year per couple, $19 for 3 years.

Golden Age Travellers Club: Pier 27, The Embarcadero, San Francisco 94111; 800-258-8880, 415-296-0151.

Grand Circle Travel: 347 Congress St, Boston 02110; 800-221-2610, 617-350-7500.

Grandtravel: 6900 Wisconsin Ave, Suite 706, Chevy Chase MD 20815; 800-247-7651, 301-986-0790.

Mature Outlook: P.O. Box 10448, Des Moines, IA 50306-0448; 800-336-6330.

Natl Alliance of Senior Citizens: 1744 Riggs Place, NW, 3rd Floor, Washington DC 20009; 202-986-0117. $10 individual, $15 per couple, $100 lifetime.

Natl Association of Retired Federal Employees (NARFE): 1533 New Hampshire Ave, NW, Washington DC 20036; 202-234-0832. $18 to $25, depending on the location of the chapter.

Saga Holidays: 222 Berkeley St, Boston 02116; 800-343-0273. Cruises, call 800-952-9590. Smithsonian Odyssey Tours, call 800-258-5885. Road Scholars, call 800-621-2151.

United Airlines: *Silver Wings Club,* P.O. Box 50159, Dallas, TX 75250; 214-760-0022; fax 214-760-9979.

SINGLES TRAVEL

Globus and Cosmos: 5301's Federal Circle, Littleton CO 80123; 800-221-0090 (reservations), 800-323-3796 (information). Guaranteed double-occupancy rates on tours to Canada, Europe, and within the United States (including Hawaii). Additional charge for single shares.

Going Solo: Box 123, Apalachicola FL 32329; 800-451-5294, 904-653-8848. A bimonthly publication focusing on solo travel. One year, $29. Sample copy, $6 plus $1 postage. Checks or money orders only.

Solo Flights: 10 Greenwood Lane, Westport CT 06880; 203-256-1235; fax 203-259-7113. Works with cruise lines and resorts that permit shared accommodations and arranges about 30 tours per year; dozens of tours are available at any time for singles of all ages (including the Mature Tours Division, for "youthful spirits over 50").

Travel Companion Exchange: Box 833, Amityville NY 11701; 800-392-1256, 516-454-0880. Same- or opposite-sex pairing: $99 for eight months, $159 per year. Bimonthly newsletter and a free profile of another member each month, $2 per additional profile. Sample copy, $50.

This chapter was adapted from the 1996 edition of Consumer Reports Best Travel Deals.

Buying Package Tours and Cruises

One of the main appeals of cruises and packaged tours is the possibility of hassle-free travel at an all-in-one price. Both can be found in a range that should suit just about any travel taste, temperament, and pocketbook. But that's not to say that either can be bought blindly; Hefty savings reward the careful shopper.

A PACKAGE-TOUR PRIMER

When you buy a package tour, you get two or more travel elements—air transportation, lodgings, meals, ground transportation, entertainment, car rental, airport transfers, sightseeing, and so on, for a single price. Put together by organizations known as wholesalers or tour operators, such tours are available for every conceivable interest and destination, from golfing in Scotland to bicycling through Asia.

Basic packages to city or sun-sand-surf locations (e.g., Florida, Hawaii, the Caribbean, or Mexico) are often good deals. You get a price break from the packager's ability to buy air, hotel, ground transfers, and sightseeing in bulk. Long available from tour operators, packages are also available from major hotel chains, airlines, and other providers.

Escorted tours handle virtually *everything* for you, including what you see, eat, and do once you reach your destination. Most local touring is by bus, with either a local guide or an escort who accompanies you throughout your trip.

Such tours have several disadvantages. A lot depends on the quality of your tour guide and the personalities of your fellow travelers; both factors are out of your control. Some people find the regimented schedules unpleasant. The pace of activities is generally only as fast as the pace of the slowest person on the tour. And your whole tour is prepaid, pretty well locking you in even if the tour turns out to be unsatisfactory.

The advantages include minimal effort and fuss (unless you get a bad tour), camaraderie and, in some cases, lower prices, particularly at hotels. Sometimes an escorted tour is the only way to take part in activities or get to places that are otherwise inaccessible to tourists. You also benefit because the facilities and itinerary on a quality tour have been carefully selected and prescreened.

TRAVEL ON YOUR OWN. To suit people who don't need hand-holding when they travel, many tour operators provide à la carte options that let you travel independently once you reach your destination. And, of course, you can always have a travel agent or tour operator tailor a trip to your specifications—though that's the most expensive way to travel.

CHOOSING A TOUR. A travel agent or the advertisements in newspaper travel sections can lead you to attractive tours. If you already know where you want to travel, you might also check your travel agent's copy of the *Official Tour Directory*. Some tour operators offer a range of choices for different budgets. Cosmos and Trafalgar specialize in low-cost, no-frills travel.

You usually won't find big discounts on tours (except perhaps cruises). Margins are thin. At best, you can get a rebate of 5% or so by buying through a discount travel agency (see chapter 1).

With careful shopping, you can sometimes discover a smaller tour operator that's a real gem. Small firms may specialize in a particular destination, run offbeat tours, or find interesting lodgings that don't accept large groups.

ZINGERS IN FINE PRINT. The specifics of a tour package are found not in the tour brochure's color pictures and colorful prose but in its fine print. Don't skip that tiny, boring type—what you don't know can hurt you. Some tour operators aren't completely frank about what they re offering.

The brochure's fine print normally applies to all the tours listed. Necessarily, some of it deals with boilerplate (official corporate names, tour numbers) and purchase conditions (minimum time for paperwork, cancellation provisions, possible children's reductions). Beyond those basics, the fine print seems designed mainly to protect the operator in case things go wrong. Some of the fine print from the more consumer-oriented tour operators also tries to inform the traveler of potential problems. (You can tell a lot about a tour operator's concern for its customers by whether the fine print is even readable.)

Here's what to look for:

•**How much?** Brochure prices are often subject to change—reasonable enough, since prices are set far in advance. But a traveler should be informed of the actual price and conditions before buying. The fine print may also reserve the operator's right to increase the price or modify what a tour provides after a traveler has paid a deposit or even paid in full (with such changes specifically ruled out as grounds for a full refund). Avoid such tours if you can. Some operators guarantee the price in the brochure.

Some brochures quote a package price with a firm airfare component.

Others list the lowest airfare available at the time of printing (usually a regular Coach/Economy excursion, or a tour-based fare available only for a tour package), adding that it's subject to change if the airline raises fares. Most never list an airfare.

US regulations are stricter for charter flights (and tours based on charter flights) than for those using scheduled airlines. A traveler must be given a full refund if, before departure, the operator imposes any major change—a price increase of 10% or more, say, or a switch in departure/arrival dates. But many important changes don't qualify as major: A price increase of less than 10%, a change in departure time, or a rerouting to pick up extra passengers at another city, for example, doesn't entitle you to an automatic refund on a charter-based tour.

- **The airline you'll fly.** If an airline sponsors a tour, it generally provides the transportation. Independent tour operators may list several airlines, any of which could be used on a given tour, or a single airline with a provision that it's subject to change. Whenever you're not promised a specific airline or if the airline is subject to change, you may wind up with below-average Economy service and have to put up with cramped seating or inconvenient routing.

- **Cancellation/change.** Brochures should spell out specifics on cancellations and itinerary changes. Typically, travelers who cancel well in advance are eligible for full refunds (less a fee). After a cutoff date (15–60

days before departure), there's commonly a sliding scale of penalties or even—on many tours—no refund at all.

Many operators let you change travel dates or accommodations, subject to availability, for an additional $20–100 per change; a few waive the fee for the first change. A few operators impose especially stringent cancellation provisions for tours during seasonal events at a popular destination—Carnival in Rio, say, or Christmas in Hawaii.

- **Complaints.** Some operators specify a maximum period in which to file complaints and refund requests; they may also specify the method for resolving conflicts and complaints. Those provisions may not be legally binding, but they're often intimidating.

- **Documents.** A few operators state how many days before the tour they will send tickets or vouchers to you. You may incur an additional delivery charge if you make a reservation within the final month before travel. Some operators include a section that describes the documents you must have to participate in the trip (visas, passport, medical certificates, and so forth) and disavow any responsibility for conditions that result from your failure to have the appropriate paperwork with you during the tour.

- **In- and exclusions.** Most tour brochures list inclusions and exclusions—specifics about charges that might be subject to question. Some package prices include services you might not consider obvious—e.g., tips to airport and hotel porters for handling your bags. Other things being equal, the more inclusions the better.

Most exclusions are unsurprising —charges for excess baggage, telephone calls, room service, laundry, and so on. Ski-tour operators may disclaim responsibility for lack of snow. Some brochures commit operators to refunds for services that were promised and not delivered. But others allow the operator to make minor changes without refund, and the operator is the judge of what's minor.

- **Accommodations**. Tour operators generally reserve the right to substitute "comparable" or "equivalent" hotels for those featured in the brochure. Some make specific promises —for instance, limiting substitutions to hotels of at least the same rating as those featured in the brochure. The basis for the rating may also be stated (a government system in Europe, for example). If not, the rating is often taken from the *Official Hotel Guide,* a standard industry reference. (See chapter 14.) Other brochures promise not only comparable *quality* but also similar *location* within or near a city center or close to a major attraction—a useful protection.

Note what else the brochure promises—or doesn't promise—about room quality and location. If nothing is said, you're usually assigned a run-of-the-house room, which can be anything with the promised number of beds and bath facilities. Be prepared for the worst room in the hotel if you're not guaranteed anything better.

- **Food.** Typically, the fine print sets forth meal policy. Interpret "continental breakfast" to mean bread and coffee or tea laid out for self-service. Unless a brochure specifically promises lunch and dinner choices from a menu, you may end up with assembly-line, dollop-it-out meals. A few premium operators include alcoholic beverages on some occasions, but most don't.

- **Itineraries.** The fine print usually doesn't say anything more about routings than the tour description in the front of the brochure. A few brochures, however, add some specific disclaimers. Several operators reserve the right to make minor adjustments in sightseeing itineraries and to vary the order of cities or attractions visited in a multistop tour.

- **No-smoking tours.** If you want to avoid secondhand smoke, choose a tour with a ban on smoking. Omission of such a ban in the fine print may mean there will be a smoking section on the bus. Ask in advance to be sure.

- **Consumer protection.** Several trade associations offer consumer protection plans. The US Tour Operators Association (USTOA), to which a few of the larger tour operators belong, requires its members to post a surety of $1 million—a useful protection but not enough to make good on all claims if a big operator fails. (See *Where to Find It,* pages 28–30.)

The National Tour Association

(NTA) maintains a consumer-protection fund to cover traveler claims resulting if a member tour operator defaults because of bankruptcy. The American Society of Travel Agents (ASTA) offers several forms of consumer protection, but they're all voluntary, not mandatory. It operates an escrow account that tour operators can use to safeguard clients' deposits. It lists tour operators that offer consumer protection through USTOA or NTA. And it has arranged for an umbrella insurance program that individual travel agencies can buy to protect clients against supplier default of any kind. Most operators recommend trip-interruption insurance as a way of hedging your risk and sell it as a tour add-on. If you decide you need coverage, we recommend you buy it directly from an independent insurance provider. (See chapter 24.) If you do buy from the tour operator, be sure to watch out for unexpected insurance charges added in with other elements of the tour.

DEALING WITH PROBLEMS. Try to resolve any tour problems as they crop up. Complain early to your tour guide or other company representative if you're on an escorted tour, or to the tour operator's headquarters or your travel agency back home. Keep your cool, and be specific about the problem and what resolution you desire.

If no resolution is possible, it may be best to bail out. That might be expensive, but it may also prevent further grief, and it may strengthen your

case for a refund or a chargeback (a credit from the charge-card issuer for the disputed charge). You'll then have to pursue your complaint with care, patience, and a series of letters setting forth your problem and the resolution you expect. As a last resort, consider filing a formal complaint with USTOA or NTA (for tour operators) or ASTA (for travel agencies).

CRUISING FOR DISCOUNTS

The cruise market is booming, and it's easy to see why: Hotel prices have ballooned, but you can still buy a week-long cruise for under $200 a day per couple—not much more than you'd have paid 10 years ago. Cruise lines openly promote price cuts for customers who book early, and they push backdoor discounts through a variety of discount agencies. That can provide good values for careful shoppers who know how the system works.

Think of a cruise as a seagoing package tour with the works thrown in. The price of a cruise covers almost all your costs: transportation, accommodations, food, entertainment and, sometimes, even wine with meals.

If you're picking your first cruise, don't choose solely for price. Lines and ships have different personalities that cater to different vacation styles. First-time cruisers who buy the cheapest cruise, disregarding cruising area, shipboard facilities, or clientele, may be in for unpleasant surprises.

Your main choices are where to cruise, when to go, and which ship to take. Probably the most popular areas are the Caribbean and the Alaska Inside Passage. But you can also cruise the US Canadian east coast, Hawaii, Mexico's Pacific coast, the Mediterranean and Aegean, the Norwegian coast, various European rivers, the Orient, and the South Pacific. Occasional longer cruises may cross the Pacific or circumnavigate South America.

Many ship and barge cruises sail the Mississippi/Ohio system in the United States, the Danube, Elbe, Moselle, Rhine, and Volga rivers in Europe, and the canal systems of Britain and France.

What sort of cabin should you select? Ignore the brochure pictures, which are taken with wide-angle lenses. Budget cabins usually measure 9x12 or 10x13 feet. On most ships, they're inside, with no portholes or windows.

Some expensive cabins have windows facing a deck. They're like motel rooms on an outside corridor: You can enjoy either your privacy or the view, but not both at the same time. Few cabins at any price have double beds.

For more information, ask friends with cruise experience for recommendations. Get advice from a travel agent. Some agents specialize in cruises, but they may also have contracts with preferred suppliers who give them commissions in return for steering you to their ships.

You may want to check a published cruise reference. Several guidebooks offer an overview of cruise lines and the areas in which they operate. While they tend to sell cruising rather than just evaluate it, they do provide useful ship-by-ship comparisons and details about major ports of call. Among the better ones are:

- *Berlitz Complete Guide to Cruising and Cruise Ships '96,* Douglas Ward (Macmillan, NY, 1995, $19.95).
- *Fodor's Cruises and Ports of Call '96* (Fodor Travel Publications, NY, 1995, $18.50). Straight talk about the world's most popular ships, and what to see and do in everyone's favorite ports.
- *Frommer's Cruises '95-'96,* Marylyn Springer and Donald A. Schultz (Prentice-Hall, NY, 1994, $19).
- *The Star Service,* available at many travel agencies, has a section on cruise ships, with objective reports and without any obvious attempt to sell.
- *The Unofficial Guide to Cruises* by Kay Showker with Bob Sehlinger (Macmillan, New York, 1995; $18).
- *Cruising: Answers to Your Questions,* a free booklet from Cruise Lines International Association (CLIA), which represents 31 North American cruise lines and about 22,000 travel agency affiliates who sell cruises. The booklet won't help you find discounts, but it can help you learn more about what to expect on a cruise.

WHICH AGENCY? The first rule of cruise buying—especially for first-timers—is to deal with someone who has been around the industry long enough to have first-hand knowledge of individual ships, lines, and popular destinations and ports. A good price on an inappropriate ship or uninteresting itinerary is not a good deal.

Cruising remains one of the few travel services that you can usually buy only through a travel agent (although some cruise lines are reported to be considering direct consumer sales). Several kinds of agencies sell cruises:

- Because a *cruise-only* agency concentrates on one aspect of the travel business, it can give real advice, rather than just take orders. Many cruise-only agencies promote themselves as "discounters." Though just about any cruise-only agency has access to the cruise lines' major promotions, the big discounters sometimes beat their competition. Recently, a few big cruise discounters have gone bust, leaving customers with neither their prepayment nor their cruise. If you deal with a discounter, check its credentials before you buy. A cruise-only agency should, at a minimum, be affiliated with the Cruise Lines Intl Assn (CLIA) or the National Assn of Cruise-Only Agencies (NACOA): While neither organization has a consumer-protection program, members must fulfill modest training and financial requirements. It's also a good idea to check the Better Business Bureau in the agency's home location for complaints or problems.

- Many *full-service* agencies book cruises as well as other travel services. The big, multibranch chains often have discount deals as good as those available through cruise-only agencies. Even a small, independent agency should have at least one agent who keeps up with the cruise industry or has an arrangement with a cruise discounter.

If you get a mere order-taker on the line when you inquire about a cruise, try another agency or ask to speak to someone who knows about a particular cruise that interests you.

WHEN TO BOOK. The best deals, cabins, and dates go to early-bird buyers. Early booking prices—and deadlines—are listed in the cruise brochures. Early typically means four to six months before departure date. All the big lines guarantee, if they later undercut their early-booking rates, to refund customers the difference.

Still, you don't necessarily need to book early to get a good price, especially if you're flexible. Last-minute deals, at least for passengers from certain regions, are often available for some ships that aren't full one month before sailing. Among the best bets for bargain rates are repositioning cruises, between-season trips on which a ship moves from one region to another—from a summer in Alaska to a winter in the Caribbean, say.

Instead of giving cash discounts to early buyers, some lines offer credit for shipboard purchases or free hotel accommodations before or after the cruise. In addition to their published advance-purchase fares, many lines offer two-for-one specials, kids-free programs, or unpublicized reductions for prior customers.

In addition to the price reduction, advance-purchase travelers have the best selection of cabins. Early booking may also be the only way to get a discount on very popular cruises.

UPGRADING YOUR CABIN. The discount market offers another attraction: the chance to combine a discount price with a free upgrade. Upgrades become available when a cruise ship sells a higher percentage of inexpensive than expensive cabins—a fairly common occurrence. Upgrades can be used either as rewards—for repeat customers or for travelers who book early—or as incentives to attract first-time cruisers.

It's no longer true that you're necessarily more likely to be offered an upgrade as an incentive for buying late. Today, when a line decides to cut prices, it may upgrade early bookers and sell the freed-up cabins at lowered rates.

However, cruise lines know that a good number of travelers who book early are seeking a specific cabin or location. Many of those early bookers wouldn't consider a change, even to a larger cabin, an upgrade. Accordingly, a cruise line may hesitate to reassign a traveler who booked early unless it's sure that the traveler really wants an upgrade.

If you book early but would welcome an upgrade, make sure your agent adds a specific notation in your reservation file that you are interested in upgrading if offered.

ALMOST **ALL-INCLUSIVE.** Cruise prices, despite their hype, aren't all-inclusive. Here are the main extras you'll face:

• **Tipping.** Can easily add as much as $10 a day per person to the cost of a cruise.
• **Shore excursions.** Almost always extra, easily adding $30-40 a person for each stop. We recommend you shun the cruise lines' tours and arrange your own after you arrive in port. Rent a car or hire a taxi and go where you want, when you want.
• **Liquor.** Excluded from most cruise

rates. And, of course, whatever you spend on-board for shopping or gambling is extra. Some ship lines offer "shipboard credits" toward such expenses as an added booking incentive for some sailing.

• **Port charges.** Can add as much as $200 to the price of a cruise. The cruise line may well add a bigger port charge than the port actually charges them and pocket the difference.

WHERE TO FIND IT

TOUR OPERATORS

Globus and Cosmos: 5301 S Federal Circle, Littleton CO 80123; 800-221-0090. Bookings accepted only through travel agents, but you can write Cosmos directly for a brochure.

Trafalgar Tours, Inc.: 11 E 26th St, Suite 1300, NYC 10010-1402; 800-854-0103, 212-689-8977.

TRADE ORGANIZATIONS

American Society of Travel Agents (ASTA): 1101 King St, Suite 200, Alexandria VA 22314; 703-739-2782.

Cruise Line International Association: For free brochure, *Cruising: Answers to Your Questions,* send a self-addressed, stamped envelope (58¢ postage) to CLIA, 500 Fifth Ave, Suite 1407, NYC 10110; 212-921-0066.

National Tour Association (NTA): 546 East Main St, Lexington KY 40508; 800-682-8886, 606-226-4678.

United States Tour Operators Association (USTOA): 211 E 51st St, Suite 12B, NYC 10022; 212-750-7371. Call or write for free brochures *How to Select* *a Package Tour* and *The Standard for Confident Travel* (about the Consumer Protection Plan).

CRUISE-ONLY AGENCIES

Here is a listing of representative, large cruise-only agencies. Many describe themselves as discounters.

All About Cruises: 9720 W Sample Rd, Coral Springs FL 33065; 800-329-3839, 954-344-3838, fax 954-755-0090.

Ambassador Tours: 120 Montgomery St, Suite 400, San Francisco 94104; 800-989-9000, 415-981-5678, fax 415-982-3490.

California State Automobile Assn Travel Agencies: 150 Van Ness Ave, San Francisco 94102; 415-565-2141. Call for nearest office.

Castaway Cruises: 311 Center St, Old Town ME 04468; 800-359-7447, 207-827-3645, fax 207-827-3645.

Cruise Company of California: 19742 Beach Blvd, Huntington Beach CA 92648; 800-872-7847, 800-992-7847 in CA, fax 714-964-2818.

Cruise Directors of NY: 234 5th Ave, 4th Floor, NYC 10001; 800-348-0009, 212-213-8224, fax 212-213-3078.

Cruise Fairs of America: Century Plaza Towers, 2029 Century Park E, Suite 950, Los Angeles 90067; 800-456-4386, 310-556-2925, fax 310-556-2254.

Cruise Headquarters: 4225 Executive Sq, Suite 1600, La Jolla CA 92037; 800-424-6111, 619-453-1201, fax 619-453-0653. Deluxe cruise lines only.

Cruise Holidays: 9665 Chesapeake Dr, Suite 401, San Diego 92193; 800-866-7245, fax 800-666-7245. Network of cruise-only agencies with 48 Canadian

and 141 US offices. Call corporate office for nearest agency.

The Cruise Line Inc.: 150 NW 168th St, N Miami Beach 33169; 800-777-0707, 305-653-6111, fax 305-653-6228.

The Cruise Market Place: 939 Laurel St, San Carlos CA 94070; 800-826-4333, 415-595-7750, fax 415-594-9048.

Cruise Masters: 300 Corporate Pointe, Suite 100, Culver CA 90230; 800-242-9444, 800-242-9000 in CA, 310-397-7175, fax 310-568-2044.

Cruise Pro: 2527 E Thousand Oaks Blvd, Thousand Oaks CA 91362; 800-222-7447, 800-258-7447 in CA, 805-371-9884, fax 805-371-9084. Voyagers Club, $15 one-time fee, includes notices of extra deals and a newsletter.

Cruise Quarters of America: 600 Anton Blvd, Unit B, Costa Mesa CA 92626; 800-648-2444, 714-754-0280, fax 714-850-1974.

Cruise Shoppe Operations: 19900 NE 21st Court, N Miami Beach 33179; 800-338-9051, 305-931-1509, fax 305-932-9693.

Cruise Stars: 6322 Fallbrook Ave, Woodland Hills CA 91367; 800-732-7287, 818-226-5555, fax 818-340-2464.

Cruise Time: 1299 Church St, San Francisco 94114; 800-338-0818, 415-677-0777, fax 415-550-8492.

Cruises by Brennco: 508 E 112th St, Kansas City MO 64131; 800-955-1909, 816-942-1000, fax 816-942-1288.

Cruises Inc: Pioneer Business Park, 5000 Campuswood Dr, E Syracuse NY 13057; 800-854-0500, 315-463-9695, fax 315-434-9175.

Cruises of Distinction: 2750 S Woodward Ave, Bloomfield Hills MI

48304; 800-634-3445, 810-332-2020, fax 810-333-9743.

Cruises Only: 1011 E Colonial Dr, Orlando FL 32803; 800-683-7447, 407-898-5353, fax 407-895-0244.

Cruiseworld: 24 Danbury Rd, Wilton CT 06897; 800-588-7447, 203-834-2828, fax 203-834-2171. Also has several local offices in the NY/NJ area.

Don Ton Cruise Tours: 3151 Airway Ave, Suite E-1, Costa Mesa CA 92626; 800-318-1818, 714-545-3737, fax 714-545-5275.

Go Ahead Vacations: 1 Memorial Dr, Cambridge MA 02142; 800-590-1104, 617-621-1900, fax 617-621-1997.

Golden Bear Travel: 16 Digital Dr, Novato CA 94949; 800-551-1000, 415-382-8900, fax 415-382-9086.

Hartford Holidays: 626 Willis Ave, Williston Park NY 11596; 800-828-4813, 516-746-6670, fax 516-746-6690.

Just Cruising: 65 Brookside Place, Newbury Park CA 91320; 800-272-1784, 805-375-8244, 888-272-1784, fax 805-375-8240.

Kelly Cruises: 1315 W 22nd St, Suite 105, Oak Brook IL 60521; 800-837-7447, 630-990-1111, fax 630-990-1147.

National Discount Cruise: 1409 N Cedar Crest Blvd, Allentown PA 18104; 800-788-8108, 610-439-4883, fax 610-439-8086.

Peter Berlin's Travel Center: 1180 S Powerline Rd, Pompano Beach FL 33069; 800-874-6040, 954-974-6040, fax 954-974-6774. Web site *http://www.univox.com/travelcenter/*, E-mail *cruise @gate.net*. Also has office in Boca Raton FL.

Spur of the Moment Cruises: 411 N Harbor Blvd, Suite 302, San Pedro CA

90731; 800-343-1991, 310-521-1070, fax 310-521-1061.

Time to Travel: 582 Market St, San Francisco 94104; 800-524-3300, 415-421-3333, fax 415-421-4857.

Travel Advisors: 668 Las Golinas Ave, San Rafael CA 94903; 800-423-8271, 415-479-4200, fax 415-479-8546.

The Travel Company: 3351 El Camino Real, Suite 250, Atherton CA 94027; 800-367-6090, 415-367-6000, fax 415-367-6040.

Trips 'n Travels: 1024 Kane Concourse, Bay Harbor Islands FL 33154; 800-331-2745, 305-864-2222, fax 305-861-8809.

Vacations at Sea: 4919 Canal St, New Orleans 70119; 800-749-4950, 504-482-1572, fax 504-486-8360.

Village Travel Service/Last Minute Cruise Club: 870 9th St, San Pedro CA 90731; 310-519-1717, fax 310-519-1184.

White Travel Service: 127 Park Rd, West Hartford CT 06119; 800-547-4790, 860-233-2648, fax 860-236-6177. Also has cruise hot line at 860-236-6176.

Whole World of Travel: 4949 Marconi Ave, Carmichael CA 95608; 800-458-3636, 916-488-8000, fax 916-488-8873.

World Wide Cruises: 8059 W McNab Rd, Ft Lauderdale FL 33321; 800-882-9000, 954-720-9000, fax 954-720-9112.

Worldwide Travel/Cruises Worldwide: 16585 Von Karman, Suite A, Irvine CA 92606; 800-627-8473, 714-975-1211, fax 714-975-1849.

This chapter was adapted from the Consumer Reports Travel Letter *article "Cruising for Discounts" (May 1996) and from the 1996 edition of* Consumer Reports Best Travel Deals.

Spend Your Way to Freebies?

You needn't travel to earn frequent-flier mileage—more than two dozen charge cards available to individuals give you frequent-flier credit for any purchase billed to the card. Rack up enough mileage and you get a free air ticket to a destination of your choice (see chapter 9). This chapter gives a rundown on how the major cards operate, what they charge, and what credit you earn.

WHAT'S OUT THERE

Travel cards fall into several broad categories:

• **Airline cards.** All big US airlines but Southwest cosponsor a charge card with a bank. You get one mile of credit in the cosponsoring airline's frequent-flier program for each dollar in purchases you charge to the card; cash advances usually don't count. Most cards are *MasterCards* or *Visas* (some lines offer both); Delta's is an *Optima* card from American Express. Typically, the airlines offer both a plain-vanilla card and a *Gold* option with additional features.

What you earn on purchases goes into your account with the airline. That credit is virtually the same as mileage earned by flying or from an airline partner: It counts toward any award the airline offers—free trips, premium-class trips, travel on a partner airline, and upgrades—and it expires on the same schedule. However, it doesn't count toward reaching very-frequent-flier (VFF) status.

If you're interested in a high-credit award, try to concentrate your mileage-earning in one or two airline accounts. Airline-sponsored cards (along with T&E—travel & entertainment—cards; see page 32) are a good way to further that objective.

• **Bank cards.** Several banks issue charge cards (*MasterCard or Visa*) on which you earn credit in a frequent-flier account maintained by the bank. When you rack up enough credit for a free trip, the bank buys you a ticket at the lowest available fare from whichever line offers it the best deal.

There's often a dollar cap on the value of the free ticket but, in some programs, you can apply the bank's maximum allowance toward a more expensive ticket.

Since the bank buys your tickets, you're not limited by the route structure of any single airline nor by the airlines' stingy allotment of seats to frequent fliers. You also earn airline (but not bank) frequent-flier credit for taking the trip. Furthermore, in some programs you can earn a free short-haul ticket for fewer than the 20,000-25,000 miles most airline programs require.

On the downside, you can't combine bank credit with your airline credit: It's totally separate. Because the bank buys tickets, you can't use bank credit for upgrades or, in most cases, for Business or First Class tick-

ets. And the ticket you get is usually saddled with the 21-day-advance-purchase and Saturday-night-stay requirements typical of a cheap ticket.

•**T&E cards.** The two giant travel-and-entertainment cards, *AmEx* and *Diners Club*, offer optional, extra-cost programs that let you earn mileage in several airline programs. As you charge purchases, credit accumulates in the card's account, where it has no expiration date. When you want to use some or all of that credit, you transfer it to a participating airline. It then becomes subject to the airline's rules on use and expiration. You needn't pick in advance the airline programs in which you'll use the credit. (Although *Optimas* aren't strictly T&E cards, we list them along with the other *AmEx* cards.)

Diners Club's *Club Rewards* in-

PLATINUM TWOFERS

The *American Express Platinum* card offers a unique travel benefit that can be worth thousands of dollars: international airline twofers in Business or First Class. In effect, a couple enjoys a 50% discount on premium-class tickets, on which big discounts are rare. You must book through the *Platinum* card's travel service; there's no limit to the number of trips you can take.

The 1996 program (it runs until April 1997) includes Aeromexico, Air New Zealand, Alitalia, Asiana, Continental, Iberia, LanChile, Lufthansa, Sabena, and Swissair. All the airlines impose some restrictions. Twofer flights were limited on Swissair to May–Aug 1996, and on Lufthansa to May–Aug 1996 and Nov 1996–Apr 1997.

Even at 50% off, Business Class isn't cheap. But for travelers who want comfortable seats, this is one of the best deals we know of—more than enough to justify the stiff $300 annual cost of a *Platinum* card. AmEx offers it "by invitation" to heavy users of *AmEx* cards, but you can call your *AmEx* card service office to see if you qualify.

HOTEL AND CRUISE CARDS

Last year saw the debut of two new hotel cards, both *Optima* cards cobranded with American Express. Both have no annual fee and offer an APR (after an introductory period) of prime plus 9.9% (18.15% at this writing).

- **Sheraton.** With the new *ITT Sheraton ClubMiles* credit card from American Express, you get one Club Mile for every eligible dollar charged to the card for purchases at any establishment that accepts the *American Express Card*. Cardmembers are automatically enrolled in, or upgraded to, gold membership status in the ITT Sheraton Club International (SCI) frequent guest program for one year. During the time that Cardmembers maintain Gold status, they receive four GoldMiles for every eligible dollar charges with the Card at participating ITT Sheraton hotels and resorts—that's one ClubMile for using the Cards, plus three ClubMiles for every dollar spent on the Card at ITT Sheraton properties. New Cardmembers will also receive a 1000 ClubMiles bonus upon their first charge.

  ClubMiles can be redeemed for free hotel stays and room upgrades at participating ITT Sheraton hotels and resorts or car rentals. ClubMiles can also be transferred to the frequent-flier programs of 17 major international carriers, most at the rate of one ClubMile to one frequent-flier mile. In addition, each year cardmembers receive a certificate for 50% off the "rack rate" (list price) for one stay of up to five nights at participating ITT Sheraton locations.

  There's no charge for additional cards on the same account. To apply for the ITT Sheraton ClubMiles credit card, call 800-467-8462.

- **Hilton.** With the *Hilton Optima* card, travelers receive two points in Hilton's *HHonors* frequent-stay program for every dollar they charge to the card and three points per dollar for charges at Hilton (US) and Conrad (overseas) hotels. That's a better payoff than you get using the American Express *Membership Rewards* program, which provides only one *HHonors* point per dollar.

  For most travelers, the Hilton card has a somewhat lower payoff than an airline card. In Hilton's frequent-stay program, you get 10 *HHonors* points for each dollar you spend at a Hilton hotel, for a payoff of about 4%. The value of the extra points you earn by using the new charge card amounts to 1.2% of your Hilton purchases and 0.8% of other charges. Even the higher increment is below the 2% figure at which we value one frequent-flier mile per dollar.

  If you use Hiltons extensively but travel mainly by car, the card makes some sense (to enroll, call 800-467-8462). But if you're interested in earning free airline trips, stick with an airline card, *Membership Rewards,* or *Diners Club.*

- **Cruise cards.** Carnival (800-847-7378) and Norwegian-American (800-515-5020) cruise lines sponsor *MasterCard* and *Visa* cards. Both offer $3 worth of cruise credit for every $100 charged—a more generous payout than airline cards give.

cludes virtually all major North American airlines. The American Express *Membership Rewards* program, however, excludes some of the nation's biggest lines (notably American, Northwest, and United). Neither T&E card is accepted in as many locations as *MasterCard* or *Visa*.

CHARTING YOUR COURSE

The table on pages 36–39 lists the most important features of the travel cards. The first columns identify the cosponsoring travel supplier and program name, the bank that issues and supports the card, whether the card is a *MasterCard,* a *Visa,* or some other brand, and whether it's an ordinary or a *Gold* card.

Next come financial details. *Annual fee* shows how much you pay per year for the card (plus any surcharge to

DIALING UP MILES

AT&T, MCI, Sprint, and several smaller telephone companies give up to seven frequent-flier miles in a participating line's program for each dollar spent on qualifying phone services —offers often limited to residential customers. Since those programs aren't confined to phone-card billings, we didn't include them in the table. However, you do get airline credit for billings to your phone card. And, of course, if you run your phone bill through a mileage-earning charge card, you also earn that card's usual one mile per dollar.

enroll in its travel-credit program). Travelers who don't charge much over the course of a year and so won't earn much mileage should look for a low-fee card. *APR* is the annual percentage rate that's applied to outstanding balances. If you typically run big credit balances, look first at the few cards with low APRs—some are as low as 8.25%. (If you don't run a balance, even a high APR doesn't matter.)

Grace period is the maximum time that can elapse after a purchase before you start to incur an interest charge. The interest-free grace period applies to new purchases only if you don't have an outstanding credit balance; otherwise, you incur interest from the day of purchase. Most cards provide a grace period only when your account is paid in full; the *Optima True Grace* card provides a grace period on all new purchases. The T&E cards have no official grace period—you're supposed to pay off your bill in full every month.

The next entries show the fee, if any, for extra cards on a single account, any bonus credit you receive when you sign up, and the credit you earn for each dollar charged to the card. Note that an enrollment bonus doesn't always loom large over time—the most generous bonus we list, 5000 miles, is worth $100.

Next come the airlines on which you earn credit, and, in *Combine credit,* an indication of whether the credit you earn on purchases can be combined with the credit you earn by flying.

Round-trip, North America is a benchmark for comparing the earning

THREE SPECIAL-INTEREST CARDS

Charge cards that earn travel credit on every purchase just keep coming. Here are the three latest entrants in a crowded field. Each appeals to a narrow segment of the traveling public, but you may find one to your liking.

For visitors to Hawaii. The *Hawai'i Advantage* card, issued by First Hawaiian Bank as a *Visa* card, either regular or *Gold,* provides up to a 1% rebate that you can apply toward Vacation Packages from Classic Hawaiian. In addition, you receive discounts up to 20% on interisland airfares, discounts up to 25% at more than 50 participating Hawaiian restaurants, reductions up to $50 a day on greens fees at participating golf courses, and a variety of other deals.

The annual fee is $25 for the regular card, $45 for the *Gold,* either waived if you charge $2500 or more each year. (The first year is free.) The APRs are prime plus 7.5% on the regular card and prime plus 6.5% on the *Gold.* The grace period for both is 25 days if you pay your balance in full.

The 1% payout on *Hawai'i Advantage* is lower than that of airline cards, typically 2%. The card clearly is aimed mainly at frequent Island visitors. If that fits you, call 800-342-2778 to apply.

For golfers. American Express has announced a card that earns golf credit. As with other cards in this proliferating field, you earn one point for each dollar charged. Once earned, points last indefinitely. The payoff appears to be about 2%.

Golf awards include equipment, greens and cart fees, instruction, and golf vacations; the suppliers include Callaway golf equipment, David Leadbetter Golf Academy, Bobby Jones apparel, American Golf courses, and several resort chains that feature golf courses and golf vacation packages. Sample awards include one off-peak greens fee plus cart at a Marriott golf resort for 3000 points, a Callaway *War Bird Big Bertha* driver for 8000 points, and two nights at a Hilton golf resort (including two rounds of golf for two guests) for 50,000 points.

In addition to awards, you receive a variety of golf-course perks, which don't require using any credit, at more than 160 courses nationwide. Among them: advance starting-time reservations at courses managed by American Golf and (even if you aren't a hotel guest) at courses associated with Hilton Golf Resorts, Marriott Golf Resorts, Golf Hyatt Resorts, and Prince Resorts in Hawaii.

The card is another Optima variant, with no annual fee and an APR of 18.15% (after an initial six months at 7.9%). It includes the usual Optima features—notably free secondary collision-damage coverage on rental cars. Call 800-297-4653 to enroll.

For cruisers. *Transmedia* has added yet another partner. Now you can opt to have 25% of your dining bill at participating restaurants returned as *Orient Dollars.* Each *Dollar* is worth $1 when applied toward a future cruise on Orient Lines. So far, Orient is sending memberships only to its list of past passengers. If you missed out, call *Transmedia* (800-422-5090).

Travel Plastic: Fees and Features*

PROGRAM	BANK/COMPANY	PHONE NUMBER TO ENROLL	TYPE OF CARD	ANNUAL FEE (a)	APR% (b)	GRACE PERIOD (c)
PROGRAM BASICS				**FEES AND CHARGES**		
AIRLINE CARDS						
Air Canada Aeroplan	CIBC	800-465-2422	V Gold	C$120	17.5	17 days
Alaska Airlines Mileage Plan	Seattle-First National	800-552-7302	MC, V	45	17.9	21
			MC/V Gold	45	16.4	21
American AAdvantage	Citibank	800-359-4444	MC/V	50	17.65	20-25
America West FlightFund	Bank of America	800-508-2933	V	45	18.15	21
British Airways Executive Club	Chase Manhattan	800-282-4273	V	50	19.15	30
			V Gold	65	17.65	30
Canadian Intl Plus	Royal Trust	800-769-2511	V Gold	C$120	17.5	21
Continental OnePass	Marine Midland	800-850-3144	MC/V	55(k)	9.4	25
			MC/V Gold	75(k)	18.4	25
Delta SkyMiles	American Express	800-759-6453	Optima	55(m)	17.65	25
Midwest Express Frequent Flier	Elan Financial Services	800-388-4044	MC	40	18.15	25
			MC Gold	65	18.15	25
Northwest WorldPerks	First Bank	800-360-2900	V	55	18	25
			V Gold	85	18	25
TWA Frequent Flight Bonus	European American	800-322-8921	MC/V	50	17.15	25
United Mileage Plus	FCC National	800-637-5555	V	60	18.15	20-25
			MC/V Gold	100	18.15	20-25
USAir Frequent Traveler	Nations	800-835-5715	V	35	(q)	20
			V Gold	55	(q)	20
BANK CARDS						
Chase Flight Rewards	Chase	800-581-7770	MC/V	25	17.65	30
			MC/V Gold	25	17.65	30
First Air	First of America	800-835-9373	V	35	18.15	25
			V Gold	49	18.15	25
ASTA Travel Plus	Bank One	800-945-2023	V	25	18	20
			V Gold	55	18	20
Stop & Shop SupeReward	Bank of New York	800-997-9116	MC	—	17.15	25
			MC Gold	—	17.15	25
Frequent Buyer Program	Huntington National	800-480-2265	MC/V	25	16.15	25
			MC/V Gold	25	13.15	25
			MC/V	75	8.25	25
			MC/V Gold	75	8.25	25
StarMiles	Star	800-999-0619	MC/V	70	8.25	25
			MC/V	25	11.75	25
			MC/V Gold	80	8.25	25
			MC/V Gold	25	11.75	25

ADDT'L CARDS	ENROLLMENT BONUS	TRAVEL CREDIT					RENTAL CAR CDW(e)
		CREDIT PER DOLLAR	AIRLINE (d)	COMBINE CREDIT	ROUND-TRIP N.A.	EXPIRATION OF CREDIT	
C$50	2500 mi	1 mi	AC	✔	30,000 mi	unlimited(f)	
free	1000 mi	1 mi	AS	✔	20,000 mi	3 years	—
free	1000 mi	1 mi	AS	✔	20,000 mi	3 years	✔
free	—	1 mi	AA	✔	25,000 mi	3 years	
free	2500 mi	1 mi	HP	✔	20,000 mi	3 years(g,h)	✔
free	4000 mi (i)	1 mi	BA	✔	25,000 mi	5 years	—
free	4000 mi (i)	1 mi	BA	✔	25,000 mi	5 years	✔
C$50	2500 mi (j)	1 pt	CP	✔	25,000 mi	unlimited(f)	✔
$25	—	1 mi	CO	✔	25,000 mi	unlimited(l)	—
$25	—	1 mi	CO	✔	25,000 mi	unlimited(l)	✔
free	5000 mi	1 mi(n)	DL	✔	25,000 mi	unlimited(h)	✔
free	1000 mi	1 mi	YX	✔	20,000 mi	3 years(h)	—
free	2500 mi	1 mi(o)	YX	✔	20,000 mi	3 years(h)	✔
free	1000 mi	1 mi	NW	✔	25,000 mi	3 years(p)	—
free	1000 mi	1 mi	NW	✔	25,000 mi	3 years(p)	✔
free	3000 mi	1 mi	TW	✔	20,000 mi	unlimited	
free	(q)	1 mi	UA	✔	25,000 mi	3 years(p)	—
free	(q)	1 mi	UA	✔	25,000 mi	3 years(p)	✔
free	2500 mi	1 mi	US	✔	25,000 mi	unlimited	✔
free	2500 mi	1 mi	US	✔	25,000 mi	unlimited	✔
free	1000 pts	1 pt	any	—	25,000 pts	5 years(p)	—
free	1000 pts	1 pt	any	—	25,000 pts	5 years(p)	✔
free	5000 pts	1 pt	any	—	25,000 pts	3 years(p)	—
free	5000 pts	1 pt	any	—	25,000 pts	3 years(p)	✔
free	1000 pts	1 pt	any	—	24,000 pts(r)	5 years	—
free	1000 pts	1 pt	any	—	24,000 pts(r)	5 years	
free	—	1 pt(s)	NW	—	30,000 pts(t)	3 years	
free	—	1 pt(s)	NW	—	30,000 pts(t)	3 years	✔
free	—	1 pt	any	—	25,000 pts	3 years(p)	—
free	—	1 pt	any	—	25,000 pts	3 years(p)	✔
free	—	1 pt	any	—	25,000 pts	3 years(p)	—
free	—	1 pt	any	—	25,000 pts	3 years(p)	✔
free	1000 pts	1 pt	any	—	25,000 pts	4 years	—
free	1000 pts	1 pt	any	—	25,000 pts	4 years	
free	1000 pts	1 pt	any	—	25,000 pts	4 years	✔
free	1000 pts	1 pt	any	—	25,000 pts	4 years	✔

TRAVEL PLASTIC: FEES AND FEATURES* (continued)

				FEES AND CHARGES		
		PROGRAM BASICS				
PROGRAM	BANK/ COMPANY	PHONE NUMBER TO ENROLL	TYPE OF CARD	ANNUAL FEE (a)	APR% (b)	GRACE PERIOD (c)
BANK CARDS (continued)						
TravelMax	MBNA	800-858-0905	V	—	19.15	—
Mileage Checking	American Savings	800-788-7000	V Gold(v)	72(w)	—	—
CMA Global Gold(x)	Merrill Lynch	800-637-7455(y)	V Gold(v)	25	—	—
Sky Key Gold Card(z)	Key PrivateBank	800-539-2968	MC/V Gold	50	16.65	25
TRAVEL & ENTERTAINMENT CARDS						
Club Rewards	Citibank/ Diners Club	800-234-6377	DC	80	—	—
Membership Rewards	American Express	800-843-2273	Personal (Green)	80	—	—
			Gold	100 (ee)	—	—
			Platinum	300	—	—
			Rewards Plus Gold	125	—	—
			Optima	50 (hh)	14.25	25
			Optima Gold	—	12.25	25
			Optima True Grace	25	17	25(ii)

---

* As of May 1996; subject to change.

(a) Annual fee, if any, plus extra fee, if any, for mileage program.
(b) Current annual percentage rate on unpaid balance.
(c) Time allowed between purchase and start of interest accrual (with no outstanding balance).
(d) Any means use credit on any airline.
(e) Free collision-damage coverage for car rented on card.
(f) By law, Canadian credit must have an expiration date, but the dates have always been extended.
(g) Certificates issued every 20,000 mi expire after 3 years.
(h) Extended indefinitely every 3 years with qualifying account activity.

(i) Plus an additional 1000 mi after you charge $1000.
(j) Plus 2500 mi for each annual renewal.
(k) Waived first year.
(l) Credit may be canceled if no account activity in an 18-month period.
(m) Waived annually if you maintain another American Express charge card (Personal, Gold, etc.).
(n) 1.5 mi for purchase of Delta ticket or tour; 20% bonus when credit balance is carried.
(o) 2 mi for any Midwest Express ticket or tour, through Dec 31.
(p) Dec 31 of third or fifth year after year in which credit is earned.
(q) Varies by promotion.

ADDT'L CARDS	ENROLLMENT BONUS	TRAVEL CREDIT					RENTAL-CAR CDW(e)
		CREDIT PER DOLLAR	AIRLINE (d)	COMBINE CREDIT	ROUND-TRIP N.A.	EXPIRATION OF CREDIT	
free	—	1 pt	any	—	20,000 pts(u)	5 years	✔
free	—	1 pt	any	—	25,000 pts	5 years	✔
free	—	1 pt	any	—	25,000 pts	5 years	✔
free	2500 pts	1 pt	any	—	25,000 pts	4 years	✔
$35	—	1 pt(aa)	(bb)	✔	(cc)	unlimited	✔(dd)
$30	—	1 pt(aa)	(ff)	✔	(cc)	unlimited	✔
$35	—	1 pt(aa)	(ff)	✔	(cc)	unlimited	✔
$150	—	1 pt(aa)	(ff)	✔	(cc)	unlimited	✔
free	—	1 pt(aa,gg)	(ff)	✔	(cc)	unlimited	✔
free	—	1 pt(aa)	(ff)	✔	(cc)	unlimited	✔
free	—	1 pt(aa)	(ff)	✔	(cc)	unlimited	—
free	—	1 pt(aa)	(ff)	✔	(cc)	unlimited	—

(r) Anywhere in the US; 16,000 points for free ticket within one of three US zones.
(s) 2 points for Stop & Shop purchases.
(t) Ticket discounts available at lower mi/point levels.
(u) Anywhere in the US; 12,000 points for free ticket within one of two US zones.
(v) Debit card.
(w) $6/month.
(x) You must have a Merrill Lynch CMA account with at least $20,000 cash or securities.
(y) Extension 1352.
(z) Must have a Private Banking account, minimum annual income of $75,000, and $100,000 in assets.
(aa) With most airlines, 1 point = 1 mi.

(bb) AA, AC, AF, AS, BA, CO, DL, HA, HP, MX, NW, QF, SA, SN, TG, TW, UA, US, WN, YX, plus Latin Pass lines: Aces, Avianca, Aviateca, Copa, Faucett, Lacsa, Ladeco, LanChile, Lloyd Aereo, Nica, Saeta, Taca, Transbrasil.
(cc) Varies by airline.
(dd) Primary coverage.
(ee) $60 for senior card.
(ff) AM,CO,DL,HA,KE,LY,MX,OS,SN,SR,US,WN.
(gg) First year, earn 2 points/$ for all airline and hotel partners; subsequent years, 1.5 points/$.
(hh) $15 for Green and Gold cardmembers, free for Platinum.
(ii) Applies to all new purchases, even with outstanding balance.

power of various frequent-flier programs. Those entries show the miles (or "points," a mileage equivalent used in some programs) required for a free Coach round-trip to anywhere a participating airline flies in the lower 48 states plus adjacent areas (within Canada, for the Canadian lines). In airline-sponsored programs, that figure is usually 25,000 miles, regardless of trip length. However, two of the bank programs—*ASTA Travel Plus* and *Travel Max*—offer a short-haul trip for less mileage.

Expiration shows how long credit, once earned, remains valid. Obviously, indefinite or at least long credit life is important to travelers who don't earn mileage credit quickly.

The last column, *Rental-car CDW,* is also key. It shows the cards that provide free collision-damage coverage for rental cars. As the table shows, most plain-vanilla *MasterCard* and *Visa* cards (as well as *Discover)* don't cover collision. Most coverage is secondary: The

card picks up only what you can't recover from other insurance. Only *Diners Club* offers primary coverage—the card picks up the entire tab, regardless of what other insurance you have.

THE DINING OPTION

Dining cards are the newest wrinkle in frequent-flier programs. The standard dining card offers a cash discount or rebate, usually 20–25% of the food and beverage bill, at hundreds of participating restaurants throughout the US and overseas. But airline dining-card programs rebate airline mileage rather than cash; the table below highlights the key features of six programs:

•*Dining a la Card Miles* (earns credit on TWA) and *Mileage Plus Dining* (earns United credit) are the most generous programs, overall. When you enroll, you receive a directory of participating restaurants. You get 10 miles per dollar spent, equivalent to a 20% cash rebate, when you patronize those restaurants. The rebate

MILES FROM DINING CARDS*

PROGRAM NAME	AIRLINE (a)	ANNUAL FEE	MILES PER DOLLAR CHARGED	CREDIT FOR FOOD AND BEVERAGE	CREDIT FOR TAXES	CREDIT FOR GRATUITY
AAdvantage Dining	AA	—	3	✔	✔	—
Dine Air	AS	—	3	✔	—	—
Dining a la Card Miles	TW	$49.95(b)	10(c)	✔	✔	✔
Dining for Miles	NW	—	2(e)	✔	—	—
Mileage Plus Dining(f)	UA	—	10(c)	✔	✔	✔
Transmedia	UA,CO	$ 9.95(g)	10	✔	—	—

Note: * As of May 1996; listed alphabetically.
(a) AA = American, AS = Alaska, CO = Continental, NW = Northwest, TW = TWA, UA = United.
(b) First 60 days free.
(c) Limited to user's first visit to a restaurant each month.
(d) Maximum party of six.

applies to the entire tab: food, beverage, tax, and tip. The main limitation is that you get credit at any one restaurant only for your first visit of the month. And the United program, as of now, is restricted to VFF members of its frequent-flier program.

When you enroll in either program, you "register" up to three *AmEx, MasterCard,* or *Visa* cards that you plan to use at restaurants. If you choose to register an airline card (from any airline), you still get the one mile per dollar charged that the airline card provides, along with the 10 miles you get from the dining program. At the restaurant, you need only present one of your registered cards; the mileage is calculated and transferred automatically. The card and restaurant program needn't be from the same airline: You could, for example, enroll your American Airlines charge card in the United dining program.

• The *Transmedia* card also gives 10 miles per dollar, but only on the food and beverage portion of the bill. Transmedia, the industry leader, issues its own card, which you use at restaurants as if it were a charge card; Transmedia transfers airline credit to your account upon request.

• *Three airline programs* are considerably less generous, giving only two or three miles per dollar charged for food and beverages (the American program also gives credit for taxes, but none gives credit for gratuities). Members of American's frequent-flier program must request a special card (no fee). With Alaska and Northwest, you just show your airline frequent-flier membership card at the restaurant and ask that you be credited.

Where there's no enrollment fee, signing up for a mileage-earning dining card is a no-brainer. At a restaurant that participates in both an airline program and a regular dining-card program, you always have the choice of a discount or rebate, if you

MIN./MAX. RESTAURANT CHARGE PER VISIT	AUTOMATIC TRANSFER	PARTICIPATING RESTAURANTS	CARD NECESSARY TO RECEIVE CREDIT	PHONE NUMBER TO ENROLL
—/—	✔	3000	AAdvantage Dining	800-267-2606
$20/—	✔	154	Alaska Mileage Plan	800-207-8232
—/$600(d)	✔	5200	Any 3 registered cards	800-804-7169
$25/—	✔	125	Northwest WorldPerks	800-447-3757 ext. 4
—/$600(d)	✔	5200	Any 3 registered cards	800-555-5116
—	—/—(h)	6266	Transmedia	800-806-3463

(e) Request a Dining for Miles voucher to receive credit.
(f) Limited to VFF members.
(g) Enrollment bonus: 1,000 miles if the card is used within first 30 days.
(h) Parties of 7 or more must reserve through Transmedia in advance.

prefer, rather than mileage. And at a restaurant that participates only in an airline program, the mileage represents a substantial value that you'd otherwise lose.

WHICH FOR YOU?

Though all the mileage-earning cards work on the same principle, they differ in important details. Here's how to pick your personal best:

- If you travel a lot—and charge a lot—you should probably carry one of the travel-and-entertainment cards and sign up for its mileage program. Credit doesn't expire, and it's transferable to any of several airlines.
- For places that don't take T&E cards, or if you want to use just one card, consider a *MasterCard* or *Visa* sponsored by the airline you fly the most.

You can use card mileage to top up the mileage you earn by flying.

- The independent bank cards are attractive mainly to people who earn little or no credit by flying and who have no interest in flying Business or First Class.
- If your primary interest is in hotel stays or cruises, consider a hotel or cruise card.
- No matter what other cards you use, note that a dining card gives you a bigger bang for the buck than any other mile-earning card.

This chapter was adapted from the Consumer Reports Travel Letter *articles "Three New Charge Cards" (September 1996) and "Travel Plastic: Trip Payoffs for Every Dollar Charged" (June 1996).*

WINGS AND WHEELS

STRATEGIES FOR CUTTING AIRFARES

For many travelers, getting the best airfare is more than just an exercise in smart shopping: It's a challenge to beat a system they perceive as unfair and capricious. This chapter provides a kit of fare-cutting tools.

RECOGNIZING BARGAINS

These days, only a tiny fraction of travelers pay full Coach fare. Yet airlines continue to use that standard as a basis for their discount claims.

To recognize a bargain, compare any domestic fare you're considering with the Coach excursion fare on a major airline. Those fares, known by such trade names as *Super Saver* and *Max Saver,* are the lowest the big lines offer except during true fare sales. For international flights, the equivalent is the cheapest Economy excursion, usually called *Apex* or *Super Apex.*

The big airlines call those low-end prices discount fares, but that's a misnomer—they're list prices for highly restricted tickets. Those tickets are nonrefundable but usually exchangeable—you can't get a cash refund, but you can generally apply their dollar value toward the purchase of another ticket, less a processing fee (currently $50 on big lines). A few tickets are still truly nonrefundable: If you don't use them as originally issued, they become worthless.

Coach/Economy excursion seats are limited: An airline may offer no more than 10% of its seats (or none at all, on some flights) at the lowest advertised prices.

SALE FARES: HARD TO BEAT

American travelers have enjoyed an almost steady stream of domestic airfare sales over the past few years. Typically, the purchase window is quite small—some sales last just one day—but buyers usually have several months to complete travel at the sale prices. Domestic sale fares can run as much as 50% below regular Coach-excursion fare levels (though 30–40% reductions are more common). Typical transcontinental sale fares hover around the $400 mark.

You'll have a tough time beating a sale airfare on a major line. (The other strategies we discuss come into play most often when you can't accept the advance-purchase or Saturday-night-stay restrictions that apply to most sale fares.) Such promotions may offer straight fare reductions, free or low-cost companion tickets, or free tickets to one area if you buy a ticket to another.

Even the cheapest regular Coach excursions can also be a good buy, especially for longer trips. But you may find it hard to get seats at the lowest fares.

The restrictions and buying limitations on all those attractive list-price tickets are designed to make them difficult for business travelers to use. But the limits often prevent vacation travelers from using them too: You must usually make reservations and buy tickets long before departure. Travel may be limited to certain days or dates or require a Saturday-night stay. And seats may not be available when you want them.

Sale fares are usually advertised early in the week in major newspapers. But you can get a head start by having a travel agent check the computer reservation system over the weekend. All new fares, including some that aren't advertised in the papers, show up there first.

If your preferred airline doesn't have a seat when you want it, check another carrier. Competitors almost always match sale fares, even if they don't advertise the fact. However, the airline that started the fare war will most likely have more sale seats than its competitors.

It also pays to be flexible. Flights at nonpeak times—midday, late at night, or midweek—will have far more sale seats available. If the flight or day you want is sold out, there's still hope. Try calling the reservation number in the late evening or early morning. That's when airlines reevaluate their pricing and release some high-priced seats at lower prices. After about 10 P.M. Eastern time, you may be able find a cheap seat on a flight that had none earlier in the day.

What if you've just missed an advertised sale's midnight deadline? Try calling directory assistance in a city in an earlier time zone. Ask for the local reservation number—not the 800 number —of the airline, then call it to reserve your seat. If it's not midnight yet in Honolulu, the sale is still on there.

Once you've paid, watch for even better fares. Nonrefundable tickets can almost always be reissued for a lower sale price. The airlines charge a fee—generally $50 per ticket—for the reissue, but the price difference could still make the switch worth the effort.

SPECIAL TWO DISCOUNTS

You can fly TWA for 20% off just about any advertised TWA ticket, domestic or international, First Class to sale-priced Coach. The tickets earn TWA frequent-flier credit and carry the same restrictions that would apply without the discount.

A few TWA tickets are excluded, most notably senior and student coupons. And you can't get a discount for travel on TWA-labeled flights that are actually flown by other airlines under a code-sharing agreement. That includes TWA's affiliated commuter lines.

As part of a financial restructuring, TWA contracted to sell tickets to investor Carl Icahn for 40% or more off the advertised price. Icahn, in turn, is selling them to the public for 20% off through his own distribution arm: Global Discount Travel, Las Vegas; 800-497-6678 *(AE, Disc, MC, V)*.

You can also buy the tickets at local offices of Omega World Travel, a large chain with 220 locations throughout the US *(DC, MC, V)*. Omega says it needs three to five business days to deliver tickets. If you can't find a local Omega office in your phone book, call 800-955-2582 for the office nearest you.

LOW-FARE AIRLINES

As another way to save, try a low-cost carrier. Low-cost lines, in fact, often make it possible to combine two short-haul flights for less than it costs to fly direct. That "split-ticket" method has limitations, though: You'll have to stop and change planes. If your carrier doesn't automatically switch your bags to another carrier, you'll have to recheck them yourself. And you may have to wait a long time for your connecting flight at the intermediate airport—the separate low-fare lines don't coordinate schedules.

There has been quite a bit of come and go in recent years, but a few of the new lines seem to be showing some staying power. All those listed below offer low unrestricted fares, and several offer even lower fares if you reserve in advance, fly at off-peak times, or buy a round-trip ticket. Most provide only very tight Coach/Economy seating. Except as noted, none has a frequent-flier program. (All information is as of a *CRTL* report in early 1996 and is subject to change.)

On ticketless airlines, you book with a charge card by phone and receive a confirmation number that you give to an airline agent at the boarding gate. Ticketless lines can also be booked through travel agents—though some aren't listed in the computer reservation systems (CRSs) that travel agents use.

Air South flies from Columbia SC to Savannah, Greenville, Spartanburg, and Jacksonville (all located in SC). *Air South* also flies to Chicago/Midway, Norfolk, and New York/JFK.

AirTran Airways flies from its Orlando hub to points in the Northeast, Midwest, and South. All flights are nonstop.

Air 21 links Fresno with Las Vegas, Palm Springs, and San Francisco. It's one of several small lines that use full-sized jets to compete with commuter airlines' turboprops. The line is ticketless and isn't listed in CRSs.

American Trans Air links the Midwest with sun destinations—Arizona, California, Florida, Hawaii, Las Vegas, and the Caribbean. Some routes are seasonal.

Carnival Air Lines flies from Florida hubs to the Northeast, Los Angeles, and the Caribbean. Most flights are one class, but premium seating is available on flights that use A300 Airbus equipment. The line has a simple frequent-flier program—you earn points good for flights,

Carnival cruises, and other awards.

Eastwind is the first big-jet airline to use Trenton-Mercer Airport, located in New Jersey between the New York/Newark and Philadelphia areas. It flies from there to Atlanta, Boston, Greensboro, Orlando, and Richmond.

Frontier flies from Denver to Albuquerque, Chicago/Midway, El Paso, Las Vegas, Los Angeles, Minneapolis/St. Paul, Omaha, Phoenix, Salt Lake City, San Diego, San Francisco, Seattle, and St. Louis. Flights that use 737-200s provide very generous legroom; unfortunately, most seats in the line's 737-300s are rather tight. Frontier participates in Continental's *OnePass* frequent-flier program, which also includes a long list of partner airlines, car-rental companies, and hotels. Travelers can also opt instead for Frontier's own program.

Jet Express is one of several lines that have found the Southeast receptive to a new arrival. It flies between Myrtle Beach and Chicago/Midway, Cleveland, Detroit, New York (JFK, Newark), and Philadelphia. It's a ticketless airline and isn't in CRSs.

Kiwi Intl has suspended operations as of press time.

Laker flies from Ft Lauderdale to Europe.

Reno Air flies from Reno, San Jose CA, or both to Alaska, Albuquerque, Anchorage, Chicago/O'Hare, Colorado Springs, Denver, Las Vegas, Laughlin, Los Angeles, Orange County, Palm Springs (winter route), Portland OR, San Diego, Seattle, Tucson, and Vancouver. Like Midway, Reno is a participant in American's frequent-flier program, and it has some other important advantages over its regional low-fare competitors: roomier seating and a low-cost First Class option.

Spirit goes from Florida to Atlantic City, Boston, Detroit, Myrtle Beach, and Philadelphia.

Sunair hopes to carve a niche in Cincinnati by undercutting Delta on flights to Ft Lauderdale, Orlando, and Tampa. It's not in CRSs.

Sunjet Intl is one of the few small lines that have targeted medium- and long-haul trips. It flies from Newark to Florida points, Dallas/Ft Worth, and Long Beach, and between Dallas/Ft Worth and St Petersburg/Clearwater.

Tower Air flies from New York/JFK to Amsterdam, Los Angeles, Miami, Oakland, Paris, San Juan, Sao Paulo, and Tel Aviv. Its unrestricted (and nonrefundable) Coach/Economy fares are a good deal, if you can conform to the line's infrequent schedules on some routes. And its Business Class is one of the best deals for anyone who wants a comfortable seat at a moderate price.

Tristar's flights have pulled back lately but still link Los Angeles and San Francisco with some important regional vacation destinations.

ValuJet, as of press time, has resumed service and is rebuilding its system. ValuJet's outlook for 1997 is uncertain.

Vanguard flies routes that extend from its Kansas City hub to Chicago/Midway, Dallas/Ft Worth, Denver, Des Moines, Los Angeles, Minneapolis/St Paul, San Francisco, and Wichita. Vanguard is ticketless. It has a simple frequent-flier program: 16 one-way flights over a 12-month period earn one free round-trip; no partner airlines, car-rental companies, or hotels.

Western Pacific is one of the main reasons Colorado Springs is giving the Denver airport some stiff competition. *West Pac* flies to 22 cities on the East or West Coasts, in the Midwest, or in the South. Not in CRSs/ticketless.

CHECK OUT CHARTERS

Charter flights also offer savings opportunities over the cheapest Coach/Economy fares on a major line (see chapter 6). Domestic charters fly mainly from large cities to popular tourist and gambling destinations: Las Vegas, Florida, Hawaii, and the Caribbean, plus ski centers in the winter and Europe in the summer.

HUBBING REDUCTIONS

On a few long-haul routes, some lines offer travelers a lower fare if they connect through one of the line's hubs than for a nonstop flight. (On the other hand, hubbing makes each one-way trip take about two hours longer than a nonstop flight, risks missing a connection, and increases the chance of losing baggage.)

In addition to providing a fare saving, a hubbing connection sometimes lets you use an airport that's handier to your origin or destination point than a major airport. The airlines don't fly transcontinental nonstops to or from such airports as Burbank, LaGuardia, Long Island/MacArthur, Oakland, or National, but they fly frequently between those airports and one or more midcountry hubs. A hub connection to or from one of those secondary fields can save you a bit extra (in ground-transportation cost) and partially offset the extra travel time.

DISCOUNT TICKETS

Airlines often unload some tickets through consolidators—outlets that sell those tickets to the public for less than the airlines say they should cost (see chapter 5). The most consistent consolidator deals are for travel across the Pacific, where they're available most of the year at prices as much as $300 below the cheapest advertised Economy excursions. Similar reductions are available across the Atlantic during the summer, when advertised fares are high. During the winter, the airlines' advertised low-season fares are hard to beat.

Consolidator tickets are rare for travel within the US. Even when available, they seldom cost less than the cheapest advertised Coach excursions, but they often carry less onerous restrictions.

The biggest risk with consolidator tickets is in buying them: All too many discount agencies are slow to deliver tickets and reluctant to provide any assistance once they've made the sale. Your best protection is to buy with a charge card. Other problems are minor but worth noting: The cheapest ticket may entail extra connections or layovers. If something goes wrong, the airline on which you're ticketed isn't likely to transfer you to another line. You may not earn frequent-flier mileage. And you may not have a choice of seats or meals.

DISCOUNT COUPONS

Airlines frequently offer dollars-off coupons, with the amount of reduction usually keyed to the price of the ticket. You can get those coupons from a variety of sources—many *Entertainment* half-price books have them, for example (see chapter 15). You also see them in promotions from such sources as retail stores, banks, and charge cards.

Airlines sometimes even accept coupons issued by a competing line. When planning a trip, check the acceptance of any airline discount coupon you happen to have (except one for a frequent-flier promotion, which typically isn't transferable). If you prefer to use a line other than the issuer—for a better schedule, perhaps, or to concentrate your frequent-flier benefits—ask the competitor if it will match the discount.

There's no risk to coupons, but they often impose restrictions on where or when you can travel, and you may not be able to use them with sale fares. Use them if you can accept the limitations.

TWOFERS

Airlines often offer free or cut-price companion tickets: One traveler pays the full price, and a companion traveling on an identical itinerary gets a free or discounted ticket. Southwest's ongoing *Friends Fly Free* promotion is the most prominent example, but it changes fairly frequently, so check the airline.

There's certainly no risk to twofers. The biggest problem is that the purchased ticket must usually be at full fare. That makes twofers a good deal in Business or First Class, where other reductions are rare. But you can often buy a ticket for Coach/Economy for less than half the base fare required for a twofer.

REBATES

All airlines pay travel agents a commission. The standard rates are 10% on domestic tickets, 8% on international. However, most big US lines have capped commissions on domestic tickets at $25 for a one-way ticket, $50 for a round-trip. So far, several smaller lines have not adopted the cap. Initially, the cap didn't apply to international tickets. However, there have been many industry rumors about a possible international cap sometime soon.

Cap or no, airlines continue to offer "commission overrides" for agents who meet volume quotas. Overrides can range from 1–5% of the ticket price for domestic flights and can be as much as 40% or so on international tickets. Some agencies pass on part of their commissions to travelers in the form of rebates. You can save 7–10% on just about any domestic ticket by buying from one of those agencies. (See chapter 1.)

Many bank charge cards and travel clubs also offer a ticketing service that rebates 4–5% of the ticket price—about half the usual commission.

STATUS FARES

Special fares for groups—known as status fares—provide discounts, though not necessarily attractive ones. Discounted fares for meetings and conventions, for instance, are minor: usually 5% off the lowest regular excursion fare. Most airlines also give an underwhelming 10% discount to seniors for domestic or international travel.

But the senior coupon still affords some great bargains. Certain status fares provide some savings for youngsters. Compassionate fares—discounted fares for travelers going to a funeral or the bedside of a gravely ill relative—also are helpful for last-minute travel in an emergency. (See chapter 8.)

OTHER COST CUTTERS

Adroit use of loopholes in ticket-buying rules can also cut your costs substantially. Three popular strategies:

- **Back-to-back tickets.** Sometimes called "nested tickets," those let travelers avoid the Saturday-night stay that the cheapest Coach excursions normally require. (They must, however, comply with all the other restrictions—advance-purchase period, seat limitations, and nonrefundability.)

  Instead of buying one expensive round-trip that doesn't require a Saturday-night stay, the travelers buy two cheap round-trip excursions, each of which does require a stay—one from their home city to their destination and back, the other from their destination to their home city and back. They use the "going" portion of the first ticket to start their trip and the "going" portion of the second ticket to return. The two tickets are separate, so the airline can't tell how long they stay at their destination.

  Back-to-back tickets save money whenever the cheapest Coach excursion is less than half the unrestricted round-trip fare. If Coach excursion tickets are bought during a fare war, the savings can be even larger.

  In the simplest version of the stratagem, a traveler actually takes just one round-trip, throwing away the "return" portion of both round-trips. But of course back-to-back tickets can save far more if used for two trips (the "return" coupons of the tickets provide the second trip). As the major limitation, the traveler must typically take both trips within 30 days, the maximum stay allowed on many of the cheap excursions.

  Airlines say that back-to-back tickets violate their rules. For a while, they tried to police their use through ticket audits. But passengers quickly figured out how to get around that barrier (by buying each of the two tickets on different airlines or from different travel agencies), and some airlines have apparently stopped trying to collect. Nevertheless, travelers run some risk of airline retaliation in using back-to-back tickets.

  There are also two other gambits, but they're risky and invite cancellation of your ticket if you're caught:

- **Hidden-city ploys.** Now and then, you can save by overshooting your mark: A traveler headed from A to B buys a cheaper ticket from A to C by way of B, and gets off the plane (or doesn't get on the connecting flight) at B, the real destination.

  For example, you can't check baggage to the intermediate city where you plan to get off. If your ticket says you're going through to New York, your bags would have to be checked through to there, too.

Hidden-city works best on one-way tickets. While you might use the "going" portion of a round-trip ticket to New York for a trip from San Francisco to Cincinnati, you'd run a big risk on the return trip. These days, airlines typically issue boarding passes for both flights of a connecting itinerary when you check in for the first flight. Showing up at the departure gate in Cincinnati with a ticket to San Francisco (rather than a boarding pass) for what is supposed to be a connecting flight will immediately arouse the agent's suspicion.

Airlines have been checking for hidden-city ticketing, a violation of their rules. If you're detected, you or your travel agency may receive a bill for the difference between what you paid and what you should have paid for the shorter flight.

On round-trip tickets, your return space may also be canceled. And if you check in for the final destination of a through flight and get off at an intermediate stop, you could delay the flight several hours while the airline investigates the "loss" of one passenger.

• **Frequent-flier coupons.** An entire underground industry has developed to broker frequent-flier awards, which are primarily used for upgrades. A broker pays a frequent flier to obtain an award, then sells it to someone else at a profit. If you see a discount

---

TRAVEL AS A COURIER?

International express-delivery companies need travelers to act as couriers for high-priority shipments. Those companies subsidize part of a courier's airfare. Express companies generally rely on a handful of specialized agencies to sell those heavily subsidized courier tickets—don't bother to contact a shipping company directly.

At popular times, the reduction from published fares may be small. But couriers can sometimes fly for less than half the cheapest Economy excursion fare. If a delivery company needs a last-minute courier, the trip may be almost free.

Courier trips are available only to large commercial centers overseas and only from a few of the biggest US gateways to a few dozen of the world's major business centers. If you want to start out at, say, Kansas City, you must pay your own way to Chicago, Los Angeles, Miami, New York, or San Francisco.

Most courier tickets are round-trips, and you may have to return on a specified date—often as soon as one week after you arrive. You usually can't check baggage, so you have to travel out of a carry-on bag. Each trip is available to only one courier, so couples must either travel on separate days or one member must buy a

agency's newspaper ad for "Business and First Class, up to 70% off," it's probably selling frequent-flier awards.

Buying such an award isn't illegal, but it's risky. Airlines are scrutinizing frequent-flier awards more carefully; if a carrier thinks you bought your ticket from a broker, the carrier may not honor it. Furthermore, airlines allot so few premium-class seats for free frequent-flier travel that, even if you buy a coupon, you'll have a tough time using it. Don't buy someone else's coupons unless you enjoy taking big-time financial risks.

PREMIUM SEATS AT A BETTER PRICE

The world's major airlines have adopted a bizarre pricing strategy: They offer cheap, poor-quality service and eye-poppingly pricey deluxe options, with nothing in between. But it's not impossible to find a comfortable, premium seat at a reasonable price, at least as we define the terms:

- To be *reasonable*, a premium seat should cost either no more than twice the cheapest regular Coach/Economy excursion seat on a major line or no more than half a major line's full-fare Business or First Class seat.
- To qualify as *premium*, a seat should measure at least 22 inches between armrest centers, and the pitch (the front-to-rear spacing of seat rows) should be at least 34 inches. All the seats should be in pairs, to eliminate the chance that you'll be in a middle seat or seated next to somebody fid-

regular ticket. You may or may not receive frequent-flier credit.

There's little risk to courier travel, and not much to do. Typically, a representative of the shipping company hands the shipment over to you at the check-in counter, and another representative retrieves it at baggage claim. You may have to repeat the process on your return trip. The biggest risk is no-showing: You stand to lose your entire ticket prepayment, to say nothing of having the courier agency blacklist you for future flights.

For an overview of agencies, fares, and procedures, read *Air Courier Bargains,* by Kelly Monaghan ($14.95 at bookstores, $17.95 from Intrepid Traveler, 800-356-9315; *AE, Disc, MC, V*). To keep up with current trips and fares, consider joining a courier "club." The Intl Assn of Air Travel Couriers publishes a bimonthly newsletter detailing trips and fares available from dozens of courier-booking agencies in the US and overseas (P.O. Box 1349, Lake Worth FL 33460, 407-582-8320, $45 a year). The Air Courier Assn (ACA) provides about the same mix of services (191 University Blvd, Suite 300, Denver CO 80206, $58 for the first year, $28 for subsequent years).

geting in one. The least roomy domestic First Class or intercontinental Business Class seats about meet those criteria, with a *CRTL* Comfort Score of 95 (see chapter 7).

At an average comfort score of about 74, no major-airline Coach/Economy cabin comes close to meeting those standards. But certain small lines do offer comfortable options, at least some of the time, that pass our reasonableness test. Here are your best bets, as of our most recent report, in mid-1995.

ROOMY SEATS IN COACH

One small US airline—Midwest Express —offers comfortable one-class seating at regular Coach and Coach excursion prices. Its seating, in DC9s and MD80s, is almost as roomy as First Class on other lines: The seats are four across (2-2, with no middle seats) at 33- and 34-inch pitch, a setup that earns Comfort Scores of 98 and 100. The line serves major cities in the East, Southeast, Midwest, and California via a Milwaukee hub.

As far as we know, the only other line in the world to use the Midwest Express formula is ACES, a small Colombian line that fits only 98 seats, arranged in pairs, into its 727-200s.

Coach/Economy seating on United's new 777 is a bit better than on their competition. However, the advantage over regular Coach/Economy is slight —far below our comfort standard.

PREMIUM COACH/ECONOMY

A few foreign lines offer a separate premium Economy cabin in addition to ordinary Economy. The most notable is Taiwan-based EVA: Its *Evergreen Deluxe* cabin, on 747s, provides eight-across (2-4-2) seating at 38-inch pitch, for a comfort score of 95. Between the US and Taipei, the minimum round-trip fare for that cabin, as of this writing, easily passed our test of a reasonable surcharge.

On flights to Tel Aviv, Tower Air offers an Economy Premium option that, as of late 1996, was $350 more each way than its cheapest Economy fare. The seats were standard Economy triples, with the middle seats kept unoccupied.

A few other lines (including Air India and Virgin Atlantic) also have premium Economy cabins, with seating similar to EVA's. But those lines reserve their extra roomy Economy seats for travelers on full-fare Economy tickets or for certain frequent fliers, putting them on the wrong side of our reasonableness threshold. The same holds true for the convertible seats USAir uses on some planes.

CHEAP PREMIUM CLASS

A few airlines offer Business or First Class tickets at a lot less than you'd expect to pay:

- Carnival (on some flights) and Reno Air offer premium seats at fares well below what the big lines charge.
- Tower Air offers low premium fares on most of its scheduled flights from New York to Los Angeles, Miami, Paris, San Francisco, San Juan, and Tel Aviv.
- Hawaiian Airlines sells low-cost First Class tickets from Los Angeles, San Francisco, and Seattle to Honolulu

(seniors 60 or over and kids 2–11 get a 10% discount).

- On El Al flights from the US to Tel Aviv, you can upgrade from any Economy ticket, including the cheapest excursions, to Business Class for a reasonable surcharge.
- On its scheduled flights from New York to Tel Aviv, World Airways offers its premium class for just double the regular round-trip Economy fare.

DISCOUNTED PREMIUM SEATS

While discount-ticket brokers often handle premium-class tickets, few offer more than about 15–20% off—far too little to pass our reasonableness test. Now and then, however, a premium fare is discounted enough to make the grade.

POSH FREQUENT-FLIER SEATS

On most lines, you can use frequent-flier mileage for free Business or First Class tickets if you can find the seats to most parts of the world.

- The big lines require 35,000–45,000 miles for domestic off-peak, round-trip travel in their first level of premium seating: First Class on two-class planes, Business Class on three-class planes. (Chapter 9 tells what mileage each major line requires.) A free "domestic" trip normally includes nearby cities in Canada and the Caribbean.
- To Hawaii, the big lines ask 50,000–60,000 miles for an off-peak premium seat; to Europe, you need 55,000–100,000 miles.

Figuring mileage at 2¢ a mile, the typical 40,000-mile award for a domestic premium trip is worth $800. That passes our reasonableness test (double the cheapest Coach excursion) only when you use it for a long-haul flight —and even then, during a fare war, it's a stretch.

Similarly, using 60,000 miles (worth

NO "OLD STANDBY"

You sometimes hear someone talk about going out to the airport "to get a cheap standby seat." However, it's been years since any of the big airlines routinely offered cheap seats to standby travelers. Travelers who show up at the last minute usually pay the highest available fare, not the lowest—in fact, airlines often refer to their top price as the walk-up fare.

Still, there are a few cases when heading for the gate makes sense:

- The East Coast "shuttles" from New York to either Boston or Washington offer a true standby service, but it isn't cheap. The so-called shuttles in the West are cheap, but only if you buy tickets 21 days ahead.
- Most lines let travelers on Coach excursions stand by for an earlier flight on the day they're ticketed.
- Travelers on senior and youth coupons (see chapter 8) can usually travel standby at the same price they pay with an advance reservation.

$1200) for a free premium trip to Hawaii makes sense mainly for travelers from the East Coast, Midwest, or South. West Coast travelers are better off buying a cheap First Class seat on Hawaiian or Northwest for $700 or so and saving their mileage for some other trip.

MILEAGE UPGRADES

Most US lines let you use frequent-flier credit to upgrade a Coach/Economy ticket, including most of the cheapest excursions. Mileage upgrades provide a firm premium-class reservation.

- The big domestic lines typically require a 20,000-mile award to upgrade a Coach excursion ticket to the next higher class of service. While several lines let you upgrade a full-fare Coach

ticket for less mileage, starting out with a full-fare ticket automatically flunks our reasonableness test.

- To Europe, upgrades from Economy excursion fares require 40,000 miles on most lines. USAir and British Airways don't provide those mileage upgrades at all. At a minimum value of $800, mileage upgrades to Europe are especially good deals for travelers from the West Coast. Even though the value of the mileage required for an upgrade can exceed the cost of an Economy excursion from the East, an upgrade is still attractive to some travelers looking to spend their frequent-flier credit to maximize their comfort.

At our benchmark 2¢ a mile, it's generally less efficient to use mileage

STANDBY TO EUROPE

Airhitch operates a de facto standby service for airlines (mainly charter lines) from major US gateway cities to Europe. Travelers interested in a cheap trip register and prepay with *Airhitch,* specify a zone (Northeast, Southeast, Midwest, or West Coast) from which they want to depart, a five-day date range during which they want to leave, and three preferences from *Airhitch's* list of available destinations.

Airhitch provides a flight voucher and a call-in date on which it will provide a list of available flights and, for each, the airline and flight schedule, origin city and airport, destination city and airport, and probable number of seats available. Travelers decide which flight(s) to try for, then head to the airport. Standby priority goes by registration date. Travelers who don't make a flight during their date range receive a full refund.

The system works the same way coming home. *Airhitch* maintains a year-round office in Paris and additional seasonal offices in other large European cities.

Two affiliated programs serve other areas. *Sunhitch* arranges standby winter-season flights from the northeastern US to Caribbean and Mexican beach resorts. Most are round-trips with a one-week stay, and most confirm a return seat to

for upgrades than to apply it toward a free ticket. However, airlines are very stingy with free seats, but upgrades of a purchased ticket are less restricted. When you can't find a free seat, a mileage upgrade may be the only practical way to trade mileage for comfort.

PURCHASED UPGRADES

Several lines sell books of coupons or stickers that their frequent fliers can use to upgrade Coach tickets, either within a few days of departure or standby. The number of coupons required is based on the length of the flight. Unless you're a very frequent flier, however, you can't use purchased upgrades with the airlines' cheapest Coach excursion tickets.

BECOME A VFF MEMBER

Upgrades that don't require ordinary frequent fliers to use mileage are elusive. But the picture changes radically for those who reach even the first level of a major-line's VFF (very frequent flier) program (see chapter 9).

United's program provides a good example. On that line, travelers at the first VFF level can purchase coupons to upgrade Coach excursion tickets. Sold in books of four, coupons covering 1000 flight miles cost $50 apiece as of January 1, 1997; those covering 500 flight miles cost $40 each. A Los Angeles–New York trip, at 2463 miles, requires two 1000-mile coupons and one 500-miler, for a total of $140 each way—easily passing our reasonableness test.

travelers who make the standby departure. And *Airhitch USA* offers one-way standby flights on a few long-haul domestic routes.

In late 1996, the standard *Airhitch* one-way fares to Europe, regardless of destination, were $169 from the Northeast, $229 from the Southeast or Midwest, and $269 from the West Coast. (Those fares compare with discounted Economy excursions and list-price charter fares of about $400–700 from the East Coast, $600–800 from the West.) *Sunhitch* flights cost $189, round-trip. *Airhitch USA* flights cost $79–129 one-way.

Like any standby operation, *Airhitch* can't promise a seat—it says only that it has a good track record in getting travelers to their destinations. Similarly, while it promises only to get them to somewhere in Europe, it claims it gets them to their preferred destinations most of the time.

Airhitch deals mainly with charter airlines, so flights operate only a few days of the week and on a limited number of routes. The service appeals mainly to students and other travelers who plan an extended visit to Europe and don't mind a variation of a day or two in their transatlantic itineraries or a switch in gateways. (Call *Airhitch* at 212-864-2000 in NYC, 310-726-5000 in Los Angeles, 011-33-1-4700-1630 in Paris.)

First-level VFF travelers reserve and ticket in Coach. Then they call the airline 24 hours before departure: If seats are available, they get a firm reservation in Business or First Class. If not, they can stand by for an upgrade. Higher VFF levels provide extended privileges.

The other big lines provide similar upgrades for VFF members. TWA passengers attain the line's first VFF level by flying only 5000 miles, much fewer than on other lines, but they can use upgrade coupons only on a standby basis.

VFF status doesn't guarantee a comfortable trip every time. In our experience, there are seldom enough First Class seats left by flight time to satisfy all eligible travelers—especially on 727s, 737s, DC9s, Fokkers, and MD80s, which may have as few as eight First Class seats. But the situation is usually better on larger planes, which have a higher ratio of premium to Coach seats and, thus, provide better upgrade odds.

Unfortunately, the airlines' relative generosity with domestic VFF upgrades doesn't extend to overseas flights. For the most part, first-level VFF fliers can't buy upgrades from Economy excursions.

Despite the problems, the ability to use coupons to upgrade Coach excursions is, to many travelers, the most important single benefit of VFF status. If you travel upward of 25,000 miles a year, it's a powerful incentive to concentrate that flying on a single line. In fact, if you're close to VFF status near the end of the year, it may pay to take a cheap long-distance flight merely to push your year's mileage over the top.

TRY A PREMIUM CHARTER

A few charter lines (and Martinair, which operates on a charterlike schedule) offer premium seating at reasonable prices. Premium charter fares are typically 75–150% higher than charter Economy fares, but they're a lot less than half the Business Class fares on major lines.

- Tower uses its two-class 747s for charters to many of the same cities it serves with its scheduled flights.
- Condor, Lufthansa's charter subsidiary, flies to Frankfurt from several US gateways. Its premium Comfort Class seating is available for a reasonable surcharge over the regular Economy fares.
- In 1996, Martinair Holland flew to Amsterdam from Denver, Edmonton, Ft Lauderdale, Los Angeles, Miami, Newark, Oakland, Orlando, Seattle, Tampa, and Toronto. Its premium Star Class was available at about double its regular Economy fares.

Other charter lines we've checked didn't offer a premium option. For some flights, however, tour operators charter planes with a premium-class cabin. Whenever you consider a charter, ask if there are premium options.

WATCH FOR TWOFERS

You'll often see pitches for free premium-class companion tickets from various sources, including airline frequent-flier programs and hotels: Buy one

Business or First Class ticket at the regular fare and get a free second ticket for a companion who travels on an identical itinerary. (Separate return schedules are occasionally allowed.) For two travelers, a free-companion deal is a 50% discount and, by definition, passes our reasonableness test.

Those deals are most attractive for flights to Asia, where a list-price Business Class ticket often costs about the same as two Economy excursion tickets. To Europe, however, Business Class fares are so high that, even at half price, a Business Class seat can cost three times as much as an Economy excursion.

WHERE TO FIND IT

Tickets (or equivalent—airlines marked * are ticketless) for all listed lines can be purchased from any travel agency.

ACES: 800-846-2237.
Air South: 800-247-7688.
AirTran Airways (ticketless if airline is called directly): 800-247-8726.
Air 21*: 800-359-2472.
American Trans Air: 800-225-2995.
Balair: 800-322-5247.
Carnival: 800-824-7386.

Condor: 800-524-6975.
Eastwind*: 800-644-3592.
El Al: 800-223-6700.
EVA: 800-695-1188.
Frontier: 800-432-1359.
Hawaiian: 800-367-5320.
Jet Express: 800-386-2786.
Laker: 888-525-3724.
Martinair: 800-366-4655.
Midwest Express: 800-452-2022.
Northwest: National, 800-225-2525; international, 800-447-4747.
Rebel Tours: 800-227-3235.
Reno Air: 800-736-6247.
Spirit: 800-772-7117.
Sunair: 800-786-2476.
Sunjet Intl: 800-478-6538.
Tower: 800-348-6937.
Tristar: 800-218-8777.
TWA: 800-221-2000.
United: 800-241-6522.
Valujet*: 800-825-8538.
Vanguard*: 800-826-4827.
Western Pacific*: 800-930-3030.
World Airways: 800-967-5350.

This chapter was adapted from the Consumer Reports Travel Letter *article "Small Low-Fare Airlines" (February 1996) and the 1996 edition of* Consumer Reports Best Travel Deals.

Consolidators for Discount Airfares

Consolidators have emerged as an effective weapon in consumer battles against excessive travel costs. Those brokers function as outlet stores, selling air tickets for less than the airlines' lowest list prices.

Airlines, naturally, would like to unload all their tickets at list price. But even their sale fares don't always tempt enough customers. Rather than slash prices openly (and invite competitive cuts from other lines), many then peddle some seats through consolidators.

As with outlet stores, consolidators ordinarily won't mention brand names (that is, airlines) in ads or promotions. But you do find out what line you'd fly on when you call to inquire about tickets.

The airlines price consolidator tickets in one of two ways. That's useful to know if frequent-flier benefits (or rock-bottom deals) matter to you:

- **Net fares.** Some consolidators contract with an airline to buy tickets at a "net" rate for each route. That's a bargain price that remains fixed even if the airline's advertised fares change.

To that, the consolidators add their own markup.

You generally won't find any dollar figure in the "fare" box on net-fare tickets, they typically don't earn frequent-flier mileage credit, and they can't be upgraded by frequent-flier mileage. Moreover, the airlines' advertised Economy excursion fares may well drop below the consolidators' best net prices in low seasons or during the short-term fare wars that airlines sometimes wage.

- **Padded commissions.** Other consolidators negotiate extra-large commissions (perhaps up to 40%) with one or more lines. On resale, consolidators retain only a fraction of that commission. They pass the rest of the reduction along to the retail agent or the customer to provide the discount. Prices for those tickets fluctuate with changes in the published fares.

No matter what price you actually pay, consolidator tickets discounted with extra-large commission overrides typically do show the airline's advertised fare in the "fare" box. Depending on the airline, such tickets often earn frequent-flier mileage and can be upgraded with the use of a frequent-flier award.

How much extra should you pay for a ticket that earns frequent-flier mileage? Figure that credit is worth 2¢ a mile. On a round-trip from the East Coast to Europe, you'd earn about $140 worth of credit; from the West Coast to Hong Kong, twice that. If the no-credit ticket doesn't save you more than the value of the mileage, forget it.

WHO'S WHO

The airfare discounters listed at the end of this chapter come in two basic flavors:

- *Consolidators* are agencies that have contracted with one or more airlines to distribute discount tickets. Some are strictly wholesalers; they sell only to travel agencies that retail the tickets. Others sell directly to the public. Some do both.
- *Discount agencies* are travel agencies that sell consolidator tickets (or other discounted travel services) to the public. Some act as their own consolidators; others buy their tickets from wholesalers. Most discount agencies tend to specialize in just one type of travel service—air trips, cruises, or hotel accommodations.

Some discount agencies don't sell consolidator tickets at all. Instead, they rebate a part of their commission on travel services they sell at list price (see chapter 1). Whatever else it may be, each agency listed in the main section of our *Discount Ticket Directory* is a retail discount agency that sells consolidator tickets to the public.

Consolidators listed in *For Travel Agents Only* (see page 70) are wholesalers that sell only to travel agencies, not to the public. We include them for the benefit of our travel-agency readers, as well as for travelers who might want to show the list to the agencies they normally patronize. Readers shouldn't contact any of those agencies directly.

WHAT YOU CAN SAVE

How much you'll save with a consolidator ticket depends on where you're going and when. You'll often save hundreds of dollars on flights to Asia and Latin America at any time of the year. On flights to Europe, the biggest discounts are for summer travel, when advertised Economy excursion fares are high. In winter, the airlines' regular excursion fares are often no higher than the best deals consolidators offer. Even in summer, fare wars often slash regular rates below typical consolidator offerings.

For domestic travel, consolidator prices are rarely any lower than the airlines' cheapest advertised excursion fares. Moreover, consolidator deals are rare: Usually only one or two big domestic lines offer them at any given time, and they may cover only a few routes.

While consolidators often don't beat the airlines' lowest advertised fares, they may still offer an advantage: a comparable ticket price without the advance-purchase or Saturday-night-stay limitations the airlines impose. True, consolidator tickets sometimes have their own advance-purchase or minimum-stay limits. But those—if any—are considerably less stringent than the limits the airlines impose on their cheapest tickets.

Sometimes you hear that only undesirable airlines sell tickets through discounters. That's not so. Discount agencies handle tickets from the world's top lines (as well as some obscure carriers). If you're after a really rock-bottom international ticket, you may have to fly on a minor airline, but you can usually fly on a major line for only a bit more. You can always specify which airlines you prefer (or which you refuse to fly) when you check prices.

FRONT-CABIN DISCOUNTS

Though the discount market focuses on Coach/Economy tickets, some lines discount Business and First Class tickets. A premium-seat discount, if you can find one, will usually be smaller as a percentage of the fare—usually no more than 20%, and often less—than the discount on Coach/Economy travel. Still, check with a discounter if you use premium-class tickets: Even a small percentage off an expensive ticket can tot up to quite a few dollars. But the discount generally won't cut the cost of premium-class travel to anywhere near the level of even list-price Coach/Economy excursions.

Once in a while, however, you find a really big discount on a premium fare. In 1996, for instance, several consolidators were selling tickets for less than the advertised price.

A FEW ANNOYANCES

Buying consolidator tickets presents some drawbacks that you don't find with tickets on scheduled airlines:

- •Discount agencies sometimes advertise charter tickets as "discount" airfares. That's deceptive. Charter fares are usually lower than major-airline fares, but they're certainly not discounted. Charter flights are cheaper because passengers have to put up with more inconvenience: Check-in takes a lot longer, seating is extremely tight, and all the seats are usually filled. The planes also fly less frequently than scheduled-line flights, posing major headaches for passengers if there's any slippage in flight schedules.
- •Discount tickets can be even less flexible than Coach/Economy excursions. If your ticketed flight is canceled or delayed, the airline isn't obligated to find you a seat on another airline (though it sometimes may). And you can get a refund only through the discount agency, if at all.
- •Consolidator tickets may require compromises—an airline you don't like, an awkward schedule, or an indirect route with extra stops. You may also have to forgo frequent-flier mileage, advance seat assignment, and special-order meals.
- •Discount agencies often don't have tickets at the fares promised in their ads. Furthermore, some agencies highlight fares "from" some low figure that's available on only a tiny number of the seats. When you price-shop, always phone for a fare quote for your precise dates and destinations.
- •A few discount agencies show obvious signs of tight cash flow: They're slow

to deliver tickets and to respond to any inquiry that doesn't represent a new sale—especially after tickets are paid for. The risk, however, is in buying the ticket, not in using it. Once you have a discount ticket in hand, you're as safe as you would be with any other highly restricted ticket.

- A few agencies that advertise big Business and First Class discounts are actually coupon brokers who buy other people's frequent-flier awards for resale. But a coupon-based ticket is not a discount ticket. Moreover, flying on such a ticket violates airline rules; it won't be honored if you're caught. Anyway, so few premium seats are allocated to frequent-flier awards during peak travel seasons that you'd have a tough time using a coupon after buying it.

MAKING YOUR DEAL

You needn't deal with a discount agency to get a consolidator ticket: A regular full-service travel agency can easily get one for you. But some agents won't want to—consolidator-ticket prices aren't in the reservation computers that agencies use, they require a bit of extra work, and they may carry a smaller commission than tickets at an advertised fare. An agency that does get one for you may add an extra markup, reducing any saving.

If your regular agency can't be bothered or you want to try for the absolutely lowest price, you may want to dicker directly with a discounter. But heed these precautions:

- Buy with a charge card. If you don't

get your ticket in good time or if something's wrong with it, you can get your money back through a chargeback (bill-cancellation) claim.

That charge-card protection is so important that we don't list any agency that doesn't accept at least some charge cards for at least some of the tickets it sells. In many cases, agencies impose a surcharge up to 5% on some charge-card transactions. To get around charge-card regulations, some disguise the surcharge by stating that the advertised prices reflect a "cash discount."

Either way, we believe that the charge-card protection is well worth a modest surcharge. To keep prices on a common base when you compare prices, ask each agent what your final price will be for the specific charge card you plan to use.

- At the outset, mention any special requirements—a ticket that earns frequent-flier mileage, for example, or a nonstop flight. That way, the discounter won't waste time chasing down options you aren't prepared to accept.
- Comparison-shop the discount market—between discount tickets and advertised sale fares, and among various discounters.
- Though many discounters promote nationally, with 800 phone numbers, deal with one in or near your home city. Should a problem develop, it's easier to complain to the agent, or even to use small-claims court.

Our list of discount-ticket outlets is arranged by state, then alphabetically. If it doesn't include a discounter in your area, check the travel section of your local newspaper or one from a nearby big city. Look for ads with extensive listings of discount airfares.

In addition to agency names and phone numbers, our listing shows other useful information:

- **Major destinations.**
- **US gateways served.**
- **Other discounts.** Some discounters claim to sell discounted tickets for Business and First Class as well as for Coach/Economy. Many also arrange hotel rooms, cruises, and tours, though not always at discount prices. And some agencies arrange hotel discounts only for travelers who buy air tickets through them.
- **Charge cards.** Acceptance may vary, depending on the airline issuing the ticket. Try to use an agency that accepts cards without surcharge (or, failing that, with a surcharge of no more than 2%).

DISCOUNT TICKET DIRECTORY

Unless noted, the agencies below sell tickets to the general public from all major US gateways. **Metro** = handles mainly trips from own metropolitan area; **NG** = handles mainly trips from nearby gateway cities. All listed agencies sell discounted Coach/Economy tickets; those noted **Prem** also sell discounted premium (Business or First Class) tickets. **Stu** = caters mainly to students; **Sr** = caters mainly to seniors. Destinations served are listed alphabetically: *Afr* (Africa), *Asia, Carib* (Caribbean), *Cen Am* (Central America), *Eur* (Europe), *HI* (Hawaii), *Intra-Asia* (within Asia), *Intra-Eur* (within Europe), *Mex* (Mexico),

WHAT'S A DISCOUNT?

The airlines tout any fare lower than full, unrestricted Coach/Economy as a discount fare. But probably no more than 2% of today's travelers pay those full fares. And the so-called discount fares are widely advertised and available at the same price from all major competitors. Such "discounts" are really just hype.

Even worse is reference to airlines such as Southwest and several of the start-ups as discount lines. Their tickets are sold at list price. They're cheaper than the majors because their costs are lower.

We think that the label "discount fares" should be applied in only two cases:

- To sale fares, offered during short-term fare wars, that are lower than the lowest advertised year-round excursion fares.
- To unpublished ticket prices that are lower than the airlines' lowest advertised prices for those or similar tickets.

Consolidator fares fall into the second group. At least some of the time, they're lower than the lowest fares the airlines advertise for tickets with the same or similar conditions.

RTW (Round-the-World), *So Am* (South America), *So Pac* (South Pacific), *US/Can* (US/Canada).

Most agencies impose a surcharge of 1–5% on charge-card purchases; charge-card acceptance and surcharge may depend on the ticket purchased or the airline. For multioffice agencies, complete information is listed under the state where the head office is located.

Consolidators that sell only to travel agencies are listed at the end of the directory.

Listing does not imply endorsement by *CRTL*.

ARIZONA

Cefra Discount Travel: Scottsdale; 800-264-5055, 602-948-5055, fax 602-948-6896. Asia, Eur, So Pac. Prem. Also charters, cruises. *AE, Disc, MC, V.*

Southwest Travel Systems: Phoenix; 800-787-8728, 602-255-6900, fax 602-255-0593. Afr, Asia, Eur, Intra-Asia, Intra-Eur, So Am, So Pac, US/Can. Prem. Also charters, hotels, tours. *AE, Disc, MC, V.*

CALIFORNIA (NORTHERN)

Airbound: San Francisco; 415-834-9445, fax 415-834-9447. Asia, Eur, Carib, Cen Am, HI, Intra-Eur, Mex, So Am, So Pac, US/Can. Also charters. *AE, MC, V.*

Air Brokers: San Francisco; 800-883-3273, 415-397-1383, fax 415-397-4767. Asia, Eur, Intra-Asia, RTW, So Am, So Pac. Prem. *AE, MC, V.*

All Continents Travel: Burlingame; 800-325-2553 except in CA, 415-548-9477, fax 415-579-7387. See California (Southern).

All Star Travel: Santa Clara; 408-247-9743, fax 408-247-2762. Asia, RTW. Metro. *AE, Disc, MC, V.*

Anglo California Travel: San Jose; 408-257-2257, fax 408-257-2664. Asia, Eur, Cen Am, Intra-Asia, Intra-Eur, So Am, So Pac. Prem. Also charters, cruises, hotels, tours (including handicapped groups). *AE, Disc, MC, V.*

ANZ Travel/Australia New Zealand Travel: Laguna Hills; 800-281-4449, 714-586-1112, fax 714-586-1124. Asia, Eur, HI, So Pac, US/Can. Also hotels, tours. *AE, CB, DC, Disc, MC, V.*

B.E.T. World Travel: San Jose; 800-747-1476, 408-229-7880, fax 408-365-1101. Asia, Carib, Cen Am, Eur, HI, Intra-Asia, Intra-Eur, Mex, RTW, So Am, So Pac, US/Can. Prem. Also charters, cruises, tours. *MC, V.*

Budget Traveler: Sausalito; 415-331-3700, fax 415-331-1377. Asia, Cen Am, Eur, HI, Mex, So Am, So Pac. Prem. Also charters. *AE, MC, V.*

Festival of Asia: San Francisco; 800-533-9953, 415-693-0880, fax 415-693-0884. Asia, Intra-Asia, RTW, So Pac. Prem. Also hotels, tours. *AE, Disc, MC, V.*

Global Access Travel Group: San Francisco; 800-938-5355, 415-896-5333, fax 415-227-4641. Asia, Cen Am, Eur, Mex, RTW, So Am, So Pac. Prem. Also hotels. *AE, MC, V.*

Magical Holidays: San Francisco; 800-433-7773, 415-781-1345, fax 415-781-4544. See New York.

Scan the World: Palo Alto; 800-775-0200, 415-325-0876, fax 415-325-0893. Cen Am, Eur, Intra-Asia, Intra-Eur, RTW, So Am, So Pac. *AE, Disc, MC, V.*

Skytours: San Francisco; 800-246-

8687, 415-777-3544, fax 415-777-9290 (E-mail: *Travlfile@skytours.com*). Asia, Carib, Cen Am, Eur, RTW, So Am, So Pac. *AE*, *DC*, *Disc*, *MC*, *V*.

STA Travel: Berkeley; 510-642-3000, fax 510-649-1407. San Francisco; 415-391-8407, fax 415-391-4105. See California (Southern).

Sunco Travel: San Francisco; 800-989-6017, 415-291-9960, fax 415-291-9950. Afr, Asia, Cen Am, Eur, Intra-Asia, Intra-Eur, RTW, So Am, So Pac. Prem. Also hotels. *AE*, *Disc*, *MC*, *V*.

Sun Destinations: San Francisco; 415-398-1313, fax 415-398-1399. Asia, Cen Am, Eur, HI, Mex, So Am, So Pac, US/Can. Prem. Also charters, cruises, hotels, tours. *AE*, *Disc*, *MC*, *V*.

Travel Design Unlimited: Mountain View; 415-969-2000, fax 415-966-8262. Asia, Cen Am, Eur, HI, So Am, So Pac, US/Can. Metro. *AE*, *Disc*, *MC*, *V*.

Travel Time: San Francisco; 800-235-3253, 415-677-0799, fax 415-391-1856. Asia, Eur, Cen Am, Mex, RTW, So Am, So Pac. Also charters, cruises, hotels, tours. *AE*, *Disc*, *MC*, *V*.

CALIFORNIA (SOUTHERN)

All Continents Travel: Los Angeles; 800-368-6822, 310-337-1641, fax 310-645-0412. Asia, Eur, Intra-Eur, So Pac. Prem. Also tours. *AE*, *MC*, *V*.

Cathay Travel: Monterey Park; 818-571-6727. Asia, Cen Am, Eur, Intra-Asia, Mex, So Am, US/Can. Also charters, hotels, tours. *AE*, *MC*, *V*.

Continental Travel Shop: Santa Monica; 310-453-8655, fax 310-453-5093. Eur, Intra-Eur. Also charters. *AE*, *MC*, *V*.

Discover Wholesale Travel: Irvine; 800-576-7770, 714-833-1136, fax 714-833-1176. Asia, Cen Am, Eur, So Am, So Pac. Also charters, hotels. *AE*, *Disc*, *MC*, *V*.

Fare Deal Travel: San Diego; 800-298-2785, 619-298-8869, fax 619-298-8927. US/Can. *AE*, *Disc*, *MC*, *V*.

Flight Coordinators: Santa Monica; 800-544-3644, 310-581-5600, fax 310-581-5620. Asia, Cen Am, Eur, So Am, So Pac. *AE*, *Disc*, *MC*, *V*.

K & K Travel: Fullerton; 800-523-1374, 714-525-4494, fax 714-525-4586. Afr, Asia, Cen Am, Eur, Mex, So Am, So Pac. *AE*, *MC*, *V*.

Rebel Tours: Valencia; 800-227-3235, 805-294-0900, fax 805-294-0981. Asia, Eur. Prem. Also charters, hotels. *MC*, *V*.

South Star Tours: El Segundo; 800-654-4468, 310-416-1001, fax 310-416-8703. Cen Am, So Am. Prem. Also cruises, hotels, tours. *AE*, *Disc*, *MC*, *V*.

STA Travel: Los Angeles (West Hollywood); 213-934-8722, fax 213-937-6008. Los Angeles (Westwood); 310-824-1574, fax 310-824-2928. Santa Monica; 310-394-5126, fax 310-394-4041. Asia, Carib, Cen Am, Eur, HI, Intra-Asia, Intra-Eur, Mex, RTW, So Am, So Pac, US/Can. Metro. Stu. Also charters, hotels, tours. *MC*, *V*.

TS Travel: Woodland Hills; 818-346-8600, fax 818-883-4624. Asia, Cen Am, Eur, Intra-Asia, Intra-Eur, RTW, So Am, So Pac, US/Can. Metro, Prem. Also charters, cruises, hotels, tours. *Disc*, *MC*, *V*.

World Link Travel Network: Los Angeles; 310-342-1280, fax 310-342-1288. Santa Monica; 310-453-8884, fax

310-453-7924. Afr, Asia, Eur, Carib, Cen Am, HI, Intra-Asia, Intra-Eur, Mex, RTW, So Am, So Pac, US/Can. Prem. Also cruises, hotels, tours. *AE, MC, V.*

COLORADO

Fare Deals Travel: Englewood; 800-878-2929; 303-792-2929, fax 303-792-2954. Asia, Carib, Cen Am, Eur, HI, Intra-Asia, Mex, RTW, So Am, So Pac, US/Can. Prem. Also charters. *AE, Disc, MC, V.*

Overseas Travel: Aurora; 800-783-7196, 303-337-7196, fax 303-696-1226. Asia, Carib, Cen Am, Eur, HI, Intra-Asia, Intra-Eur, RTW, So Am, So Pac. Prem. Stu. Also charters, cruises, hotels, tours. *AE, Disc, MC, V.*

CONNECTICUT

Tread Lightly: Washington Depot; 800-643-0060, 860-868-1710, fax 860-868-1718. Cen Am, So Am. *AE, Disc, MC, V.*

DISTRICT OF COLUMBIA

Democracy Travel: Washington; 800-536-8728, 202-965-7200, fax 202-342-0471. Asia, Eur, HI, Intra-Asia, RTW, So Am, So Pac, US/Can. Prem. *AE, Disc, MC, V.*

STA Travel: Washington; 202-887-0912, fax 202-887-0031. See California (Southern).

FLORIDA

Arnsdorff Travel: Apopka; 407-886-1343, fax 407-886-5959. RTW, NG, Prem. *Disc, MC, V.*

Cosmopolitan Travel Center: Ft Lauderdale; 800-548-7206, 954-523-

0973, fax 954-523-8324. Cen Am, Eur, So Am. Prem. *AE, Disc, MC, V.*

Direct Line Travel: Miami; 800-422-2585, 305-385-2585, fax 305-382-9429. Asia, Cen Am, Eur, So Am. Also charters, cruises, tours. *AE, Disc, MC, V.*

Getaway Travel Intl: Coral Gables; 800-683-6336, 305-446-7855, fax 305-444-6647. Asia, Cen Am, Eur, So Am. *AE, Disc, MC, V.*

Guardian Travel: St Petersburg; 800-741-3050, 813-367-5622, fax 813-367-4597. Eur. Specializes in Israel. *Disc, MC, V.*

Hostway Travel: Ft Lauderdale; 800-327-3207, 954-966-8500, fax 954-966-7815. Asia, Carib, Cen Am, Eur, So Am, So Pac, US/Can. Also charters, cruises. *AE, Disc, MC, V.*

Interworld Travel: Coral Gables; 800-468-3796, 305-443-4929, fax 305-443-0351. Afr, Eur, So Am. Specializes in flights out of London. *AE, Disc, MC, V.*

Mena Tours and Travel: Miami; 800-327-4514, 305-649-7066, fax 305-643-4615. See Illinois.

Rebel Tours: Orlando; 800-732-3588, 407-352-3600, fax 407-352-3609. See California (Southern).

Smart Traveller: Miami; 800-448-3338, 305-448-3338, fax 305-443-3544. Asia, Carib, Cen Am, Eur, Mex, RTW, So Am, So Pac. Also cruises. Accepts all credit cards.

TFI Tours Intl (Miami Travel Center): Miami; 305-895-8115, fax 305-895-4653. See New York.

Travac: Orlando; 800-872-8800, 407-896-0014, fax 407-896-0046. See New York.

GEORGIA

All World Travel: Atlanta; 770-578-8408, fax 770-578-8408. Asia, Cen Am, Eur, RTW, So Am, US/Can. *AE*, *MC*, *V.*

Alpha Travel: Marietta; 800-793-8424, 770-988-9982, fax 770-988-9986. Asia, Eur, Carib, Intra-Asia, Intra-Eur, RTW, US/Can. Prem. Also charters, cruises, tours to Holy Land. *AE*, *Disc*, *MC*, *V.*

JC Tour & Travel: Doraville; 800-239-1232, 404-451-1236, fax 404-451-9969. Asia, Cen Am, Eur, So Am, So Pac. NG, Prem. *AE*, *Disc*, *MC*, *V.*

McAbee Travel: Atlanta; 800-622-2335, 770-396-9988, fax 770-393-0084. Asia, Eur, So Pac. NG, Prem. *AE*, *MC*, *V.*

Midtown Travel Consultants: Atlanta; 800-548-8904, 404-872-8308, fax 404-881-6322. Afr, Asia, Cen Am, Eur, Intra-Asia, So Am. Prem. Also hotels. *AE.*

HAWAII

Asia Travel Service: Honolulu; 808-926-0550, fax 808-924-2177. Asia, Eur, HI, RTW, So Pac, US/Can. Prem. Also charters. *AE*, *Disc*, *MC*, *V.*

Pali Travel: Honolulu; 808-533-3608, fax 808-524-2483. Asia, Carib, Cen Am, Eur, HI, Intra-Asia, Intra-Eur, Mex, RTW, So Am, So Pac, US/Can. Metro. Also charters, cruises, hotels, tours. *AE*, *Disc*, *MC*, *V.*

ILLINOIS

Austin Travel: Elmwood Park; 800-545-2655, 708-452-1010, fax 708-452-9264. Asia, Eur. NG, Prem. Also charters, cruises. *AE*, *Disc*, *MC*, *V.*

Chisholm Travel: Chicago; 800-359-6388, 312-263-7900, fax 312-759-9234.

Asia, So Pac. Prem. *AE*, *Disc*, *MC*, *V.*

Cut Rate Travel: Deerfield; 800-388-0575, 847-405-0575, fax 847-405-0587. Asia, Cen Am, Eur, RTW, So Am, So Pac. Prem. Also charters, hotels, tours. *AE*, *Disc*, *MC*, *V.*

Mena Tours and Travel: Chicago; 800-937-6362, 312-275-2125, fax 312-275-9927. Carib, Cen Am, Mex, So Am. Also hotels, tours. *AE*, *MC*, *V.*

Overseas Express: Chicago; 800-343-4873, 312-262-4971, fax 312-262-4406. Asia, Cen Am, Eur, Intra-Asia, Intra-Eur, RTW, So Am. Prem. Caters to missionary travel. *AE*, *MC*, *V.*

STA Travel: Chicago; 312-786-9050, fax 312-786-9817. See California (Southern).

Travel Avenue: Chicago; 800-333-3335, fax 312-876-1254. Asia, Carib, Cen Am, Eur, HI, Intra-Asia, Intra-Eur, Mex, RTW, So Am, So Pac, US/Can. Prem. Also cruises, hotels, tours. *AE*, *Disc*, *MC*, *V.*

Travel Core of America: Lincolnshire; 800-992-9396, 847-948-1300, fax 847-948-5446. Afr, Eur. *AE*, *Disc*, *MC*, *V.*

LOUISIANA

Dixieland Tours: Baton Rouge; 800-256-8747, 504-273-9119, fax 504-273-0199. Metairie; 800-489-8747, 504-833-1991, fax 504-837-8371. Eur, US/Can. Also hotels. *MC*, *V.*

Globe Tours: New Orleans; 800-374-8352, 504-522-6697, fax 504-522-6703. Asia, Eur. *AE*, *Disc*, *MC*, *V.*

MARYLAND

AESU Travel: Baltimore; 800-638-7640, 410-323-4416, fax 410-323-4498.

Eur. Stu. Also tours. *AE*, *Disc*, *MC*, *V*.

Fare Deals: Owings Mills; 800-347-7006, 410-581-8787, fax 410-581-1093. Asia, Carib, Cen Am, Eur, HI, Mex, RTW, So Am, So Pac, US/Can. Prem. Also charters, cruises, tours. *AE*, *MC*, *V*.

Hans World Travel: Rockville; 800-421-4267, 301-770-1717, fax 301-770-0650. Asia, Cen Am, Eur, HI, Intra-Asia, RTW, So Am, US/Can. Prem. Also charters. *AE*, *Disc*, *MC*, *V*.

MASSACHUSETTS
STA Travel: Boston; 617-266-6014, fax 617-266-5579. Cambridge; 617-576-4623, fax 617-576-2740. See California (Southern).

MICHIGAN
GTI Travel Consolidators: Holland; 800-829-8234, 616-396-1234, fax 616-396-7720. Asia, Eur, Intra-Asia, Intra-Eur. Prem. Also missionary travel. *AE*, *Disc*, *MC*, *V*.

MINNESOTA
Campus Travel/Euroflights: Minneapolis; 800-328-3359, 800-292-4176 in MN, 612-338-5616, fax 612-338-6798. Eur, So Am. *AE*, *MC*, *V*.

Travel Beyond: Wayzata; 800-876-3131, 612-475-9975, fax 612-475-1029. Afr. Also tours. Specializes in South Africa, soft adventure, and luxury travel. *AE*, *Disc*, *MC*, *V*.

MISSOURI
Group & Leisure Travel: Blue Springs; 800-874-6608, 816-690-4040, fax 816-690-8665. Asia, Carib, Cen Am, Eur, HI, Mex, RTW, So Am, So Pac,

US/Can. Prem. Sr, Stu. Also charters, cruises, hotels, tours. *AE*, *Disc*, *MC*, *V*.

UniTravel: St Louis; 800-325-2222, 314-569-0900, fax 314-569-2503; Afr, Asia, Cen Am, Eur, HI, Mex, So Am, US/Can. Prem. *AE*, *Disc*, *MC*, *V*.

NEW JERSEY
British Network: Upper Montclair; 800-274-8583, 201-744-8814, fax 201-744-0531. Eur. Also tours. *AE*, *Disc*, *MC*, *V*.

Gary Marcus Travel: West Orange; 800-524-0821, 201-731-7600, fax 201-731-1775. Africa, Asia, Carib, Cen Am, Eur, Intra-Asia, Intra-Eur, Mex, RTW, So Am, So Pac, US/Can. Prem. Also charters, cruises, hotels, tours. Specializes in Caribbean and Las Vegas hotel packages. *AE*, *Disc*, *MC*, *V*.

Paul Laifer Tours: Parsippany; 800-346-6314, 201-887-1188, fax 201-887-6118. Eur, Intra-Eur. Prem. Also hotels, tours. *MC*, *V*.

Rupa Travel: Edison; 800-206-8869, 908-572-5000, fax 908-572-3456. Asia, Carib, Cen Am, Eur, HI, Mex, RTW, So Pac, US/Can. Also cruises, hotels, tours. *AE*, *Disc*, *MC*, *V*.

Worldvision Travel Services: West Orange; 800-545-7118, 201-736-8210, fax 201-736-9659. Africa, Asia, Eur, Intra- Asia, Intra-Eur, RTW, So Am, So Pac, US. Prem. Also charters. *AE*, *Disc*, *MC*, *V*.

NEW YORK
Air Travel & Tours: NYC; 800-938-4625, 212-714-1100, fax 212-714-2180. Afr, Asia, Cen Am, Eur, HI, So Am, So Pac. *AE*, *Disc*, *MC*, *V*.

Air Travel Discounts: NYC; 800-888-2621, 212-922-1326, fax 212-922-1547. Afr, Asia, Eur, RTW, So Am, US. *AE, Disc, MC, V.*

All Continents Travel: NYC; 800-525-3632, 212-751-9051, fax 212-751-9053. See California (Southern).

Asensio Tours & Travel: NYC 800-221-7679, 212-213-4310, fax 212-689-3021. Cen Am; So Am (80% of business). Prem. Also tours. *AE, MC, V.*

Balkan Holidays: NYC; 212-573-5530, fax 212-573-5538. Afr, Eur, Intra-Eur. Prem. Also hotels, tours. *AE, Disc, MC, V.*

Cedok Central European Tours: NYC; 800-800-8891, 212-689-9720, fax 212-481-0597. Eur, Intra-Eur. Prem. Also hotels, tours. *AE, Disc, MC, V.*

Favored Holidays: Sheepshead Bay; 718-934-8881, fax 718-934-4115. Former Soviet Union and Eur. *AE, MC, V.*

Flytime Tours & Travel: NYC; 212-760-3737, fax 212-594-1082. Asia, Cen Am, Eur. Prem. *AE, MC, V.*

French Experience: NYC; 212-986-3800, fax 212-986-3808. Eur. Also hotels, tours. *MC, V.*

Homeric Tours: NYC; 800-223-5570, 212-753-1100, fax 212-753-0319. Eur. Metro, NG, Prem. Also charters, cruises, hotels, tours. *MC, V.*

KTS Services: Jamaica; 800-531-6677, 718-454-2300, fax 718-454-9491. Eur. NG. *AE, Disc, MC, V.*

LT & Travel: NYC; 800-295-3436, 212-682-2748, fax 212-682-4663. Eur, HI, So Am, US. Prem. *AE, Disc, MC, V.*

Magical Holidays: NYC; 800-228-2208, 212-486-9600, fax 212-486-9751. Afr, Cen Am, Eur, Intra-Eur, Mex, So Am. Prem. Caters to missionary travel. Also tours. *AE, MC, V.*

Payless Travel: NYC; 212-573-8980, fax 212-573-8878. Asia, Cen Am, Eur, Mex, So Am, So Pac. Prem. Also hotels, tours. *AE, Disc, MC, V.*

STA Travel: NYC (Columbia); 212-865-2700, fax 212-316-0523. NYC (NYU); 212-627-3111, fax 212-627-3387. See California (Southern).

TFI Tours Intl: NYC; 800-745-8000, 212-736-1140, fax 212-564-4081. Asia, Carib, Cen Am, Eur, HI, Mex, So Am, So Pac, US/Can. *Disc, MC, V.*

Travac: NYC; 800-872-8800, 212-563-3303, fax 212-563-3631. Afr, Eur, Intra-Eur. Also charters. *MC, V.*

Travel Center: NYC; 800-419-0960, 212-545-7474, fax 212-545-7698. Asia, Cen Am, Eur, Intra-Asia, RTW, So Am, So Pac, US/Can. Prem. Also charters, cruises, tours. *AE, DC, Disc, MC, V.*

Tulips Travel: NYC; 800-882-3383, 212-490-3388, fax 212-490-3580. Asia, Cen Am, Eur, Intra-Asia, HI, Mex, RTW, So Am, So Pac, US/Can. Also charters, hotels. *AE.*

United Tours: NYC; 800-245-0203, 212-245-1100, fax 212-245-0292. Eur, Intra-Eur. Prem. Also hotels. *AE, Disc, MC, V.*

Zig Zag Travel: Forest Hills; 800-726-0249, 718-575-3434, fax 718-575-5135. Lynbrook; 800-726-0249, 516-887-0776, fax 516-887-3682. Asia, Eur, Intra-Eur. NG, Prem. Also charters. *AE, Disc, MC, V.*

OHIO
American Travel: Cleveland; 216-781-7181, fax 216-781-7214. Eur. Metro. *AE, MC, V.*

PENNSYLVANIA

Holiday Travel Intl: N Huntingdon; 800-775-7111, 412-863-7500, fax 412-863-7590. HI, US/Can. Prem. Also tours. *AE, Disc, MC, V.*

Pennsylvania Travel: Paoli; 800-331-0947, 610-251-9944, fax 610-644-2150. Asia, Cen Am, Eur, So Am, US/Can. Also charters, cruises, hotels, tours. *AE, Disc, MC, V.*

STA Travel: Philadelphia; 215-382-2928, fax 215-382-4716. See California (Southern).

TEXAS

Airfare Busters: Houston; 800-232-8783, 713-961-5109, fax 713-961-3385. Asia, Eur, RTW, So Am, So Pac. Prem. *AE, Disc, MC, V.*

Aries Tours & Travel: Dallas; 214-638-7008, fax 214-638-1907. Asia, Eur, HI, Intra-Asia, Intra-Eur, Mex, RTW, So Am, So Pac, US/Can. Metro, NG. Also cruises, hotels, tours. *AE, Disc, MC, V.*

Carefree Getaway Travel: Roanoke; 800-969-8687, 817-430-1128, fax 817-430-0522. Afr, Asia, Carib, Cen Am, Eur, HI, Intra-Eur, Mex, RTW, So Am, So Pac, US/Can. Prem. Also hotels, tours, cruises. *AE, Disc, MC, V.*

Embassy Tours: Dallas; 800-299-5284, 214-956-9600, fax 214-357-2580. Asia, Cen Am, Mex, So Am. Prem. Also hotels, tours. *AE, Disc, MC, V.*

Katy Van Tours: Houston; 800-808-8747, 713-492-7032, fax 713-492-0586. Afr, Asia, Eur, Middle East, So Am, So Pac. Also tours. *AE, Disc, MC, V.*

New World Travel: Houston; 713-779-9562, fax 713-779-3656. Asia, Carib, Cen Am, Eur, HI, Intra-Asia, Intra-Eur, Mex, RTW, So Am, So Pac, US/Can. Metro, NG, Prem. Also cruises, tours. *AE, Disc, MC, V.*

Royal Lane Travel: Dallas; 800-329-2030, 214-340-2030, fax 214-340-2082. Asia, Carib, Cen Am, Eur, HI, Intra-Eur, Mex, So Am, So Pac. Caters to Russian-speaking travelers. Also charters. *AE, Disc, MC, V.*

Skypass Travel: Dallas; 800-381-8687, 214-634-8687, fax 214-634-0559. Austin; 512-467-8687, fax 512-467-9353. Asia, Cen Am, Eur, HI, Intra-Asia, RTW, So Am, So Pac, US/Can. *AE, Disc, MC, V.*

TCI-Access Travel: Dallas; 800-272-7359, 214-630-3344, fax 214-630-3477. Cen Am, Eur, HI, So Am, US. *AE, Disc, MC, V.*

UTAH

Panorama Tours: Salt Lake City; 800-527-4888, 800-276-5757, fax 801-276-5760. Afr, Asia, Cen Am, Eur, HI, Intra-Asia, Intra-Eur, So Am, So Pac, US Prem. Also hotels, tours. *AE, Disc, MC, V.*

VIRGINIA

Fellowship Travel Intl: Richmond; 800-235-9384, 804-264-0121, fax 800-262-6724. Asia, Cen Am, Eur, Intra-Asia, Mex, RTW, So Am, So Pac. Prem. *AE, Disc, MC, V.*

Landmark Travel Services: Alexandria; 800-556-7902, 703-750-3411, fax 703-941-7535. Asia, Cen Am, Eur, HI, So Am, US. *AE, Disc, MC, V.*

South American Fiesta: Hampton; 800-334-3782, 804-825-9000, fax 804-826-1747. Cen Am, So Am. Prem. *AE, Disc, MC, V.*

WASHINGTON

Americas Tours: Seattle; 800-553-2513, 206-623-8850, fax 206-467-0454. Cen Am, Mex, So Am. *AE, Disc, MC, V.*

C & G Travel: Seattle; 206-363-9948, fax 206-365-8559. Asia, Cen Am, Eur, HI, Intra-Asia, Mex, So Am, So Pac, US/Can. *AE, Disc, MC, V.*

Cathay Express Travel: Seattle; 206-622-9988, fax 206-621-9213. Asia, Cen Am, Eur, So Am, So Pac, US/Can. *AE, Disc, MC, V.*

New Wave Travel: Seattle; 800-220-9283, 206-527-3579, fax 206-527-3241. Asia, Carib, Cen Am, Eur, HI, Intra-Asia, Intra-Eur, Mex, RTW, So Am, So Pac, US/Can. Prem. *AE, Disc, MC, V.*

STA Travel: Seattle; 206-633-5000, fax 206-633-5027. See California (Southern).

Travel Network: Bellevue; 800-933-5963, 206-643-1600, fax 206-649-9756. Carib, Cen Am, HI, Mex, So Am, US/Can. *AE, Disc, MC, V.*

Travel Team: Seattle; 800-788-0829, 206-632-0520, fax 206-301-0697. Asia, Carib, Cen Am, Eur, HI, Intra-Asia, Mex, RTW, So Am, So Pac, US/Can. Also charters, cruises. *AE, DC, Disc, MC, V.*

WISCONSIN

Value Holidays: Mequon; 800-558-6850, 414-241-6373, fax 414-241-6379. Eur. NG. Also tours and group travel. *AE, MC, V.*

FOR TRAVEL AGENTS ONLY

Readers should not call the following agencies; if your travel agency doesn't have a consolidator source, show your agent this list. We do not note charge-card acceptance by consolidators that deal only with travel agencies, since agencies make their own arrangements for payment.

CALIFORNIA (NORTHERN)

Alta Tours: San Francisco; 800-338-4191, 415-777-1307, fax 415-434-2684. Cen Am, Eur, So Am. Also hotels, tours. Specializes in Argentina, Chile, Portugal, and Spain.

Charterways: San Jose; 800-869-2344, 408-257-2652, fax 408-257-2664. Asia, Cen Am, Eur, Intra-Asia, Intra-Eur, So Am, So Pac. Prem. Also charters, hotels, tours.

CL Thomson Express Intl: San Francisco; 800-833-4258, 415-398-2535, fax 415-398-5062. Also offices in Honolulu, Los Angeles, New York, Hong Kong. Afr, Asia, Cen Am, Eur, HI, Intra-Asia, Intra-Eur, So Am, US/Can.

Diplomat Tours: Sacramento; 800-727-8687, 916-972-1500, fax 916-481-4728. Asia, Cen Am, Eur, Intra-Asia, Intra-Eur, So Am, So Pac. Prem. Also cruises.

CALIFORNIA (SOUTHERN)

Brendan Air: Van Nuys; 800-491-9633, 818-785-9696, fax 818-901-2685. Asia, Cen Am, Eur, So Am, So Pac. Prem. Also charters.

CL Thomson: Los Angeles; 800-423-4488, 310-337-9982, fax 800-423-4424. Also offices in Chicago, New York, Honolulu, and San Francisco. Afr, Asia, Eur, HI Intra-Asia, Middle East RTW, SO Pac., So Am. US/Can. Also hotels in China.

DER Tours: Los Angeles; 800-717-

4247, 708-692-4141, fax 800-282-7474. Also offices in Chicago and Toronto. Eur. Also hotels, tours.

Express Discount Travel: San Diego; 800-266-8669, 800-266-2639, fax 619-563-8437. Mex.

J & O Air: San Diego; 800-877-8111, 619-282-4124, fax 619-282-4164. Afr, Asia, Cen Am, Eur, Intra-Asia, Intra-Eur, RTW, So Am, So Pac. Prem.

Pacifico Creative Service: Los Angeles; 800-221-1081, fax 213-239-2410. Also offices in Atlanta, Chicago, Dallas, Houston, Miami, New York, San Francisco, Seattle, Washington DC. Asia, Cen Am, So Am. Specializes in travel to Japan and other Asian countries.

Queue Travel: San Diego; 800-356-4871, 619-260-8577, fax 619-260-0832. Also office in Miami. Asia, Cen Am, Eur, Intra-Asia, Intra-Eur, So Am, So Pac, US/Can. Prem. Also hotels.

DISTRICT OF COLUMBIA

Solar Tours: Washington; 800-388-7652, 202-861-5864, fax 202-452-0905. Also office in Sarasota FL. Carib, Cen Am, Eur, Mex, So Am. Also hotels, tours.

FLORIDA

Golden Pacific #1 Travel: Brandon; 800-500-8021, 813-684-6365. Asia, Intra-Asia, So Pac. Prem. Also hotels, tours.

Intervac: Miami; 800-992-9629, 305-670-8990, fax 305-670-6168. Carib, Cen Am, So Am. Also hotels, tours, cruises.

Passport Travel Management Group: Tampa; 800-950-5864, 813-931-3166, fax 813-933-1670. Asia, Intra-Asia, RTW. Prem. Also hotels.

Travel Leaders Intl: Coral Gables;

800-323-3218, 305-443-7755, fax 800-694-7772. Afr, Asia, Eur, Cen Am, Intra-Asia, Intra-Eur, Mex, RTW, So Am, So Pac. Prem.

ILLINOIS

Pleasure Break Vacations: Rolling Meadows; 800-777-1566, 847-670-6300, fax 847-670-7682. Carib, Cen Am, Eur, Mex, So Am. Prem. Also charters, hotels, tours.

TravNet: Chicago; 800-359-6388, 312-759-9200, fax 312-759-9234. Asia, So Pac. Prem.

MICHIGAN

Anderson Intl Travel: East Lansing; 800-365-1929, 517-337-1300, fax 517-337-8561. Afr, Asia, Eur, So Am, So Pac.

NEW YORK

American Intl Consolidators: Elmsford; 800-888-5774, 914-592-0206, fax 914-592-2889. Afr, Eur, US.

Marnella Tours: Huntington Station; 800-937-6999, 516-271-6969, fax 516-271-8593. Asia, Cen Am, So Am. Also tours.

Orbis Polish Travel Bureau: NYC, 800-876-7247, 212-867-5011, fax 212-682-4715. Eur. Also hotels, tours.

Skylink Travel: NYC; 800-247-6659, 212-599-0430, 212-573-8980, fax 212-557-4339, 212-573-8878. Also offices in Chicago, Los Angeles, and Washington DC. Afr, Asia, Eur, Intra-Asia, Intra-Eur, RTW. Prem.

Sunrise Tours: NYC; 800-872-3801, 212-947-3617, fax 212-947-3618. Asia, Carib, Cen Am, Eur, So Am. Prem. Also tours; specializes in travel to Russia.

Travel N Tours: Beacon; 800-854-5400, 914-838-2600, fax 914-831-4160. Afr, Asia, Cen Am, Eur, Intra-Eur, So Am. Prem. Also hotels, tours.

OREGON
Pacific Gateway: Portland; 800-777-8369, 503-294-6478, fax 503-294-2199. Afr, Asia, Cen Am, Eur, Mex, So Am, So Pac.

STT Worldwide Travel: Portland; 800-348-0886, 503-641-8866, fax 503-641-2171. Also offices in Atlanta, Los Angeles, Seattle. Asia, Eur, HI, Mex, So Am, So Pac, US/Can.

PENNSYLVANIA
Airplan: Pittsburgh; 800-866-7526, 412-257-3199, fax 412-257-8421. Afr, Asia, Cen Am, Eur, Mex, So Am, US/Can. Prem.

HTI Tours: Philadelphia; 800-441-4411, 215-563-8484, fax 215-563-4411.

Afr, Asia, Cen Am, Eur, Intra-Asia, RTW, So Am.

TEXAS
D-FW Tours: Dallas; 800-527-2589, 972-980-4540, fax 972-386-3802. Afr, Asia, Cen Am, Eur, So Am, So Pac. Prem. Also hotels, tours.

VIRGINIA
Trans Am Travel: Alexandria; 800-822-7600, 703-998-7676, fax 703-824-8190. Also office in NYC. Asia, Cen Am, Eur, Intra-Asia, Intra-Eur, Mex, So Am, So Pac.

Travel Wholesalers: Fairfax; 800-487-8944, 703-359-8855, fax 703-359-8895. Afr, Asia, Carib, Eur, So Am, So Pac. Prem. Also hotels, tours.

This chapter was adapted from the 1996 edition of Consumer Reports Best Travel Deals.

Charters: Sometimes Good Bets

In the summertime, charter operators fly from dozens of US and Canadian cities to popular vacation spots in other big US cities, Europe, the Caribbean, Hawaii, and Mexico. When winter arrives, nonstop charters wing off to sun-sand-surf or ski destinations.

Those charters are usually cheaper than flights on scheduled airlines. Even when a scheduled line seems to have a price advantage, it may offer only a few seats at the come-on fare. A charter seat may be your only low-fare alternative when scheduled lines sell out their allotments of seats at lowball, promotional fares.

Even when charters don't save you money, they often offer the convenience of nonstop flights to destinations that other lines serve only with tedious connections. In addition, a few charter lines offer premium seats to Europe at modest cost. The seats and service may not match First or Business Class on a scheduled line, but they're far better than a big line's Economy and far cheaper than its premium.

As still another plus, charter tickets ordinarily aren't restricted: The minimum advance-purchase period depends on how long it takes to complete the paperwork, and the minimum stay depends on how often the charter line flies a particular route.

ANY DRAWBACKS?

But charters aren't always the cheapest way to fly:

- More and more small scheduled low-fare lines operate around the country —on long-haul as well as short-haul routes—at fares that may match or beat charter prices.
- Scheduled-line prices may drop below charter prices when there's a fare war. Even when there isn't, the major lines' advertised fares to Europe in winter are usually low enough to discourage charter competition, and discount tickets from consolidators may also undercut charter fares.

Charter flights have other shortcomings, too:

- Most charters operate less frequently

than scheduled airlines—sometimes only once or twice a week. Unless the flight days correspond to the beginning and end of your vacation, you could lose quite a bit of time waiting for a charter trip.

- Some travel agents don't like to sell charter flights, since most can't be checked out readily in computer reservation systems.
- You may have a tough time getting a refund if you have to cancel a charter flight, and your ticket may not be as easily exchangeable as a Coach/Economy excursion ticket on a scheduled line. If a ticket isn't exchangeable, you can protect yourself with trip-interruption insurance, at a typical cost of $5.50 per $100 of coverage (see chapter 24).
- A charter virtually guarantees an ex-tremely crowded trip (unless you pay more for a premium seat). Seating on charter flights isn't always tighter than on a scheduled line, but it's hardly ever better, and most flights fly close to full.

- Check-in, boarding, and baggage claim are often much slower for a charter than for a scheduled flight.
- Charter flights may arrive or depart at oddball hours. And any significant flight delay can throw a charter line's schedule out of whack for days.

BUYING YOUR TICKET

The built-in disadvantages of a charter always tip the balance in favor of a scheduled airline if fares, schedules, and comfort are close to equal. So don't take a charter unless it provides a tangible advantage over a scheduled

CHARTER INS AND OUTS

The main distinction between a charter flight and a scheduled one is legal: With a charter, a tour operator charters a plane and crew from the airline that actually operates the flight. Your contract is with the tour operator, and the operator —not the airline—is responsible if something goes wrong.

But there are also some important operational differences:
- Charter lines typically don't sell seats directly to the public or list fares, schedules, and available seats in the computer reservation systems travel agencies use.
- Charter flights serve very limited routes, generally without hubs or connections —flights go point to point between a few major cities and a few major vacation spots.

Note that airline nomenclature here is a bit misleading. "Scheduled" isn't really a good way to describe lines ranging from giant American and United to the commuters. Charter lines, of course, also adhere to schedules. As a further complication, some small airlines in effect run scheduled service under charter rules. That's because it's easier to start up a charter than a scheduled line. On the other hand, a few airlines that function like charters (notably Germany's LTU) have chosen to register as scheduled lines.

flight, a cheaper ticket, a more direct route, or a bargain premium seat.

You can buy almost any charter "air only." You can also buy most of them as part of a complete package that includes lodgings, airport transfers, and sightseeing.

Charters are ordinarily available through your regular travel agency. Some of the tour operators listed in *Where to Find It,* below, also sell directly to the public, but you won't save any money that way. In fact, you're probably better off buying from a local travel agency, and buying with a charge card: Should anything go wrong, it's apt to be easier for you to get redress.

One of the largest European charter lines (Martinair) acts as its own tour operator: It sells directly to the public, as well as through travel agencies. Martinair lists its schedules in computer-reservation systems, though it's technically still a charter line.

Many tour operators that run big summer charter programs advertise winter flights, too. But for the most part, those winter flights are actually on scheduled airlines, often at a price lower than the airline normally charges. (In effect, the tour operators are acting as consolidators.) Among the large tour operators running such programs are Council Travel and Skytours; see chapter 5 for addresses.

WHERE TO FIND IT

The following organizations sell charter flights and tours. Those marked *(A)* are airlines; the others are wholesale tour operators. Tour operators

marked *(T)* sell through travel agencies only and do not accept calls from individual travelers.

Adventure Tours: 800-999-9046.
Ah Wee World Travel: 718-584-2100.
Apple Vacations East *(T).*
Apple Vacations West *(T).*
Condor *(A,T).*
Conquest Tours *(T).*
Euram Flight Center: 800-848-6789.
Fantasy Holidays: 800-645-2555.
France Vacations: 800-332-5332.
Funjet Vacations *(T).*
GG Tours *(T).*
GWV Intl: 800-225-5498.
Hamilton, Miller, Hudson & Fayne Travel (HMHF) *(T).*
Homeric Tours: 800-223-5570.
Hot Spot Tours: 800-433-0075; in NY area, 212-421-9090.
LTU Intl Airways *(A):* 800-888-0200.
Martinair Holland *(A):* 800-366-4655.
MLT Vacations *(T).*
New Frontiers: 800-677-0720.
Pleasant Holidays: 800-242-9244.
PleasureBreak: *(T).*
Rebel Tours: 800-732-3588.
Sceptre: 718-738-9400.
Skytours: 800-246-8687.
Sunbird Vacations *(T).*
SunTrips: 800-786-8747 (CA only); 408-432-1101.
TransGlobal Vacations *(T).*
Travel Charter: *(T).*

This chapter was adapted from the Consumer Reports Travel Letter *articles* "Charters for Summer '96" *(May 1996) and* "Winter Charters: Sun, Snow" *(November 1995), and from the 1996 edition of* Consumer Reports Best Travel Deals.

THE SEAT SQUEEZE ALOFT

In a rational marketplace, travelers would have a wide choice of seating options and fares. But today's airline pricing doesn't work that way. On any given route, airlines typically charge the same fares: low for crowded, highly restricted Coach/Economy tickets and hair-curlingly high for a roomy seat in Business or First Class, with nothing in between.

Individual airlines, not aircraft manufacturers, decide how constricted the seating will be. So when fares don't differ and schedules are equally convenient, it makes sense to choose your flight for the seat room you get.

That's almost critical for Coach/Economy, where seats are generally so straitjacket-tight that even small differences in roominess can have a big effect on your temper. But judicious flight choices affect your comfort even in Business Class. This chapter will lead you to the most comfortable seats in the Coach/Economy and Business Class cabins of a broad spectrum of US and foreign lines.

YARDSTICKS OF COMFORT

Airline seating comfort depends on three factors:

- **Seat pitch,** or the front-to-rear spacing of seat rows. Pitch governs both legroom and your upper-level space for reading or working. Aircraft seats are fastened to the floor on tracks, so airlines can give you as much or as little legroom as they choose in increments of an inch or less.
- **Seat width** determines side-to-side space, both at the seat cushion and at shoulder level. Airlines have less flexibility here—once they figure out how many seats they want in each row, they usually install the widest seats the cabin allows.
- **Configuration,** how seats are grouped within a row, determines your risk of being crammed into a middle seat or of sitting next to someone squirming in one.

For ready reference, *CRTL* (*Consumer Reports Travel Letter*) combines the effects of those three factors into a single **seat-comfort score.** A score of

100 represents the tightest seating that we judge to be comfortable for a long trip in a full plane. That score corresponds to premium Coach/Economy seating on a few airlines and to some of the less roomy international Business Class seating.

FLYING IN COACH/ECONOMY

Over the past few years, travelers have made it increasingly clear that they consider tight, uncomfortable seating in Coach/Economy a major problem:

- Surveys show that it's the most important *predictable* deficiency in air travel. Safety, on-time arrival, and timely delivery of baggage, while more important, aren't predictable for any given flight.
- Seating is also the most *pervasive* problem. On the average, about 80% of the nation's airline flights arrive within 15 minutes of schedule, and relatively few bags are lost. But on most planes, a Coach/Economy seat is always tight. And on the average, you can count on getting a bit of extra space by sitting next to an unoccupied seat only about 25% of the time.

True, tight seating promotes low fares—the more seats stuffed into a plane, the less it costs to haul each passenger. That's a point to remember the next time you're jammed into an unforgiving but relatively cheap Coach/Economy airline seat.

CRTL periodically compiles data on the Coach/Economy seating of all large US airlines and most important international lines that serve North America (JAL, KLM, and several Latin American lines didn't respond to our survey). Our latest results (from a mid-1995 report) show that airborne comfort remains elusive.

The *Coach/Economy Seat Comfort* table beginning on page 80 shows the pitch used in more than 200 aircraft models, flown by over 60 airlines. Door and emergency exit placement affects seat setup in a few locations.

The table *Stuffing 'Em In* on page 84 shows which seat widths are standard in which planes. Depending on a specific seat's design, widths may vary from the figures we tabulate, but by no more than a fraction of an inch.

The *Stuffing 'Em In* table also shows the typical configuration in various planes (as well as some nonstandard setups): Numerals indicate how many seats are in each unit, hyphens represent aisles. Thus, 2-3-2 designates a row whose central three-seat unit has an aisle and a two-seat unit on each side.

In most cases, number of seats per row determines configuration. However, in planes with nine seats per row, a few lines use a 3-4-2 or a 3-3-3 configuration instead of the usual 2-5-2.

For each configuration, the table also shows a middle-seat factor—the percentage of travelers whose comfort is impaired by sitting in a middle seat or next to someone in one (when seats have been assigned to minimize the use of middle seats). Our middle-seat factors are based on an occupancy that ranges from 40% to 100% on individual flights but that averages 70% for all flights. For charter lines, we assume

100% occupancy on all flights, so their middle-seat factors are higher.

Since airlines claim that their planes typically fly only 65–70% full, you might conclude that middle seats aren't used very often. The real situation is worse. Actual occupancies (load factors, in airlinese) are higher, because travelers on frequent-flier tickets and airline employees aren't counted in. Moreover, the reported occupancy is an average of flights that range from full to light. On a typical narrow-body plane (such as the 737), middle seats come into use whenever occupancy rises above 67%. And while the heavily loaded flights—those with an occupancy of 80% or higher—account for only 43% of the number of trips, they carry 55% of the passengers.

As the table shows, the 2-3-2 arrangement used in 767s is the best of the standard Coach/Economy configurations. The 2-3, 2-4-2, and 2-5-2 setups used in some other models are also good. On the other hand, the 3-3, 3-3-3, and 3-4-3 arrangements in certain models are at the bottom.

Some airlines use nonstandard widths and configurations. The best setups have no middle seats, an arrangement used extensively in Business and First Class cabins but only rarely in Coach/Economy. All seats are in pairs: 2-2 in narrow-body planes, 2-2-2 in wide-bodies. Midwest Express, for example, uses 2-2 seating on its DC9s and MD80s—more like other lines' Business or First Class than their Coach/Economy seating. In addition to stan-

SUPER SEATS?

Certain seats have extra space, even on planes with the most limited legroom. Here are some you may want to ask for:

•**Door rows.** Most wide-bodies and a few narrow-bodies have exit doors in the middle of the cabin. The seat rows right behind those doors have extra legroom. (However, those seats may be at a bad angle for viewing an in-flight movie, be narrower than usual because of a folding tray in their armrest, or be in a high-traffic area near the galley, a lavatory, or an area where the cabin crew congregates.)

•**Exit rows.** In narrow-bodies, seats next to the over-wing emergency exits generally have extra pitch. (However, the airline may require occupants of those seats to be able to assist in an emergency evacuation, and it may not assign those seats in advance.)

•**Bulkhead rows.** If you sit right behind a cabin divider, you may get extra legroom, and nobody in front can recline a seatback into your face. (However, those seats are sometimes reserved for disabled travelers or people with babies, and they may be too close to the movie screen for easy viewing.)

•**Twin side seats.** On most 767s, DC10s, MD11s, and L1011s, seats along both

dard Coach/Economy seating, a few international airlines offer a premium configuration such as the 2-4-2 in 747s and 2-3-2 in A300s and MD11s used in EVA's *Economy Deluxe,* Virgin's *Mid Class,* or both.

At the opposite end, a few lines stuff ten 18½-inch seats into each row of a DC10, MD11, or L1011, using the undesirable 3-4-3 configuration. And some cram nine narrow seats into each row in A300-310s, rather than the standard eight.

The scores range from 58 to 100, but most are somewhere between 66 and 80. You're apt to find a plane with a score of 76 or over marginally acceptable, one scoring 70–75 noticeably cramped, and one scoring 69 or less a miserable cattle car.

SOME GOOD NEWS . . .

A few lines scored markedly higher than most:

- •The winner was tiny Midwest Express (comfort scores of 98 and 100). It's the only US airline that can claim comfortable Coach seating even when its planes are full, largely because of the wide seats and lack of middle seats. Its premium seating and meal service are available at competitive Coach and Coach excursion fares from its Milwaukee hub to major cities in the East, Midwest, and California.
- •TWA's relatively good comfort scores reflect seating in its *Comfort Class* as of mid-April '95. Unfortunately, *Comfort Class* seems to have been a box-office failure—its extra legroom

sides of the cabin are in two-seat units; on DC9s, MD80s, and Fokkers, you find two-seat units along one side. If you ask for a seat in a two-seat group, you'll never be in a middle seat or next to anyone writhing in one.

On most airlines, you can reserve specific seats a month or more before departure. But many lines block out the best seats for travelers on full-fare Coach/Economy tickets or those with VFF status, so travelers on cheap Coach/Economy excursions can't reserve them. Some lines won't assign seats in advance to travelers on discount (consolidator) tickets, either. If you want a particular seat, ask if and when you can get an advance assignment. If you can't get an advance assignment, check in early for departure and ask then for the seat you want.

If you want to try for a specific seat, check the *Official Airline Guide,* available at many travel agencies and in corporate travel departments. It has seating charts for some of the larger domestic and foreign airlines. Seating charts are also available in Carlson Publishing Co's *World Annual Airline Seating Guide,* $39.95 for both the US and overseas editions (Box 888, Los Alamitos CA 90720, 310-493-4877; *MC, V*).

COACH/ECONOMY SEAT COMFORT*

AIRCRAFT	PITCH (INCHES)	COMFORT SCORE	AIRCRAFT	PITCH (INCHES)	COMFORT SCORE
AER LINGUS			**ALITALIA** (cont'd)		
A330	34	78	DC9	30	72
BAe146	31	64	MD11	33	79
737-300/400	32	69	MD80	30	72
737-500	33	71	**ALL NIPPON**		
747	34	77	747	34	74
AEROFLOT			**ALOHA**		
IL96	34	74	737	31	66
AEROMEXICO			**AMERICA WEST**		
757	32	69	A320	32	74
767	32	78	737	32	69
DC10	34	83	757	32	69
DC9	30	72	**AMERICAN**		
MD82/3/7/8	31	75	A300	31	75
AEROPERU			727	31	66
727	32	69	737	31	66
757	31	66	757	32	69
AIR CANADA			767-200	32	78
A320	34	76	767-300	31	76
A340	33	78	DC10	31	75
747-100/200	32	69	F100	31	72
747-400	33	74	MD11	33	80
767-200	32	76	MD80	31	75
767-300	33	78	**AMERICAN TRANS AIR**		
L1011	34	80	727	31	66
AIR FRANCE			757	30	64
A300	34	83	L1011	32	67
A310	34	83	**AUSTRIAN**		
A320	31	66	A310	32	75
A340	34	83	A340	32	75
737	31	66	MD81/2/7	32	75
747	34	77	MD83	30	70
767	34	83	**BRITISH AIRWAYS**		
AIR INDIA			A320	34	79
A300	33	78	737	34	74
A310	32	75	747	31	67
747-200	31	69	757	32	69
747-300	33	72	767	32	78
AIR JAMAICA			DC10	32	73
A300	33	78	**CANADIAN INTL**		
727	33	71	A320	32	71
AIR NEW ZEALAND			737	31	66
737	32	69	747	34	77
747	34	74	767	33	78
767	32	78	DC10	33	80
AIRTRAN			**CARNIVAL**		
737	31	66	A300	31	75
ALASKA			727	32	66
737	33	71	737	31	64
MD80	33	80	**CATHAY PACIFIC**		
ALITALIA			A330	32	75
A300(a)	32	73	A340	32	75
A300(b)	31	64	747	33	72
747	33	74	L1011	32	67

* As of May 1995; subject to change.
† Now out of business.

AIRCRAFT	PITCH (INCHES)	COMFORT SCORE	AIRCRAFT	PITCH (INCHES)	COMFORT SCORE
CHINA (Taiwan)			**ICELANDAIR**		
A300	34	80	757	33	71
737	33	71	**KIWI †**		
747	34	77	727	34	74
MD11	34	80	**KOREAN**		
CONTINENTAL			A300	33	75
A300	32	75	727	32	69
727	31	64	747	34	74
737	32	69	DC10	34	80
747	33	72	F100	31	72
DC10	31	73	F28	32	72
DC9	32	72	MD11	34	78
MD80	32	72	MD82	31	72
CSA CZECH			**LADECO**		
A310-300	32	73	727	31	66
DELTA			737	28	59
A310	33	80	757	31	66
727	33	71	**LAN CHILE**		
737	32	69	737	31	66
757	33	71	767	32	78
767	33	81	**LOT POLISH**		
L1011	33	80	767	33	81
MD11	33	80	**LTU(d)**		
MD88	33	80	A330/340	31	64
MD90	33	80	757	33	65
EL AL			767	33	72
747	32	69	L1011	33	63
757	32	69	MD11	33	63
767	32	73	**LUFTHANSA**		
EVA			A300	34	80
747-400	34	74	A310	34	78
747-400(c)	38	95	A310(e)	32	73
767	34	83	A340	32	73
MD11	34	78	737	34	74
MD11(c)	37	93	747	32	72
FINNAIR			**MARKAIR †**		
DC10	31	75	737-200	31	66
DC10(e)	31	64	737-300/400	29	61
DC9-40	31	75	**MARTINAIR(d)**		
DC9-50	32	77	767	30	65
MD11	32	78	747	31	60
MD82/7	30	72	MD11	31	58
MD83	29	70	**MIDWAY**		
FRONTIER			F100	34	80
737	34	74	**MIDWEST EXPRESS**		
HAWAIIAN			DC9	34	100
DC10	32	75	MD80	33	98
DC9	32	75	**NORTHWEST**		
IBERIA			A320	32	69
A300	34	80	727	32	69
727	32	69	747	32	69
747	34	74	757	32	69
DC10	34	78	DC10-30	31	75
DC9	31	72	DC10-40	30	68

COACH/ECONOMY SEAT COMFORT* *(continued)*

AIRCRAFT	PITCH (INCHES)	COMFORT SCORE
NORTHWEST *(cont'd)*		
DC9-10/50	31	75
DC9-30	32	77
DC9-40	30	72
MD80	32	77
PHILIPPINE		
A300	33	80
BAC1-11	31	70
737	31	66
747	34	77
DC10	33	78
F50	29	70
QANTAS		
747	32	72
767	32	73
RENO		
MD80/1/2/3/7/8	32	77
ROYAL JORDANIAN		
L1011	33	80
SABENA		
A300	34	80
747	34	77
DC10	34	80
SAS		
737	30	61
767	32	76
DC9	31	75
F28	32	72
MD80	31	75
SINGAPORE		
A300	32	75
747-200/300	34	74
747-400	32	72
SOUTHWEST		
737-200	31	66
737-300/500	32	69
SPIRIT		
DC9	31	75
SWISSAIR		
A310	31	75
A320	32	74
747	34	77
F100	31	72
MD11	34	81
TAP AIR PORTUGAL		
A300/310/340	35	85
A320	35	81
727	34	74
737	34	74
L1011	37	89

AIRCRAFT	PITCH (INCHES)	COMFORT SCORE
THAI		
A300	34	80
747	34	77
DC10	34	80
MD11	34	80
TOWER		
747	32	72
UNITED		
A320	31	71
727-100	34	74
727-200	31	66
737-200	32	69
737-300/500	31	66
747	31	67
757	31	66
767-200	32	78
767-300	31	76
777	32	80
DC10-10	33	75
DC10-30	31	70
USAIR		
727	31	66
737	31	66
757	32	69
767	32	78
DC9	31	75
F100	32	75
F28	32	72
MD80	31	75
VALUJET		
DC9	31	75
VANGUARD		
737	30	64
VASP		
MD11	32	78
VIRGIN ATLANTIC		
A340	31	73
A340(c)	37	93
747-200	30	67
747-400	31	69
747/200-400(c)	38	95

Note: Excludes commuter planes and some planes used only for domestic flights by overseas lines.

(a) Used for international flights.
(b) Used for domestic flights.
(c) Economy Deluxe (EVA) or Mid Class (Virgin Atlantic).
(d) Charter line or scheduled line that operates like a charter; comfort score based on 100% occupancy.
(e) Long-range version.

apparently didn't translate into improved ticket sales. TWA added back at least some of the seats removed to create *Comfort Class.*

•The nine-across seats in United's 777s are wider than those in the Coach/ Economy cabin of any other major US or international airline, earning the plane a comfort score of 80. Unfortunately, the legroom for some seats is at a stingy 31-inch pitch.

•Among international lines, Taiwan-based EVA earned good marks for its premium *Economy Deluxe* service. Transpacific fares for a seat in that cabin are only a modest amount more than in standard Economy, a rare case in which travelers can opt for comfort at a reasonable price. Virgin Atlantic's *Mid Class* also earned a good score, but those seats are available only to those travelers who pay full-fare Economy, so they aren't attractive.

•Despite airline-to-airline differences, on average the 767 scored highest in comfort of any airplane type. That's mainly because its seven-across, 2-3-2 seating minimizes the unfavorable effects of middle-seat use. If you're comparing flights on lines we didn't rate, you're most apt to be comfortable in a 767.

. . . BUT MOSTLY BAD

The number of unacceptably crowded planes remains sadly high. The table beginning on page 82 identifies all the culprits, but a few are worth noting here:

•The 28-inch pitch on Ladeco's 737s was the tightest we've ever recorded

and its comfort score (59) the lowest ever for a noncharter line. That's an unfortunate reversal for Ladeco, which once featured extra legroom.

•Virgin Atlantic is another line that has abandoned an extra-legroom formula in its main Economy cabin.

•A few scheduled lines (and most charters) fly DC10s, MD11s, and L1011s with 10-across seating, a double whammy for comfort that combines extra-narrow seats and a 3-4-3 configuration. Among the offenders are American Trans Air, Finnair (in some planes), Cathay Pacific, Garuda, and Malaysia. Other offenders—Air France, Alitalia, Finnair, and Pakistan—use ultratight, nine-across seating in some or all of their A300-310s.

•The charter and charter-style lines show generally poor scores—their seats are tight and they're usually full or close to full.

SEAT STRATEGY

To use our comfort ratings, you need to know what planes your airline flies on your route. That information is noted in the reservation computers and the *Official Airline Guide,* but not usually in the airline's own timetable. If you're not sure, call the airline or ask your travel agent.

When considering a line we didn't rate, note that the 767 is a clear winner among popular airplanes. Avoid the worst cattle cars if you can, especially on long flights: charter-style DC10s, L1011s, and MD11s with 10 seats in each row (rather than the usual nine), and tight-pitch 727s, 737s, and 757s.

You can put up with even the worst airline seating if you're next to an empty seat. Here's how to increase your odds of sitting next to an empty:

- On a wide-body plane, airline people report, middle seats in the center section are considered the least desirable, so they're the last to be assigned. You can boost your chances of having an empty next to you by requesting an *aisle seat in the center section*.

- Airlines normally assign adjacent seats to couples. If most of the seats on a plane are in groups of three, as they are in several models, one of the couple will almost always be assigned to a middle seat. Couples can sometimes beat that system by asking for an *aisle and a window seat in a three-seat row*. Unless the plane is close to full, there's a good chance that the middle seat won't be assigned to anyone. If the plane does fill up, the unfortunate who is supposed to sit in the middle seat will doubtless be overjoyed to exchange it for either an aisle or a window position.

STUFFING 'EM IN*

PLANE	SEAT WIDTH(a)	CONFIGURATION(b)	IMPAIRED COMFORT(c)
A300(d)	20	2-4-2	18%
	18.5	3-3-3(e)	50
A320	20	3-3	50
DC9/MD80(f)	20	2-3	21
	23	2-2(g)	0
DC10/MD11	20	2-5-2	20
	18.5	3-4-3(e)	46
	20.5	2-3-2(g)	15
F100/200	20	2-3	21
L1011	20	2-5-2	20
	18.5	3-4-3(e)	46
727	19	3-3	50
	22	2-3(g)	21
737	19	3-3	50
747	19.5	3-4-3	46
	20.5	2-4-2(g)	18
757	19	3-3	50
767	19	2-3-2	15
777	20.5	2-5-2	20

*As of May 1995; subject to change.

Note: All data apply to Coach/Economy seating.
(a) In inches measured between armrest centers.
(b) As used by most scheduled airlines except as noted.
(c) Percentage of travelers occupying a middle seat or next to an occupied middle seat when airline's average occupancy is 70% (see text).
(d) Includes A310, A330, A340.
(e) Undesirable charter configuration; also used by a few scheduled airlines.
(f) Includes MD81, 82, 83, 87, 88.
(g) Desirable nonstandard (premium) Coach/Economy configuration used by a few small airlines.

• Several large lines (including American and United) now try to reserve a section of the Coach/Economy cabin for very-frequent-flier members of their frequent-flier (VFF) programs. Those lines say they assign middle seats in those sections only when planes are full. If you're a VFF member, that's a big advantage. But if you're not, your odds of being in a middle seat or next to an occupied middle seat increase.

HOW ABOUT BUSINESS CLASS?

Compared with Coach/Economy, all Business Class seats are comfortable—at least on planes designed primarily for intercontinental flights. But there's a big difference between the best and worst of the lot. In fact, there's far less consistency among competing versions of Business Class than you find in either First Class or Economy. Given those substantial differences and the lack of widespread discounts, travelers who pay stiff Business Class fares should search for the best service they can find.

FIGURES OF MERIT

The table on pages 87–89 shows Business Class seating arrangements of more than 100 airplane models, as of summer 1996:

• **Configuration.** In 747s (main deck), 777s, A300-310-330-340s, DC10s, L1011s, and MD11s, the usual Business Class arrangement was either 2-3-2 (two-seat units on the outside and a three-seat unit in the center) or 2-2-2 (all seats in pairs). Obviously, at any given cabin width, seats in a

2-2-2 arrangement can be wider than those in 2-3-2; also, the 2-2-2 arrangement has no middle seats—a big plus. (On the narrow upper deck of 747s, 2-2 seating was the norm.)

In 767s, Business Class seats were typically 2-2-2. But since that plane is the narrowest of the wide-body planes, those seats aren't as roomy as 2-2-2 seats on larger models. A few lines had only one seat in a 767's center section (2-1-2).

In narrow-body planes, such as 757s, 737s, and A320s, most lines used 2-2 seating, although a few used 2-3. Seats in those arrangements are wide enough to be comfortable, even when the plane is full.

In Coach/Economy, on the other hand, airlines usually put 10 seats in each row of a 747 (3-4-3); nine in 777s, DC10s, L1011s, and MD11s (2-5-2); seven in 767s (2-3-2); six in most single-aisle planes (3-3); and five in the narrower DC9s, MD80s, and Fokkers (2-3). Those seats generally aren't wide enough to provide a comfortable trip if someone is sitting next to you.

• **Seat pitch.** Ordinarily, today's Business Class pitch is even better than the 36–38 inches in most domestic First Class seating. We think that 36-inch pitch is the minimum for adequate space. (Coach/Economy seat pitch is usually 30–32 inches.)

• **Comfort score** combines the effects of seat width, arrangement, and pitch (again, 100 represents the lowest figure that guarantees a comfortable flight even in a full plane). On average, most current Business Class comfort scores exceeded 100, some considerably. And they were far higher than the typical Coach/Economy scores of 65-80.

Many airlines use more than one version of a plane model; we list variants separately. Planes with different "dash" numbers (such as 747-200 and 747-400) are normally identified as such in the *Official Airline Guides* and other references, so you can determine which plane is used on each flight. But when an airline flies more than one variation of a single dash-number model, the references don't note which version is used for any given flight.

•**Video at seat** shows which planes had individual video screens at each seat —a feature that's rapidly becoming a standard in First and Business Class and is gradually catching on in Economy, as well.

HOW THEY MEASURED UP

On the whole, the products the airlines lump under the rubric of "Business Class" showed surprising variations:

•Aerolineas Argentinas, Alitalia, Ansett Australian, Continental, TWA, and Virgin Atlantic provided extraroomy sleeper seats (at least on some planes) that reclined almost fully and provided an extensible leg rest; their seat pitch was 54 inches or better. American provided 55-inch pitch on the MD11s it used across the Atlantic (but not across the Pacific, where

per-mile fares were lower and the competition wasn't so severe). Comfort scores were a bit less consistent, thanks to differences in seat widths and arrangements.

•A large group of airlines (including Air France, Air New Zealand, British Airways, Canadian Intl, LanChile, Northwest, Qantas, Singapore, and United) offered a still-generous pitch of 47-50 inches. Typically, those seats also offered a leg rest, but they didn't recline as fully as those in the first group. Still, they were much roomier than typical First Class seats in planes configured for purely domestic travel.

•Another group (including Delta, Lufthansa, and Swissair) provided the equivalent of standard domestic First Class seating, with a pitch of 38-42 inches.

•Trailing the pack were a few planes that European lines used for short-haul, regional flights. Seat widths were no better than in Economy, with at best only an inch or two of extra leg-room. Calling such a service Business Class looks like deceptive advertising. Comfort scores were as low as 74—a sorry excuse for anything labeled Business Class.

This chapter was adapted from the Consumer Reports Travel Letter *article "Business Class Seats: Wide, Roomy, Expensive" (August 1996) and from the 1996 edition of* Consumer Reports Best Travel Deals.

BUSINESS CLASS: COMFORT AT A PRICE*

AIRLINE/ AIRCRAFT	CONFIG.	PITCH	VIDEO AT SEAT	COMFORT SCORE
AER LINGUS				
A330	2-2-2	52	✔	150
AEROLINEAS ARGENTINAS				
A310	2-2	55	—	168
B747	2-2	55	—	168
AIR CANADA				
A320(a)	3-2	38	—	107
A320(a)	2-2	38	—	125
A340	2-2-2	58-60	✔	168
B747-100	2-2-2	55	✔	168
B747-200	2-2-2	55	✔	168
B747-400	2-2-2	55	✔	168
B767-200	2-1-2	55	✔	168
B767-200	2-2-2	45	—	123
B767-300	2-1-2	55	✔	168
DC9(a)	2-2	38	—	105
AIR FRANCE				
A320(a,b)	2-2	34	—	105
A340	2-2-2	48	✔	140
B747-200	2-3-2/2-2	48	—	144
B747-400	2-3-2/2-2	48	✔	144
B767	2-1-2	48	✔	150
B737(a,b)	2-2	34	—	105
AIR INDIA				
A300	2-2-2	39-40	—	118
A310	2-2-2	40-47	✔	130
B747-200	2-2	38-40	—	128
B747-300	2-2	38	—	125
B747-400	2-2	38	✔	125
AIR NEW ZEALAND				
B747-200	2-2	50	✔	155
B747-400	2-2	50	✔	155
B767-200	2-2-2	50	✔	135
B767-300	2-2-2	50	✔	135
AIR PACIFIC				
B737(a)	2-2	40	—	130
B747-200	2-2	40	—	130
B767-300	2-2-2	40	—	110
ALITALIA				
A300(a)	2-3-2	34	—	93
A321(a)	3-3	34	—	79
B747	2-2	55	—	168
B767	2-2-2	52	—	140
F70(a)	2-2	34	—	95
MD11	2-2-2	54	✔	155
MD80(a)	2-2	33	—	9
ALL NIPPON				
B747-200	2-3-2/2-2	50	✔	149
B747-400	2-3-2/2-2	50	✔	149
B767-300	2-1-2	50	✔	155
B777-200	2-2-2	40	—	130
AMERICAN				
B767-200	2-2-2	50	—	135
B767-300	2-2-2	48	—	130
MD11(c)	2-3-2	51	—	136
MD11(d)	2-3-2	55	—	146
ANSETT AUSTRALIAN				
A320-200	2-2	35	—	118
B727-200	2-2	35	—	118
B737-300	2-2	36	—	120
B747-300	2-2-2	54	✔	165
B767-200	2-2-2	39	—	128
B767-300	2-2-2	55	—	168
AUSTRIAN				
A310	2-2-2	47	✔	138
A340	2-2-2	47	—	138
BRITISH AIRWAYS				
A320(a)	3-2	34	—	97
B737-200(a)	3-2	34	—	97
B737-400(a)	3-2	34	—	97
B747-100	2-3-2/2-2	50	✔	149
B747-200	2-3-2/2-2	50	✔	149
B747-400	2-3-2/2-2	50	✔	149
B757-200	2-2	50	✔	155
B767-200(a)	2-2-2	34	—	95
B767-300	2-2-2	50	✔	135

BUSINESS CLASS: COMFORT AT A PRICE* *(continued)*

AIRLINE/ AIRCRAFT	CONFIG.	PITCH	VIDEO AT SEAT	COMFORT SCORE
BRITISH AIRWAYS *(cont'd)*				
B777	2-3-2	50	✔	143
DC10-30	2-3-2	50	✔	133
BRITISH MIDLAND				
B737-300(a)	3-2	32	—	92
B737-400(a)	3-2	32	—	92
B737-500(a)	3-2	32	—	92
F70(a)	3-2	32	—	77
F100(a)	3-2	32	—	77
CANADIAN INTL				
A320	2-2	38	—	125
B737	2-2	39	—	128
B747	2-2	50	✔	155
B767	2-2-2	50	—	135
DC10	2-2-2	50	✔	145
CATHAY PACIFIC				
B747-400	2-3-2/2-2	50	✔	149
CHINA				
A300	2-2-2	40	—	120
B747-200	2-3-2/2-2	42	—	129
B747-400	2-3-2/2-2	41	✔	127
B747SP	2-2	42	—	135
MD11	2-3-2	42	✔	123
CONTINENTAL				
B747	2-2-2/2-2	55	✔	168
B757-200	2-2	55	✔	168
DC10-10	2-2-2	55	✔	158
DC10-30	2-2-2	55	✔	158
DELTA				
B767-300	2-2-2	40	—	110
L1011-250	2-3-2	41-43	—	113
L1011-500	2-3-2	39-40	—	106
MD11	2-3-2	42	✔	113
EL AL				
B747-200	2-2-2/2-2	38-40	—	128
B747-400	2-3-2	38-40	✔	116
B757	2-2	38	—	125
B767	2-2-2	38	—	105
EVA				
B747-400	2-2	44	✔	140
B767-200	2-2-2	38	✔	105
B767-300	2-2-2	43-45	✔	120
MD11	2-2-2	44	✔	130
FINNAIR				
MD11	2-2-2/2-3-2	42	—	113
JAPAN				
B747-100,300	2-3-2	36-40	—	113
B747-400	2-3-2	50	✔	143
B747-400	2-3-2	40	✔	118
DC10	2-3-2	36-40	—	103
MD11	2-3-2	39-40	✔	106
KLM				
B747-300	2-2	47	—	148
B747-400	2-2	47	✔	148
B767	2-2-2	47	—	128
MD11	2-3-2	47	—	126
LANCHILE				
B737	2-2	43	—	138
B757	2-2	50	—	155
B767-200	2-2-2	50	—	135
B767-300	2-2-2	50	—	135
LUFTHANSA				
A300-600(a)	2-3-2	34	—	93
A310-300(a)	2-3-2	34	—	93
A320-200(a)	3-3	34	—	79
A321-100(a)	3-3	34	—	79
A340	2-2-2	40	✔	120
B737-200(a)	3-3	34	—	74
B737-300(a)	3-3	34	—	74
B737-400(a)	3-3	34	—	74
B737-500(a)	3-3	34	—	74
B747-200	2-2-2,2-3-2	40	✔	124
B747-400	2-2-2,2-3-2	40	✔	125

AIRLINE/ AIRCRAFT	CONFIG.	PITCH	VIDEO AT SEAT	COMFORT SCORE
MARTINAIR				
B747-200	2-2	39	—	128
B767-300	2-2-2	36	—	100
MD11	2-3-2	36-37	—	98
NORTHWEST				
B747	2-3-2	48	✔	138
DC10	2-2-2	48	✔	140
QANTAS				
B747-400	2-3-2/2-2	50	✔	149
SABENA				
A310-300	2-2-2	47	—	113
A340	2-2-2	47	✔	118
DC10	2-2-2	62	—	175
SAS				
B767	2-2-2	48	✔	130
SINGAPORE				
A310-200	2-2-2	37	—	113
A310-300	2-2-2	44	—	130
B747-200	2-3-2/2-2	39	—	122
B747-300	2-3-2/2-2	47	—	142
B747-300(e)	2-2	38	—	125
B747-400	2-3-2/2-2	47	✔	142
SWISSAIR				
A310-221(a)	2-3-2	34	—	93
A310-322	2-3-2	36	—	98
A310-325	2-2-2	40	—	120
A319(a)	2-3	34	—	97
A320(a)	2-3	34	—	97
A321(a)	2-3	34	—	97
B747-300	2-3-2/2-2	40	—	124
F100(a)	2-2	35	—	88
MD11(f)	2-2-2	40	—	120
MD11(f)	2-2-2	49	—	143
MD81(a)	2-2	34	—	85
TAP AIR PORTUGAL				
A310	2-3-2	43	—	116
A320	2-2	34	—	115
A340	2-2-2	46	✔	135
B737-200(a)	3-3	34	—	74
B737-300(a)	3-3	34	—	74
L1011	2-3-2	38	—	103
THAI				
B747-400	2-2	39-40	—	128
TWA				
B747	2-2	57	—	173
B767	2-2-2	57	—	153
UNITED				
B747-100	2-3-2/2-2	38-40	—	122
B747-200	2-3-2/2-2	48-50	—	147
B747-200	2-3-2/2-2	40	—	124
B747-400	2-3-2/2-2	48-50	—	147
B747-400	2-3-2/2-2	40	—	124
B767-200	2-2-2	39-40	—	108
B767-300	2-2-2	48	—	130
B777	2-3-2	49	✔	141
USAIR				
B767-200	2-2-2	44	✔	120
VARIG				
B747	2-3-2	42	—	123
B767-200	2-2-2	42	—	115
B767-300	2-2-2	41	—	113
DC10	2-3-2	42	—	113
MD11	2-3-2	42	—	113
VIRGIN ATLANTIC				
A340	2-2-2	55	✔	158
B747-200	2-2	55	✔	168
B747-400	2-2	55	✔	168

* As of mid-1996; subject to change.
(a) Used for domestic or regional flights.
(b) Standard 3-3 Economy seating with the middle seat blocked.
(c) On Pacific routes.
(d) On Atlantic routes.
(e) Combined passenger/ cargo configuration.
(f) Pitch to be extended from 40 to 49 inches during winter of '96-97.

For Seniors, Youth, and the Bereaved

Status airfares are fare breaks that target particular classes of traveler —among them the elderly, the young, and relatives of a deceased or gravely ill person. Some status fares are better than any deal available otherwise. In fact, many are simply extra discounts that can make good deals better. Others are better deals than regular tickets for some trips, but not as good for others.

Travelers who use status fares must be prepared to prove their eligibility when they buy tickets and possibly again when they travel. That means presenting age ID for senior, children's, and youth fares and a funeral or death notice or equivalent documentation for a compassionate (also called bereavement) ticket.

The table on pages 94–95 highlights the most important status fares for travel within North America. (See *For Overseas Travel*, page 91, for a brief summary of transatlantic programs.)

A BARGAIN FOR SENIORS

The best status airfares are aimed at senior travelers. Retirees have the time to travel, usually unconstrained by work or school schedules, and they have money to spend on themselves. As a happy side effect, seniors who are still active in business can enjoy a minor windfall.

SENIOR COUPONS. Despite modest but steady price increases, coupons remain the best deal for seniors traveling over long-haul domestic routes. Most big lines offer travelers 62 and over books of four coupons, each good for a one-way trip within the lower 48 states. Lines that fly to nearby points in Canada, Puerto Rico, and the US Virgin Islands typically include those points. On some lines, you can fly to Alaska or Hawaii using two coupons each way. Connecting flights with no stopover at the connection point count as a single trip.

Travel stipulations are similar on all the big US lines: Seats are limited; you can either reserve 14 days or more in advance or travel standby. Unlike other low-fare promotions, senior coupons require no minimum stay. Travel on senior coupons qualifies for frequent-flier credit. Each senior traveler requires a separate book—a couple can't share a four-coupon book to take one round-trip together. Once issued, the coupons are valid for a year.

Otherwise, as the table shows, there are differences worth noting (prices and conditions as of spring 1996):

•Coupons on America West, Continental, and TWA are a bit cheaper than the "standard" price adopted by American, Delta, Northwest, United,

and USAir. However, senior coupons require that you take a minimum of two round-trips a year. Accordingly, routes and schedules from your home city are probably more important in your choice of airline than the relatively small price differences.

•America West, Continental, and TWA retain the option, dropped by other lines, of eight-coupon books, with a lower per-coupon price than on the

FOR OVERSEAS TRAVEL

Most US and Canadian airlines give senior travelers to Europe the same 10% discount that they receive within North America. The minimum age is 62 on US lines, 60 on Canadian lines.

Most overseas-based transatlantic lines we checked also give 10% senior reductions; El Al gives 15%, and Aer Lingus and Air India don't offer senior reductions. The minimum age is 62 on most lines, 60 on British Airways, LTU, and Lufthansa. The reduction applies to most fares but may not apply to all; check with each airline for particulars. And seniors are often targeted for special short-term promotions. We found no US or foreign line that gives comparable senior reductions to Asia.

On most international flights, infants under two pay 10% of the accompanying adult's fare, but get no seat. Typically, children 2–11 pay 25–75% of the adult fare (including Economy excursion fares).

Many US and European airlines offer youth fares for Europe-bound youngsters age 12–24. Typically, they can make reservations only within 72 hours of departure; the return portion of a round-trip is left open, with the same 72-hour reservation limit. Seats are restricted and may be blacked out on some dates. Often, youth tickets are no cheaper than discount (consolidator) tickets available to anybody. Always compare both options before you buy.

Most charters to Europe charge everyone the same fare. Thus, even though their adult fares may be higher, a scheduled line can often beat a charter for family travel. However, a few charter operators also offer children's reductions.

Only two of the overseas lines we checked offer compassionate fares. Aer Lingus offers 50% off unrestricted Economy, and British Airways offers a fare equal to the seven-day advance-purchase Economy excursion.

now-standard four-coupon books.

- For $648, TWA sells a coupon book for a companion of any age who accompanies a qualifying senior. Four-coupon TWA books (senior, companion, and youth) also contain a coupon that gives a 20% reduction on a ticket to Europe.
- USAir permits seniors to use their coupons for an accompanying child, age 2–11.

For a transcontinental round-trip, the cost of travel with the most expensive four-coupon book works out to $298. That's less than half the cheapest regular Coach excursion (in the absence of a fare war) and a bit cheaper than even the best current fare-war prices. Coupons may be a good deal even for a flight as short as Chicago–New York, where the cheapest Coach excursion normally costs about $300.

SENIOR REDUCTION. Except for Southwest, all the big US and Canadian lines offer a 10% senior discount to travelers 62 or over on virtually any published fare, from First Class to Coach/Economy excursions, for travel within North America. (So do some smaller lines, including American Trans Air, Midway, Midwest Express, and Reno.) Most lines give the same reduction to a companion of any age who follows the same itinerary as a qualified senior traveler.

Southwest is the stingiest of the big lines. It offers a 30% reduction, but from only its highest, walk-up fare.

Senior reductions may not be available on short-term sale fares; you have to check with each airline on each promotion. Frequent-flier credit and upgrade policies are generally the same as for the any-age fares on which the domestic senior fares are based.

On a typical Coach excursion, 10% generally won't save big bucks. For long trips, you're usually better off with a coupon book.

FREEDOM PASSPORT. Continental sells a pass that allows a one-way trip each week, including connecting flights, for a full year (subject to a few blackout periods). You must be at least 62 to buy the pass, but a companion of any age can buy a second one for travel when you travel.

The basic *Freedom Passport* covers travel within the lower 48 states and the US Virgin Islands. It currently costs $1999 in Coach, $3499 in First Class. Passholders may buy a limited number of add-ons for trips to Alaska, the Caribbean, Central America, Europe, Hawaii, and Mexico at less than regular fares. A Global option, at $4499 in Coach/Economy, $6999 in Business/

LOW STUDENT AND TEACHER AIRFARES

Council Travel, especially geared toward students and teachers, offers low airfares for domestic and international flights. Council also issues Eurail and Britrail passes, hostel cards, work abroad programs, and advice on how travelers can best stretch their travel dollars. Call Council's National Reservation Center for more information (800-226-8624).

First Class, combines the travel the basic pass allows plus the maximum nine add-ons for less than you'd pay separately. A four-month variant is also available, providing about one-third as much travel for about half the price.

You can visit any city up to three times a year. You can make advance reservations only for travel noon Monday through noon Thursday and all day Saturday, but you can try for a standby seat at any time. (International travel days vary.) Seats are limited; you may make reservations during peak periods of the year no earlier than seven days in advance (30 days for international travel). Travel on the pass does not qualify for frequent-flier credit.

Theoretically, the basic yearly pass would provide trips in Coach worth as much as $12,000 (24 long-haul round-trips a year at $500 a trip). That's a lot of travel. Indeed, the pass beats senior coupons any time you take seven or more round-trips a year. With coupons, however, you have a choice of airlines —including, perhaps, ones with routes that suit you better than Continental's.

The First Class passes look like a tremendous value, compared with regular First Class fares. However, some readers tell us that *Freedom Passport* travelers are pretty low on the upgrade totem pole. Continental apparently allocates only a minuscule number of First Class seats to passholders, and plenty of business travelers chase First Class seats. Overall, we recommend it only to travelers who are willing to lay out the money but forgo actually getting a First Class seat some of the time.

SHORT-TERM DEALS. Airlines occasionally offer short-term promotions for senior travelers.

FARES FOR YOUNGSTERS
Though the old fare better, the young too can find a few good deals.

YOUTH/STUDENTS. US airlines have finally become a bit more generous with deals for the young. Probably the best news is TWA's youth coupons, essentially the same as TWA's senior coupons except that there's no companion option. They're attractive whenever the cheapest regular round-trip Coach excursion is over $274—as it is on a large number of routes.

Air Canada and TWA also offer youth discounts. And USAir offers youth fares (to age 22) on selected routes. But Southwest's youth/children option is underwhelming: a mere 5% off the line's highest, walk-up fare.

In the recent past, several US lines have run short-term promotions for young travelers. Canadian Intl has also offered special standby youth fares within Canada. There will probably be more such promotions this year.

INFANTS. Children under two travel on domestic airlines at no charge—and with no seat reservation. When the plane is full, fare-paying adults have to hold infants in their lap. Of course, if a seat is empty, cabin attendants normally allow an infant to use it.

US airlines are now required to accommodate infant safety seats if parents want their infants to use them. But despite pressures from safety interests, neither the Dept of Transportation nor any airline has established a safety-seat requirement. The big stumbling block: A child in a safety seat must have a separate seat reservation and ticket. So far, Southwest is the only domestic line we know of that offers reduced fares for infants who occupy a safety seat. Otherwise, parents must purchase the cheapest available adult ticket.

CHILDREN. Except for occasional promotions, kids 2–11 years old typically get no important breaks on domestic travel. They must buy the cheapest available adult ticket.

COMPASSIONATE FARES

On big airlines, the cheapest tickets must usually be bought up to 21 days in advance. Until the airlines formally adopted compassionate fares, travelers suddenly called to a relative's funeral or sickbed were hit with last-minute walk-up fares, usually the highest.

Each airline has its own rules about just how distant a family connection qualifies a traveler for the fare. There are also variations in the circumstances that qualify: All the lines include attendance at a relative's funeral. But only some include serious illness or imminent death.

Compassionate fares are typically a bit higher than the cheapest advance-purchase Coach/Economy excursion. In some cases, they're the same as the slightly higher, seven-day fare with the advance-purchase restriction waived.

NORTH AMERICAN STATUS FARES

AIRLINE	SENIOR COUPONS (BOOK OF 4)	SENIOR COUPONS (BOOK OF 8)	SENIOR REDUCTION	CHILDREN'S REDUCTION
Air Canada	—	—	10%(a)	10%
Alaska	—	—	10%	33%(d)
America West	$495	$920	10%	—
American	596	—	10%	—
American Trans Air	—	—	10%(g)	10%(h)
Canadian	—	—	10%(a)	10%
Continental	579	999	10%	(f)
Delta	596(j)	—(j)	10%	—
Midwest Express	—	—	10%	—
Northwest	596	—	10%	—
Reno	—	—	10%	(f)
Southwest	—	—	30%(b)	5%(b)
TWA	548(m)	1032	10%	—
United	596	—	10%	10%(p)
USAir	596(q)	—	10%	10%(r)

Note: Prices as of March 1996; subject to change. Coupon prices include the 10% US transportation tax, temporarily suspended; subtract 10% if tax has not been reinstated. Unless otherwise noted, minimum age for senior fares is 62; age limits for children's fares are 2-11.

(a) Age 60 or over.

(b) Reduction from full Coach/Economy fare.
(c) In case of a death only.
(d) To Mexico, Russia only.
(e) Advance-purchase waived on 7-day Coach excursion fare.
(f) No fixed discount; dollar fares published on specific routes.
(g) Age 55 or over.

But in all cases, they're lower than the walk-up fare that business travelers pay.

It pays to check all the possibilities. If you want to use one of the big lines, check to see if the nature of the crisis (death or serious illness) and your relationship to the person involved qualify. If one airline says no, try another.

Also check to see if a low-fare line flies to your destination (see chapter 5). Some of them don't impose advance purchase requirements on any traveler —bereaved or otherwise.

GETTING YOUR TICKET

You can buy status-fare tickets directly from an airline or through any travel agency. Most sellers require some sort

of documentation to confirm your eligibility (proof of age, student status, a physician's or undertaker's statement, or the like). Senior, youth, and children's fares are considered "published" fares, so you can get an additional 4–8% discount by purchasing your ticket through a rebating agency such as Travel Avenue (800-333-3335) or All-American Travel Club (800-451-8747). For more on rebating travel agencies, see chapter 1.

This chapter was adapted from the Consumer Reports Travel Letter *article "Airfares: 'Status' Counts" (April 1996) and from the 1996 edition of* Consumer Reports Best Travel Deals.

YOUTH/STUDENT REDUCTION	YOUTH/STUDENT COUPON	YOUTH/STUDENT SPECIAL FARES	COMPASSIONATE REDUCTION
65%(b)	—		50%(b,c)
—	—		30%(b,c)
—	—		(e)
—	—	(f)	(c,f)
—	—	(f)	50%(b,i)
—	—		50%(b)
—	—(j)	(f)	50%(i,k)
—	—	(g,l)	50%(i,k)
—	—		70%(i,k)
—	—		—
5%(b)	—	(f)	—
10%(n)	4 for $548(o)		50%(b,c)
—	—	(f)	35-45%(b,c)
(f)	—		50%(b,c)

(h) Age 2-17.
(i) In case of death or serious illness.
(j) Also senior and youth (age 12-24) coupons for Shuttle flights: four for $227, eight for $418.
(k) Off some fares.
(l) Age 17-26.
(m) Coupons for companion of any age, $648; both books include coupon for 20% discount on ticket to Europe.
(n) Age 16-26.
(o) Age 14-24; includes coupon for 20% discount on ticket to Europe.
(p) On some routes only.
(q) Coupons can be used by companion age 2-11.
(r) When traveling with senior.

AWAY ALONE – YOUNG OR OLD

Say you have to arrange a long plane flight for your 7-year-old grandson or your 92-year-old mother. What happens if he or she misses a connection or suffers an extended delay in a distant hub?

UNACCOMPANIED MINORS

Most major US airlines accept children of 5 years or older on nonstop or through (no change of plane) flights, or at a minimum age of 8 years if there's a plane change. Southwest's minimum is also 5 years, but the line accepts only minors who don't need to make a connection.

Most lines let an unaccompanied minor travel at no extra charge on a nonstop or through flight, but they charge an escort fee of $30 each way when a connection is required. Midwest Express doesn't charge a fee.

Kids flying alone generally pay the lowest applicable adult fare. The adult making reservations and buying tickets should make sure the reservation agent (or travel agent) knows the ticket is for an unaccompanied minor. That fact is made a permanent part of the flight-reservation record, so that it's accessible to any airline employee who needs to check. Minors traveling solo normally wear a conspicuous tag, button, or pouch that hangs around the neck.

Airlines require a form that includes the full name, address, and phone number for the responsible adult at the trip's origin and for the person who will meet the child at the destination.

The responsible adult hands a youngster over to an agent at the departure airport. The agent packs tickets and other documents into the pouch (or some other secure document holder) and escorts the child to the plane and the care of a flight attendant.

It's a good idea to stay in the boarding area until the flight has left the ground, not just the gate. That way, you're still on hand if a mechanical problem requires a return to the gate and, possibly, a switch to another plane.

If a plane change is necessary, an airline representative escorts an unaccompanied minor from the arrival to the departure gate, remaining there until the child can be handed over to a flight attendant on the connecting flight. Some airlines maintain special supervised rooms, equipped with games and amusements, for children making connections at their major hub airports.

An adult meeting a minor should arrive at the airport well before the flight is to arrive and check in at the counter. The minor is escorted off the plane, normally by a flight attendant, and is turned over to the adult named in the paperwork. The airline will require the adult to show valid photo ID.

If there's a missed connection or an extended delay, the airline will have an adult staffer supervise an unaccompanied minor at all times. Should overnight housing be necessary, a staff member will stay with the minor in a hotel, at no additional charge. If the designated adult fails to meet a minor on arrival, the airline will contact one of the adults named in the paperwork. If necessary, airline personnel will keep a minor overnight, with hotel charges billed to the parent or guardian.

To avoid problems, Alaska Airlines does not accept unaccompanied minors if bad weather is likely to alter or delay routing or arrival schedules. United doesn't accept unaccompanied minors on the last flight of the day on any route that involves a connection.

Airlines assume that most kids of 12 or over can cope as adults with the vagaries of air travel. But if you're dealing with a young teenager who isn't mature enough to handle the challenge, you can request America West, Continental, Delta, Northwest, TWA, and United to treat children through age 17 as unaccompanied minors. The $30 fee applies for connecting flights, just as it does with younger minors. Midwest Express provides the same service at no fee.

To prepare children for a trip, brief them about it as thoroughly as their maturity permits, and be sure to provide them with the name and phone number of the adult who's to meet them at the arrival airport. If a child is old enough, explain how to work a pay phone. In addition to the itinerary given to the airline, put a separate copy of the child's itinerary in a secure pocket. Provide children with enough entertainment to keep them busy throughout the flight—books, coloring books, a cassette player, games, or the like.

THE FRAIL ELDERLY

Only a few lines have policies covering seniors who can't fend for themselves. Upon request, Alaska, America West, Northwest, and United will treat seniors in about the same way (and at the same fee) as they handle unaccompanied minors. The other lines (except Southwest) say they make special arrangements for seniors as required.

Free Trips for Frequent Fliers

Join a frequent-flier program? Why not? It doesn't cost you anything and you earn credits toward free trips, upgrades to better seats, and various other benefits. Even if you never earn enough credits for payoffs like those, you usually get in on members-only airfare deals, mileage bonuses on certain routes, occasional free upgrade certificates, and bonuses for using certain hotel or car-rental partners.

Basic frequent-flier award schedules haven't changed all that much recently. Since the big devaluations of 1994, the major changes have been primarily in partnerships—travel suppliers, airline and nonairline, that award mileage credit whenever you use their services.

For this chapter, we've analyzed the earning and award schedules of the 10 US and 2 Canadian lines that run full-scale, complex programs. We also take a brief look at the limited programs of Southwest and several smaller lines (see *The Other Players*, page 112). And we evaluate the perks offered to very frequent fliers.

HOW THE BASIC PLANS COMPARE

Frequent-flier programs aren't all alike. They may differ in any of seven important factors: payoff, ease of earning credit, destinations offered, mileage life, extent of travel blackouts, ease of upgrading from a Coach/Economy excursion ticket, and the relative availability of free seats. To choose a program, you should match its particular benefits to your own travel patterns. The *Ratings* table on page 100 shows how we ranked each one, but here's an overview.

FIGURING YOUR PAYOFF

The most important ratings factor is probably payoff, the miles you must fly to earn one free trip. We rated payoffs for three popular awards: a Coach ticket within the lower 48 states (often including a few nearby points in the Bahamas, Canada, Mexico, or the Caribbean), a Coach trip to Hawaii, and an Economy trip to Europe.

We also figured the average payoff on free trips in a premium class

(Business or First Class, whichever required less credit) to those same three areas. And for couples, we developed a similar payoff index for two tickets, since you can earn two tickets in a few programs for less than double the credit required for one ticket.

HOW YOU EARN CREDIT

The table on pages 102–107 shows the credit you can earn on each line, as published in late 1996 (but subject to change) for travel in 1997 and thereafter. On all the lines, you earn a mile of credit for each mile flown, but at least 500 or 750 miles for even the shortest flight (except on United's Shuttle flights, where you get only the miles you actually fly).

Even the cheapest Coach/Economy excursions and, on most lines, senior coupons earn credit (but a few kinds of discount and group-tour tickets don't). Most lines award a bonus for flying Business or First Class; America West gives a bonus for full-fare Coach.

Some lines are more generous than others:

- On both Canadian lines, travelers who fly cheap Economy excursions within Canada earn only half credit—a major drawback.
- America West and TWA are relatively openhanded: Both give a minimum of 750 miles a flight. That's a substantial advantage for travelers who earn credit mainly on short-haul trips.
- Most lines give credit for flights on one or more partner airlines, but with notable differences. On some code-shared flights (flights operated

by certain other airlines that also carry the sponsoring line's flight numbers), you get the same credit you'd get on the sponsoring line, including the minimum mileage and premium-class bonuses. But on other partner lines, neither the minimum nor the bonus applies. The big lines also give credit on affiliated commuter lines (not shown).

Some partner lines are even more restrictive. Cathay Pacific and Singapore don't give credit on their US partner lines for any Economy flight. You get no credit on some US partners when you use one of the cheaper Economy excursion tickets on Air India and Philippine; Qantas gives full credit on Alaska and American, but not on Continental. And some overseas partner airlines severely limit the routes beyond their home-base area on which they give credit. Those limitations are often buried in the program's fine print.

- All the lines also give mileage credit for doing business with nonairline partners—car-rental companies, hotel chains, long-distance phone companies, tour operators, cruise lines, and even restaurants and sellers of flowers or mutual funds. The more such partners there are, the greater your opportunity to earn credit. However, in some cases, you earn car-rental and hotel credit only when you fly to or from the rental or hotel location on the sponsoring airline.
- All the lines co-brand a charge card that gives one mile of credit for each dollar billed to the card. American

Express and Diners Club also run programs that let you earn credit on the same basis and convert it to airline credit when you choose, thus bypassing any credit-life limitations (see chapter 3). Since you can earn credit through charge cards on any of the US lines we list, we didn't score that factor.

WHERE YOU CAN GO

Our destinations-offered Ratings reflect the number of major areas to which you can get free trips, weighted to favor those of greatest interest to readers of *Consumer Reports Travel Letter*. We think that makes more sense than a simple count of the cities an airline and its partners serve. (Of course, if any line's program gets you where you want to go, who cares where it doesn't go?)

The table on pages 108–09 spells out the mileage required for a free trip on some popular routes. We've listed the lowest-credit award, which may require off-peak travel, be usable during just a few months of the year, be subject to severe limitations on the number of seats available, or be on a partner airline:

- On some lines, you can bypass seat limitations or fly at peak periods if you're willing to spend more of your credit.
- All the lines provide free flights within the lower 48 states (or within Canada, for the Canadian lines). However, Alaska, America West, and Midwest Express have limited ser-

HOW THE PROGRAMS RATE*

	AIR CANADA AEROPLAN	ALASKA MILEAGE PLAN	AMERICA WEST FLIGHTFUND	AMERICAN AADVANTAGE	CANADIAN CANADIAN PLUS
PAYOFF					
US, Coach(b)	O	+	+	O	O
Hawaii, Coach	–	–		+	O
Europe, Economy	O	+	O	+	+
Premium Class(d)	+	+	O	–	–
Couples(e)	–	+	O	+	O
OTHER BENEFITS					
Ease of Earning Credit	O	–	+	+	O
Destinations Offered	+	–	–	+	+
Mileage Life	+	+	O	O	+
When You Can Fly	O	O	+	+	O
Upgrades	O	–	+	+	O
Seat Availability	–	+	–	+	

*As of October 1996; subject to change.
+ Above average   – Average   O Below average
(a) Listed ratings based on off-peak program; payoff on standard program would be rated lower.

(b) May include some nearby points in the Bahamas, Canada, the Caribbean, and Mexico.
(c) Frequent-flier trips to Hawaii not available.
(d) Based on extra credit required for a premium-class

vice areas; on those lines, you must fly on a partner line to reach some areas of the US.

- •All lines can also get you to Asia and Europe, either on their own flights or on a partner line—but only in Business or First Class on TWA.
- •Only USAir can't get you to Hawaii, either on its own flights or on those of a partner.
- •All lines except Alaska, Midwest Express, and Northwest offer their own or partner travel to South America. And all of these airlines but TWA can get you to the South Pacific.

HOW WELL CREDIT AGES

As the *Earning Frequent-Flier Credit* table shows, some programs cancel unused credit after three years. That could be a big disadvantage—an infrequent traveler may not fly enough in three years to earn even one free trip, while a very frequent traveler may not be able to use up a large credit balance that fast. Delta and Midwest Express are a bit more lenient—they reset their three-year clock each time you take a flight. Alaska, TWA, USAir, and the Canadian lines let you sit on your credit as long as you want.

Most lines maintain an account of your credit, similar to a bank account, with periodic statements of deposits and withdrawals. When you want to take a free flight, you ask for an award. America West still issues certificates each time you rack up a certain num-

CONT'L ONEPASS	DELTA SKYMILES	MIDWEST EXPRESS FREQUENT FLYER	NORTHWEST WORLD-PERKS(a)	TWA FREQUENT FLIGHT-BONUS	UNITED MILEAGE PLUS	USAIR FREQUENT TRAVELER
O	Ⓞ	+	+	+	Ⓞ	O
–	+	–	+	–	+	O(c)
–	–	+	+	+	–	–
O	–	–	+	O	–	–
O	–	+	+	O	–	O
+	+	O	–	+	+	–
+	+	–	–	O	+	O
–	–	O	Ⓞ	+	Ⓞ	+
+	Ⓞ	+	Ⓞ	O	–	O
+	+	(f)	+	–	+	O
O	Ⓞ	–	–	+	+	–

award, relative to average for all lines.
(e) Based on extra credit required for a two-ticket award, relative to average for all lines.
(f) Upgrades not required for online flights; rated Below

Average for partner-line upgrades.

ber of miles; it's up to you to keep track of the certificates and submit them when you want an award.

BLACKOUTS AND LIMITS

The programs also differ substantially in the number of days during a year on which you can use the lowest-credit awards. Our blackout ratings are based on the number of days per year on which you can take trips within the lower 48 states, to Hawaii, and to Europe for the least mileage credit. (We used the off-peak credit requirement for lines that offer off-peak awards, the standard credit requirement for others.)

Almost all the programs impose blackouts during major holiday periods —up to about 30 days a year. But some lines ban frequent-flier trips on some routes for entire seasons—up to 100 days a year. And in an offset to their relatively generous award schedules, the Continental and Northwest programs limit some low-credit travel to

DON'T WASTE YOUR CREDIT

Applied to a long-haul trip, frequent-flier credit is worth about 2¢ a mile. Don't waste a domestic award, worth about $500, on a short-haul trip—one where you could buy a ticket for less than half that value. Don't waste 30,000 to 40,000 miles for a Coach trip from the West Coast to Hawaii when you could buy a round-trip ticket for under $300.

EARNING FREQUENT-FLIER

	AIR CANADA AEROPLAN
EARNING CREDIT	
Minimum per Trip(a)	500 miles(b)
Mileage Life	Unlimited(d)
BONUSES(a)	
Business Class	25%
First Class	—
PARTNERS	
Airlines	Austrian, British Midland, Cathay Pacific, Continental, Finnair, Lufthansa, SAS, Swissair, United Airways
Hotel Chains	Crowne Plaza, Hilton, Hilton Intl, Holiday Inn, Hotel des Gouverneurs, Keddy's, Marriott, Radisson, Sheraton, Westin
Car Renters	Avis, Budget, Hertz(q)
Charge Cards	Diners Club, Visa
Phone Services	Participating Canadian companies
Tour Operators	Air Canada Vacations
Other	Park 'N Fly

CREDIT

ALASKA MILEAGE PLAN	AMERICA WEST FLIGHTFUND	AMERICAN AADVANTAGE	CANADIAN CANADIAN PLUS	CONT'L ONEPASS
500 miles Unlimited	750 miles 3 years(e)	500 miles 3 years	500 miles(b) Unlimited(d)	500 miles Unlimited(f)
— 50%	— 50%(i)	25% 50%	25% 50%	25% 50%
British Airways, Horizon, Northwest, Qantas, TWA	Aeromexico, Air France(j), Air New Zealand, British Airways, Continental, Northwest(j)	British Airways(j), British Midland(j), Canadian Intl, Cathay Pacific(k), Hawaiian(l), Japan, Midway, Qantas, Reno, Singapore(k), South African	Air New Zealand, Aloha, American, British, Qantas	Aer Lingus, Aerolineas, Argentina, Air Canada, Alitalia, America West, BWIA, CSA, Czech, Frontier, Iberia, LanChile, Malaysia, Qantas (m), SkyWest
Coast, Hilton, Holiday Inn, Hyatt, Kimpton, Preferred, Princess, Red Lion, Sheraton, West Coast, Westin, Westmark	Crowne Plaza, Hilton, Holiday Inn, Radisson, Westin	Crowne Plaza Fairmont, Fiesta, Forte, Forum, Hilton, Hilton Intl, Holiday Inn, Hyatt, Inter-Continental, Loews, Marriott, Meridien, Radisson Red Lion, Sandals, Sheraton, Westin, Wyndham	Best Western, Canadian Pacific, Coast, Delta, Evaz, Fiesta, Forum, Howard Johnson, Inter-Continental, Loews, Prince, Ramada, Renaissance, Shangri-La, West Coast, Westmark	Aston(q), Camino Real(q), Fiesta Hilton, Marriott, Melia(q), Radisson Sheraton, Sol(q)
Alamo, Budget, Hertz(q)	Alamo, Avis, Dollar, Thrifty	Alamo, Avis, Hertz (q), National(r)	Alamo, National (r), Thrifty	Avis(q), Hertz(q), National(q,r), Thrifty(q)
Diners Club, MasterCard, Visa	Visa	MasterCard, Visa	American Express (s), Visa	American Express, Diners Club, MasterCard, Visa
AT&T Alascom, Sprint	Sprint	MCI participating cellular companies	Participating Canadian companies	MCI
Alaska Airlines Vacations, Horizon Air Holidays	America West Vacations	Fly AAway Vacations	Canadian Holidays	—
DineAir	Flower Club, Phoenix Club	AAdvantage Dining, AAdvantage Funds, Computer City, FTD Direct	Atlas Van Lines, Aeropark Edmonton, Brewster Transportation, Flowers 24 Hours, Holt Renfrew, Park & Jet Calgary, YVR Airport Parking	—

EARNING FREQUENT-FLIER CREDIT* *(continued)*

	DELTA SKYMILES	MIDWEST EXPRESS FREQUENT FLYER	NORTHWEST WORLDPERKS	TWA FREQUENT FLIGHT BONUS
EARNING CREDIT				
Minimum per Trip(a)	500 miles	500 miles	500 miles	750 miles
Mileage Life	3 years(g)	3 years(g)	3 years(h)	Unlimited
BONUSES(a)				
Business Class	25%	—	25%	50%
First Class	50%	—	50%	50%
PARTNERS				
Airlines	Aer Lingus, Aeromexico, Air New Zealand, All Nippon, Austrian, Finnair, Malaysia, Sabena, Singapore(k), Swissair, Varig	Air New Zealand, Northwest(j,n), Swissair, Virgin Atlantic	Air New Zealand, Alaska, Hawaiian, Horizon, KLM	Aerolineas Argentinas, Air India(m), Alaska, Horizon, Philippine(m)
Hotel Chains	Crowne Plaza, Forte, Forum, Hilton, Hilton Intl, Holiday Inn, Hyatt, Inter-Continental, Marriott, Meridien, Preferred, Radisson, Renaissance, Sheraton, Swissotel	Hilton, Loews, Wyndham	Courtyard, Crowne Plaza, Fairfield Inn, Golden Tulip, Hilton, Holiday Inn, Hyatt, Marriott, NewOtani, Peabody, Radisson, Shangri-La, Sheraton Tulip Inns, Westin	Adam's Mark, Forte, Hilton, Inter-Continental, Marriott, Radisson, Renaissance
Car Renters	Alamo, Avis(q), Hertz(q)	Alamo(q), Avis (q), Hertz (q), National(q,r)	Alamo(q), Avis(q), Hertz(q), National(q)	Alamo, Avis, Thrifty(q)
Charge Cards	American Express, Optima	Diners Club, MasterCard	Diners Club, Visa	Diners Club, MasterCard, TWA, Getaway Card, Visa
Phone Services	MCI	MCI	MCI	Global One, Sprint, WorldCom
Tour Operators	—	Holidays With Style, Midwest Express Vacations	Northwest WorldVacations, Packages	TWA Getaway Vacations
Other	Charles Schwab, Flower Club, Renaissance Cruises, SkyMiles Dining	Amtrak, Baumgarten Krueger Florists, Midwest Express Floral Club	Dining for Miles, 800 Music Now, Flower Club	Ambassadors Club, Better Homes & Gardens real estate, Dining a la Card Miles, Flower Club

UNITED MILEAGE PLUS	USAIR FREQUENT TRAVELER
500 miles(c) 3 years(h)	500 miles Unlimited
25% 50%	25% 50%
Aeromar, Air Canada (b,m), Air France, ALM Antillean, Aloha, Ansett Australia, British Midland, Gulfstream Intl, Lapa, Lufthansa, National of Chile (m), SAS, Thai(m)	Air France, Alitalia, All Nippon, British Airways (o), LatinPass lines(p), Northwest, Qantas, Sabena, Swissair
Crowne Plaza, Forum, Hilton, Hilton Intl, Holiday Inn, Inter-Continental Libertel, Marriott, Melia, Radisson, Ritz Carlton,Shangri-La, Sheraton,Sol, Westin	Hilton, Hyatt, Marriott, Radisson, Renaissance, Westin
Alamo(q), Avis(q), Budget(q), Dollar, Hertz(q), National(q,r)	Alamo, Avis, Hertz(q), National(r)
Diners Club, MasterCard, UA Travel Card, Visa	Diners Club, Visa
AT&T, GTE Airfone	AT&T
United Vacations	—
Countrywide Home Loans, cruise lines(t), 800-Flowers, Mileage Plus Dining, Namco, PMP Relocation	Flower Club

(a) On primary carrier; partner airline's mileage and bonus may vary.
(b) Earn 50% of actual miles on Economy excursions within Canada; minimum 250 mi.
(c) Shuttle by United earns actual miles flown.
(d) By law, Canadian credit must have an expiration date, but the dates have always been extended.
(e) Mileage certificates are issued automatically at 20,000 mi and expire 3 years after issue; unused credit expires if there is no account activity for 36 months.
(f) Credit may be canceled if no activity over 18-month period.
(g) Extended indefinitely with qualifying account activity every 36 months.
(h) December 31 of third year.
(i) Also 50% bonus on full-fare coach.
(j) Award travel only.
(k) No credit on Economy flights.
(l) Earn 50% of actual miles on Economy excursions between Hawaii and mainland.
(m) No credit for some or all Economy excursion fares.
(n) Northwest awards available only for credit earned on flights to or from Milwaukee and Omaha.
(o) Partnership expires 3/29.
(p) Aces, Avianca (Colombia), Apa Intl (Dominican Republic), Aviateca (Guatemala), Copa (Panama), Faucett (Peru), Lacsa (Costa Rica), Lapsa (Paraguay), Ladeco Chilean, LanChile, Mexicana, Nica (Nicaragua), Saeta (Ecuador), Taca (El Salvador).
(q) Earning may be limited to stays or rentals in conjunction with flight on sponsoring airline.
(r) Includes affiliates Europcar in Europe, Tilden in Canada.
(s) For Canadian American Express cards only.
(t) Crystal, Norwegian, Renaissance.

just a few months of the year. In fact, although off-peak awards may appear generous, Northwest imposes limits so harsh that off-peak travel is virtually out of reach.

Several lines provide optional free-trip awards that bypass blackouts and seat limitations. Typically, those peak awards require about twice the credit of off-peak awards.

UPGRADES TO BETTER SEATS

To some travelers, upgrade opportunities are the most important feature of a frequent-flier program. We scored each line's upgrade potential by considering the mileage required to bump up Coach/Economy excursion tickets within the US and to Europe and whether the upgrade can be applied to the cheapest advertised excursion fare.

- Most big lines let you use 20,000 miles of credit to upgrade a domestic Coach excursion ticket to the next higher class (Business on three-class planes, First on two-class planes). Those are "positive space" upgrades, confirmed at the time you reserve. However, on some lines, you can't use those upgrades with a few of the cheapest advertised Coach excursions or with senior coupons. The Canadian lines don't offer credit-based upgrades. Neither does Midwest Express for online (non-partner) flights, but it doesn't need to—it offers near First Class service at Coach fares.

- Most US lines let you upgrade an Economy excursion to Europe for 40,000 miles of credit. But again, the upgrade may not be valid with the cheapest advertised Economy ticket.

- Several lines sell books of coupons or stickers that their frequent fliers can use to upgrade domestic Coach tickets, either within a few days of departure or standby. The number of coupons required is based on the length of the flight. However, only VFF (very-frequent-flier) members can use them to upgrade Coach excursions. Unfortunately, no such upgrades are available for overseas travel.

TWA has the most liberal VFF program: Frequent fliers reach its first level after completing just 5000 miles. They can then use coupons to upgrade a Coach excursion if seats are available at departure time. However, TWA's higher-level VFF members can reserve upgrades a day or more in advance, so few Business or First Class seats are apt to be left by departure day.

- A number of lines provide for easy and inexpensive upgrades from full-fare Coach/Economy. But those upgrades are worthless to all but those few of our readers who buy such tickets.

In our experience, mileage-based upgrades work well—if you're willing to use almost as much credit as you'd need for a free trip in Coach/Economy. However, upgrades based on coupons or stickers are problematic: On most flights we've observed, the demand for such upgrades vastly exceeds the meager supply.

FINDING A SEAT

Having enough credit for frequent-flier trips is one thing, getting seats can be quite another. The big US airlines report the percentage of their passenger-miles flown by frequent fliers, as well as the year-end outstanding balance of unclaimed frequent-flier awards. Our availability index is the number of free-trip awards outstanding at the end of 1995 divided by the number of free-trip seats actually offered during that year—in effect, it shows the number of potential free trips chasing each available seat. The lower the resulting number, the more generous the frequent-flier program.

Alaska, American, TWA, and United were the most generous, with fewer than two outstanding awards per available seat. Continental and Delta were stingiest, with four to five awards per available seat. America West, Northwest, and USAir showed intermediate figures, all close to three outstanding awards per seat.

WHAT'S BEST FOR YOU

You may not really have a choice among frequent-flier programs. If you live in Atlanta, you'll probably find yourself flying mainly on Delta no matter what you think of the line or its frequent-flier program. Similarly, St Louis residents will probably log most of their miles on TWA. Even if you live in a city with lots of airline service, such as Boston or San Francisco, you may still be locked into one line if most of your trips are to that line's major hub.

We didn't rate the programs overall, because each one's value to you depends on how you earn and use your credit. But these points are worth noting:

- **American, Delta,** and **United** offer very similar programs: full-service, with no extra-generous features but

no serious disadvantages either. Use them as a benchmark for measuring other lines.

- **Air Canada.** *Disadvantages:* Half-credit for Economy excursion trips inside Canada—a fatal flaw for most travelers. High credit required for travel to Europe and Asia. No upgrades.
- **Alaska.** *Advantages:* Generous free-trip and upgrade awards for online travel in the line's limited service area. *Disadvantage:* No upgrades to Europe on Economy excursions.
- **America West.** *Advantages:* Generous free-trip awards for online travel in the line's limited service area. 750-mile minimum credit per trip, attractive for travelers who earn credit mainly on short hauls. Alternative participation in Continental's program (less generous but with more options). *Disadvantages:* Limited destinations; no upgrades to Europe through the line's own generous program.
- **Canadian Intl.** *Disadvantages:* Half-credit for Economy excursion trips in Canada and a high mileage requirement for Hawaii. No off-peak Economy flights to Europe for at least 150 days of the year.
- **Continental.** *Advantage:* Mileage doesn't expire (but Continental has been canceling accounts of inactive travelers). *Disadvantages:* High credit (100,000 miles) required for Business Class trip to Europe. Saturday-night-stay requirement on a domestic round-trip—a gratuitous limitation that makes an award less valuable to frequent fliers without any benefit to the airline.
- **Midwest Express.** *Advantages:* Gen-

CREDIT REQUIRED FOR FREE TRIPS*

CLASS		AIR CANADA AEROPLAN	ALASKA MILEAGE PLAN	AMERICA WEST FLIGHTFUND	AMERICAN AADVANTAGE	CANADIAN CANADIAN PLUS
ONE FREE TRIP (b)						
US/Canada(c)	Coach	25	20(d)	20(d)	25	25
	Business	30	—	—	40(f)	30
	First	—	30(d)	40(d)	60	—
Hawaii	Coach	40	40(g)	45(g)	35	60
	Business	50	—	—	60(f)	75
	First	—	60(g)	60(g)	—	—
Europe	Coach	60	40(g)	60(g)	40	40
	Business	75	80(g)	—	80	75
	First	—	85(g)	100(g)	100	—
Asia	Coach	75	55(g)	70(g)	50(h)	50(h)
	Business	100	90(g)	—	90(h)	80(h)
	First	—	120(g)	120(g)	120(h)	—
Caribbean	Coach	40	35(g)	35(g)	30	60
	Business	50	—	—	60(f)	75
	First	—	50(g)	60(g)	—	—
TWO FREE TRIPS(b)						
US/Canada(c)	Coach	50	40(d)	40(d)	50	50
	Business	60	—	—	80(f)	60
	First	—	60(d)	80	120	—
Hawaii	Coach	80	80(g)	90(g)	70	120
	Business	100	—	—	100(f)	150
	First	—	120(g)	120(g)	—	—
Europe	Coach	120	80(g)	120(g)	80	80
	Business	150	160(g)	—	140	150
	First	—	170(g)	200(g)	160	—
Asia	Coach	150	110(g)	140(g)	100(h)	100(h)
	Business	200	180(g)	—	150(h)	160(h)
	First	—	240(g)	240(g)	180(h)	—
Caribbean	Coach	80	70(g)	70(g)	60	120
	Business	100	—	—	100(f)	150
	First	—	100(g)	120(g)	—	—
UPGRADES(b)						
US/Canada(c)	Miles	—	10(d)	20	20	—
	Fare	—	Any	Any	Any	—
Europe	Miles	—	—	—	40	—
	Fare	—	—	—	Any	—
Asia	Miles	—	—	—	25	—
	Fare	—	—	—	Some	—

*As of October 1996; subject to change.
(a) Awards shown for separate off-peak program.
(b) All credit shown in 000s; requirements based on lowest-mileage award subject to peak-period blackouts and seat limitations on primary carrier.
(c) Credit shown for travel in the contiguous 48 states; may include travel to nearby Canadian and Caribbean points.
(d) For online trip within line's limited service area.
(e) Saturday-night stay required.
(f) First class on two-class planes.

CONT'L ONEPASS	DELTA SKYMILES	MIDWEST EXPRESS FREQUENT FLYER	NORTHWEST(a) WORLDPERKS	TWA FREQUENT FLIGHT BONUS	UNITED MILEAGE PLUS	USAIR FREQUENT TRAVELERS
25(e)	25	20(d)	20	20	25	25
—	—	—	—	—	40	—
45(e)	40	40(g)	35	60	60	40
45	30	40(g)	30	40	35	—
60	—	—	—	—	60	—
—	60	60(g)	50	60	80	—
50	50	40(g)	35	35	50	50
100	80	80(g)	55	—	80	80
—	100	100(g)	65	85	100	100(g)
70	60	70(g)	45	—	60	50(g)
100	90	90(g)	60	—	90	90(g)
—	120	120(g)	80	—	120	120(g)
35	30	40(g)	30	20	35	35
—	—	—	—	—	60	—
60	60	60(g)	50	60	80	50
50(e)	50	40(d)	40	40	50	5
—	—	—	—	—	80	—
90(e)	80	80(g)	70	120	120	80
90	60	80(g)	60	80	70	—
120	—	—	—	—	100	—
—	120	120(g)	100	120	140	—
100	100	60(g)	70	70	100	100
200	160	160(g)	110	—	140	160
—	200	200(g)	130	170	160	200(g)
140	120	140(g)	90	—	120	100(g)
200	180	180(g)	120	175(g)	150	180(g)
—	240	240(g)	160	250(g)	180	240(g)
70	60	80(g)	60	40	70	70
—	—	—	—	—	100	—
120	120	120(g)	100	120	140	100
20	20	—	20	20	20	(i)
Some	Some	—	Some	Any	Some	Some
40	40	60(g)	40	40	40	—
Some	Some	Some	Some	Any	Some	—
50	50	—	50	—	50	—
Some	Some	—	Some	—	Some	—

(g) Award flights to some or all destinations are on partner airlines; lowest option is shown where more than one airline serves destination.

(h) For trips to Japan; trips to other Asian destinations require higher mileage.

(i) 2500 miles of credit required for each 799 flight miles (one way).

erous free-trip awards for online travel in the line's limited service area. Partnership with Northwest, limited to "qualifying" mileage earned for travel to and from Milwaukee or Omaha. (Since Milwaukee and Omaha are the line's hubs, we include those Northwest awards in our tables and ratings.) *Disadvantage:* Extremely limited choice of travel awards for fliers who don't qualify for the Northwest partnership.

- **Northwest.** *Advantage:* Very generous awards on off-peak program—if you can concentrate your free trips into the very short off-peak season. Otherwise, unexceptional standard program. *Disadvantage:* No free travel to South America.
- **TWA.** *Advantages:* Mileage doesn't expire. Generous free-trip awards for domestic online travel. 750-mile minimum credit per trip, attractive for travelers who earn credit mainly on

EARN MILES WITH PHONE CALLS

All three big long-distance telephone carriers—AT&T, MCI, and Sprint—let you earn frequent-flier mileage on your phone charges. Once enrolled (free), residential customers get five frequent-flier miles per dollar spent on long-distance calls billed to their residential phone or a calling card. That's a good payoff. Each mile is worth about 2¢, so the frequent-flier mileage you get amounts to a rebate of 10% of your long-distance charges.

AT&T TRUE REWARDS

As of May 1, 1996, participants in AT&T's basic *True Rewards* program no longer accumulate points toward awards redeemable for products, services, and discounts. Instead, long-distance customers who charge at least $5 a month in AT&T long-distance service—and sign up for the revised *True Rewards* program—receive on-the-spot access to travel premiums and promotions, along with nontravel options.

Among the more valuable discounts are those on Alamo rental cars (15% domestic, 10% international), 25% off companion tickets on Amtrak, 15% off rack (regular) rate at Choice Hotels (Clarion, Comfort, Econo Lodge, Quality, Rodeway, and Sleep), 10% off lunch and dinner charges (food and beverage) at participating Marriott hotels, 20% off vacation packages at Marriott Vacation Clubs, a one-time certificate for $25 off any United ticket costing $200 or more, and a one-time certificate worth $100 per person on a Club Med vacation of seven days or longer. Participants simply show their membership card (or submit a certificate) when they want to take advantage of the various discount offers.

AT&T customers who spend $50–74.99 a month on long distance continue to earn points convertible to mileage credit in the British Airways, Delta, United, or USAir frequent-flier programs. Callers who spend $75 a month or more earn double points.

short-haul trips. *Disadvantages:* No off-peak Economy award to Europe for at least 150 days of the year. High credit required for premium-class domestic travel. Extremely limited free trips to Asia (two-ticket premium awards on Philippine Airlines or Air India only). No travel to the South Pacific. Limited travel to Hawaii: You must fly via St Louis (even if you start on the West Coast), and the only eastbound trip is an overnight red-eye.

•**USAir.** *Advantage:* Mileage doesn't expire. *Disadvantages:* No travel to Hawaii—a major fault. No off-peak Economy flights to Europe for at least 150 days of the year. No upgrades from Economy excursion to Europe.

This chapter was adapted from the Consumer Reports Travel Letter *article "Frequent-Flier Programs: How They Measure Up" (December 1996).*

True Rewards customers who spent at least $25 a month on qualifying calls were enrolled automatically in the revised program. Present and prospective customers who spend $5–25 a month can enroll by calling 800-773-9273.

MCI

Calls earn frequent-flier credit on American, Continental, Northwest, or Southwest. When you enroll, you must specify which line you want credited. Credit is automatically transferred to your account monthly, as you earn it, so it has the same expiration as credit earned by flying. There is no spending minimum.

MCI customers should call 800-624-6453. They can earn an extra mile per dollar by having a residential MCI account billed to a charge card that gives frequent-flier mileage, an airline *MasterCard* or *Visa,* or *American Express.*

SPRINT

You can earn five miles of America West or TWA credit per dollar spent on Sprint long-distance calls (seven miles if you're a TWA very-frequent-flier, or VFF, member). Credit is transferred monthly, as you earn it. As with MCI, you can earn an extra mile per dollar by charging a residential Sprint bill to a charge card that earns mileage. To enroll, phone 800-755-1093 and register your airline account number.

As an alternative, you can enroll in Sprint's *Priority Rewards* program (800-366-7587). With that option, you earn 10 points per dollar charged to your residential phone account. Points earn a variety of travel awards (but not frequent-flier mileage) from United Airlines, Hertz, Marriott, and Royal Caribbean Cruise Line. Members of TWA's frequent-flier program receive a 200-mile bonus for signing up with Sprint.

THE OTHER PLAYERS

Low-fare Air South, Carnival, Southwest, and Vanguard run simple frequent-flier programs. Southwest's *Rapid Rewards* program is typical: 16 one-way trips or eight round-trips during one year earn one free round-trip. That's relatively generous, especially if you earn credit mainly by taking short flights. But your free travels are confined to the cities served by each line—a minor problem with Southwest, a major failing with the others.

Southwest's recently revised program now includes credit from partners: Alamo, Budget, and Hertz car rentals, and MCI long-distance phone service. Award vouchers are issued automatically as soon as you log the required 16 flight credits. As long as a seat is available, you can get it for a free trip: There are no blackouts or seat limitations.

Southwest's program still lags far behind the big lines' programs in choice of destinations: Although you can now reach Florida on Southwest, you still can't get to New York, Hawaii, or Europe. And of course, since Southwest is all-Coach, there's no such thing as an upgrade.

Instead of running their own programs, four small lines have linked up with a giant line's program: Frontier with Continental's, Hawaiian with Midway's, and Reno with American's. On those lines, you effectively get the same schedule of earning and awards that you get on the affiliated giant line. Typically, commuter lines participate in the programs of their large-line partners.

At press time, Pan Am had a new program that was developing a list of partner airlines to provide free travel to areas of the US that Pan Am doesn't serve and to Europe and South America. By the time you read this, other low-fare lines may well have formed comparable alliances or joined with Pan Am.

10

LOUNGE CLUBS: AIRPORT OASES

With their blaring flight announcements, pushing crowds, and background din, big airports are about as jarring an environment as you're apt to face. Fortunately, relief is easy to find. All big US and Canadian airlines but Southwest operate lounges, a string of members-only clubrooms at the most important airports in their systems. If you fly a lot, consider joining—for convenience, comfort, and help when you need it.

Your own travel patterns and the pattern of airline service to your home city may leave you only one realistic choice. But where more than one club is feasible, this chapter will steer you to your best option.

WHAT MEMBERS GET

An airline lounge is usually quieter and more pleasant than an airport's gate area (though clubrooms in the biggest hub airports are occasionally so busy they aren't much more peaceful than the public areas). If nothing else, every clubroom provides a comfortable space

where you can await a flight or meet people after you arrive.

You'll find good seats, tables for your work papers or beverages, a rack full of newspapers and magazines, and access to a television set. There'll generally be monitors displaying current arrivals and departures. Most clubs have some sort of bar and snack service, too. (A few locations, at relatively minor airports, may be a bit more spartan.)

Most clubrooms have storage areas where you can leave coats, hats, and carry-on baggage, at least while you have a meal, buy a magazine, change money, or get a ticket reissued. (For security reasons, however, overnight storage may not be permitted.) Some clubs have their own rest rooms.

A visit to a lounge club can often let you bypass the line at a check-in counter or departure gate. Most clubrooms have a full-time attendant, usually an airline employee, who has access to the airline's computer reservation system. The attendant can issue boarding passes, get or change seat assignments, adjust reservations, and handle other airline business.

But lounge-club attendants aren't airfare experts: If you have a complicated problem that can't be answered by a simple computer inquiry, you'll probably have to go to a ticketing desk. And, of course, you can't check your baggage in at a clubroom.

A clubroom makes a good temporary communications center or home base. It's one of the few places in an airport where you can be pretty sure of receiving an incoming call, and it provides a fixed point for meeting other travelers or family members. If you don't connect with someone meeting you or with someone you're meeting on an arriving flight, the attendant can take and relay messages—especially important in case of a delay or cancel-lation. (But beware of a misconnect at a big airport, where your airline may have clubs at several locations.)

Lounge clubs increasingly provide special facilities and services for business travelers: copiers, personal computers and printers, fax machines, express-delivery pickup stations, meeting rooms, and such. (A few clubs charge for use of their meeting rooms, and most require you to reserve one in advance.)

Originally, membership in US-line lounge clubs was free, but by invitation only; it was in effect the first frequent-flier perk. After a court challenge, however, the airlines were forced to open their lounge clubs to all comers (which they did, but for a price). Now the clubrooms are more democratic—and generally more hectic, especially during

VIP AIRPORT LOUNGE

Travelers who usually fly on a single airline probably do best with that line's own lounge-club program: The lounges are usually reasonably close to the gates the line uses, and they'll have access to its current flight information. If, however, you spread your business among different airlines, you might be better off with an independent airport club.

Once such program, *Priority Pass,* provides access to airport VIP lounges at more than 170 major airports around the world. US locations include Albuquerque, Boston, Chicago, Cleveland, Columbus, Dallas, Dayton, Denver, Honolulu, Houston, Kansas City, Los Angeles, Miami, New York, Newark, Phoenix, Pittsburgh, San Francisco, St. Louis, Washington, D.C., and West Palm Beach. Overseas, most major cities are represented. Specific facilities vary by location.

Priority Pass doesn't limit access to travelers holding tickets on a sponsoring airline for a flight that day, as several airline clubs do. There are several different pricing plans to fit the different needs of frequent business travelers. To learn more about *Priority Pass* and the membership options available, call 800-430-1001.

weather delays or at heavy traffic times (between 5 and 8 P.M. on a Thursday or Friday evening, say).

Members could once use a clubroom at any time, too—even if flying on a competitor or not flying at all. But now, some clubs limit admittance to members with tickets for departing or arriving flights on the sponsor airline (see *Use limitations,* page 116). At big airports, that's a small loss: airline gate areas are so far-flung that it's impractical to use the club of a line you're not flying with.

WHAT PRICE TRANQUILLITY?

Aloha and the Canadian lines charge no enrollment fee. With the others, you pay up to $100 at sign-up, then $105–225 a year. An optional, separate membership that lets your spouse use the club when traveling alone adds $55–100 a year (again, the Canadian lines and Aloha are exceptions). The *Costs and Benefits* table gives the details.

Some lines offer multiyear or even "lifetime" memberships, at an average yearly cost that's usually quite a bit lower than the regular one-year cost. (But there's a risk: If your travel patterns change, you move to a different city, or the sponsoring airline changes its routes, you may stop flying that line. You'll then have little or no use for its lounge club.) And some lines let you use frequent-flier credit to join their lounge clubs. The table doesn't note those variations.

The clubrooms do welcome a few nonmembers: Some admit Business and First Class travelers. And some let in holders of certain charge cards (check your charge-card information packet for particulars).

SOME SPECIAL FEATURES

Your choice of a lounge club, as of a frequent-flier program, may be limited to just one airline by your own travel patterns or the pattern of flights at your home airport. But if you have alternatives, there are some differences to note among the major programs:

•**Locations.** The two *Club Locations* tables (see pages 118 and 122) list all US and Canadian as well as most overseas facilities of the airlines they cover. For reasons of space, those tables omit lines with five or fewer locations. Alaska has five (Anchorage, Los Angeles, Portland, San Francisco, and Seattle). So does Aloha (Hilo, Honolulu, Kahului, Kona, and Lihue). Outside North America, Alaska, Aloha, Delta, and USAir have no clubrooms; Hawaiian has one in Pago Pago. We also didn't include airlines based outside the US or Canada, many of which operate lounge clubs. If you fly any of those lines often, ask for a brochure.

Most clubrooms are exclusive to one airline. However, code-sharing airlines may honor memberships in their partners' clubs, and a few of the listed locations are shared by two different lines. In those cases, use limitations may vary substantially—check individual program brochures for details.

Overseas, club membership sometimes provides access to an airport-run VIP lounge or a First Class lounge, rather than an airline-run clubroom. Similarly, a First Class or Business Class ticket by itself is often enough to get you into an airline's lounge club abroad—member or not.

- **Use limitations.** America West, Canadian Intl, and Delta admit you only on days when you arrive or depart on the sponsoring airline (you must show a ticket). Other clubrooms let you in any time.

- **Bars.** Air Canada, Alaska, Canadian Intl, Delta, and Northwest operate free bars: Some have a bartender, others are pour-your-own. American and United run cash bars in US clubs, free bars at most overseas spots. America West, TWA, and USAir have cash bars at all locations, Conti-nental at most. With standard drinks typically $3–5 each at an airport bar, a free bar can make a consider-able difference in your annual cost of using a lounge club.

- **Other features.** The *Costs and Benefits* table below lists other lounge-club features and services: the maximum number of guests each member can take in (often waived for large family groups); the availability of meeting rooms, check-cashing, personal com-puters, and copying and fax services; and any additional fees for those extras.

Lounge Clubs: Costs and Benefits*

AIRLINE	CLUB	ENROLLMENT FEE(a)	ANNUAL FEE		ENROLLMENT BONUS (MILES)
			MEMBER	SPOUSE	
Air Canada	Maple Leaf Club	—	C$175(f)	—	—
Alaska	The Board Room	$100	$150	$ 70	(g)
Aloha	Executive Club	—	120	—	—
America West	Phoenix Club	50	150	75	2500
American	Admirals Club	100	200	100	—
Canadian Intl	Empress Lounge	—	C$195	—	—
Continental	Presidents Club	50	150	75	—
Delta	Crown Room Club	100	200	100	—
Hawaiian	Premier Club	20	105	55	(g)
Northwest	WorldClubs	75	195	95	(g)
TWA	Ambassadors Club	25	125	75	5000
United	Red Carpet Club	100	200	100	—
USAir	USAir Club	50	175	75	—

* As of mid-1996; subject to change.

(a) New memberships.

(b) Including shared locations, reciprocal locations, and airport VIP locations.

(c) Free unless otherwise noted; advance reservations rec-ommended or required.

(d) Amount may be limited outside the US.

(e) Fees and services may vary by location; C=computer, F=fax, P=printer, X=copier.

(f) US$75 for US citizens.

(g) Bonuses offered during occasional promotions.

(h) Or immediate family.

VALUE FOR MONEY?

Joining a lounge club doesn't make sense if you take only a few flights a year. If you calculate that each visit is worth $10–15 in added convenience and comfort, you'd have to take a dozen or so round-trips yearly (depending on the airline and its annual fee) to offset the cost of membership.

But sometimes use of a clubroom can have an imponderable value. Every year or two, you may encounter some special circumstance—a need to meet someone in an airport, say, or to rearrange a schedule after a canceled flight—in which one use justifies the annual cost.

Here's how to compare your options:

•Check out any locations at your home airport. Presumably, close to half your airport transits will be at home base. Next time you have a few extra minutes at your airport, buzz the door and ask the attendant to show you around.

•Then check which lounge clubs have locations at the airports where you most often make connections—often, you'll find that the hub-airport clubroom will be the most important location in the system. Visit that clubroom, as well.

•Now scan the *Locations* tables to see if a lounge club you're considering

NUMBER OF LOCATIONS (b)	USE LIMITATIONS	BAR	GUESTS PERMITTED	LOCATIONS WITH MEETING ROOMS(c)	CHECKS CASHED(d)	OTHER SERVICES(e)
43	—	Free	1	Most	—	C,F,P,X
5	—	Free	2(h)	Most	50	F
5	(i)	—	1	—	—	F,X(j)
20	(k)	Cash	1	Some/2hr free(l)	100	C,F,X
42	—	Cash(m)	2(h)	Most(l,n)	100	C,F,P,X
31	(k)	Free	1	Some	—	F,P,X
33(o)	—	Cash(p)	2(h)	Most	100	F,P,X
39	(k)	Free	2	Most	50	F,P,X
10	—	—	2	(j)	—	—
26	—	Free	2(h)	Some	50	C,F,P,X
24	—	Cash	2(h)	Some(l)	50	F,P,X
35	—	Cash(m)	2(h,q)	Most(l)	100	F,P,X
20	—	Cash	2	Most(l)	100	F,X

(i) First Class passengers also allowed access.
(j) Honolulu only.
(k) Must be ticketed on flight on day of use.
(l) $20-50 fee charged for use.
(m) Free at most foreign locations.
(n) Some, in foreign locations.

(o) *Presidents Club* members admitted to Air Canada *Maple Leaf Clubs* worldwide.
(p) Free in Honolulu, London, and Paris.
(q) One guest in foreign locations.

North American Club Locations[*]

CITY	AIR CANADA	AMERICA WEST	AMERICAN	CANADIAN INTL
Albuquerque	—	—	✔	—
Atlanta	✔	—	✔	—
Austin	—	—	✔	—
Baltimore	—	—	✔	—
Birmingham	—	—	—	—
Boston	✔(a)	✔(a)	✔	—
Buffalo	—	—	—	—
Calgary	✔	—	—	✔
Charlotte	—	—	—	—
Chicago/O'Hare	✔(a)	✔(a)	✔	—
Cincinnati	—	—	—	—
Cleveland	✔(a)	✔(a)	✔	—
Columbus OH	—	✔(a)	—	—
Dallas/Ft Worth	—	—	✔	—
Dayton	—	—	—	—
Denver	✔(a)	✔(a)	✔	—
Detroit/Metro	—	—	✔	—
Edmonton/Intl	✔	—	—	✔
Ft Lauderdale	—	—	✔	—
Greensboro	—	—	—	—
Halifax	✔	—	—	✔
Hartford	—	—	✔	—
Hilo	—	—	—	—
Honolulu	✔(a)	✔(a)	✔	✔
Houston/ Intercontinental	✔(a)	✔(a)	—	—
Indianapolis	—	—	—	—
Jacksonville	—	—	—	—
Kahului	—	—	—	—
Kansas City	—	—	✔	—
Kona	—	—	—	—
Las Vegas	—	—	—	—
Lihue	—	—	—	—
Los Angeles	✔(a)	✔(a)	✔	✔(a)
Memphis	—	—	—	—
Miami	✔(a)	—	✔	—
Milwaukee	—	—	—	—
Minneapolis/StPaul	—	—	—	—
Montreal/Dorval	✔	—	—	✔
Montreal/Mirabel	✔	—	—	—

CONTINENTAL	DELTA	HAWAIIAN	NORTHWEST	TWA	UNITED	USAIR
—	—		—	✔	—	
✔(a)	✔	—	—	—	—	
✔(a)	—	—	—	—	✔	✔
—	✔	—	✔	✔	✔	✔
—	✔	—	—	—	—	✔
✔(a)	✔	—	—	—	—	✔
✔	✔	—	✔	✔(a)	✔	—
✔	✔	—	✔	—	—	✔
✔	—	—	—	✔	—	—
—	✔	—	—	✔	—	—
—	—	—	—	✔	—	—
✔	✔	—	—	—	✔	—
—	✔	—	✔	—	—	—
✔(a)	—	—	—	—	—	—
—	✔	—	—	—	—	✔
✔(a)	—	—	—	—	—	✔
—	✔	✔	—	—	—	—
✔	✔	✔	✔	—	✔	—
✔	✔	—	—	—	—	—
—	—	—	—	—	✔	✔
—	✔	—	—	—	—	—
—	—	✔	—	✔	—	—
—	✔	✔	—	—	—	—
—	✔	—	—	—	—	—
—	—	✔	—	—	✔	—
✔	✔	✔	✔	✔	✔	✔
—	✔	—	✔	—	—	—
—	✔	—	—	—	✔	—
—	—	—	✔	—	—	—
✔(a)	✔	—	—	—	—	—
✔(a)	—	—	—	—	—	—

NORTH AMERICAN CLUB LOCATIONS* *(continued)*

CITY	AIR CANADA	AMERICA WEST	AMERICAN	CANADIAN INTL
Nashville	—	—	✔	—
Newark	✔(a)	✔(a)	✔	—
New Orleans	—	—	✔	—
NewYork/JFK	—	—	✔	—
NewYork/LaGuardia	✔(a)	✔(a)	✔	—
Orange County	—	—	✔	—
Orlando	—	—	✔	—
Ottawa	✔	—	—	✔
Philadelphia	—	—	✔	—
Phoenix	✔(a)	✔	✔	—
Pittsburgh	—	—	—	—
Portland OR	—	—	—	—
Quebec City	✔	—	—	—
Raleigh/ Durham	—	—	✔	—
Regina	✔	—	—	—
Rochester	—	—	—	—
St John's	✔	—	—	✔
St Louis	—	—	✔	—
Salt Lake City	—	—	✔	—
San Diego	—	—	✔	—
San Francisco	✔(a)	✔(a)	✔	✔
San Jose	—	—	✔	—
San Juan	—	—	—	—
Seattle/ Tacoma	✔(a)	—	✔	—
Syracuse	—	—	—	—
Tampa	—	—	—	—
Toronto	✔	—	✔	✔
Vancouver	✔	—	—	✔
Washington/Dulles	—	—	✔	—
Washington/National	—	—	✔	—
West Palm Beach	—	—	—	—
Winnipeg	✔	—	—	✔
TOTAL	26	12	28	12

* As of mid-1996; subject to change.   (a) Shared with another airline or airport lounge

CONTINENTAL	DELTA	HAWAIIAN	NORTHWEST	TWA	UNITED	USAIR
—	✔	—	—	—	—	—
✔	✔	—	—	✔	✔	✔
—	✔	—	✔	✔	—	—
✔	✔	—	✔	✔	✔	—
—	✔	—	—	—	✔	✔
✔(a)	—	—	—	—	✔	✔
✔(a)	✔	—	✔	✔	—	✔
—	✔	✔	—	—	✔	—
✔(a)	—	—	—	—	—	✔
✔(a)	—	—	—	—	—	✔
✔(a)	—	—	—	—	—	—
—	—	—	—	✔	—	—
—	✔	—	—	—	—	—
✔	—	—	—	✔	—	—
✔	✔	✔	✔	—	✔	—
—	✔	—	—	—	—	—
—	✔	✔	✔	✔(a)	✔	—
—	✔	—	✔	—	—	✔
✔(a)	✔	—	—	—	—	✔
✔(a)	—	—	—	—	—	—
—	—	—	—	✔	✔	—
✔(a)	✔	—	✔	✔	✔	✔
—	✔	—	—	✔	—	✔
✔(a)	—	—	—	—	—	—
26	39	9	16	19	19	20

has clubrooms at the cities you visit most frequently.

- If more than one lounge club passes that test, compare the features in our *Costs and Benefits* table to see which club offers the most attractive mix of facilities and services at the best price.

A HUBBER'S SURVIVAL GUIDE

All the hassles of dealing with airports multiply when you have to hub (wait for a connection at some airport between your origin and destination). A late arrival or delayed connecting flight can turn an ordinary inconvenience into a major debacle. But you can retain more control of the process than you think. Here are some tips on coping.

HEADING OFF TROUBLE. Good planning can minimize your chances of problems:

- Reserve a nonstop flight whenever possible. Next best is a direct flight on which you stop but don't change planes. But watch out for a trap: Some airlines use a single number for a flight that requires a change of aircraft. While such changes are noted in the *Official Airline Guides (OAG)* and on agents' computer screens, an airline reservation agent may not volunteer the information if you reserve directly.
- Don't schedule a trip so tightly that a delay of several hours throws you into chaos.
- If you can't avoid changing planes, try to stay with the same airline for your connecting flights. Airlines are

FOREIGN CLUB LOCATIONS*

CITY	AIR CANADA	AMERICA WEST
EUROPE		
Amsterdam	—	—
Berlin	✔(a)	—
Dusseldorf	✔(a)	—
Frankfurt	✔(a)	—
Glasgow	✔(a)	—
London/Gatwick	✔(a)	✔(a)
London/Heathrow	✔	—
Lyons	✔(a)	—
Madrid	—	—
Manchester	✔(a)	—
Milan	—	—
Nice	✔(a)	—
Paris/deGaulle	✔(a)	—
Paris/Orly	✔(a)	✔(a)
Rome	—	—
Vienna	✔(a)	—
Zurich	✔(a)	—
PACIFIC		
Auckland	—	—
Bangkok	—	—
Beijing	—	—
Delhi	✔(a)	—
Guam	—	—
Hong Kong	✔(a)	—
Kuala Lumpur	—	—
Manila	—	—
Melbourne	—	—
Nadi	—	—
Nagoya	—	—
Osaka	✔(a)	—
Saipan	—	—
Seoul	✔(a)	—
Singapore	—	—
Sydney	—	—
Taipei	—	—
Tokyo	—	—
CARIBBEAN/SOUTH AMERICA		
Acapulco	—	✔(a)

AMERICAN	CANADIAN INTL	CONTINENTAL	NORTHWEST	TWA	UNITED
—	—	—	✔	—	—
—	—	—	—	—	✔
✔	✔	✔(a)	—	✔	✔
✔	—	✔	✔	✔(a)	—
✔	✔(a)	✔(a)	—	—	✔
—	—	—	—	—	—
—	—	✔(a)	—	—	—
—	—	✔(a)	—	✔	—
—	—	—	—	✔	—
—	✔	—	—	✔	—
✔	—	✔	—	✔	—
—	✔(a)	—	—	✔	—
—	—	—	—	—	—
—	—	—	—	—	—
—	✔(a)	—	—	—	✔
—	✔	—	✔	—	✔
—	✔(a)	—	—	—	—
—	—	✔	—	—	—
—	✔	—	✔	—	✔
—	✔(a)	—	—	—	—
—	—	—	✔	—	✔
—	—	—	—	—	✔
—	✔(a)	—	—	—	—
—	✔(a)	—	—	—	—
—	—	—	✔	—	—
—	—	—	—	—	—
—	—	—	✔	—	✔
—	—	—	—	—	✔
—	✔(a)	—	✔	—	✔
—	✔(a)	—	✔	—	✔
—	✔	—	✔	—	✔
—	—	—	—	—	—
—	—	—	—	—	—

more likely to hold connecting flights for their own passengers who arrive late. Often, the connecting flight will be in the same area of the airport where you arrive.

•In winter, try to schedule yourself through a good-weather hub (Dallas/Ft Worth, Houston, Las Vegas, Phoenix) rather than one with frequent weather problems (Chicago, Denver, Detroit). Avoid the busiest hubs (Atlanta, Chicago) in favor of less frantic Charlotte, Memphis, or Salt Lake City.

•Don't book the last flight of the day that connects to your final destination. If that flight is canceled, you'll be stuck at the hub overnight.

•Minimum connecting times (noted in the *OAG*) often don't allow enough slack if your plane is late. At some airports, you have to take a shuttle bus to another terminal, and the bus may be held up in terminal-area traffic. (The easiest airports for hubbing are those with people movers: Atlanta, Chicago/O'Hare, Dallas/Ft Worth, Houston, Seattle-Tacoma, Tampa.) Ask for an earlier flight to give you leeway to make your connection, but not so early that you have to pay for a stopover (generally defined as four hours or more).

•Before you leave for the airport, phone the airline's reservation (or separate flight-information) number to find out if your plane is on time. If your itinerary looks iffy, ask if you can make alternate arrangements.

•If you're a frequent flier, consider joining the airport lounge club of the airline you fly most often.

•In the event that your checked baggage is lost or you miss a connection, pack enough clothes and personal items in your carry-on to last you for 48 hours.

SORT THINGS OUT ALOFT. Before you land at a hub:

•Listen to the connecting-flight announcements the flight attendant makes before you land. When you hear your flight called, look up its departure gate on the airport diagram (usually found in the airline's in-flight magazine).

•If it becomes obvious during the flight that you've missed your connection, ask a flight attendant to reseat you near the exit door for

---

FOREIGN CLUB LOCATIONS* *(continued)*

CITY	AIR CANADA	AMERICA WEST
CARIBBEAN/SOUTH AMERICA *(continued)*		
Bogota	—	—
Buenos Aires	—	—
Caracas	—	—
Guadalajara	—	✔(a)
Lima	—	—
Merida	—	✔(a)
Mexico City	—	✔(a)
Panama City	—	—
Rio de Janeiro	—	—
San Juan PR	—	—
Santiago	—	—
Santo Domingo	—	—
Sao Paulo	—	—
Tijuana	—	✔(a)
Veracruz	—	✔(a)
TOTAL	17	8

*As of mid-1996; subject to change.

landing (so you can get started on an alternate flight quickly) or ask the airline to arrange a "protecting" reservation for you.

GETTING HELP. Airline staff at hub airports are quickly overloaded during major delays. Your best bet is often to bypass the line at the passenger-service counter:

- Use a travel agency that provides 24-hour telephone assistance. At any time, you can then call the agency for help if you miss a connection or face a delay.
- If you don't have a 24-hour agency, call the airline reservation number. You'll almost always be able to make alternative arrangements faster by phone than by standing in line at an airline counter.

- Unless your ticket is unrestricted, the airline on which you are ticketed will be much more likely than some other airline to accommodate you without asking you to pay extra. It helps to have a copy of your airline's pocket schedule (pick one up at the airline counter). Or have your travel agent copy the appropriate pages of the *OAG* for you.

WAITING OUT DELAYS. What happens if your flight arrives at your intermediate stop too late for you to make a connection?

- If your connecting flight is scheduled to leave just as you arrive, head for the departure gate anyway. Flights don't always leave quite on time, even though the arrival and

AMERICAN	CANADIAN INTL	CONTINENTAL	NORTHWEST	TWA	UNITED
✔	—		—		—
✔	✔(a)		—		✔
✔	—		—		—
✔	—		—		—
	—		—		—
✔	✔(a)		—		✔
✔	—		—		—
✔	✔(a)		—		✔
✔	—		—		—
	✔(a)		—		—
✔	—		—		—
✔	✔(a)		—		✔
	—		—		—
14	**19**	**7**	**10**	**5**	**16**

(a) Shared with another airline or airport lounge.

departure monitors indicate that they've gone.

- Don't expect much sympathy in case of a weather delay—the airlines don't consider themselves responsible for blizzards. But sometimes they'll provide something (a meal, less likely a hotel room) to alleviate crowding in the waiting area, to avoid having to call in more personnel, or to ensure that the gate for the next departure won't be besieged.

- If you have to spend the night in a nearby hotel and the airline isn't providing a hotel room, ask an airline agent which hotels provide "distressed passenger" rates. Those are usually much lower than rack rates, especially if it's late at night. If you just need a few hours, a few airport hotels—including the Hilton at Chicago/O'Hare and the Marriott at Newark—offer short-term (half-day or hourly) room rates.

- Consider using airport services in case of a long delay. You can get a haircut and a shoeshine, do some minor shopping, or have a meal.

- Be courteous to the airline's customer-service staffers in case of a delay. The agents can often sign your ticket over to another airline or offer you hotel accommodations or meals at airline expense. They're more likely to respond favorably to suggestions from a reasonable, civil passenger.

This chapter was adapted from the Consumer Reports Travel Letter *article "Airline Lounge Clubs: Peace—For a Price" (September 1996) and the 1995 edition of the* Consumer Reports Travel Buying Guide.

Airport Shuttles: Cheap and Fast

Door-to-door airport shuttles are a good choice for many travelers—especially solo travelers. A shuttle offers much of the speed and convenience of a taxi at a price that isn't much higher than that of a fixed-route airport bus.

For a late-1995 report, we checked the 35 busiest airports in the US and Canada and located 25 where two-way shuttle service was available. (Shuttle service was slated to start sometime in 1996 at Washington/Dulles.) As with most transportation systems, the fares and schedules we note here are subject to change without notice.

HOW SHUTTLES WORK

We focused on shuttles that pick you up at or deliver you to any street address—hotel, residence, office, or whatever—within their service area. Some idiosyncrasies to note:

- Unlike taxis, shuttles may carry more than one travel party on each trip, picking up or delivering at multiple destinations. (At some loca-

tions, shared-cab programs provide the same sort of service, at least for arriving travelers.) Though shuttles may make an extra stop or two, however, they provide the same convenient one-vehicle transport as a taxi.

- Unlike airport buses, shuttles operate on demand, rather than on fixed schedules and routes. Travelers needn't wait for a scheduled departure time and needn't take two separate vehicles—one between the airport and a downtown terminal, another between the terminal and their starting or final destination point.

Shuttle operators generally use minivans. However, a few use sedans or vehicles as large as 21-passenger minibuses. Unless they're overcrowded, shuttle vans are usually more comfortable than typical airport buses—and considerably more comfortable than public-transit buses. For one or two people, a cab is usually more comfortable than either a bus or a shuttle. But for three passengers, van seating normally wins out over the back seat of a cab.

SOME CAUTIONS

The main problem with shuttles is occasional circuitous travel. That crops up when passengers leaving from or heading to widely separated parts of a big-city area wind up in the same van:

- In big metropolitan areas, large shuttle companies typically operate routes in several different zones. That way, trips can (theoretically) be scheduled to avoid roundabout routings and minimize pickup time: Normally, you won't be taken far out of your way, even if you're the first person picked up or the last one delivered. Even so, you may occasionally find yourself on an extended—and unwelcome—tour of an urban area.

- Smaller companies that specialize in serving only certain adjacent parts of town can also avoid excessive driving. But some small companies try to serve an entire area. With those, the first few travelers to be picked up or the last to be delivered can find themselves on lengthy, unanticipated detours through much of a city. Because of potential detours, departing travelers usually should allow a half hour to an hour more time for airport access than they'd require with a cab.

In a few cities—notably the midtown Manhattan area of New York—shuttles offer door-to-door service at residence or office addresses only to arriving travelers. Travelers who are departing must find their own way to a

hotel to catch a shuttle to the airport.

Shuttles (and cabs) are less subject to traffic delays than airport or transit buses: They can skirt problem areas while buses have to keep to assigned routes. But often neither van nor cab can escape rush-hour tangles. To avoid traffic snarls, use the rail transit that's available at a few US airports.

THE PRICE YOU PAY

The table starting on page 132 lists shuttle companies that operate at major US airports, along with the destinations they serve and sample fares to their most popular destinations, as of late 1995.

The shuttle fare for one person is almost always much less than the cab fare. But shuttle rates aren't always consistent. Some companies charge a flat rate, regardless of distance; others have distance-based fares. Some charge the same fare, regardless of how many travelers in a party; others charge less per person for groups of two or more. Some offer discounts for children and seniors. Many offer round-trips at less than the cost of two one-ways. In addition to the fare, our surveys show that readers of *Consumer Reports Travel Letter* generally tip a shuttle driver the same percentage of the fare as they tip a cab driver.

Shuttle fares are usually somewhat higher than airport-bus fares (and you don't generally tip bus drivers). But airport buses enjoy that cost advantage only if your origin or final destination is at or close to a scheduled bus stop—if you have to take a taxi to get to or from the bus, the combination will usually be more expensive than a shuttle. Because shuttles save time and hassle as well as money, they've largely displaced traditional airport buses in some cities.

Public mass transit is usually much cheaper than either a shuttle or an airport bus dedicated solely to airport access. Except in the few cases in which there's a rail link to the airport, however, public transit is usually much slower and less convenient than either a shuttle or an airport bus. And, of course, public transport doesn't serve all local airports.

ARRANGING YOUR TRIP

When you arrive at an airport, you usually either call for a pickup, request a pickup from a dispatcher or at a ground-transportation booth, or hail a circulating shuttle at a designated curbside point; if you aren't sure, ask at the airport's ground-transportation desk. If your shuttle isn't full, it may wait around a bit—or make an additional circuit of the airport—before taking you to your destination.

For departure, you normally arrange a pickup by calling the shuttle's local office. You give your address and flight time; the operator dispatches a shuttle, usually by radio, that picks you up at your door and delivers you to the airport. While many shuttle operators won't guarantee a pickup without a minimum 24-hour advance notice, many can arrange a pickup at shorter notice— even within an hour or two—if a previously scheduled vehicle will be passing near your neighborhood and its available space isn't already fully reserved.

The table shows the shuttle companies that serve each airport we list, the regions for which service is available, sample fares for one and two passengers, discounts given, whether 24-hour service is available, and the number of vehicles each company operates (a guide to the company's size and scope of operation). Use that information to see if shuttle service is available to and from a specific zone within a metropolitan area.

In *Where to Find It,* we list at least one primary phone number for each shuttle system. Some systems have additional numbers for various local communities within their primary area. We also show the colors each company uses to help you locate the right van.

WHERE TO FIND IT

The following shuttle companies operate at the airports listed in the table. We list phone numbers, distinctive vehicle colors, and charge-card acceptance for each company. Some systems have additional phone numbers in local communities within their primary service area.

ATLANTA

AAA Airport Express: 800-354-7874, 404-767-2000. Vehicle colors: White/blue. *AE, Disc, DC, MC, V.*

Atlanta Airport Shuttle: 800-842-2770, 404-524-3400. Vehicle colors: Green/white. *AE, MC, V.*

Dixie Excursions: 334-887-6294. Vehicle colors: White/black. *AE, Disc, MC, V.*

BALTIMORE

Airport Connection: 800-284-6066, 301-459-2402. Vehicle color: Green. *AE, MC, V.*

Baltimore Airport Shuttle: 800-287-4227, 410-821-5387. Vehicle color: Yellow. *AE, DC, MC, V.*

Delaware Express Shuttle: 800-648-5466, 302-454-7634. Vehicle colors: Red/white/blue. *AE, DC, Disc, MC, V.*

SuperShuttle: 800-258-3826, 301-369-2854, 410-792-4776, 202-562-1234. Vehicle colors: Blue/gold. *AE, MC, V.*

BOSTON

Dartmouth Mini-Coach: 603-448-2800. Vehicle colors: Green/white. *MC, V.*

Donahue Limousine Service: 800-523-7171, 508-537-7882. Vehicle color: Varies. *AE, Disc, MC, V.*

Flight Line: 800-245-2525, 603-893-8254. Vehicle colors: Red/gold.

Knight's Airport Limousine: 800-822-5456, 508-839-6252. Vehicle colors: Maroon/white. *AE, Disc, MC, V.*

Little Daddy Limousine: 800-535-7676, 508-987-8295. Vehicle color: White. *Disc, MC, V.*

Marlboro-Westboro Airport Shuttle: 800-242-0064, 508-481-7300. Vehicle color: Varies. *AE, Disc, MC, V.*

North Shore Airport Limo: 800-328-2292, 617-595-3200. Vehicle color: Varies.

R&A Shuttle Service: 800-927-0190, 617-598-0190. Vehicle colors: White/blue.

Thomas Transportation Services: 800-526-8143, 603-352-5550. Vehicle colors: Red/silver. *Disc, MC, V.*

US Shuttle: 800-449-4240, 617-894-3100. Vehicle colors: Red/white. *AE, MC, V.*

Worcester Airport Limousine: 800-660-0992, 800-343-1369 outside MA, 508-756-4834. Vehicle color: Varies. *AE, Disc, MC, V.*

CINCINNATI

DART Airport Shuttle: 800-953-2785, 513-299-7906. Vehicle colors: Blue/yellow. *AE, DC, Disc, MC, V.*

Door to Door Transportation: 800-783-0088, 513-641-0088. Vehicle color: Varies. *AE, Disc, MC, V.*

DALLAS/FT WORTH

Classic Shuttle: 214-841-1900. Vehicle colors: White/blue. *AE, Disc, MC, V.*

Discount Shuttle & Tours: 800-748-0789, 817-267-5150. Vehicle colors: Orange/blue. *AE, DC, Disc, MC, V.*

SuperShuttle Dallas/Ft Worth: 800-258-3826. Vehicle colors: Blue/gold. *AE, MC, V.*

DENVER

Airport Shuttle to Colorado: 800-222-2112, 970-945-9400. Vehicle color: Varies. *AE, DC, Disc, MC, V.*

Boulder Airporter: 303-444-0808. Vehicle color: Varies. *AE, MC, V.*

Colorado Mountain Express: 800-525-6363, 970-949-4227. Vehicle colors: Gray/red/white. *AE, DC, MC, V.*

Golden West Commuter: 303-342-9300. Vehicle color: Varies. *AE, Disc, MC, V.*

Home James Transportation: 800-451-4844, 970-726-5060. Vehicle colors: White/black. *AE, MC, V.*

Overland Airport Express: 303-646-

0100. Vehicle color: Varies. No credit cards accepted.

Resort Express: 800-334-7433, 970-468-7600. Vehicle color: White. *AE, MC, V.*

DETROIT

Robert Q's Airbus: 800-265-4948, 519-573-6804. Vehicle colors: White/burgundy. *AE, MC, V.*

FT LAUDERDALE

Gray Line Airport Shuttle: 800-244-8252, 954-561-8888. Vehicle colors: Navy/white. *AE, DC, MC, V.*

LOS ANGELES

3R Express Shuttle: 310-373-1443. Vehicle color: Silver. *AE, Disc, MC, V.*

AAA Airport Shuttle: 213-730-1111, 310-215-6729. Vehicle colors: Blue/yellow. *Disc, MC, V.*

ABC Shuttle: 800-400-8060, 805-582-1923. Vehicle colors: Silver/red/black. *AE, Disc, MC, V.*

Airtrans Express: 800-870-7474, 310-410-0800. Vehicle colors: Blue/white. No credit cards accepted.

Apollo Shuttle: 800-342-9949, 213-480-1112, 310-215-6729. Vehicle colors: White/red. *Disc, MC, V.*

Best Shuttle: 800-499-2378, 310-338-8088. Vehicle colors: White/green. *AE, Disc, MC, V.*

Coast Shuttle: 800-310-8267, 310-417-3988. Vehicle colors: Brown/beige. *AE, Disc, MC, V.*

Dani's Shuttle: 800-500-3264, 818-244-9977. Vehicle color: Blue. *AE, MC, V.*

E-Z Shuttle & Charter Service: 800-541-7009, 800-499-7717, 805-581-1451. Vehicle colors: White/green/red/black.

AE, Disc, MC, V.

Inland Express Services: 909-626-6599, 310-215-6744. Vehicle colors: Blue/ rainbow stripe.

LAX Chequer Van: 800-545-7745, 310-215-9950. Vehicle colors: Blue/white.

LA Xpress: 800-427-7483, 310-641-8000. Vehicle colors: Yellow/blue. *AE, DC, Disc, MC, V.*

Metropolitan Express: 800-338-3898, 310-417-5050. Vehicle color: Varies. *AE, Disc, MC, V.*

Prime Time Shuttle Intl: 800-733-8267, 818-504-3600. Vehicle colors: Red/white. *AE, Disc, MC, V.*

Roadrunner Shuttle: 800-247-7919, 805-389-8196. Vehicle colors: White/ blue. *AE, MC, V.*

Shuttle 2000: 800-977-7872, 310-352-3550. Vehicle colors: Turquoise/orange. *AE, MC, V.*

Shuttle One: 800-400-7488, 310-670-6666. Vehicle color: Silver. *AE, Disc, MC, V.*

Southern California Coach: 800-232-6224, 714-978-6415. Vehicle colors: White/blue/orange. *AE, MC, V.*

SuperShuttle/Los Angeles: 310-782-6600, 213-775-6600. Vehicle colors: Blue/gold. *AE, DC, MC, V.*

SuperShuttle/Orange County: 714-517-6600. Vehicle colors: Blue/gold. *AE, MC, V.*

SuperShuttle/San Fernando Valley: 800-660-6042, 818-556-6600. Vehicle colors: Blue/gold. *AE, DC, Disc, MC, V.*

SuperShuttle/San Gabriel: 909-467-9600, 818-443-6600. Vehicle colors: Blue/gold. *AE, DC, Disc, MC, V.*

Valencia Airport Shuttle: 805-294-0100. Vehicle color: Green. *AE, MC, V.*

AIRPORTS WITH SHUTTLE SERVICE*

AIRPORT/ COMPANY(a)	MAIN COUNTY/ REGION SERVED	SAMPLE FARES(b) (1 PERSON/2 PERSONS)	DISCS. (c)	24 HRS(d)	FLEET SIZE
ATLANTA HARTSFIELD INTL (ATL)					
AAA Airport Express	Metro Atlanta, Northeast Georgia	Athens $25/50; Gwinnett $18/36	I,R	✔	100
Atlanta Airport Shuttle	Metro Atlanta	Alpharetta $40/50; Marietta $28/38	I	—	50
Dixie Excursions	Eastern Alabama	Auburn AL $39/65; Opelika AL $40/75	R	—	11
BALTIMORE/WASHINGTON INTL (BWI)					
Airport Connection	Metro Baltimore/ DC	Bethesda $25/33; DC $30/37	C,I,R,S	—	10
Baltimore Airport Shuttle	Baltimore, Howard	Downtown Baltimore $15/20; Waverly $19/24	I	—	3
Delaware Express Shuttle	Chester, New Castle	Newark DE, Wilmington $60/$78	I,D	✔	44
SuperShuttle	DC, Prince Georges, Montgomery	Bethesda $21/26; DC $21-26/$26-31	I,D	✔	34
BOSTON LOGAN INTL (BOS)					
Dartmourth Mini-Coach	Upper Valley NH	Hanover NH $35/70	C	—	6
Donahue Limo Svc	Northern Worcester	Fitchburg, Leominster, Lunenburg $38/40	R	✔	13
Flight Line	Southern NH, Merrimack Valley	Andover MA $31/38; Nashua NH $35/38	I	✔	18
Knight's Airport Limo	Central MA, Framingham, Worcester	Framingham, Natick $21/36;Worcester $24/41	I,D,R	—	16
Little Daddy Limo	Western MA	Oxford $40/59; Webster $45/64	I	✔	10
Marlboro-Westboro Airport Shuttle	Eastern MA	Marlboro, Westboro $20/40	I,D,S	✔	8
North Shore Airport Limo	North shore	Marblehead, Swampscott $25/30	—	✔	10
R&A Shuttle Svc	North shore	Beverly, Salem $25/30	—	—	5
Thomas Tptn Svcs	Keene NH, Brattleboro VT	Keene NH $52/70; Brattleboro VT $68/86	C	✔	12
US Shuttle	Metro Boston, Eastern MA	Downtown Boston $7/14; Cambridge $10/17	I,S	✔	30
Worcester Airport Limo	Central MA	Auburn $32/52; Worcester $28/48	I,R	—	21

AIRPORT/ COMPANY(a)	MAIN COUNTY/ REGION SERVED	SAMPLE FARES(b) (1 PERSON/2 PERSONS)	DISCS. (c)	24 HRS(d)	FLEET SIZE
CINCINNATI/NO KENTUCKY INTL (CVG)					
DART Airport Shuttle	Dayton, Miami Valley	Dayton, Kettering $35/53	I,R,S	✔	5
Door to Door Tptn	Metro Cincinnati	Downtown Cincinnati $17/17; Oxford $43/50	D,S	—	17
DALLAS/FT WORTH INTL (DFW)					
Classic Shuttle	Metro Dallas/Ft Worth	Downtown Dallas $10/18; Downtown Ft Worth $12/22	I,C,D,R,S	✔	37
Discount Shuttle & Tours	Metro Dallas/Ft Worth	Downtown Dallas $14/18; Plano $24/28	D	✔	100
SuperShuttle	Metro Dallas/Ft Worth	Downtown Dallas $14-25/19-30; Plano $23-27/28-32	I,D	✔	70
DENVER INTL (DEN)					
Boulder Airporter	Boulder area	Boulder, Gunbarrel, Lafayette $16/32	I,C,D	—	18
Colorado Mountain Express	Ski areas	Aspen $79/$79; Vail $50/50	I,D	✔	140
DIA Airporter/ Commuter	Metro Denver	Arvada, Westminster, $25/30; Aurora $20/25	—	—	22
Golden West Commuter	Wheat Ridge, Golden, Lakewood	Denver west side; $20/32; Federal Center $16/28	I,D,S	—	18
Home James Tptn	Grand	Silvercreek $40/78; Winter Park $33/66	I,C,D	—	16
Overland Airport Express	Castle Rock, Highlands Ranch, Parker	Castle Rock $22-30/31-35; Parker $22-27/31-32	I,S	✔	6
Resort Express	Ski areas	Breckenridge, Copper Mtn, Keystone $76/152	I	—	60
Vans to Vail/Vans to Breckenridge/ Aspen Limo	Ski areas	Aspen $75/150; Breckenridge $38/76; Vail $49/98	I,C,S	—	126
DETROIT METRO WAYNE COUNTY (DTW)					
Robert Q's Airbus	Southwestern Ontario	Chatham $36/61; London $41/71(e)	I,C,R,S	✔	31
FT LAUDERDALE/HOLLYWOOD INTL (FLL)					
Gray Line Airport Shuttle	Broward, Dade, Palm Beach	Ft Lauderdale Beach, Hollywood, Hallandale $6/12	—	✔	70

AIRPORTS WITH SHUTTLE SERVICE* *(continued)*

AIRPORT/ COMPANY(a)	MAIN COUNTY/ REGION SERVED	SAMPLE FARES(b) (1 PERSON/2 PERSONS)	DISCS. (c)	24 HRS(d)	FLEET SIZE
LOS ANGELES INTL (LAX)					
3R Express Shuttle(f)	Los Angeles, Orange	Long Beach $20/27; Palos Verdes peninsula $15/22	I,R,S	✔	10
AAA Airport Shuttle	Los Angeles	Downtown Los Angeles $5/10; Pasadena $9/16	—	✔	3
ABC Shuttle(f)	Los Angeles, Orange	Century City $14/21; West Hollywood $18/25	I,R	✔	5
Airtrans Express	Los Angeles, Orange	Anaheim, Covina $25/32; Pomona $42/49	I,S	✔	7
Apollo Shuttle(f)	Los Angeles, Orange	Downtown Los Angeles; Hollywood $10/17	I,S	✔	14
Best Shuttle(f)	Los Angeles, Orange	Costa Mesa $38/45; Long Beach $20/27	I,D,R,S	✔	30
Coast Shuttle	Los Angeles, Orange	Santa Monica $12/15; Westwood $15/20	I,D,R,S	✔	15
Dani's Shuttle(f)	Los Angeles, Orange	Altadena $23/30; Eagle Rock $21/28; Orange $30/37	I,R,S	✔	9
E-Z Shuttle & Charter Svc(f)	Los Angeles, Ventura	Glendale $29/36; Simi Valley $32/37	I,C,D,R,S	✔	11
Inland Express Svcs(f)	Inland Empire	Ontario $41/49; Riverside, San Bernardino $49/57	S	✔	16
LAX Chequer Van	Los Angeles, Orange	Anaheim $35/40; Hollywood $15/20	I,C,D,R,S	✔	2
LA Xpress(f)	Los Angeles, Orange	Huntington Beach $35/44; West Los Angeles $16/19	I,D,R,S	✔	35
Metropolitan Express(f)	Los Angeles, Orange	Hollywood $17/24; Pasadena $22/28	I,C,D,S	✔	6
Prime Time Shuttle Intl(f)	Los Angeles, Orange	Burbank $26/35; Mid-Wilshire $21/30; Reseda $29/38	I,D,R,S	✔	150
Roadrunner Shuttle(f)	Ventura	Camarillo $35/44; Thousand Oaks $30/39	—	✔	15
Shuttle 2000(f)	Los Angeles, Orange	Century City $13/20; Universal City $25/35	I,R,S	✔	8
Shuttle One(f)	Los Angeles, Orange	Hollywood, Beverly Hills,Century City $14/21	I,C,R,S	✔	14
Southern California Coach(f)	Los Angeles, Orange	Mission Viejo $45/53; Yorba Linda $41/49	—	✔	20

AIRPORT/ COMPANY(a)	MAIN COUNTY/ REGION SERVED	SAMPLE FARES(b) (1 PERSON/2 PERSONS)	DISCS. (c)	24 HRS(d)	FLEET SIZE
SuperShuttle(f,g)	Metro Los Angeles	Downtown Los Angeles $12/22; Simi Valley $37/46	I,D,R	✔	210
Valencia Airport Shuttle	Santa Clarita Valley	Canyon Country, Newhall $37/44	R	—	3
MIAMI INTL (MIA)					
SuperShuttle	Broward, Dade, Palm Beach	Hollywood $24/32; Kendall $25/33; downtown Miami $8-9/15-16	I,D	✔	75
NEW YORK JOHN F KENNEDY INTL (JFK)					
Classic Airport Share-Ride(h)	Long Island	Hempstead $29/29; Huntington $33/33; Seaford $30/30	I	✔	40
Gray Line Air Shuttle	Manhattan	23rd-63rd Sts $16/32(i)	—	—	90
Long Island Limo Svc(h)	Long Island	Hauppauge $31/31; Huntington $28/28; Westbury $25/25	I,C,D,R,S	✔	50
Marc 1 of New York	North counties(j)	Rye $25/37; Tarrytown $30/45	I,C,D,R,S	✔	50
Westchester Express	Westchester	Tarrytown, White Plains $35/50; Yonkers $32/47	I	—	60
Winston Airport Shuttle(h)	Long Island	Amityville $31/31; Huntington $32/32; Massapequa $25/25	I,S	✔	40
NEW YORK LA GUARDIA (LGA)					
Classic Airport Share-Ride(h)	Long Island	Hempstead $29/29; Huntington $33/33; Seaford $30/30	I	✔	40
Gray Line Air Shuttle	Manhattan	23rd-63rd Sts $13/26(i)	—	—	90
Long Island Limo Svc(h)	Long Island	Hauppauge $31/31; Huntington $28/28; Westbury $25/25	I,C,D,R,S	✔	50
Marc 1 of New York	North counties(j)	Rye $20/30; Tarrytown $25/40	I,C,D,R,S	✔	50

AIRPORTS WITH SHUTTLE SERVICE* *(continued)*

AIRPORT/ COMPANY(a)	MAIN COUNTY/ REGION SERVED	SAMPLE FARES(b) (1 PERSON/2 PERSONS)	DISCS. (c)	24 HRS(d)	FLEET SIZE
NEW YORK LA GUARDIA (LGA) *(continued)*					
Winston Airport Shuttle(h)	Long Island	Amityville $31/31; Huntington $32/32; Massapequa $25/25	I,S	✔	40
NEWARK INTL (EWR)					
Gray Line Air Shuttle	Manhattan	23rd-63rd Sts $18/36(i)	—	—	90
Long Island Limo Svc(h)	Long Island	Huntington $63/63; Westbury $60/60	I,C,D,R,S	✔	50
Marc 1 of New York	North counties, Queens(j)	Bayside, Forest Hills $29/39; Rye $37/56; Tarrytown $39/58	I,C,D,R,S	✔	50
State Shuttle	New Jersey	Morristown, Somerset, Sparta $35/45, Secaucus $20/40	C	✔	30
ORLANDO INTL (MCO)					
Cocoa Beach Shuttle	Brevard Space Coast area	Cocoa Beach $20/38; Cape Canaveral $20/40	C,D,S	—	8
DOTS (Daytona Orlando Transit Svc)	Orange, Volusia	Daytona $26/52; De Land $20/40; Palm Coast $55/75	I,C,D	—	7
Lake Limo	Lake Marion	Lady Lake $35/51; Leesburg, Mt Dora, Tavares $31/47	D	✔	21
Polk Airport Transit	Polk	Lake Wales $37/47; Winter Haven $33/43	—	—	4
Spaceport	North/South Brevard	Cape Canaveral, Cocoa Beach, Titusville $25/45	I,C,D	—	4
PHILADELPHIA INTL (PHL)					
Airport Express	Philadelphia, South NJ	Center City $10/20; Northeast Philadelphia $24/30	I,D,R,S	—	11
Airport One	Philadelphia, South NJ	Center City $10/20; Northeast Philadelphia $30/40	I,C,D,R,S	✔	25
American Penn Express	Philadelphia, Bucks	Center City $8/16; Northeast Philadelphia $18/35	I	✔	6
Bennett's Main Line Airport Svc	Montgomery	Ardmore, Bryn Mawr, Haverford, Radnor $18/25	I,R	—	6

AIRPORT/ COMPANY(a)	MAIN COUNTY/ REGION SERVED	SAMPLE FARES(b) (1 PERSON/2 PERSONS)	DISCS. (c)	24 HRS(d)	FLEET SIZE
Dave's Best Limo	Philadelphia, Bucks, Montgomery	Bensalem $20/31; Northeast Philadelphia $17/25	D,R	✔	22
Delaware Express Shuttle	Chester, New Castle	Newark DE $27/44; Wilmington $22/39	I,D	✔	44
Limelight Limo	Philadelphia, Bucks, South NJ	Center City $10/20; Holland $30/36	R	✔	15
Metro's Rapid Rover	South NJ	Cherry Hill $20/28; Mt Laurel $22/30	I,C	✔	35
Philadelphia Airport Shuttle	Philadelphia, Atlantic City	Center City $10/16; Northeast Philadelphia $17/23	R	✔	50
Rainbow Cab/Limo	Chester, Delaware	Lionville $29/58; West Chester $27/54	I,C	—	5
Sky Shuttle	South NJ	Cherry Hill $20/28; Medford $23/31	I,C,D	✔	15
SuperShuttle	Delaware, Southeast PA	Northeast Philadelphia $17/23; Wilmington $21/32	I	✔	50
PHOENIX SKY HARBOR INTL (PHX)					
A1 Airport Tptn	Sun cities	Sun City, Sun City West, Youngtown $14/20	I,C	✔	6
Sun City Express	Sun cities	Sun City $13/19; Sun City West $14/20	I	✔	17
SuperShuttle	Metro Phoenix	Glendale $16-21/21-26; Mesa $14-24/19-29	I,D	✔	107
PITTSBURGH INTL (PIT)					
Airport Limo Svc	Allegheny	McKeesport, Monroeville, South Hills $20/35	I,C,D	—	12
Pittsburgh North Aire Ride	Western PA	Butler, Kittanning $25/42;Indiana $35/52	—	✔	30
Southern Park Limo	Northeast OH, Western PA	Boardman OH $33/58; Youngstown OH $40/65	C	—	12
PORTLAND INTL (PDX)					
Blue Star Svcs	Metro Portland	Oregon City $18/20; Vancouver WA $10/15	I,C,D,R	—	18
Metropolitan Shuttle	Metro Portland	Beaverton $25/30; Lake Oswego $27/32	I,S	✔	12
Raja Tours	Metro Portland	Beaverton $20/25; Lake Oswego $20/30	I,C,R,S	—	3

AIRPORTS WITH SHUTTLE SERVICE* *(continued)*

AIRPORT/ COMPANY(a)	MAIN COUNTY/ REGION SERVED	SAMPLE FARES(b) (1 PERSON/2 PERSONS)	DISCS. (c)	24 HRS(d)	FLEET SIZE
PORTLAND INTL (PDX)					
Blue Star Svcs	Metro Portland	Oregon City $18/20; Vancouver WA $10/15	I,C,D,R	—	18
Metropolitan Shuttle	Metro Portland	Beaverton $25/30; Lake Oswego $27/32	I,S	✔	12
Raja Tours	Metro Portland	Beaverton $20/25; Lake Oswego $20/30	I,C,R,S	—	3
ST LOUIS LAMBERT INTL (STL)					
Alton Airport Limo	Metro St Louis	Downtown St Louis $16/18; Collinsville IL $28/30	I	✔	15
BART (Bootheel Area Rapid Transit)	Southeast MO, South central IL	Cape Girardeau MO $40/70; Carbondale IL $40/70	C	✔	17
Springfield Shuttle Svc	Springfield IL	Lincoln IL $50/70; Springfield IL $40/60	—	—	4
Tiger Air Express	Central MO	Columbia $40/60; Jefferson City $43/65	I,C,D,S	—	120
SALT LAKE CITY INTL (SLC)					
Airport Express	Metro Salt Lake City, Ski areas	Deer Valley, Park City $20/40; Provo $18/36	I,C,R	—	6
All Resort Express	Ski areas	Deer Valley, Park City $19/38	—	✔	14
Lewis Bros Stages	Ski areas	Alta, Snowbird $19/$38; Deer Valley, Park City $15/30	I	✔	60
Park City Tptn	Ski areas	Alta, Snowbird $18/36; Park City $20/40	I,C,D	✔	25
Rocky Mtn Tptn	Metro Salt Lake City	Ogden $22/44; Park City $19/38; Provo $21/42	I,C,D	—	15
Super Express	Metro Salt Lake City	Downtown Salt Lake City $15/20; Provo $18/36	I,C,R	—	11
Wasatch Mtn Svc	South Davis	Bountiful, North Salt Lake City $20/20; Centerville $25/25	—	✔	4
SAN DIEGO LINDBERG FIELD INTL (SAN)					
California Sunshine Shuttle	San Diego	Carlsbad, Oceanside $25/25; Rancho Bernardo $20/20	I,C,D,R,S	✔	25
Cloud 9 Shuttle	San Diego	La Jolla $15/21; Mission Valley $11/17;	I,D,R,S	✔	75

AIRPORT/ COMPANY(a)	MAIN COUNTY/ REGION SERVED	SAMPLE FARES(b) (1 PERSON/2 PERSONS)	DISCS. (c)	24 HRS(d)	FLEET SIZE
Coronado Livery	San Diego	Poway $15/18 Chula Vista $15/30; Coronado $8/16; North Island $10/20	I,C,D,R	✔	6
Prime Ride Shuttle	San Diego	Downtown San Diego $5/10; Del Mar $20/25	I,D,R,S	✔	15
Seaside Shuttle	San Diego	Carlsbad $24/28; Del Mar $18/22; Oceanside $27/31	—	✔	15

SAN FRANCISCO INTL (SFO)

AIRPORT/ COMPANY(a)	MAIN COUNTY/ REGION SERVED	SAMPLE FARES(b) (1 PERSON/2 PERSONS)	DISCS. (c)	24 HRS(d)	FLEET SIZE
Advanced Airporter(k)	San Francisco	San Francisco $10/20	I,C,R,S	✔	8
Airport Connection(k)	Bay Area	Berkeley, Palo Alto $20-35/30-35	C,S	✔	45
Bayporter Express(k)	East Bay, South Bay	Berkeley $16/26; Oakland $21/31; Palo Alto $17/27	C,D	—	32
Bay Shuttle	San Francisco	San Francisco $10/20	I,C,D,R,S	✔	7
Designated Driver Group(k)	Bay Area	Berkeley, Oakland $35/35; Concord $45/45	I,C	—	3
East Bay Connection(k)	Contra Costa, Solano	Concord $20/40; Orinda, Walnut Creek $20/35	I,C,D	—	12
EZ Way Out Shuttle(k)	Bay Area	Berkeley $25/35; Sausalito $35/45	I,D,S	✔	17
Lorrie's Travel & Tours	San Francisco	San Francisco $10/20	C,S	—	19
M&M Luxury Airport Shuttle	San Francisco	San Francisco $10/20	I,C,R,S	✔	7
Marin Door to Door(k)	Marin	Central San Rafael $28/38; Sausalito $20/30	I,C,D,S	—	9
Quake City Airport Shuttle	San Francisco	San Francisco $10/18	I,C,D,S	—	6
Pacific Airport Shuttle	San Francisco	San Francisco $9/18	I,C,D,R,S	—	16
South & East Bay Airport Shuttle(k)	East Bay, South Bay	Mountain View $19/24; Palo Alto $15/20; Sunnyvale $21/26	D,S	✔	17
SuperShuttle(k)	San Francisco, South Bay	Downtown San Francisco $11/19; Belmont, San Carlos $13/21	I,D,S	✔	100

AIRPORTS WITH SHUTTLE SERVICE* *(continued)*

AIRPORT/ COMPANY(a)	MAIN COUNTY/ REGION SERVED	SAMPLE FARES(b) (1 PERSON/2 PERSONS)	DISCS. (c)	24 HRS(d)	FLEET SIZE
SAN FRANCISCO INTL (SFO) *(cont'd)*					
VIP Airport Shuttle(k)	East Bay, South Bay	Palo Alto $15/20; San Mateo $12/17	D,R,S	✔	8
Yellow Airport Express Shuttle	San Francisco	San Francisco $10/20	I,C,S	✔	10
SEATTLE-TACOMA INTL (SEA)					
Capital Aeroporter	Tacoma, Olympia, Grays Harbor	Olympia $22-25/30-35; Tacoma $16/22	I,C,D,R,S	—	8
SuperShuttle	King, Pierce, Snohomish	Downtown Seattle $18/24; Downtown Tacoma $21/28	I,C	✔	80
TAMPA INTL (TPA)					
Airport Express	Hernando	Brookville $27/44; Spring Hill $22/39	I,C	—	5
Astro Limo Svc	Hernando, Pasco	Newport Richey $15/26; Spring Hill $18/30	—	✔	19
Central Florida Limo	Hillsborough, Polk	Lakeland $24-35/36-53; Temple Terrace $15/15	D	—	13
Pony Express Limo	Pasco	Hudson, Newport Richey $15/25	C,D,R	—	5
Red Line Limo	Pinellas	Clearwater Beach, St Petersburg $12/23	I,C,R	✔	15
The Limo	Hillsborough, Pinellas	Clearwater, Tampa $13/26; Sun City center $16/32	I,C,D,R	✔	63
TORONTO LESTER B PEARSON INTL (YYZ)					
Airlink Tptn Svcs	Brant, Haldimand Norfolk	Brantford, Paris C$45/57; Simcoe, Delhi C$64/76	C,D	✔	8
Airways Transit Svc	Hamilton, Kitchener	Hamilton C$43/62; Kitchener, Waterloo C$45/62	I,C,D	✔	85
Century Airline Svc	Peterborough, Victoria	Lakefield C$73/88;	C	✔	11

AIRPORT/ COMPANY(a)	MAIN COUNTY/ REGION SERVED	SAMPLE FARES(b) (1 PERSON/2 PERSONS)	DISCS. (c)	24 HRS(d)	FLEET SIZE
Niagara Airbus	Niagara, Buffalo NY	Niagara Falls, St Catharines C$38/71; Welland, C$42/79	C,R,S	✔	60
Northern Airport Svc	North Bay Ontario	Gravenhurst C$43/86; North Bay C$30/6	I,C,R,S	—	6
Red Car Airport Svc	Wellington	Fergus C$45/59; Guelph C$36/50	I,C,R	✔	12
Robert Q's Airbus	Southwestern Ontario	London C$40/62; Sarnia C$46/72; Woodstock C$36/57	I,C,R,S	✔	31
Simcoe County Airport Svc	Simcoe	Barrie C$34/45; Orillia, Midland C$41/52	—	✔	9
Stratford Airporter	Mitchell, Stratford, St Marys	St Marys, C$53/80; Stratford, C$39/66	—	✔	6
Symcha Charter	Metro Toronto, York	Richmond Hill, Markham, Vaughan C$35/35	S	✔	105

* As of October 1995; subject to change.

(a) Company names shortened; see Where to Find It for complete versions of names.

(b) Fares shown are just a sampling of many possible destinations and rounded off to the nearest dollar; two-person rate is for transportation to or from same address. Lower rates may apply for larger parties, groups, or charters; tip, airport-access fees, late-hour surcharges, road tolls not included in base rate. Area rates may vary according to ZIP code; Toronto fares do not include Goods & Services Tax (GST). Door-to-door service may be combined with scheduled shuttle operations or limited to certain sections or cities. Advance reservations required by many companies.

(c) C = children's fares, D = discount coupons or frequent-rider discount, I = infants free, R = reduced round-trip discounts, S = senior fares. Check with company for other discounts for corporate customers, students, military personnel, etc.

(d) Hours may vary by season or time of airport activity.

(e) Reservations made by phone in Canada quoted in C$.

(f) Also serves Burbank, Long Beach, Ontario, or Orange County airports.

(g) Served by Los Angeles, Orange County, San Fernando Valley, and San Gabriel franchises, coordinated at airport by central dispatcher. See Where to Find It for reservations numbers for home pickups.

(h) Also serves Long Island MacArthur (Islip) Airport.

(i) Door-to-door service city-bound only; service to airport available from major hotels and pickup points.

(j) Shared-ride service available to and from the Bronx, Putnam, Rockland, and Westchester counties; Queens shared-ride available for Newark Airport only.

(k) Also serves Oakland or San Jose airports.

MIAMI

SuperShuttle: 305-871-2000. Vehicle colors: Blue/gold. *AE, MC, V.*

NEW YORK

Classic Airport Share-Ride: 800-666-4949, 516-567-5100. Vehicle colors: White/blue. *AE, MC, V.*

Gray Line Air Shuttle: 800-451-0455, 212-757-6840. Vehicle color: Burgundy/white.

Long Island Limo Service: 516-234-8400, 718-656-7000. Vehicle colors: White/blue/orange. *AE, DC, MC, V.*

Marc 1 of New York: 800-309-7070, 718-729-7475. Vehicle color: Maroon. *AE, MC, V.*

State Shuttle: 800-427-3207, 201-729-0030, 908-542-6505. Vehicle colors: Red/yellow. *AE, Disc, MC, V.*

Westchester Express: 800-532-3730, 914-592-9200. Vehicle color: Blue. *AE, MC, V.*

Winston Airport Shuttle: 800-424-7767, 516-924-1200. Vehicle colors: Orange/brown/red. *AE, Disc, MC, V.*

ORLANDO

Cocoa Beach Shuttle: 800-633-0427, 407-784-3831. Vehicle color: Red. *Disc, MC, V.*

DOTS (Daytona Orlando Transit Service): 800-231-1965, 904-257-5411. Vehicle color: Varies. *MC, V.*

Lake Limo: 800-448-2808, 352-742-2808, 352-622-2292. Vehicle colors: White/blue. *MC, V.*

Polk Airport Transit: 941-967-6293. Vehicle colors: Red/white.

Spaceport: 407-383-0374. Vehicle colors: Brown/white.

PHILADELPHIA

Airport Express: 215-745-8519. Vehicle color: Varies. *AE, DC, Disc, MC, V.*

Airport One: 800-535-5466, 215-535-4040. Vehicle color: Gray. *AE, Disc, MC, V.*

American Penn Express: 800-326-4148, 215-938-7235. Vehicle color: Varies. *AE, MC, V.*

Bennett's Main Line Airport Service: 800-427-3464, 610-525-0513. Vehicle color: White. *MC, V.*

Dave's Best Limousine: 215-288-1000. Vehicle color: Varies. *MC, V.*

Delaware Express Shuttle: 800-648-5466, 302-454-7800. Vehicle colors: Red/white/blue. *AE, Disc, MC, V.*

Limelight Limousine: 800-327-5466, 215-342-5557. Vehicle color: Varies. *MC, V.*

Metro's Rapid Rover: 800-322-8062, 609-428-1500. Vehicle colors: Yellow/green. *AE, MC, V.*

Philadelphia Airport Shuttle: 800-774-8885, 215-551-6600. Vehicle colors: Blue/yellow. *AE, Disc, MC, V.*

Rainbow Cab/Rainbow Limo: 800-322-4470, 610-696-6060. Vehicle color: Varies. *AE, Disc, MC, V.*

Sky Shuttle: 800-825-3759, 609-770-1313. Vehicle colors: Red/white/blue. *AE, Disc, MC, V.*

SuperShuttle: 215-551-6600, 302-655-8878. Vehicle colors: Blue/yellow. *AE, Disc, MC, V.*

PHOENIX

A1 Airport Transportation: 800-474-3321, 602-979-7330. Vehicle color: Varies.

Sun City Express: 800-238-1508, 602-

933-9300. Vehicle colors: White/black/blue. *AE, MC, V.*

SuperShuttle: 800-258-3826, 602-244-9000. Vehicle colors: Blue/gold. *AE, MC, V.*

PITTSBURGH

Airport Limousine Service: 412-664-4777. Vehicle colors: White/green.

Pittsburgh North Aire Ride: 800-647-4331, 412-548-8536. Vehicle color: White. *AE, MC, V.*

Southern Park Limo: 800-528-9663, 216-726-2800. Vehicle colors: Blue/grey.

PORTLAND OR

Blue Star Services: 800-247-2272, 360-573-9412, 503-249-1837. Vehicle color: Varies.

Metropolitan Shuttle: 800-817-1885, 503-331-2335. Vehicle colors: Varies. *AE, MC, V.*

Raja Tours: 503-260-9802. Vehicle colors: Mocha/brown. *AE, Disc, MC, V.*

ST LOUIS

Alton Airport Limousine: 800-946-0103, 314-741-6550. Vehicle color: Varies. *AE, Disc, MC, V.*

BART (Bootheel Area Rapid Transit): 800-284-2278, 314-335-0844. Vehicle color: Varies. *MC, V.*

Tiger Air Express: 800-333-3026, 314-443-3544. Vehicle colors: Black/gold. *AE, DC, Disc, MC, V.*

SALT LAKE CITY

Airport Express: 800-682-6743, 801-269-9977. Vehicle color: Varies. No credit cards accepted.

All Resort Express: 800-457-9457,

801-649-3999. Vehicle color: Varies. *AE, Disc, MC, V.*

Lewis Bros Stages: 800-826-5844, 801-359-8677. Vehicle color: Varies. *AE, DC, Disc, MC, V.*

Park City Transportation: 800-637-3803, 801-649-8567. Vehicle color: White. *AE, Disc, MC, V.*

Rocky Mountain Transportation: 800-397-0773, 801-576-0772. Vehicle color: Varies. *AE, MC, V.*

Super Express: 800-321-5554, 801-566-6400. Vehicle colors: Varies. *AE, Disc, MC, V.*

Wasatch Mountain Service: 800-365-8511, 801-295-4666. Vehicle colors: Varies. *MC, V.*

SAN DIEGO

California Sunshine Shuttle: 619-443-7900. Vehicle color: Varies. No credit cards accepted.

Cloud 9 Shuttle: 800-974-8885, 619-278-8877. Vehicle colors: White/blue. *AE, MC, V.*

Coronado Livery: 800-204-2287, 619-435-6310. Vehicle colors: White/blue.

Prime Ride Shuttle: 619-855-9696. Vehicle colors: White/burgundy. *AE, Disc, MC, V.*

Seaside Shuttle: 800-570-3700, 619-281-6451. Vehicle colors: Blue/ white. *AE, MC, V.*

SAN FRANCISCO

Advanced Airporter: 415-550-1112. Vehicle color: Burgundy. No credit cards accepted.

Airport Connection: 800-247-7678, 415-877-8300. Vehicle colors: Black/white. *AE, Disc, MC, V.*

Bayporter Express: 800-287-6783, 415-467-1800. Vehicle colors: Green/silver. *AE, MC, V.*

Bay Shuttle: 415-564-3400. Vehicle color: Blue. *AE, MC, V.*

Designated Driver Group: 510-261-6321, 415-861-3374. Vehicle colors: Silver/black.

East Bay Connection: 800-675-3278, 510-945-0268. Vehicle colors: Gray/white. *AE, MC, V.*

EZ Way Out Shuttle: 510-430-9090. Vehicle colors: White/blue/red. *AE, MC, V.*

Lorrie's Travel & Tours: 415-334-9000. Vehicle colors: Red/yellow. *AE, MC, V.*

M&M Luxury Airport Shuttle: 800-286-0303, 415-552-3200. Vehicle colors: White/yellow. *AE, MC, V.*

Marin Door to Door: 800-540-4815, 415-457-2717. Vehicle color: Varies. *AE, Disc, MC, V.*

Quake City Airport Shuttle: 415-255-4899. Vehicle colors: Green/black/yellow. *AE.*

Pacific Airport Shuttle: 415-282-6088. Vehicle colors: Blue/red. No credit cards accepted.

South & East Bay Airport Shuttle: 800-548-4664, 408-225-4444. Vehicle colors: Yellow/blue.

SuperShuttle: 415-558-8500. Vehicle colors: Blue/yellow. *AE, MC, V.*

VIP Airport Shuttle: 800-235-8847, 408-378-8847, 408-855-1800. Vehicle colors: Red/blue.

Yellow Airport Express Shuttle: 415-282-7433. Vehicle colors: Yellow/white/black.

SEATTLE/TACOMA

Capital Aeroporter: 800-962-3579, 206-838-7431 (Seattle), 360-754-7113 (Olympia), 206-927-6179 (Tacoma). Vehicle color: Varies.

SuperShuttle: 800-487-7433, 206-622-1424. Vehicle colors: Blue/yellow. *AE, Disc, MC, V.*

TAMPA

Airport Express: 800-537-6032, 904-688-0784. Vehicle colors: Red/white/blue. *AE, Disc, MC, V.*

Astro Limousine Service: 800-303-3262, 813-848-3262. Vehicle colors: White/black.

Central Florida Limousine: 800-282-1284, 941-665-8155. Vehicle colors: Cream/orange/green.

Pony Express Limo: 800-715-4667, 813-848-7557. Vehicle colors: White/red.

Red Line Limo: 800-359-5466, 813-535-3391. Vehicle colors: White/red.

The Limo: 800-282-6817, 813-572-1111. Vehicle colors: White/blue/ green. *AE, Disc, MC, V.*

TORONTO

Airlink Transportation Services: 416-292-6200. Vehicle colors: Blue/white. *AE, MC, V.*

Airways Transit Service: 905-689-4460, 519-886-2121. Vehicle colors: White/maroon/black. *AE, MC, V.*

Classique Airline Van Service: 800-387-5450 in Canada, 905-427-6800. Vehicle colors: Blue/gold. *AE, MC, V.*

Niagara Airbus: 905-374-8111. Vehicle colors: White/blue. *AE, MC, V.*

Northern Airport Service: 800-461-4219 in Canada, 705-636-7728. Vehicle colors: White/blue. No credit cards accepted.

Red Car Airport Service: 519-824-9344. Vehicle color: Burgundy.

Robert Q's Airbus: 800-265-4948, 519-673-6804. Vehicle colors: White/burgundy. *AE, MC, V.*

Simcoe County Airport Service: 800-461-7529, 705-728-1148. Vehicle colors: White/black/red.

Stratford Airporter: 519-273-0057.

Vehicle color: White. *MC, V.*

Symcha Charter: 905-888-1122. Vehicle colors: Blue/white. *AE, MC, V.*

This chapter was adapted from the Consumer Reports Travel Letter *article "Airport Shuttles: Door to Door" (December 1995).*

The Car-Rental Game

Attracted by come-on rates for car rentals that include a weekend or a Saturday night? How about offers of free upgrades to larger models? Watch out for the vanishing-deal effect: You may have to coax the promised rate out of a reluctant reservation agent by quoting an advertisement exactly, or even by citing a code number from an ad. Furthermore, some specials are limited to renters who hold airline tickets, to discourage locals from renting at airport locations, where rentals are generally cheaper than at downtown facilities.

SCOUTING OUT BARGAINS

True, there are fine deals to be had—especially in Florida and California, with their cutthroat competition. But wherever you rent, proceed with caution. Here's how to shop:

PROMOTIONS. A few years ago, we checked to see how easy—or hard—it was for ordinary travelers to get in on advertised bargains. At that time, rental companies were trumpeting deals for the coming month or two.

In a series of calls to the companies' toll-free numbers, we asked for the lowest rates for the dates and car models the advertisements featured. But we didn't mention the ads or ask for discounts unless the agents quoted us rates other than the advertised ones.

Only a handful of reservation agents volunteered the best sale prices. It took gentle quizzing, sometimes nudging, to get other agents to offer the advertised rates. Several agents held firmly to whatever rate they quoted first, even when pressed to check further.

We found that the surest way to get an advertised discount was to quote directly from an ad or to mention the promotion's discount code. That code is usually listed in small print beneath the boldly displayed rate or in the description of the terms and conditions of the rental.

WEEKEND RATES. If your schedule permits you to rent a car over a weekend, you can often get a great deal. There's also the Saturday-night-keep, a low rate that depends on your keeping the car over a Saturday night.

Weekend rates are usually good from noon Thursday through noon the following Monday, and they often include unlimited mileage. But you have to shop carefully. Even on a simple weekend rental, you face a crazy quilt of rates. The lowest rental rate varies substantially in different cities and among companies in a given city. Some rates are based on a uniform daily rate, usually with a two- or three-day minimum. Others are flat rates pegged to the length of the rental—generally, the longer the rental, the lower the per-day rate. Some locations don't offer weekend rates.

You do have to be careful to avoid extra charges. Extra-driver charges (see page 148) are sometimes high enough to make a big difference in your total rental bill. In some locations, renting a car at an airport and returning it downtown, or vice versa, costs far more than the advertised weekend price. And with some companies, missing the return deadline causes the entire weekend rental to revert to the much more expensive weekday rate.

If there's a chance you'll keep a car beyond the usual weekend period, ask about extra-day pricing when you make the reservation, and try to rent from a company that doesn't cancel the weekend rate if you miss the return deadline. If you can't find such a deal, you can return the car by the deadline and rerent for the extra day or two at weekday rental rates.

HUNT BY COMPUTER? A travel agent's computer-reservation system doesn't necessarily make the lowest promotional rates easier to find. We spot-checked in the *System One* reservation system for two advertised promotions in several cities.

In the first promotion, we found a lower rate than the advertised rate in seven of the 12 cities we checked. In the five other cities, the promotional rates were higher than the advertised rate (though in three of those cities, the regular weekend rate was lower than the advertised rate).

For the other promotion, we checked the computer for eight cities. We found lower rates in five cities, the advertised rate in one, and higher rates in two (in one of those, the weekend daily rate was higher than the lowest weekday rate).

We didn't stop with the computer's initial standard car-rental display (although even the most competent travel agents and corporate travel managers might well have stopped there). Instead, we undertook a cumbersome search in the special promotions areas of the database. So much for the theory that the computer always spews out the best deal.

SENIOR DISCOUNTS. Some car-rental companies also extend discounts to seniors, sometimes tied in to membership in a senior organization such as AARP. However, seniors will generally do better by shopping short-term promotions—rental company discounts are usually only 5-10% off.

HIDDEN EXTRAS

Many car-rental companies won't let you drive away from the lot at low advertised rates without a struggle. A combination of enticements, threats, and fine print can more than double your rental bill. Here are the main ploys:

ADDITIONAL DRIVERS. Rental companies may add $3–9 a day or a flat $20–25 a rental for each additional driver in your travel party. Most let your husband or wife drive at no extra cost, but some may not.

Some companies won't rent to drivers younger than 21; others require renters to be at least 25. Those with the younger cutoff usually assess an additional charge for drivers aged 21–24.

Don't try to save money by neglecting to list additional drivers. If you have an accident, the company could claim you violated your contract and withhold any insurance or service benefits. If you're planning to share driving chores, shop around for a company that has a competitive rate without an extra-driver gouge.

UPGRADE HARD SELLS. Those low advertised rates are usually for a subcompact car. But when you reach the desk, you may be pressured to upgrade to a more powerful vehicle. Many agents try to convince customers that local driving conditions make the subcompact inadequate. That switch—if you fall for it—can balloon your bill. Decide exactly what kind of car you want before you reserve.

COLLISION INSURANCE. Some travelers still find it difficult to rent a car without being gouged for collision-damage waiver or loss-damage waiver (CDW/LDW). That's the quasi-insurance that yields car-rental companies fat

daily fees ($7–15 a day) for waiving their right to hold you liable if your rental car is damaged or stolen.

Most renters can cover their risk of damage or loss without CDW/LDW. Those risks are often covered by your regular auto policy for driving within the United States. But a few big auto insurers, including industry giants State Farm and Nationwide, have backed away from providing complete coverage automatically for rental cars as part of the coverage for your own car. Whether you're affected depends on your insurance company, the date on which your policy next comes up for renewal, and where you live—some state regulations will require continued coverage. If you rely on your personal insurance for business travel, be sure to check your policy. Have your agent clarify any uncertainties.

Charge cards and the *Gold* versions of credit cards typically provide CDW/LDW coverage. The *Private Issue* version of the *Discover* credit card, for instance, offers to reimburse you up to $25,000 for the costs of damage to a car you've rented.

Most cards offer secondary coverage. *Diners Club* and *Discover,* however, give primary coverage—you needn't submit a claim on your own policy first.

Most cards do have time limitations: *MasterCard Gold,* for example, now covers rentals for only up to 15 days. *Visa Gold* offers 15-day coverage within the US and 31-day coverage overseas. (Coverage on standard *MasterCard* and *Visa* cards, if any, varies by issuing bank.) *American Express* offers 30-day consecutive coverage in the United States and overseas, and *Diners Club* offers a flat 31 days anywhere. So if you rely on a credit card or charge card, don't drive a rental car beyond the card's maximum coverage. If you do rent for a longer time and you can't rerent every 15 days, consider getting a new card with a longer limit.

Some car-rental agents still use high-pressure sales tactics, which may include cautioning clients that credit card or charge-card coverage is risky or that the car-rental company doesn't have an arrangement with a given credit card or charge-card issuer. That's irrelevant—the card-issuer's deal is with *you.*

Alternatively, an agent may tell customers that, without CDW, they won't be allowed to leave the state if they have an accident until the claim is settled. But there's no way a car-rental company can restrict your freedom of movement because you (or your insurance company) owe money for repairs.

Some rental companies would like to keep CDW/LDW alive because it's immensely profitable. It also lets them headline lowball prices and still profit from the big markup on the insurance. Industry sources estimate the real cost of CDW/LDW at about $2 per day, so a $7–15 retail price provides a lot of gravy. Articles in the trade press indicate that individual rental offices and employees are rated, in part, on their success in selling CDW/LDW.

Even if you buy CDW/LDW, the fine print may exclude certain kinds of damage (such as broken or cracked glass) or contain so many loopholes that

the car-rental company can charge you for almost any damage.

Damage discovered after a car is returned remains the liability of the renter (who may by then have left the area). However, typical rental contracts have no provision for an agent to inspect and sign off for damages. You're within your rights to insist on a sign-off (but expect an argument).

CDW/LDW ABROAD. You may find it especially tough to avoid CDW/LDW when you rent from a local agency overseas. Many foreign rental companies apparently continue to rely on CDW/LDW for profits, threatening to put a big hold on your card to cover possible damage if you don't. (If you carry more than one card, your countermove is to charge your rental on one card and put day-to-day expenses on the other.)

Your best defense is to prearrange the rental through a US office or agency. Specify when you rent that you intend to use your credit card or charge card for collision protection and won't buy CDW/LDW. If you rent abroad, use a major multinational company, which should be used to dealing with Americans who rely on their cards. And if you somehow find yourself about to be denied a car unless you buy CDW/LDW, accept it, note on the contract that you accepted under duress, and demand a full refund as soon as you return home.

Liability insurance covers damage someone in a rented car might do to other persons or property. Buying CDW/LDW from the rental company does not provide liability coverage, nor do major charge cards provide it as a free extra.

Until fairly recently, car-rental companies normally included enough primary liability coverage in their basic rate to satisfy the legal minimum in the state where a car was rented. With primary coverage, an injured party's first claim is against the rental company's insurance; a renter's personal insurance picks up any excess owed. But in a number of states, large rental companies have switched to secondary coverage, shifting the bulk of accident costs to the driver's own insurance policy. In California, many companies have canceled liability coverage entirely.

If you own a car, you probably carry liability insurance that would cover you while driving a rented car. Should there be a claim that exceeds your own coverage, the car-rental company's policy would make up the difference, up to its limit. The switch simply increases the chances of a hit on your own insurance—which would probably increase your rates.

If you don't own a car and therefore don't have automobile insurance, the rental company's secondary insurance becomes de facto primary. (In California, you could be uninsured.) The liability insurance that satisfies most states' requirements is probably enough to cover repair of someone else's car or to fix minor damage to a building. But it's apt to be woefully inadequate to protect your personal assets against a big personal-injury claim. You'd be wise to buy extra liability insurance, no matter where you rent.

Those who frequently rent cars but do not own one (or drive cars borrowed from others) should consider a year-round nonowner policy—several auto insurers sell them. If you rent infrequently, you can buy $1 million in additional liability coverage from most car-rental companies for about $7–8 a day.

"ALL-IN-ONE" RATES. Alamo's optional All-in-One car-rental rates bundle a long list of charges and extras into one daily price. It includes the car with unlimited mileage, additional drivers at no extra charge, a full tank of gas, a baby seat or ski rack (if needed), collision-damage waiver (CDW) with $500 deductible, any applicable airport taxes or fees, state and local surcharges, and local sales taxes.

When we checked for a report in early 1996, the basic national All-in-One rates were about double the basic regular rates. But most travelers have no need for many of the bundled-in extras.

There's a special catch to the CDW coverage. If you accept the All-in-One rate, you accept Alamo's CDW—and so negate any collision coverage your charge card provides. *American Express, Diners Club, MasterCard,* and *Visa* all told *CRTL* that they would not cover the $500 deductible of the Alamo program. (They do pay the deductible if you rely on your regular auto insurance to cover damage to a rental car.)

PITFALLS AND POTHOLES

Here are some not-so-obvious problems that may crop up when you rent a car:

•**Documentation.** If you're renting a

car at an airport but aren't arriving or departing on a flight, check to make sure that a quoted rate doesn't require you to show a ticket.

• **Geographic limits.** Some companies that specialize in cheap car rentals limit where you can drive. For example, if you rent a car in California, the rental company may prohibit you from driving it into any other state (except for short side trips to Las Vegas or Reno). If you're heading for Arizona or Oregon, you may have to use a more expensive rental—possibly from another company.

It doesn't pay to figure that the rental company will never know whether you drive out of the permitted areas—if you run into trouble, you've violated the contract. When you're arranging your rental, let the agent know where you plan to drive, and make sure the quoted rate covers your itinerary.

• **Redlining.** Another complication is redlining—marking out certain areas where residents who rent cars locally must pay higher rates or pass extra screening. Ask about surcharges when you reserve.

• **Mileage limits.** Currently, the industry has adopted unlimited mileage as a standard for noncorporate rentals. However, unlimited mileage is not always your best deal. If you're using a rented car mainly for local errands in your destination area, a low daily or weekly rate with 100 or 150 free miles per day may be better than a competitor's unlimited mileage rate. You have to estimate how far you're going to drive on each rental and compare alternatives.

• **Being fuelish.** A number of companies rent their cars with a "full" tank, requiring it to be returned the same way or demanding a premium price if the rental company fills the tank. But sometimes the tank isn't full, though the checkout slip says it is. Always check before you drive off.

You may also take a hit when returning the car. On many fuel gauges, the needle points to F well before the tank is actually full. If, before returning a car, you fill up to the point at which a gas pump shuts off automatically, you make a gift of a dollar or so's worth of gas to the rental company. Try filling up just to the F.

• **One-way drop-off.** With a rental car, rent-it-here, leave-it-there refers to pickup and return in different cities. Some companies allow you to pick up a car from one office and drop it off at another within the same metropolitan area at no extra charge. Many travelers use that provision to rent a car downtown and drop it off at the airport. However, for most companies, local one-way drop-off policies vary by location; be sure to check before you reserve.

Franchised locations are often especially reluctant to feature attractive one-way rates. (Second-tier companies have a greater proportion of franchised locations than the Big Four—Avis, Budget, Hertz, and National.) You may find a low one-way rate at one of these locations if you're traveling between two cities with a pattern of heavy one-way rentals (or if the franchisee operates in both cities). These one-way rentals may also be limited to certain models, seasons, and dates. But if the company has to send an employee to drive the car back to its original location, you're looking at a hefty drop-off charge.

A one-way rental requires comparison shopping, even more than with ordinary rentals. To locate the least expensive rental, decide on the cities in which you plan to rent and return the car, who in the travel party will be driving, and what size car you want. Then get quotes from several rental companies, including extra-driver or underage-driver charges if applicable, and whatever discounts you may be eligible for.

Make sure one of the quotes is from National, and at least one more is from one of the second-tier renters (Dollar, Payless, or Thrifty, say). Those companies tended to offer the best deals when we checked a few years back. If you plan to drive for four or five days, get quotes for that period as well as for a full week. The weekly rate may well be better, even if you leave the car idle for a day or two.

DANGEROUS RENTALS

Holiday Which?, a British travel publication, had a mechanic check 60 rental cars in Greece and Spain a few years back. The mechanic classified 20 cars as either dangerous or very dangerous. Among the major problems: tires badly cut, bald, or with bulging sidewalls (a sign of an impending blowout); a leaking fuel tank; a missing wheel nut; inoperative or badly adjusted brakes; inoperative brake lights; and windshield wipers that didn't work. All but eight of the 60 cars were poorly maintained, too.

Beyond hazards, there are questions of financial exposure. When you sign a rental agreement, you may be agreeing that the car is in good condition. If you spot a defect later, that agreement may limit your recourse.

This prerental checklist makes good sense anywhere in the world:

- Check the tires (including the spare) for bulges, cuts, and excessive tread wear. Be sure there's a jack.
- Have obvious body or mechanical damage noted on the contract, so you won't be charged for it later.
- Test the windshield wipers, seat belts, seat adjustments, and all lights, including brake lights.
- Make sure there's an owner's manual. If not, have the agent demonstrate the use of important controls and convenience features (show you how to set the clock and the radio's push buttons, say).

•**Record checks.** A number of rental companies check driving records, at least at some locations, before they'll rent a car. Drivers are screened not when they make their reservation but when they arrive at the counter to pick up their car. That's too late to get an advance-booking rate at another rental company if they flunk the check, and perhaps too late to get a car at any price.

Typically, you can be denied a rental for three moving violations or two accidents over a 36-month period; for one instance of drunk driving, hit-and-run, driving a stolen car, or other serious offense; or for presenting a suspended or invalid license. Moreover, once you've been screened and refused, the car-rental company may carry your name on a blacklist.

The potential screenees are drivers who live in states that make the records available to online services: Alabama, Arizona, California, Connecticut, Florida, Idaho, Kansas, Maryland, Minnesota, New York, Ohio, Pennsylvania, South Carolina, and Virginia, plus Washington DC.

If you plan to rent a car, be sure you know what's in your driving record:

•If your record is clean, forget about the screening—at worst, it will extend the rental transaction by a few seconds. Rent from the company with the best deal. Ditto even if you have a questionable record, if you live in a state that doesn't disclose driving records.

•If you have a problem record and live in a state that permits screening, rent from a company that doesn't check records. Currently, that means Alamo everywhere, or Enterprise anywhere but in New York. Alternatively, have someone else in your travel party rent the car and do the driving.

•If you don't know the status of your record, check with your local motor-vehicle department.

•If you want to see exactly what the car-rental companies' computers will pull up, TML Information Services, one of the companies that operate the online data services, will send you a copy. TML charges consumers $9.95 ($7.95 for American Automobile Assn members); call 800-388-9099. The company will screen your driving records against the criteria used by the rental companies to bar risky drivers and fax or mail you the resulting report. The service is not available to California or Pennsylvania drivers.

WHERE TO FIND IT

Car-rental companies with an * are affiliated with AARP and offer member discounts.

*Alamo: 800-327-9633; "Experienced Driver Rate": 5–15% discount (varies by location) to drivers over 50. Additional discounts for members of senior organizations (varies by location).

*Avis: 800-331-1212; various discounts (5–10%, with restrictions) for AARP members.

Budget: 800-527-0700; 5% discount to AARP members (not all locations).

Dollar: 800-800-4000; discount varies by location (not all locations).

Enterprise: 800-325-8007; 10% discount to AARP members.

*Hertz: 800-654-3131; 5-15% discounts to members of AARP, Mature Outlook, National Association of Retired Federal Employees (5–10%, with restrictions), others.

*National: 800-227-7368; 10–30% discounts, with restrictions, available to members of AARP, Mature Outlook, and other senior organizations.

Payless: 800-729-5377; "Nifty Fifty Plus" program (no fee) for all drivers over 50. Discount varies by location.

Thrifty: 800-367-2277; 10% discount to seniors age 55 and older.

This chapter was adapted from the Consumer Reports Travel Letter *article "Alamo's All-In-One Rates" (March 1996) and from the 1996 edition of* Consumer Reports Best Travel Deals.

RAIL PASSES: US AND CANADA

Quite a few English-speaking travelers like to ride trains—long-haul "land cruises" are especially popular in Canada, Australia, South Africa, and the US. Extended daytime sightseeing rides are also feasible on some routes. Rail passes are an economical way to get the most out of a country's rail network.

In 1996, *Consumer Reports Travel Letter* published an overview of what was then available in North America. (We also covered Asia and the South Pacific; see chapter 22.) The prices in the listings that follow are in US dollars as of that year, converted where necessary at late-February '96 exchange rates (1997 prices weren't available at this writing). Unless noted, infants traveled free and older children paid the adult fare. Average rail speeds are based on scheduled station-to-station times (not top running speed).

Most rail passes work in much the same way: For a fixed price, you get unlimited train travel within a specified time. Some passes have only *full-time* options: You can travel on any day

on which the pass is valid. Other passes are *flexible*, good for travel on a set number of days anytime during the pass's validity period.

A rail pass usually covers just a daytime seat. Overnight sleeping accommodations, private compartments, meals, and such are usually extra. You may also have to pay an extra charge to ride some premium trains.

CANADIAN OFFERINGS

Canada's government-run VIA Rail is a mixed bag. High-speed trains (averaging up to 84 mph) in the Montreal-Toronto corridor challenge air travel in door-to-door time. Other trains offer mainly land cruises. However, Canadian trains are the only reliable means of access to a few remote areas. Top main-line trains are air-conditioned in both First and Second Class.

The *Canrailpass* on VIA Rail provided unlimited Coach Class travel on any 12 days during a 30-day period. Sleeping berths, private compartments, and meals were extra. The pass did not cover private sightseeing trains or trips on BC Rail, Ontario Northern, or other private lines.

Prices varied by season: 1996's peak season was May 15–Oct 15. Rates for adult tickets (without tax) were $390.50 high season, $266.41 low, with extra days available for $34 peak, $22 offpeak. Youth 24 or under and seniors 60 or over paid $351.81 (peak) and $240.14 (off-peak).

VIA Rail's top tourist trip is undoubtedly the run between Toronto and Vancouver, covering more than 2800 miles in just under three days at an average 41 mph. You should reserve far in advance—especially for peak season or anytime you want a private compartment. The route from Jasper to Prince Rupert is also scenic, as are several trains into the North.

A *Canrailpass* isn't for everyone. Many US residents find it easy to drive into Canada; you can also reach most of Canada's top visitor centers directly by air. But it's a good deal for train buffs and for long-haul trips: One-way from Toronto to Vancouver, at $380, cost more than a low-season pass and only slightly less than a high-season pass. Buy a *Canrailpass* from any travel agency before you arrive in Canada, and show it to obtain a train ticket. For current pass prices, you can call VIA Rail at 800-561-3949 in the US, 800-561-8630 in Canada.

PASSES FOR THE US

The US Amtrak system is really several rail services. Between New York and Washington, *Metroliners* provide frequent, high-speed service (averaging

THE FAST TRACK

One ready gauge of the sophistication of a railway system is the average speed its passenger trains attain. In Europe and Japan, average station-to-station speeds on new high-speed lines can top 150 mph, and even conventional-technology trains regularly average better than 80 mph. Amtrak's *Metroliners* and Canadian trains in the Montreal-Toronto corridor also average better than 80 mph.

High speed goes hand in hand with frequency of service. Fast passenger trains require expensive roadbeds; the investment isn't justified unless it's spread over dozens of trains a day. That's why Amtrak's once-a-day (or less) long-haul trains will probably never average better than 55 mph. And it's why average speeds in some countries are mired in the range of 30-40 mph.

In a quick review of world railway schedules, we found only two places outside Europe, North America, and Japan in which average speeds of main-line express trains exceed 60 mph: South Korea (66 mph between Seoul and Pusan) and Taiwan (62 mph between Taipei and Kaohsiung). Rail is a good way to get around in both those countries, but they don't offer rail passes.

up to 85 mph); they challenge planes for door-to-door time and beat them hands down for comfort. Amtrak also operates frequent trains (although nowhere near as fast) between Los Angeles and San Diego.

The main long-haul trains, on the other hand, are primarily recreational land cruisers. They pass through some of the country's most scenic areas at a snail's pace. The accommodations are spacious, and the cars are designed for sightseeing. Several shorter routes are hybrids—too short to be land cruises, too long and slow to compete with air travel or driving. The top main-line trains are air-conditioned in both First and Second Class.

Amtrak's program was new last year. Its *Explore America Fare* catered to US and Canadian train lovers, providing up to 30 days of travel in day coach, with roomy reclining seats on most long-distance trains. Sleeping berths, private compartments, and meal service were extra.

On most segments, you could travel only once in either direction, with unlimited stopovers, and you had to set your itinerary when you bought your pass. The pass wasn't valid on *Metroliners* (but you could ride other Northeast Corridor trains), the Alaska Railroad, private scenic railways, and non-Amtrak suburban trains.

Prices varied by season and region: Spring season continued through June 16, when the peak summer season began. Amtrak divides the US into three regions: Eastern, Central, and Western. During the spring season, coach travel was $158 within any one region, $198 within two adjacent regions, and $278 for the entire system. Peak-season prices were $50 higher. Children 2–15 paid 50% (up to two children per adult). Seniors 62 or over got a 15% reduction.

Those fares were valid as of late 1996. At the time of our report, Amtrak hadn't established prices for sale after that. Call Amtrak for current prices (800-872-7245).

AMTRAK FREQUENT-RIDER PROGRAM

Amtrak, which often tries to emulate the airlines, now has a frequent-rider program. Travelers who sign up for *Executive Privileges* earn awards for riding *Metroliner* trains between New York and Washington, and *Empire* trains between New York City and upstate New York.

Four one-way trips (or two round-trips) within a three-month period earn a 20% discount at some Choice hotels, a free *Transmedia* dining card, and a Club Class rail upgrade. Travelers who use those rail services even more frequently earn such additional rewards as a free weekend Amtrak ticket, shopping coupons at Bloomingdale's (a leading department-store chain), and cruise discounts. To enroll (no charge), call 800-836-6656.

Students who had a Student Advantage card were also entitled to 15% discounts on most Amtrak fares, including the *Explore America Fare.* The card also provided discounts from a range of other suppliers (including Dell Computers, Dollar Rent A Car, and several movie-theater chains) as well as a half-price hotel directory from *Great American Traveler* (see chapter 15). To get a card, you had to be a student (subject to verification); a card cost $20 a year (800-962-6872; *AE, MC, V*).

In addition to rail travel, travelers who used a *Visa* card to buy *Explore America Fare* tickets received a 5% reduction on Amtrak sleeping accommodations, 10% discounts from rack (list-price) rate at Choice hotels, and a variety of promotional offers from Avis.

For good daytime sightseeing in the East, the Adirondack between New York and Montreal earns high marks. In the West, top sectors include Denver–Salt Lake City and Oakland–Reno on the *California Zephyr,* Los Angeles–Oakland and Klamath Falls–Seattle on the *Coast Starlight,* and the stretch near Glacier Park on the *Empire Builder.*

Overall, Amtrak's long-haul trains are slow. The fastest is the *Southwest Chief* between Chicago and Los Angeles, averaging 55 mph, but it still doesn't quite match the time the *Super Chief* made on that route 40 years ago. Other long-haul trains are slower: The *Sunset Limited* between Miami and Los Angeles averages only 44 mph.

Amtrak's rail pass is attractive for buffs who want to log a lot of miles riding the rails. However, even they might consider an alternative: In cooperation with United Airlines, Amtrak offers excursion fares on its long-haul trains that let travelers fly in one direction and take the train in the other.

For just one trip, individual tickets may also be cheaper. The '96 round-trip fare from New York to Montreal, for example, was $144. But for a long trip, the pass beat separate tickets: Just one way on the Chicago-Oakland run was $262—about the same as a peak-season two-region pass. You can buy Amtrak passes or rail/air excursion tickets at any Amtrak station or travel agency.

This chapter was adapted from the Consumer Reports Travel Letter *article "Rail Passes: North America, Asia, and the South Pacific" (April 1996).*

BEST BUYS IN LODGINGS

SCOPING OUT HOTEL DEALS

S mart travelers rarely pay full price for a hotel room. Rates vary widely, even for the same room in the same hotel on the same day. Hotels use complex pricing systems formulated on predictions of room-occupancy rates for each date and location. Rates for empty rooms drop as a given reservation date approaches.

For most travelers, it's too risky to show up at a hotel hoping to get a room at a good price. And it's unnecessary, when there are so many good sources for bargain hunters.

WHERE THE BUYS ARE

Room deals can be had through either private or public sources.

- **Private channels**. Hotels sell off excess room capacity through half-price hotel programs, which often offer the best deals for travelers. (See chapter 15.) Their biggest drawback? You may have to be flexible about locations or dates, especially during a peak-demand period.

    Tour operators book blocks of

hotel rooms. If you ask, they may sell you just the lodging at a 20 to 40% discount without the transportation or sightseeing that normally makes up a tour package. You can also get discounted rooms through some consolidators. (See chapter 5.)

In some cities, local reservation services can provide good deals. (See chapter 16.) And if you're heading off for a week or so on an island, in the mountains, or in a distant major city, be aware that a hotel or resort isn't your only choice. A vacation rental or home exchange can be cheaper, roomier, or more fun.

- **Public channels**. Every type of hotel from economy to full-service (business), deluxe, and even resort properties gives discounts off rack rate (list price). It's generally best to call individual hotels directly to check for the best rate; national reservations operators aren't always informed of local short-term deals.

Direct discounts come in several forms:

- **Sales and promotions.** Rates at hotels that cater to business travelers during the workweek tumble on weekends. So do rates at resort hotels during off-season.
- **Bargain destinations.** Overbuilding in a region affects hotel rates dramatically. Ask your travel agent which destinations offer the best deals.
- **Advance-reservation deals.** A number of chains will reward you with lower rates if you do your booking ahead (anywhere from 7 to 29 days in advance). In one such deal, you pay for your first night's stay within a week of reserving; if you cancel without giving at least a 15-day notice, you lose your deposit. Penalties for cancellation, however, vary, as do prepayment requirements and the amount of the discount; check before you book.
- **Other sources.** Membership associations, such as the American Automobile Association (AAA) and the American Association of Retired Persons (AARP), negotiate special rates for their members with selected hotel chains (see chapter 17). And many marketing partnerships are formed around discount hotel offers. Some banks offer lodging discounts as benefits with their credit cards (usually rebates of 5–10%, often with a minimum hotel bill of $100 or so).
- **Special rates.** Most hotels that serve business travelers offer *corporate* rates—often available to any traveler who can produce even vague evidence of corporate or professional employment when checking in (a business card will usually do). Regular corporate rates are available at thousands of hotels. However, they usually run no more than 20% off rack rate, and many are even stingier. They may even be a bit higher than the lowest rack rate, to cover some extra amenity: a "superior" room, an "executive" floor, or a few pleasant but minor perks.

Preferred rates are a special kind of corporate rate, specifically negotiated by a big travel agency, an independent booking service, or a travel club. Those rates may provide substantially better deals than ordinary corporate rates—average discounts are around 20%, and some are as high as 40%. However, they're available at far fewer hotels than regular corporate rates are (perhaps a fifth to a quarter as many) and only through the individual travel agencies, travel clubs, booking organizations, and corporate travel offices that have negotiated them. Furthermore, some preferred discounts are 10% or less.

FINDING PREFERRED RATES

Three kinds of outfit run preferred-rate programs:

Big travel-agency chains, such as American Express, Carlson Travel Network, Uniglobe, and US Travel, operate their own programs. Those chains have retail locations or franchises throughout the country; check your phone book for the location of the agency nearest you.

You can also arrange a preferred-rate discount through a travel agency that operates mainly by phone. American

Express, for example, provides phone-only services for travelers with *Gold* and *Platinum* cards, and both use different lists of hotels from the AmEx storefront agencies. Phone-only agencies that are bundled with your charge card can also get you the discounts.

Independent booking services (ABC and Thor 24, for instance) provide preferred-rate programs for independent travel agencies. For a fee, any agency can buy into the ABC program. Thor 24 is a consortium that provides a range of services beyond preferred rates, as well as operating preferred-rate programs for other consortiums (independent agencies banded together to pool their purchasing power).

Certain travel clubs, such as the Intl Airline Passengers Assn (IAPA), offer a preferred-rate program as one of their benefits. (Most clubs offer a half-price program instead.) A few, including IAPA, arrange their own deals; others use a service such as ABC.

To arrange a preferred discount, ask to see your travel agency's current preferred-rate directory when you plan a trip. Check the listings and prices for the places you want to visit, then have the agent make your reservations.

Alternatively, ask to see a display of available preferred rates on your travel agent's computer screen. The big multi-office chains and large independent networks (including ABC and Thor 24) have their own preferred rates listed in most of the airline-sponsored computer-reservation systems. Computer access to those rates is restricted to participating retail travel agencies.

If your regular travel agency is a branch of a big national chain, it will certainly have a preferred-rate program. Even an independent agency, if it claims to be full service, should have a program through ABC or a consortium such as Thor 24.

Some travel agencies confine preferred rates to their steady business clients. But you needn't work for the government or a big company to get a deal. Many agencies are happy to obtain preferred rates for anyone who asks. About the only kind of agency you shouldn't expect to offer a preferred-rate program is a minimum-service airfare discounter (a consolidator).

PICKING A HOTEL

In the United States at least, the most widely used hotel grades are probably those published in the *Official Hotel Guide* (*OHG*). When a tour brochure or newspaper ad promises a certain grade

WEATHER WAKE-UP

The Weather Channel's telephone service now provides wake-up calls. Just dial 1-900-WEATHER, select "option 6," specify a time within 24 hours, and you'll receive a wake-up call with the day's weather outlook. Away from home, you can call 1-800-WEATHER and bill the wake-up to a charge card. Either way, you pay about 95¢ for the service. You can't use the service from any location where incoming calls go through a switchboard.

of hotel, the claim is probably based on *OHG* classifications.

As *Decoding Official Hotel Guide Ratings* below shows, the system has three basic classes: Deluxe, First Class, and Tourist. Each of those, in turn, has subgroups, with Superior at the top, Moderate at the bottom, and the unadorned class name in the middle.

OHG ratings combine two elements: quality of lodgings (room size and standard of furnishings) and extent of facilities (number and size of public and meeting rooms, restaurants, and shops). When you use them, or any other hotel rating, be sensitive to nuance. The travel industry is reluctant to say flatly that any hotel is really bad. So the *OHG*

DECODING *OFFICIAL HOTEL GUIDE* RATINGS

DELUXE
Superior Deluxe. An exclusive and expensive luxury hotel, often palatial, offering the highest standards of service, accommodations, and facilities. Elegant and luxurious public rooms. A prestige address. Establishments in this category are among the world's top hotels.

Deluxe. An outstanding property offering many of the same features as Superior Deluxe. May be less grand and offer more reasonable rates than the Superior Deluxe properties, yet in many instances may be just as satisfactory. Safe to recommend to most discriminating clients.

Moderate Deluxe. Basically a Deluxe hotel, but with qualifications. In some cases, some accommodations or public areas may offer a less pronounced degree of luxury than that found in fully Deluxe properties. In other cases, the hotel may be a well-established famous name, depending heavily on past reputation. The more contemporary hotels may be heavily marketed to business clients, with fine accommodations and public rooms offering Deluxe standards in comfort, but with less emphasis on atmosphere and/or personal service.

FIRST CLASS
Superior First Class. An above-average hotel. May be an exceptionally well-maintained older hotel, more often a superior modern hotel specifically designed for the first-class market, with some outstanding features. Accommodations and public areas are expected to be tastefully furnished and very comfortable. May be a good value, especially if it is a commercial hotel. May be recommended to average clients and in most cases will satisfy the discriminating ones.

First Class. A dependable, comfortable hotel with standardized rooms, amenities, and public areas. May have superior executive level or wing. May be safely recommended to average clients not expecting Deluxe facilities or special ser-

and other sources often resort to code words and euphemisms. When the description says "may not be well kept" or "should only be used in a pinch," read it as "this hotel is a dog."

Competing ratings. *OHG* is published for the travel industry, not consumers. But quite a few hotel-classification systems are designed mainly for use by the traveling public:

- **Government agencies** assign hotel ratings in many countries, among them Australia, Austria, Belgium, France, Greece, Indonesia, Italy, Mexico, the Netherlands, New Zealand, Spain, Switzerland, and the United Kingdom. Those ratings may be noted in hotel and tour brochures

vices. Should also be satisfactory for better groups.

Limited-Service First Class. A property offering full first-class quality accommodations but limited public areas, food service, and facilities. Usually moderate in size, the hotel often utilizes a residential scale and architecture, and many offer complementary breakfast and evening cocktails in the lobby or in a small, informal restaurant. Geared to the individual business/pleasure traveler.

Moderate First Class. Essentially a First Class establishment with comfortable if somewhat simpler accommodations and public areas. May be lacking in some features (e.g., restaurant). While adequate, some of the rooms or public areas may tend to be basic and functional. Usually suitable for cost-conscious clients.

TOURIST

Superior Tourist Class. Primarily a budget property with mostly well-kept, functional accommodations, some up to First Class standards. Public rooms may be limited or nonexistent. Often just a place to sleep, but it may have some charming or intimate features. May be a good value. Should satisfy individuals (sometimes even discriminating ones) or groups on a budget.

Tourist Class. Strictly a budget operation with some facilities or features of Superior Tourist Class, but usually no (or very few) First Class accommodations. Should under no circumstances be recommended to fussy or discriminating clients. Should usually be used with caution.

Moderate Tourist Class. Low-budget operations, often quite old and may not be well-kept. Should only be used in a pinch if no other accommodations are available. Clients should always be cautioned what to expect.

(Reprinted with permission of the Official Hotel Guide.)

in place of, or in addition to, *OHG* ratings.

However, many important tourist countries (including Denmark, Finland, Germany, Japan, Norway, Sweden, and the United States) don't rate hotels. Travelers headed for those countries, as well as tour operators and travel agencies, have to rely on nongovernmental sources for ratings.

• **Certain major guidebooks**—including the *AAA Tour-Books, Michelin's Red Guides,* and the *Mobil Travel Guides* —have hotel ratings of their own. Others (for instance, the *Birnbaum, Frommer, Let's Go,* and *Lonely Planet* series for consumers, and the *Star Service* for travel professionals)

BEWARE THE TIMESHARE TRAP

Many of those "free trip" come-ons you get in the mail are from timeshare promoters who will foot the bill for your weekend to get a chance to give you a hard sell. Here's the pitch: For a modest price, you can "own" a luxury condo in some fabulous beach or ski area for a week every year. For variety, you may even be able to trade your timeshare for a week in some other equally fabulous area, even overseas. But watch out: Your investment in timeshare ownership may become a trap.

Timeshares are a refinement of the condo idea. In a condo, a building is carved up into individually owned units; in a timeshare, the ownership of those units is subdivided into weekly time slots. As with a condo, you pay a purchase price plus a prorated share of the maintenance costs of the individual apartment and the building's grounds.

Beyond that, however, timeshares aren't all alike. With some, you buy a specified week each year; with others, you have a floating time slot. You may get an actual deed to a specific occupancy right. Or you may simply join a "vacation club" that promises you space every year.

PAYMENTS AND HEADACHES

With your timeshare, you usually get a chance to join (and pay a fee to) one of two big international timeshare-exchange networks: RCI or Interval International. Through either, you can trade time with other exchange members throughout the world—your week in a ski area, say, for a week in the Caribbean or Europe.

Owning a week in your own vacation condo may not be any cheaper than simply renting. With maintenance and cleaning fees, membership in RCI or Interval International, and other miscellaneous fees and charges, the cost of your week can easily hit $500 to $600. Worse, it's almost impossible to sell. When you try, you're apt to be competing with the developer, who is often still selling units in

provide only descriptive prose.

All the systems are similar to some extent. Government systems tend to rely on such statistical measures as dimensions of guest rooms and public areas, percentage of rooms with bath, and the like. The *OHG* and the guidebooks lean more on the personal judgments of authors, professional inspectors, or voluntary reports from travelers, travel agents, and travel writers.

FOR BUDGET TRAVELERS. The *OHG* system doesn't serve the needs of all travelers—it doesn't even list many low-end hotels. But in many parts of the world, hotels more basic than those *OHG* rates can be quite adequate. Budget travelers in Paris, for instance,

---

your program. Owners who try to walk away lose their investment, yet the timeshare's maintenance fees continue to mount. If there's a foreclosure, there may be a blot on the owner's credit record.

Once you've bought in, you're again in competition with the developer. When you try to claim a floating time slot, you may find that the developer tries to rent the most desirable weeks to nonowners instead. Some developers actually oversell a timeshare, figuring that a certain percentage of owners won't find a suitable time to visit. If you try to rent out your time slot on your own, the developer may try to block you—with obstacles as broad as a flat ban on rentals by individual owners, or as small as refusing to have someone on hand to give the keys to a renter. You also have very little control over the property you supposedly own.

BUYING OR SELLING

If despite those problems you still like the timeshare idea, buy a resale unit from an individual owner. There are many more sellers than buyers, so you should be able to drive a hard bargain. In some cases, you might even be able to take ownership merely by assuming the current owner's long-term maintenance obligation.

To find a motivated private seller, check the ads in newsletters and local papers in resort areas. You might also nose around some of the more attractive timeshare complexes—talking to present owners, checking bulletin boards, and looking for notices. A few real estate brokers also specialize in timeshares.

Anyone considering buying or selling a timeshare should also join the Resort Property Owners Association (RPOA), Box 2395, Northbrook IL 60062; 847-291-0710; $20 per calendar year. The group represents property owners and conducts extensive studies of timeshare markets and price trends.

can be perfectly happy in hotels with a government rating of only 1 or 2 stars, if they know what to expect. Similarly, travelers in the United States find budget hostelries a great buy even at list price. (See chapter 16.)

WHERE TO FIND IT

CHARGE-CARD TRAVEL SERVICES

American Express: Select Rates; *Gold* cardholders, 800-327-2177; *Platinum* cardholders, 800-443-7672.

CHAIN AGENCIES

American Express Vacations: P.O. Box 1525, Ft Lauderdale, FL 33302; 800-241-1700. Check phone directory for local American Express office or call travel agent.

BTI Americas: 400 Skokie Blvd, Northbrook IL 60062. Call 847-480-8400 for the name of a participating travel agent nearest you.

Carlson Travel Network: Carlson Pkwy, P.O. Box 59159, Minneapolis 55451; 800-227-5766 for name of agent nearest you.

Uniglobe Travel Intl: Key Cities Program. Call 604-662-3800 for name of participating travel agent near you.

Intl Airline Passengers Assn (IAPA): Box 870188, Dallas 75287; 800-527-5888; annual dues $99-799 (foreign plan); $149 (domestic plan) with travel insurance, $79 for either plan without the insurance; *AE, DC, MC, V.*

INDEPENDENT BOOKING SERVICES

ABC Corporate Services, a division of Reed Travel Group: Call 800-722-5179 for the name of the agency nearest you.

Thor 24: Call 800-862-2111 for the name of the agency nearest you.

This chapter was adapted from the 1996 edition of Consumer Reports Best Travel Deals.

Half-Price Hotels: Savings Coast to Coast

Membership in a half-price hotel program is one of the standard tools in a frugal traveler's kit. The ID card you receive is a key to 50% discounts—about the biggest you can expect through any source—at thousands of North American hotels. Typically, your savings from just one or two nights' use will more than pay for the membership fee (typically $20–100). Beyond that, what you save is gravy.

Like most other tools, a half-price program isn't usable in every situation. You won't get 50% off every time and in every place. Discounts are "subject to availability": Hotels halve their regular rates only when they can't fill all their rooms at full price. Furthermore, the rack rate (or list price) from which the discount is calculated may be a phony, inflated figure that nobody pays except at rare times when demand far exceeds supply.

Still, half-price programs pay off well enough to justify their cost. Every traveler, we think, should join at least one of them.

Every program we cover here lists at least a few hotels outside North America. But for the best overseas coverage, you'll be better off with one of the specialized overseas directories (see chapter 20).

A CLOSER LOOK

Hotels that give half-price rates try to get high list prices from walk-in customers while luring careful shoppers with big price breaks. Here's how they do it:

- Program operators sign up hotels that agree to cut their rates in half whenever they expect to be less than about 80% full. That way, the hotels generate some income from rooms that might otherwise go unrented.
- Travelers enroll in a "club" or buy a discount directory. The program operator then gives them a list of participating hotels plus an identification card that's good for at least a year. The bigger programs now list upward of 2000 hotels in the US and Canada, plus some overseas locations.

Before a trip, you check your program's directory for participating hotels along your itinerary. You call each appealing-looking one directly, telling the reservationist which half-price program you're using and asking if a discount room rate is available when you want it. If one is, you make your reservation (guaranteed by charge card, if necessary). On checking in, you show your ID card; you pay when you leave by cash or charge card.

Hotels sometimes offer a lesser discount if a half-price discount isn't available when you want it. You can try for a different date or check with another hotel if that's not acceptable.

Typically, a half-price ID is good for only one room a night—if you're traveling in a party that requires two or more rooms, you usually need a separate membership for each room. Half-price discounts can't be combined with any other reductions—corporate, senior, or weekend discounts, say. And half-price rates aren't commissionable, so your travel agency won't arrange them for you.

Most programs offer a wide choice of hotels—independent and chain; budget, midpriced, and deluxe; downtown, suburban, airport, and highway. The directories give some indication of each hotel's price range, usually with a symbol indicating a general price class. The entry for each individual hotel typically includes its address, phone number (*Privilege Card* also lists fax numbers) and, in some, a brief list of the services the hotel provides.

Most hotels offer half-price rates on any day of the year, subject to availability. Some directories include a supplementary list of hotels where discounts are available only off-season, or on weekends (city hotels) or weekdays (resorts); others mix full-time and heavily restricted hotels together. A few hotels impose a minimum or maximum stay.

It's well to be aware of a few facts:
• There's a fair amount of in-and-out among participants. Don't be surprised if the reservationist at a listed hotel tells you that it no longer honors a program's card.
• Don't expect to get a half-price room merely by mentioning the name of a big program: Hotel clerks generally ask you to produce a valid card.
• You must usually call ahead—at least a few hours—for a reservation, not just show up at the desk.
• That "subject to availability" limitation is real: You won't get a discount when a hotel expects to be busy. Don't join a program expecting to pay half-price for all your stays.

THE PROGRAM TO PICK

Choose the program with the most hotels in the areas you plan to visit. Unless you need a tie-breaking factor, don't pick a program because it has a low membership fee: Just one extra night at half price can more than counterbalance the extra cost of a pricey program.

The table on page 172 shows the number of North American hotels in the US, Canada, the Caribbean, and Mexico in each program's directory as of summer 1996. (The rest of this chapter is based on *CRTL's* March 1995 report; we don't expect much change for 1997.)

The table includes hotels that offer half-price rates seasonally as well as those that give year-round deals. There really isn't much difference in room availability: A hotel may claim it gives year-round discounts yet be full enough during its peak season to make the discount period, in effect, seasonal. Furthermore, some hotels will allow the discount, if business is slow, even on dates listed as not valid.

All the programs listed accept enrollments (or sell directories and coupon books) by phone. Except as noted, all directories and memberships are valid for one year from date of purchase. Some of the programs are also included as one of the benefits of full-service or special-interest travel clubs and department-store or oil-company travel programs. And some are occasionally offered as premiums in promotions and charity drives, or as an employee benefit through corporate personnel offices.

CARTE ROYALE. This relatively small program offers almost entirely First Class or better hotels (based on *Official Hotel Guide* ratings; see chapter 14), or equivalent hotel-industry or AAA ratings. It lists a few top-notch hotels that aren't available from other programs. Other hotel discounts: preferred and corporate rates (25–40% off) at over 3000 hotels through affiliated travel agency.

Extras: car-rental discounts (10–20%) from Alamo, Avis, Budget, Hertz and National; access to a rebating travel

agency (about 5% off virtually any travel purchase, plus last-minute cruise deals). $39.95 (*MC, V*). 800-847-7002.

ENCORE. One of the largest travel clubs featuring over 5500 quality hotels, motels, resorts, and country inns worldwide that offer up to 50% off. Other hotel deals include chain-wide 30% discounts at participating Choice Hotels and Vagabond Inns.

Extras: savings of up to 50% on dining at over 500 restaurants at participating hotels; car rental discounts from Alamo, Avis, Hertz, and National; two American Airlines discount certificates each good for up to $90 off per ticket; tour packages to major resort areas; membership newsletter; *ValueLine* trip publication offering discounted trip packages; $750 in cashback certificates redeemable on travel packages; savings of up to 50% at family leisure attractions across the US; customized member travel planner; and exclusive collection of over 200 getaway "Escape" packages. $49.95 per year (*AE, Disc, MC, V*). *Villas of the World* villa/condo rental program available for an additional $60. 800-638-0930.

ENTERTAINMENT PUBLICATIONS. Last year, this program reinforced its number-one position with the all-new *Ultimate Travel Savings Directory*, $59.95, which lists almost 4500 hotels in North America. That's a good 1000 more than either of its top rivals, *Encore* or *ITC-50*. In addition, the new book throws in virtually all of *Entertainment's* 800-plus European hotels as well as the program's listings in Asia and the Middle East—in effect, it offers virtually the entire *Entertainment* hotel inventory in one small volume.

Extras: The new book also includes four American Airlines coupons (up to $75 off), two Continental coupons (up to $125 off), and an assortment of cruise, car-rental, and resort coupons. However, it omits restaurant deals. For travelers willing to settle for a smaller sample of half-price offerings, the smaller *National Hotel & Dining Directory* is still available at $37.95: It incorporates some restaurant deals as well as hotel and miscellaneous coupons.

Entertainment also continues to sell more than 130 regional editions ($28–53; see Entertainment's Empire, below). A local book lists fewer hotels than the national directories, but it offers quite a few more restaurant discounts—typically 20–25% off the total bill, a free appetizer or dessert, or twofers—as well as similar deals from visitor attractions and other travel and auto-motive services. The local books also include the American and Continental dollars-off coupons.

Entertainment is your top option

ENTERTAINMENT's EMPIRE

In addition to its national and European directories, *Entertainment Publications* offers local coupon books for more than 130 individual cities. They're especially useful for the nonhotel discount offers: restaurants, admissions, rental cars, and discount coupons on American and Continental airlines. Directories cost $28–53 each. Here's a list of local directories, as published in *CRTL,* March 1995:

Arizona: Phoenix, Tucson/Southern Arizona. **Arkansas:** Little Rock. **California:** Bakersfield, East Bay/Alameda County, East Bay/Contra Costa County, Fresno/Central Valley, Long Beach, Los Angeles W/Downtown, Marin County/North Bay, Monterey Peninsula/Santa Cruz, Orange County Central N, Orange County Central S, Palm Springs, Sacramento/Gold Country, San Diego County, San Fernando Valley, San Francisco/San Mateo, San Gabriel/Pomona valleys, San Jose/Santa Clara County, Santa Barbara, Solano County, Sonoma/Napa, Stockton/Modesto. **Colorado:** Denver. **Connecticut:** Fairfield County, Hartford, New Haven/New London.

Delaware: Delaware. **DC:** DC/Maryland, DC/N Virginia. **Florida:** Ft Lauderdale, Ft Myers, Jacksonville, Miami, Orlando, St Petersburg/Clearwater, Sarasota, Tampa Bay, West Palm Beach. **Georgia:** Atlanta. **Hawaii:** Hawaii, Hawaii Visitors. **Idaho:** Boise. **Illinois:** Central Illinois, Chicago N, Chicago NW, Chicago S/SW, Chicago W. **Indiana:** Ft Wayne, Indiana NW, Indianapolis, South Bend. **Iowa:** Des Moines. **Kansas:** Kansas City, Wichita. **Kentucky:** Louisville. **Louisiana:** New Orleans. **Maryland:** Baltimore N, Baltimore S. **Massachusetts:** Boston N, Boston S, Boston W. **Michigan:** Detroit E, Detroit NW, Detroit W/SW, Grand Rapids. **Minnesota:**

for reach and diversity. But to take advantage of all the deals, you'd need to buy the *Ultimate* directory (for widest hotel coverage, including overseas), a local directory for any city you plan to visit extensively (for restaurants and attractions), and the local directory for your home area. After you buy one book, any other book (other than *Ultimate*) is $28, including shipping (*MC, V*). 800-445-4137.

GREAT AMERICAN TRAVELER. Often sold or distributed through employers, travel clubs, and other channels, this program offers a mix of budget, moderate, and First Class hotels.

Extras: car-rental discounts from Alamo, Budget, and National; Northwest discount offer (up to $100 off one ticket). $49.95 (*AE, Disc, MC, V*). For an extra $49.95 a year, you can get a *Golf Access* membership, with discounts of up to 50% on fees at courses in the US and Canada. Also offers *Recreation Access* membership with discounts up to 50% on various recreation activities such as hot-air balloon rides, river

Minneapolis. **Missouri:** St Louis. **Nebraska:** Omaha. **Nevada:** Lake Tahoe/Reno, Las Vegas. **New Jersey:** New Jersey Central/Monmouth, New Jersey Central/Middlesex, New Jersey N/Bergen, New Jersey N/Essex, New Jersey N/Morris, New Jersey S. **New Mexico:** Albuquerque/Santa Fe.

New York: Albany, Brooklyn, Buffalo, Long Island/Nassau County, Long Island/Suffolk County, Lower Hudson Valley, Mid Hudson Valley, NYC/Manhattan, NYC/Queens, Rochester, Staten Island, Syracuse/Central NY State. **North Carolina:** Charlotte. **Ohio:** Akron, Canton, Cincinnati, Cincinnati/N Kentucky, Cleveland, Columbus/Central Ohio, Dayton/Springfield, Toledo. **Oklahoma:** Oklahoma City, Tulsa/Green County. **Oregon:** Greater Oregon, Portland. **Pennsylvania:** Bucks/Montgomery, Erie, Harrisburg, Lancaster/York, Lehigh Valley, NE Pennsylvania, Philadelphia E, Philadelphia W, Pittsburgh, Reading/Pottsville. **Tennessee:** Memphis, Nashville. **Texas:** Austin, Corpus Christi, Dallas, Ft Worth, Houston, Houston N/NW, NASA/Galveston Bay Area, San Antonio. **Utah:** Salt Lake City. **Vermont:** Vermont. **Virginia:** Norfolk/Virginia Beach, Richmond. **Washington:** N Puget Sound, S Puget Sound/Peninsula, Seattle, Spokane/Inland Empire. **Wisconsin:** Appleton/Green Bay, Madison, Milwaukee.

Canada: Calgary, Edmonton, Hamilton/Burlington/Oakville, Montreal/Laval/Laurentians, Montreal/S Shore/Eastern Townships, Montreal/West Island, Okanagan, Ottawa/Outaouais, Toronto Central, Toronto W Central, Vancouver Island, Vancouver N Central, Vancouver S Central, Winnipeg.

DISCOUNTS IN NORTH AMERICA*

	CARTE ROYALE	ENCORE	ENTER. PUBS. (a)	GREAT AMER. TRAV.	IMPULSE	ITC-50	PRIV. CARD	QUEST	SEE AMER.
Alabama	3	25	20	17	3	20	13	19	17
Alaska	0	7	7	1	1	13	4	4	3
Arizona	14	99	107	45	11	77	38	58	37
Arkansas	0	8	10	4	2	7	9	8	5
California	122	522	845	286	48	480	374	378	280
Colorado	17	83	81	37	9	67	39	50	52
Connecticut	2	43	54	18	4	50	15	26	19
Delaware	1	8	13	4	1	3	1	5	4
Dist of Columbia	8	35	34	21	3	30	24	21	17
Florida	52	421	380	225	32	415	222	233	212
Georgia	13	77	63	40	7	57	52	49	42
Hawaii	37	97	73	64	15	94	45	69	18
Idaho	—	10	29	5	1	11	2	9	5
Illinois	10	70	98	32	9	65	41	48	39
Indiana	7	50	54	29	4	42	12	27	25
Iowa	—	12	19	9	2	9	7	10	5
Kansas	2	19	23	16	4	10	8	15	14
Kentucky	1	22	24	11	2	21	8	10	10
Louisiana	5	56	31	25	4	29	18	16	29
Maine	—	18	13	6	2	37	5	10	6
Maryland	10	56	61	35	7	55	29	25	37
Massachusetts	15	60	79	36	11	64	32	29	37
Michigan	9	75	96	46	10	64	39	41	22
Minnesota	2	49	61	32	5	39	16	25	15
Mississippi	—	8	5	2	1	6	2	2	6
Missouri	3	53	59	68	5	51	33	33	20
Montana	1	9	10	3	1	30	3	13	3
Nebraska	—	15	7	6	1	6	5	7	6
Nevada	5	18	47	12	4	15	8	14	10
New Hampshire	3	18	18	9	3	29	7	14	13
New Jersey	6	74	100	49	6	69	36	54	48
New Mexico	5	35	41	20	4	23	24	16	7
New York	14	119	158	52	11	122	64	64	69
North Carolina	15	47	44	43	5	63	41	49	40
North Dakota	—	4	5	1	0	2	1	—	3
Ohio	15	84	112	60	6	65	48	45	35
Oklahoma	3	22	32	14	2	17	12	16	14
Oregon	9	36	80	21	5	35	10	33	14
Pennsylvania	9	106	111	54	12	115	52	50	51
Rhode Island	—	6	9	6	2	9	3	4	5
South Carolina	2	51	44	36	3	43	26	33	12
South Dakota	—	9	6	6	1	6	4	4	6
Tennessee	3	35	29	19	6	36	18	21	26
Texas	18	142	181	83	16	117	86	89	42
Utah	1	28	24	14	6	20	11	17	10
Vermont	4	24	31	8	5	33	21	11	13
Virginia	8	97	102	55	6	100	40	53	54
Washington	10	51	153	30	8	56	24	60	20
West Virginia	—	13	6	6	1	14	7	7	6
Wisconsin	3	38	44	23	2	41	18	16	15
Wyoming	1	9	4	6	1	11	4	6	7
Total US	**468**	**3073**	**3737**	**1750**	**320**	**2893**	**1661**	**1918**	**1505**
Canada	46	308	477	57	28	377	112	100	80
Caribbean	12	68	35	4	16	37	47	8	2
Mexico	26	22	242	54	1	120	44	33	18
Total N America	**552**	**3471**	**4491**	**1865**	**363**	**3427**	**1874**	**2059**	**1605**

*As of mid-1996; subject to change.
(a) As listed in *Entertainment's Ultimate Travel Savings Directory*.

rafting, miniature golf, and theme parks (also $49.95). 800-548-2812.

IMPULSE. Like *Carte Royale,* this program concentrates on a small number of upscale hotels. Other hotel deals: weekend discounts at Residence Inns (50% off weekday rates or 10% off promotional rates), 10% discounts at certain Choice Hotels.

Extras: discounts on Avis and National car rentals. $49 (*MC, V*). 303-741-2457.

ITC-50. Among the largest programs, this one is most widely available as a membership benefit of such major motor clubs as Allstate, Amoco, First Card Road Security, Gulf, Sears, Shell, Sun Travel Club, and Texaco.

Extras: dining-discount program offering 20–50% reductions at more than 1000 restaurants; car-rental discounts through Avis, Budget, Hertz, and National. $49 (*AE, MC, V*). 800-342-0558.

PRIVILEGE CARD. This program includes a full-service travel agency (offering discounts on airlines, car rentals, and cruises), discount calling card services, low-cost condo rentals, and an Internet directory. It's available as a premium from the Amateur Golfers Assn Intl, American Federation of Teachers, Natl Automobile Assn, and the National Alliance of Senior Citizens. Other hotel deals: discounts (10–30%) at participating Best Western, Days Inn, Howard Johnson/HoJo, and Ramada hotels.

Extras: attraction and theme park discounts (15%); car-rental discounts (up to 15%) at Alamo, Avis, Hertz, and Value; discounts on cruises through affiliated travel agency; rebate coupons for airline tickets booked through affiliated travel agency. $74.95 (*AE, MC, V*). 800-236-9732.

QUEST. This program offers over 2000 participating half-price hotels in North America and abroad. A membership includes the *Quest Condo Program* (50% off weekly rates) and chainwide savings of 10% with a number of national chains.

Extras: 25% dining discounts at participating *Quest* hotel restaurants; car rental discounts with Alamo, Hertz, and National; airfare, cruise, and vacation package savings, plus travel agency services at more than 1200 Carlson Wagonlit Travel agency locations. Quarterly directory updates, including additional travel savings certificates, are included in the fee. $99 (*AE, Disc, MC, V*). 800-742-4100.

SEE AMERICA. Distributed mainly as an incentive for people to join other travel clubs or as a sales premium, this program offers hotels varying from budget to moderate. As with all discount deals, it's best to call ahead for the specifics of each program.

Extras: discounts (typically 50%) at some hotel restaurants. $99.95 (*AE, DC, Disc, V*). 410-653-2616.

This chapter was adapted from the Consumer Reports Travel Letter *article "Half-Price Blockbuster" (September 1996) and the 1996 edition of* Consumer Reports Best Travel Deals.

HOTEL BROKERS FOR EASY DISCOUNTS

Want a good hotel deal without having to fuss with memberships and directories? Just call a hotel broker (*CRTL's* term for a specific type of hotel discounter), mention where you're heading, and ask what's available. Unless there's a big convention in town, chances are that a broker will be able to get you a discounted room in at least one hotel. (The discount can be as much as 50% off the hotel's asking price.) The service costs you nothing; the hotel pays the broker's fee.

Of course, brokers can't solve all your hotel problems. They generally handle a limited number of hotels—usually midpriced and up—in a limited number of big cities. When you're looking for deals in small cities and resort areas or along the highway, you're better off with a 50%-off or preferred-rate program (see chapters 14 and 15), or perhaps a senior discount or a hotel's own promotion.

Brokers may not offer rock-bottom deals, either. You may get a lower rate through a half-price program or by calling a hotel directly to ask for current promotions. Hotels sometimes volunteer a promotional rate—well below their rack rate—to anyone who calls. The only way you can be sure that a broker's rate (or any other discount) is a good deal is to compare it with the hotel's own quote for the specific time you're considering.

Still, brokers usually provide an easy way to get at least a reasonably good deal—even when hotels black out half-price rates, as they do when they expect to be nearly full. Some brokers are especially adept at finding last-minute rooms when your direct calls to hotels are met with "Sorry, sold out."

ARRANGING THE DISCOUNT

Hotel brokers work in various ways:

- Some arrange preferred rates, typically 10–40% off rack (list-price) rates. Those are much the same deals big travel agencies negotiate for their corporate clients. Hotels usually sign up for preferred-rate programs on a yearly basis.

- Some operate like airfare consolidators. They get deals from hotels when business is slow, so their lists often change from week to week. But the discounts can be big—sometimes more than 50%.
- And some are wholesalers: They sell rooms to independent travelers at the same rate they sell them in package tours. Once set, a wholesaler's list tends to remain stable for at least a year. Discounts usually run 10–40%. Unlike other brokers, wholesalers typically quote an all-in rate that includes tax and service charges.
- Most brokers simply act as agents, selling whatever inventory the hotels give them. A few, however, pay the hotels up front for blocks of rooms. They may have rooms even when a hotel says it's full.
- Some brokers accept bookings from (and give commissions to) travel agencies. Others deal only with individual travelers.

How you pay for your room depends on the broker: When you book a room through a preferred-rate or consolidator-style broker, the broker ordinarily just makes a reservation: You pay the hotel when you check out. There's usually no fee if you cancel before the cancellation deadline—or even if you don't show up, if you haven't guaranteed. Brokers that work that way are noted in the listings as *pay at hotel*.

With wholesale brokers and those who sign up for blocks of rooms, you must usually prepay the full room charge to the broker, by major charge card or check. The broker mails you a room voucher or has it held at the hotel for your arrival. The listings note those brokers as *prepay/voucher* and list the cards they accept. There's usually a stiff cancellation penalty.

If you book through a wholesale broker, you must also cancel through the broker.

MULTICITY SPECIALISTS

Brokers in this group, listed alphabetically, arrange deals in at least two big-city areas. Some cover only a few cities; others deal with dozens of cities worldwide.

Accommodations Express, 801 Asbury Ave, Ocean City NJ 08226; 800-444-7666, fax 609-525-0111, E-mail *accom@acy.digex.net,* Web site *http:// www.accommodationsxpress.com.* Arranges preferred rates in Atlantic City, Boston, Chicago, Ft Lauderdale, Las Vegas, Los Angeles, Miami Beach, New Orleans, New York, Orlando, Philadelphia, San Francisco, and Washington DC. Also has last-minute deals and room blocks. Prepay/voucher (for gift certificates, call 800-831-4760); *AE, MC, V.*

California Reservations, 165 8th St, Suite 201, San Francisco 94103; 800-576-0003, 415-252-1107, fax 415-252-1483, E-mail *cal@cal-res.com.* Arranges preferred rates in Anaheim/ Orange County, Carmel/Monterey, Fresno/Central Valley, Los Angeles, Napa/Sonoma Valleys, Palm Springs, Portland OR, Reno, Sacramento, San Diego, San Francisco Bay Area, San Jose, Santa Barbara, Seattle, Vancouver, and Yosemite. Also has last-minute deals and room blocks at some hotels. Pay at hotel.

Central Reservation Service (CRS), 505 Maitland Ave, Suite 100, Altamonte Springs FL 32701; 800-548-3311, 407-339-4116, fax 407-339-4736, E-mail *crs@reservation-services.com,* Web site *http://www.reservation-services.com.* Arranges preferred rates in Ft Lauderdale, Los Angeles, Miami, New York, Orlando area, and San Francisco. Has 24-hour courtesy phones at LaGuardia, Miami Intl, Newark, Orlando, and San Francisco Intl airports. Staff is bilingual (English/Spanish). Pay at hotel.

Express Reservations, 3800 Arapahoe, Boulder CO 80303; 800-356-1123, 303-440-8481, fax 303-440-0166, E-mail *info@express-res.com,* Web site *http://www.express-res.com.* Arranges preferred rates in the Los Angeles area and New York—mainly at moderate to deluxe hotels. Pay at hotel.

Hotel Reservations Network (HRN), 8140 Walnut Hill Lane, Suite 203, Dallas 75231; 800-964-6835, 214-361-7311, fax 214-361-7299, Web site *http://www.hoteldiscount.com.* Arranges preferred rates in Anaheim, Boston, Chicago, London, Los Angeles, Miami, New Orleans, New York, Orlando, Paris, San Diego, San Francisco, and Washington DC. Also has room blocks. Awards 500 frequent-flier miles on Delta, USAir, Northwest, or Continental when three or more nights are booked (program subject to change). Prepay/voucher; *AE, Disc, MC, V.*

Players Express Vacations, 2980 W Meade Avenue, Suite A, Las Vegas NV 89102; 800-458-6161, 702-365-1414, fax 702-365-1448. Arranges preferred rates and packages in several areas in California, Florida, Hawaii, Nevada; also serves Branson MO, Montreal, New Orleans, Puerto Vallarta. Prepay/voucher; *AE, Disc, MC, V.*

Quikbook, 381 Park Ave S, NYC 10016; 800-789-9887, 212-532-1660, fax 212-532-1556. Arranges preferred rates in Atlanta, Boston, Chicago, Los Angeles, New York, San Francisco, and Washington DC. Pay at hotel.

Room Finders USA, 112 N Rampart St, New Orleans 70116; 800-473-7829, 504-522-9234, fax 504-529-1948, Web site *http://www.accesscom.net/roomfinders/.* Arranges preferred rates in Cancun, Chicago, and New Orleans. Prepay/voucher; *AE, Disc, MC, V.*

RMC Travel, 424 Madison Ave, Suite

FODOR BOOKS ROOMS

In addition to selecting a hotel from Fodor's extensive series of travel guides, readers can now reserve a room through Fodor's: You simply call 800-446-6245, 24 hours a day, seven days a week. The service is a joint venture of Fodor's and Intl Reservations Services Ltd. It covers hotels in the US and Intl.

Fodor's can provide "regular" discounts, such as senior (AARP) rate cuts or day-of-week specials, which are available to just about anyone. The service looks most useful for booking low-priced lodgings that normally don't give discounts beyond the standard senior or day-of-week deals. At pricier hotels, you're likely to get a better rate through some other program.

705, NYC 10017; 800-245-5738, 212-754-6560, fax 212-754-6571. Arranges preferred rates in Anaheim, Atlanta, Boston, Chicago, Los Angeles, Montreal, New York, Philadelphia, Phoenix/Scottsdale, San Diego, San Francisco, Seattle, Vancouver, Washington DC, and most other major North American cities. Also has deals in many resort cities, including Carmel, Myrtle Beach, Sun Valley, and Tahoe. Reservations should be made at least 10 days prior to departure. Prepay/voucher; *AE, Disc, MC, V.*

LOCAL BROKERS

Nine US visitor destinations are covered by one or another local broker. (They're usually covered by one or more of the multicity brokers, too.)

• ATLANTIC CITY
Atlantic City Toll-Free Reservations, Box 665, Northfield NJ 08225; 800-833-7070, fax 609-646-8655. Arranges preferred rates. Prepay/voucher; *AE, Disc, MC, V.*

Also see *Accommodations Express.*

• BOSTON
Citywide Reservation Services, 25 Huntington Ave, Suite 500, Boston 02116; 800-468-3593, 617-267-7424, fax 617-267-9408. Arranges preferred rates. Also serves other areas in New England, New York, and Washington; has room blocks. Pay at hotel.

Meegan Reservation Service, 300 Terminal C, Logan Intl Airport, East Boston 02128; 800-332-3026, 617-569-3800, fax 617-561-4840. Arranges preferred rates. Current deals include

budget to deluxe hotels at 25–50% off regular rates. Pay at hotel.

Also see *Accommodations Express, Hotel Reservations Network, Quikbook, RMC.*

• BRANSON MO
Branson Nights Reservations, 714 State Highway 248, Suite 8, Branson MO 65616; 800-329-9999, 417-335-6971, fax 417-335-6025. Arranges preferred rates. Also sells packages that include local show tickets. Prepay/voucher; *AE, Disc, MC, V.*

Also see *Players Express.*

• CHICAGO
Hot Rooms, 1 E Erie St, Suite 225, Chicago 60611; 800-468-3500, 312-468-7666, fax 312-649-0559, E-mail *Hotrooms@aol.com.* Arranges preferred rates. $25 cancellation fee anytime after booking. Pay at hotel.

Also see *Accommodations Express, Hotel Reservations Network, Quikbook, Room Finders, RMC.*

• KANSAS CITY MO
Kansas City Hotel Reservation Service, 4545 Worlds of Fun Ave, Kansas City MO 64161; 800-877-4386, 816-453-7280, fax 816-454-4655. Arranges preferred rates. Pay at hotel.

• LAS VEGAS–LAUGHLIN
Las Vegas Reservations, 101 Convention Center Drive, Suite P-125, Las Vegas NV 89109; 800-862-1155, 702-737-7621, fax 702-737-5167. Arranges preferred and regular rates. Also provides services for shows, tours, and

weddings (plus reservations in Hawaii). Prepay/voucher; *AE*, *MC*, *V*. Pay at hotel.

Also see *Accommodations Express, Players Express.*

• SAN DIEGO
San Diego Hotel Reservations (SDHR), 7380 Clairemont Mesa Blvd, Suite 218, San Diego 92111; 800-728-3227, 619-627-9300, fax 619-627-9405, Web site *http://www.savecash.com.* Arranges preferred rates in the San Diego area. Pay at hotel.

Also see *California Reservations, Hotel Reservations Network, RMC.*

• SAN FRANCISCO
San Francisco Reservations, 22 2nd St, San Francisco 94105; 800-677-1500, 415-227-1500, fax 415-227-1521, Web site *http://www.hotelres.com.* Arranges preferred rates, last-minute bookings, and bookings (from over 225 hotels) when space is tight. Pay at hotel.

Also see *California Reservations, Central Reservation Service, Hotel Reservations Network, Players Express, Quikbook, RMC.*

• WASHINGTON DC
Capitol Reservations, 1730 Rhode Island Ave NW, Suite 114, Washington DC 20036; 800-847-4832, 202-452-1270, fax 202-452-0537, Web site *http:// www.hotelsdc.com.* Arranges preferred rates; also last-minute deals. Pay at hotel.

Washington DC Accommodations, 1534 U St NW, Washington DC 20009; 800-554-2220, 202-289-2220, fax 202-483-4436. Arranges preferred rates. Pay at hotel.

Also see *Accommodations Express,*

Hotel Reservations Network, Quikbook, RMC.

OVERSEAS OPTIONS
A few brokers specialize in Europe or Asia:

• EUROPE
Hotels Plus, 2205 Thames Dr, Conyers GA 30208; 800-235-0909, 770-929-1102, fax 800-644-0422. Arranges preferred rates in London, Paris, Rome, and other major European cities. Prepay/ voucher; *AE*, *MC*, *V*.

Intl Marketing & Travel Concepts (IMTC), 3025 Maple Drive, Suite 5, Atlanta 30305; 800-790-4682, 404-240-0949, fax 404-240-0948, E-mail *imtc @mindspring.com.* Arranges preferred rates in major European cities. Prepay/ voucher; checks only.

Also see *Hotel Reservations Network, VacationLand.*

• ASIA/PACIFIC
Travel Interlink, 4348 Van Nuys Blvd, #206, Sherman Oaks CA 91403; 800-888-5898, 818-986-8354, fax 800-888-0191, 818-986-8345, E-mail *travelink @aol.com* or *travelink@ix.netcom.com.* Arranges preferred rates in Australia, Bangladesh, Bhutan, Brunei, Burma, Cambodia, China, Fiji, Guam, Hong Kong, India, Indonesia, Japan, Korea, Laos, Macau, Malaysia, Maldives, Mongolia, New Zealand, Nepal, Pakistan, Palau, Papua New Guinea, Philippines, Samoa, Singapore, Sri Lanka, Tahiti, Taiwan, Thailand, Tibet, Tonga, Vanuatu, and Vietnam. Prepay/voucher; *Disc, MC, V.*

VacationLand, 150 Post St, Suite 680, San Francisco 94108; 800-245-

0050, 415-788-0503, fax 415-788-0103. Arranges preferred rates in Asia, Australia, and major European cities. Prepay/voucher; no cards. Ask for *Hotemart* program.

This chapter was adapted from the Consumer Reports Travel Letter *article "Hotel Brokers for Easy Discounts" (April 1996).*

REWARDS FOR FREQUENT HOTEL STAYS

Frequent-stay programs have a simple aim: to reward good customers with free stays and other payoffs. Some programs are pretty generous, others are quite stingy. But either way, just about any hotel program can provide benefits worth having, at least if you travel frequently. While it usually doesn't pay to forgo a good hotel discount for frequent-stay benefits, they can tip the balance when you need a tie-breaker.

This chapter looks at some 30 frequent-stay plans that let you earn credit at any participating hotel, pool the credit earned at different locations into a single account, and use it for a free stay at any participating hotel (or for some other award). We excluded programs that offer benefits only for repeated stays at one hotel, and those that offer discounts or perks (but not free stays) to corporate clients and other major customers.

The programs we're reporting on fall into two broad groups:

- Programs with an elaborate schedule of earning options and awards and an extensive list of partners. Those resemble the frequent-flier programs of big airlines.
- Programs with just one primary benefit—one free night after you log a specified number of paid nights. Those are like the simple frequent-flier programs run by Southwest and some of the small, low-fare lines.

WHAT YOU SPEND . . .

Earning Credit, pages 182–85, shows how your hotel and other expenditures can fatten your frequent-stay account. A few highlights:

- Most of the programs give you credits, points, or whatever for each night you stay. A few give a fixed amount of credit per stay, regardless of length. Some base credit on the number of dollars you spend at the hotel—on lodgings plus, in several cases, other hotel services and even merchandise at a hotel gift shop. Westin's premium program gives you both lodging- and dollar-based points.
- About half the programs credit you for rooms occupied at discount rates

such as preferred, senior, and half-price rates (though a few of those don't give credit for the deepest discounts). The others typically limit credit to travelers who pay rack (list-price) rate or the hotel's published corporate rate.

- Only a few programs give additional hotel credit for using partner car-rental companies or airlines (in conjunction with a hotel stay).
- Several chains give credit in partner-airline programs for hotel stays. Of those, Hilton, Red Lion, and Westin allow members of their programs to double dip—travelers can rack up both hotel and airline credit for the same stay. With most other programs, you must choose between getting hotel or airline credit for any given stay. But with Marriott, you sign up at the outset for hotel credit or airline credit and must stick with your choice.

- A few programs let members earn very-frequent-stay status (similar to very-frequent-flier status in airline programs). VFS members enjoy faster earning or more generous benefits. We list the first VFS levels for Sheraton and Westin separately, because

CRUNCHING THE NUMBERS

Because of their tremendous popularity, airline frequent-flier programs are the yardstick for frequent-traveler award programs. Their payoff runs 5–20%, figured this way:

- The most popular frequent-flier award is a free domestic Coach round-trip. Because of its restrictions (blackouts and seat limitations), it's worth about the same as the cheapest Coach excursion ticket in the absence of a fare sale—about $500 for a long-haul trip. On most big lines, you need 25,000 miles of credit for that award.
- You could earn that 25,000 miles by taking five transcontinental round-trips on cheap Coach excursion tickets and use the credit for a sixth long-haul trip. That six-for-five payoff is 20%.
- The payoff could be even higher during airfare sales. A while back, when you could have bought a round-trip ticket to Europe for around $300 from the East Coast, $400 from the West, you could earn 25,000 miles by spending no more than $1100. The payoff then would have been a hefty 45%.
- On the other hand, if you earn mileage mainly on short-haul trips at full Coach fares, you could easily spend more than $10,000 to earn 25,000 miles, for a meager payoff of 5% or less.

As you can see, the actual payoff varies among individuals and airlines. But we'd say that a frequent-flier payoff of 5–20% is a good benchmark—the higher end for people who earn credit buying cheap tickets, the low end for travelers who pay high fares.

Earning Credit*

	CREDIT FROM HOTEL STAYS				HOTEL CREDIT FOR FLYING	
HOTEL CHAIN	POINTS/ DOLLAR SPENT	PAID NIGHT EARNS 1-NIGHT CREDIT	CREDIT EARNED AT DISC. RATES(a)	CREDIT FOR ANY HOTEL PURCHASES	AIRLINE PARTNERS(b)	AMT. OF CREDIT/ STAY(c)
Best Inns	—	✔(g)	—	—	—	—
Best Western	1	—	—	—	—	—
Budgetel	—	✔	—	—	—	—
ClubHouse Inn	—	✔	—	—	—	—
Courtyard	—	✔	✔	—	—	—
Cross Country Inn	—	✔	—	—	—	—
Drury Inn	—	✔(i)	✔	—	—	—
Exel Inn	—	✔	—	—	—	—
Fairfield Inn	—	✔	✔	—	—	—
Hawaiian	—	✔	✔	—	—	—
Hilton	10(k)	—	—	✔(l)	AA,AC,AS, BA,CO,DL,HP, MX,NW,UA,US	250 pts.
Holiday Inn	1(o,p)	—	✔(q)	—	—	—
Howard Johnson	—	✔	—	—	—	—
Hyatt	5(o)	—	✔	✔	DL,NW,UA,US	300 pts.
La Quinta	—	✔(t)	✔	—	—	—
Marriott						
Honored Guest	10(t)	—	✔	✔	BA,CO, DL,NW,TW,US	25% bonus
Miles	—	—	✔	—	—	—
Masters Economy Inns	—	✔	✔	—	—	—
Meridien	—	✔(w)	—	—	—	—
Omni *Gold*	—	✔(w)	✔	—	—	—
Ramada	10	—	✔	✔	—	—
Red Lion	—	✔(k)	✔	—	—	—
Renaissance	1	—	✔	—	US	40 pts.
Sheraton *Basic*	2	—	✔	✔	—	—
Gold	3	—	✔	✔	—	—
Sofitel	—	✔	—	—	—	—
Summerfield Suites	—	✔(y)	—	—	—	—
Susse Chalet	—	✔	—	—	—	—
Travelodge	—	✔	—	—	—	—
Vagabond Inns	—	✔	✔(z)	—	—	—
Westin *General*	—	✔(k,aa)	✔	—	—	—
Burgundy	1(k)	✔(k,aa)	✔	✔	—	—

HOTEL CREDIT FROM CAR RENTAL			AIRLINE CREDIT FROM HOTEL STAY			
CAR RENTAL PARTNERS(d)	AMT. OF CREDIT/STAY(c)	CHARGE-CARD CREDIT PTS.(e)	AIRLINE PARTNERS(b)	MILES/STAY	TIME TO EARN CREDIT(f)	HOTEL CHAIN
—	—	—	—	—	unlimited	Best Inns
AV	100 pts.	—	—	—	unlimited	Best Western
—	—	—	—	—	1 year	Budgetel
—	—	—	—	—	1 year	ClubHouse Inn
—	—	—	—	—	unlimited(h)	Courtyard
—	—	—	—	—	unlimited	Cross Country Inn
—	—	—	—	—	unlimited	Drury Inn
—	—	—	—	—	unlimited	Exel Inn
—	—	—	—	—	unlimited(h)	Fairfield Inn
—	—	—	—	—	1 year(j)	Hawaiian
AL,AV,NA,TH	250 pts.	2-3/$(m)	AA,AC,AS,BA,CO,DL,HP,MX(n),NW,UA,US	500(k)	unlimited(h)	Hilton
—	—	—	AA,AC,AN,DL,KL,LH,NW,OZ,QF,SN,TG,UA	(o,r)	12/31/96	Holiday Inn
—	—	—	—	—	1 year(j)	Howard Johnson
AL,AV	300 pts.	—	AS,CX,DL,MH,NW,SA,SQ,UA,US	500(o,s)	unlimited(h)	Hyatt
—	—	—	—	—	unlimited	La Quinta
						Marriott
HE	20% bonus	1-3/$(u)	—	—	unlimited	Honored Guest
—	—	—	AA,AC,BA,CO,DL,NW,TW,UA,US	500(v)	unlimited	Miles
—	—	—	—	—	unlimited	Masters Economy Inns
—	—	—	—	—	2 years	Meridien
—	—	—	—	—	1 year	Omni Gold
AL	25% bonus	3/$	—	—	unlimited	Ramada
—	—	—	AA,AS	500(k,x)	unlimited	Red Lion
AV	20 pts.	—	—	—	unlimited	Renaissance
AV	500 pts.	—	—	—	unlimited(h)	Sheraton Basic
AV	500 pts.	—	—	—	unlimited(h)	Gold
—	—	—	—	—	1 year	Sofitel
—	—	—	—	—	unlimited	Summerfield Suites
—	—	—	—	—	unlimited	Susse Chalet
—	—	—	—	—	1 year	Travelodge
—	—	—	—	—	unlimited	Vagabond Inns
—	—	—	AA,AC,AS,HP,NW,UA,US	500(k,v)	4 years(h)	Westin General
—	—	—	AA,AC,AS,HP,NW,UA,US	500(k,v)	4 years(h)	Burgundy

EARNING CREDIT* *(continued)*

* As of early 1996; subject to change.

(a) Any rate below rack or advertised corporate rates.

(b) AA=American, AC=Air Canada, AN=Ansett Australia, AS=Alaska, BA=British Airways, CO=Continental, CX=Cathay Pacific, DL=Delta, HP=America West, KL=KLM, LH=Lufthansa, MH=Malaysia, MX=Mexicana, NW=Northwest, OZ=Asiana, QF=Qantas, SA=South Africa, SN=Sabena, SQ=Singapore, TG=Thai Airways, TW=TWA, UA=United, US=USAir.

(c) Bonus points or miles added, or percent bonus applied to, credit earned for hotel stay. Earning may require proof of air flight or car rental.

(d) AL=Alamo, AV=Avis, HE=Hertz, NA=National, TH=Thrifty.

(e) Credit for billings to hotel-sponsored charge card.

(f) How long credit is valid toward earning awards.

(g) Double credit for stays with 10-day advance reservation.

(h) As long as membership is active.

(i) Credit also earned for additional rooms for immediate family members.

(j) Calendar year.

(k) Both hotel-program and airline credit given for each stay.

(l) All charges must be billed to guest room; non-Hilton concessions do not earn points.

(m) Co-branded Optima Card; 3 points per dollar for stays

you can buy your way into Sheraton's *Gold* level and you reach Westin's *Burgundy* level after just three stays or 10 nights.

• Some chains give you an unlimited time to accumulate enough credit for a free stay or other award; others give you only a year. With some, you must stay in a participating hotel at least once or twice a year to keep your credit account active.

• Hilton, Marriott, Ramada, and Sheraton cosponsor credit cards: You earn frequent-stay credit for all purchases billed to the card, not just hotel stays.

• Membership in most hotel programs is free, as it is with their airline counterparts. However, Courtyard, Fairfield Inn, Holiday Inn, Sheraton *Gold,* and Susse Chalet charge modest fees ($25 a year or less). Sofitel charges a whopping $71 a year.

. . . AND WHAT YOU GET

With almost all the programs, free hotel stays are available as awards—often the only awards. Other programs give cash-value awards, and several let you redeem hotel points for a wide range of other travel services. Some programs even let you trade in credit for merchandise.

But a laundry list of awards means nothing unless you know what you must spend to earn one. Two benchmarks in the *Awards and Payoffs* table, pages 186–87, will help you compare the programs:

• The *minimum worthwhile award* is the lowest-credit award of tangible dollar value that we judge broadly desirable. It includes free nights, room discounts, cash certificates, and such—but not awards of limited interest or intangible value, such as a room upgrade or free use of a "health club" or a "business center."

The minimum worthwhile award is a fairly good yardstick for leisure travelers. The typical minimum award is simple: one free night at any time. In a few programs, it's a free weekend night (or an off-peak night at a resort location).

If you don't stay in hotels often enough to earn a minimum award within a year or two, forget about hotel credit. Choose a program that provides benefits you can use without racking up a minimum number of

at Hiltons; 2 points per dollar for all other purchases;
you must choose between Hilton and American Express
programs.
(n) Proof of qualifying flight is required for MX only.
(o) Earn points or miles, not both.
(p) 25 points per night at Holiday Inn Express.
(q) Applies to specified discounts amounting to no more
than 30% off rack rates; valid in US only.
(r) AA,DL,NW,UA=2 miles/S; AC,LH,OZ,TG=500 miles/stay;
AN,QF= 500 points/night; KL=300 points/stay; SN=250
points/night. (Reduced levels for stays at Holiday Inn
Express.)

(s) CX,MH,SQ=1000 km in joint Passages program.
(t) For up to 3 rooms charged to same account.
(u) 2 points per dollar for stay at Marriotts; 3 points per dollar for cards issued before Mar 31, 1989; 1 point per
dollar for all other purchases.
(v) 2500-mile bonus for every 5 stays through 1996.
(w) One credit per stay.
(x) For stays at corporate rate or higher.
(y) Requires 2-night weekend stays.
(z) Half-price hotel program rates do not earn credit.
(aa) 1000 points per night.

stays (see *Just for Signing Up*, page 190) or one that awards mileage that you can add to your airline account.

•The award for staying 25 nights, a reasonable benchmark for frequent vacation travelers and many business travelers, is what you'd earn by staying (and paying for) 25 nights at participating hotels. Where a program offers alternative awards at the 25-night credit level, we list the one with the highest cash value.

In most programs, higher-credit awards are simply multiples of a basic award: If 12 paid nights get you one free night, 24 paid nights get you two, and 36 get you three. That formula also holds true for the awards of frequent-flier mileage that some plans offer: What you get is directly proportional to the number of times you stay (or the dollars you spend).

In the programs that award one free night for every 8, 9, 10, 11, or 12 paid nights, you actually attain the listed 25-night award (two or three free nights) by staying fewer than 25 nights. Even so, to have a common standard of comparison, we list those

as 25-night awards in the table.

Once you earn the credit, some programs give you an indefinite period to use it. But most impose a time limit, as the table shows.

FIGURING YOUR PAYOFF

The *Awards and Payoffs* table also shows a payoff figure for both benchmark awards. That's simply the value of the award, expressed as a percentage of what you'd have to spend to earn it. Where a program offers either hotel or airline credit, we tabulate the hotel-stay award (except for Holiday Inn, where the airline-credit payoff is quite a bit higher). However, you still may prefer to add mileage to an airline account rather than to accumulate separate hotel credit that you might not use.

•The highest payoff percentage (33%) is for Summerfield Suites, a program in which both earning and free-room awards are confined to weekend stays—an unusual limitation.

•Summerfield aside, the programs with the highest payoffs—8–13%—are, in the main, those that give one free night for every 8–12 paid nights.

Awards and Payoffs*

HOTEL CHAIN	MINIMUM WORTHWHILE AWARD(a)			AWARD FOR STAYING 25 NIGHTS(a)	
	CREDIT REQUIRED	AWARD(c)	PAYOFF	AWARD(c)	PAYOFF
Best Inns	12 nights	1 night	8%	2 nights	8%
Best Western	1200 points	$50(e) or $100 savings bond	4	$50(e) or $100 savings bond	4
Budgetel	2 nights	1 night	8	2 nights	8
ClubHouse Inn	12 nights	1 night	8	2 nights	8
Courtyard	12 nights	1 night or 1750 miles(h)	8	2 nights or 3500 miles(h)	8
Cross Country Inn	12 nights	1 night	8	2 nights	8
Drury Inn	10 nights	1 night	10	2 nights	10
Exel Inn	12 nights	1 night	8	2 nights	8
Fairfield Inn	12 nights	1 night or 1000 miles(h)	8	2 nights or 2000 miles(h)	8
Hawaiian	10 nights	1 night	10	2 nights	10
Hilton	20,000 points	1 WE night	4	1 WE night, 3000 miles	4
Holiday Inn	60 points	150 miles	5	3875 miles	5
Howard Johnson	10 nights	50% off 2 nights	10	50% off 3 nights	6
Hyatt	8000 points	1 WE night	3	1 WE night(j)	3
La Quinta	11 nights	1 night	9	2 nights	9
Marriott Honored	20,000 points	1 night(k)	5	1 night(k)	5
Guest/Miles	1 stay	500 miles	5	3000 miles	4
Masters Economy Inns	9 nights	1 night	11	2 nights	11
Meridien	5 stays	1 WE night	5	1 WE night	5
Omni Gold	6 stays	50% off WE stay	4	50% off WE stay	4
Ramada	12,000 points	50% off 2-night WE stay	5	50% off 2 night WE stay	5
Red Lion	10 nights	1 WE night	5	1 night	5
Renaissance	1000 credits	$50 savings bond	3	$100 savings bond	2
Sheraton Basic	3000 points	1 night(m)	6	1 night(n)	4
Gold	3000 points	1 night(m)	9	2 nights(m)	8
Sofitel	12 nights	2 WE nights	8	2/2 WE nights	8
Summerfield Suites	3 WE stays(o)	2-night WE stay(o)	33	2 WE stays(o)	33
Susse Chalet	8 nights	1 night(p)	13	3 nights(p)	13
Travelodge	10 nights	1 night	10	2 nights	10
Vagabond Inns	9 nights	1 night	11	2 nights	11
Westin General	10,000 points	1 WE night(r)	5	1 night, 3000 miles	6
Burgundy	10,000 points	1 WE night(s)	6	1 night, 3000 miles	6

* As of early 1996; subject to change.
(a) Hotel awards shown for programs that offer choice of hotel awards or airline mileage; mileage payoffs are usually better (see text). Minimum worthwhile awards exclude intangible-value, low-credit awards such as room upgrades. 25-night benchmark is the most valuable award available for credit earned by staying up to 25 nights. For programs based on stays, the minimum award was calculated on a 2-night stay, the 25-night award was calculated on 6 stays.
(b) May be in conjunction with or in place of hotel-stay awards.
(c) WE = weekend.
(d) From date award is issued, unless noted otherwise; a date indicates award expiration regardless of issue date.
(e) Certificate applied to future stay.

| | | OTHER AWARDS(b) | | | | |
CAR RENTAL	CLUB MEMBERSHIPS	MERCHANDISE	PHONE CALLING CARDS	TOURS/ CRUISES	AIRLINE TICKETS	AWARD LIFE(d)
						unlimited
✓	✓	✓	✓	✓	✓	1 year(f)
—	—	—	—	—	—	1 year(g)
—	—	—	—	—	—	1 year
—	—	—	—	—	—	1 year
—	—	—	—	—	—	6 months
—	—	—	—	—	—	unlimited
—	—	—	—	—	—	unlimited
—	—	—	—	—	—	1 year
—	—	—	—	—	—	1 year(i)
✓	—	✓	—	✓	✓	1 year
✓	✓	✓	✓	✓	✓	6/30/97
✓	✓	✓	✓	✓	✓	1 year
✓	—	—	—	✓	—	1 year
—	—	—	—	✓	—	18 months
—	—	—	—	✓	✓	1 year
—	—	—	—	—	—	—
—	—	—	—	—	—	unlimited
—	—	—	—	—	—	unlimited
—	—	—	—	—	—	1 year
✓	—	✓	—	—	✓	1 year
—	—	—	—	—	—	18 months(l)
—	—	—	—	—	—	1 year
✓	—	—	—	—	—	unlimited
✓	—	—	—	—	—	unlimited
—	—	—	—	—	—	14 months(g)
—	—	—	—	—	—	1 year
—	—	✓	—	—	—	1 year(q)
✓	✓	—	✓	—	—	1 year
—	—	—	—	—	—	unlimited
—	—	—	—	✓	—	1 year
—	—	—	—	✓	—	1 year

(f) 1 year in US, Canada, and Caribbean; 6 months in Europe.
(g) From date of first credit earned.
(h) American, Delta, or USAir.
(i) Calendar year.
(j) In "Regency Club" room; also additional partner discounts.
(k) May be weekend or weekday award; varies by location and season.
(l) Certificates issued beginning 7/1/96 valid through 12/31/97.
(m) At lower-priced Sheratons.
(n) At most Sheratons.
(o) Stays are 2 nights; award not available in Orlando.
(p) Receive additional night when stays include 6 different locations.
(q) From date of last credit-earning stay.
(r) At lower-priced Westins.
(s) At most Westins.

Most of them are run by the mid-priced chains.

- Payoff percentages are considerably lower—generally 3–5%—for the more complex programs run by the pricier chains.
- Payoff in frequent-flier credit, in programs that offer it, is generally low. Since a mile of credit is worth about 2¢, the 500 miles per stay you get in several programs amounts to about $10. In view of the room rent you must pay to earn it, the return is stingy.
- The table also notes the programs that offer alternatives to free rooms —discount certificates for air tickets, tours, merchandise, and such. The payoffs for those awards are almost always lower than what you'd get in free nights.

Where credit is awarded per stay (rather than per dollar or per night), we figured the cost of a minimum award on the basis of a two-night stay and assumed that the 25-night award was earned during six stays. For programs that give one night for a certain number of paid nights, the payoff calculations for the 25-night award are based on the actual number of nights needed to earn the two or three free rooms.

The calculations weren't adjusted to cover possible bonuses for nonroom expenditures or use of a partner airline or car-rental firm. Since weekend rates are often much lower than weekday rates, we valued a free weekend night (a popular low-credit award) at half the average rack rate. And since discount coupons are so widely available for a variety of travel services, we

assigned no value to discount awards.

Our payoff calculations apply to average travelers and may be quite different for other people. If, say, you normally pay discounted or promotional rates, the payoff of a program that doesn't honor promotional rates is

MEMBERSHIP BENEFITS*

HOTEL CHAIN		FREE BREAKFAST	DISC. ROOM RATES
Best Inns		—	—
Best Western		✔	—
Budgetel		—	—
ClubHouse Inn		—	—
Courtyard		—	✔
Cross Country Inn		—	—
Drury Inn		—	✔
Exel Inn		—	—
Fairfield Inn		—	—
Hawaiian		✔	✔
Hilton		—	—
Holiday Inn		—	—
Howard Johnson		—	—
Hyatt		—	—
La Quinta		—	✔
Marriott	Honored Guest	—	—
	Miles	—	—
Masters Economy Inns		—	—
Meridien		—	—
Omni	Gold	—	—
Ramada		—	✔
Red Lion		—	—
Renaissance		—	—
Sheraton	Basic(b)	—	—
	Gold	—	—
Sofitel		—	✔
Summerfield Suites		—	—
Susse Chalet		✔	✔
Travelodge		—	—
Vagabond Inns		—	—
Westin	General(b)	✔	—
	Burgundy	✔	—

* As of early 1996; subject to change.

zero. If your average stays are just a day or two, you'll pile up per-stay credit faster than you would by staying at one hotel for extended periods.

The payoff on the charge cards that Hilton, Marriott, and Ramada sponsor is about 1%. Since the payoff on airline cards is around 2%, most travelers are probably better off with an airline-sponsored card than with a hotel card. Sheraton's card, however, could be a good deal for travelers who want to earn free stays. (For more details, see *Hotel and Cruise Cards* in chapter 3.)

LATE CHECKOUT	FREE LOCAL CALLS	PRIORITY RESERVATION	FREE STAY FOR COMPANION	ROOM UPGRADE	DISCOUNT AT RESTAURANTS, SHOPS
—	✔	—	✔	—	—
—	✔	—	✔	✔	—
—	—	—	✔	—	—
—	—	—	—	—	—
—	✔	—	✔	—	—
—	—	—	—	—	—
—	—	—	—	—	—
—	—	—	✔	—	—
—	✔	—	—	✔	✔
✔	—	✔	✔	✔	✔
✔	—	—	—	✔	—
✔	—	✔	✔	—	✔
—	—	—	✔	—	—
✔	✔	—	—	✔	—
✔	—	✔	—	—	—
✔	—	—	✔	✔	—
✔	—	—	✔ (a)	—	✔
✔	—	—	✔	—	—
—	—	—	—	✔	—
✔	—	✔	✔	—	—
✔	—	✔	—	—	✔
—	✔	—	✔	—	—
—	—	✔	—	✔	—

(a) Up to 4 people stay in the same room.   (b) Basic and general programs provide only nominal benefits.

RATING THE PROGRAMS*

HOTEL CHAIN	PAYOFF	EARNING OPPS.	MEMBER. BENEFITS
ABOVE AVERAGE			
Drury Inn	+	O	O
Hawaiian	+	O	+
La Quinta	O	O	+
Masters Economy Inns	+	O	+
Ramada	–	+	+
Sheraton Gold	O	+	+
Summerfield Suites	+	–	+
Susse Chalet	+	–	+
AVERAGE			
Best Inns	O	–	
Best Western	–	–	O
Courtyard	O	O	
Fairfield Inn	O	O	
Hilton	–	+	–
Howard Johnson	–	–	+
Hyatt	–	+	+
Marriott Honored Guest	–	+	O
Red Lion	–	O	+
Sheraton Basic	–	+	+
Sofitel	O	–	+
Travelodge	O	–	
Vagabond Inns	+	O	–
Westin Burgundy	–	O	O
Westin General	–	O	
BELOW AVERAGE			
Budgetel	O	–	–
ClubHouse Inn	O	–	
Cross Country Inn	O	–	
Exel Inn	O	–	O
Holiday Inn	–	O	O
Marriott Miles	–	O	
Meridien	–	–	–
Omni Gold	–	O	+
Renaissance	–	+	O

* As of early 1996; subject to change.
+ Above Average   O Average   – Below Average
Note: Listed by group in order of estimated quality. Programs within each group are listed alphabetically.

JUST FOR SIGNING UP

About half the programs offer at least some perks just for enrolling. The *Membership Benefits* table shows which programs offer the free extras we consider to be of greatest value, either in dollars or convenience. Those include additional room or restaurant discounts, free breakfast, late check-out, free local calls, and such. While a few programs offer a long list of other freebies, many of those are picayune—a free cup of coffee or newspaper, for example or a "space-available" upgrade that nobody ever seems to get.

That table lists only extras available solely to frequent-stay members. Those extras alone justify joining a no-fee program, even for travelers who will never earn enough credit for a free stay.

Instead of a frequent-stay program, a number of big chains feature "customer-recognition" programs. Those don't offer free stays and other awards but do offer membership benefits comparable with those in our table. Other chains and independent hotels offer "volume" programs that offer price concessions or special benefits to good clients. Still others have no program at all, other than possible individual-customer deals.

WHICH PROGRAM TO JOIN?

The *Rating the Programs* table shows how the programs measure up in the three main factors:

- **Payoff**—what you get for what you spend—is probably the most important item.
- **Earning opportunities** rates ease of racking up credit, with highest marks given to programs that let you earn

credit even at promotional rates. We also gave good marks to programs that give credit for nonroom expenses and for using partner airlines and car-rental companies.

- **Membership benefits,** or the extras of real dollar value or convenience that each program offers.

Two other considerations may also be important:

- If you travel through much of the US, a program with a large number of participating locations will be much more useful than one run by a chain with only a few dozen hotels.
- If you're a relatively infrequent traveler, you may want to avoid programs that charge a fee.

WHERE TO FIND IT

The easiest way to enroll is to pick up an application (or validation card) at any chain location. Otherwise, call:

Best Inns: *BIP Club,* 800-237-8466.

Best Western: *Gold Crown Club Intl,* 800-873-4653.

Budgetel: *Roadrunner Club,* 800-428-3438.

ClubHouse Inn: *Best Guest,* 800-258-2466.

Courtyard: *Courtyard Club,* 800-321-7396; $10 per year or $15 for two years.

Cross Country Inn: *Travelers Dozen,* 800-621-1429.

Drury Inn: *Preferred Customer,* 800-325-8300.

Exel Inn: *Insider's Card,* 800-356-8013.

Fairfield Inn: *INNsiders Club,* 800-333-3914; $10 one-time fee.

Hawaiian: *Coconut Club,* 800-222-5642.

Hilton: *HHonors,* 800-446-6677.

Holiday Inn: *Priority Club,* 800-272-9273; $10 per year (fee is waived if you stay at a Holiday Inn motel once a year).

Howard Johnson: *Business Traveler Club,* 800-547-7829.

Hyatt: *Gold Passport,* 800-514-9288.

La Quinta: *Returns Club,* 800-531-5900.

Marriott: *Honored Guest* or *Miles,* 800-367-6453.

Masters Economy Inns: *Preferred Guest,* 800-633-3434.

Meridien: *L'Invitation;* ask when registering.

Omni: *Select Guest,* 800-367-6664.

Ramada: *Business Card,* 800-672-6232.

Red Lion: *Frequent Guest Dividends,* 800-733-5466.

Renaissance: *Club Express,* 800-824-3571.

Sheraton: *Sheraton Club Intl,* 800-247-2582; *Gold* $50 first year, then $25 per year (Basic members automatically enrolled in *Gold* after four stays).

Sofitel: *Exclusive Card,* 800-763-4835; 350FF (US$71) per year ($190 per year for *Business Exclusive*).

Summerfield Suites: *Family Frequent Play Card,* 800-833-4353.

Susse Chalet: *VIP Club,* 800-258-1989; $10 per year.

Travelodge: *Guest Rewards,* 800-545-5545.

Vagabond Inns: *10th Night Free,* 800-522-1555.

Westin: *Premier,* 800-521-2000; *Burgundy* level requires three stays or 10 nights.

This chapter was adapted from the Consumer Reports Travel Letter *article* "Hotel Frequent Stay Plans" (February 1996).

PROGRAMS PLAIN AND FANCY

Frequent-stay programs aren't necessarily confined to monster chains. Here are some smaller contenders:

- The **Travelodge** frequent-stay program, until last year available in just five states, is now nationwide. The "11th Night Free" promotion provides a free room-night (and automatic enrollment in the *Gold Guest Rewards* frequent-stay program) after 10 room-nights at any combination of participating Travelodges and Thriftilodges in the US and Canada. *Guest Rewards* members are also entitled to free local phone calls, special reduced room rates, and a few other minor perks.

  You receive a sticker to put on your card for each room night. When you have 10 stickers, you exchange the card by mail for a voucher good for a free night. The payoff is 10%, but to qualify for a sticker, you must pay either rack (regular) rate, a *Rewards* rate, or a corporate rate.

- **Wellesley Inns,** a small midpriced chain, also has a new frequent-stay program covering its 29 locations: 12 paid nights earn one free night, for a payoff of 8.3%. Free nights require advance reservation and are subject to availability, and blackout dates apply. Pick up an application for free membership at any Wellesley Inn or call 800-444-8888.

- **Frequent-stays deluxe.** The 205 members of **Small Luxury Hotels of the World** have introduced their own frequent-stay program, called *Passport.* The SLH group is comprised of high-priced hotels that aren't affiliated with a big-name chain. Among the members are the Mark in New York and the Argyle in Los Angeles.

  For every eight paid stays of any length, at any combination of participating hotels, you earn one free night at any participating hotel. Travelers maintain their own records by entering dates and confirmation numbers on a small card. There's no time limit to earning the eight-stay credit. You must reserve either through the chain's central reservation office (800-525-4800) or through a travel agency (using "code LX").

If each qualifying stay is just one night, the payoff is 12.5%, among the higher rates we've found. However, as the average length of stay increases, the payoff decreases proportionately. Call 713-522-3159 to enroll; there's no charge.

HOTEL DISCOUNTS FOR SENIORS

With (supposedly) scads of leisure time and disposable income, seniors are the belles of the travel industry's ball. But "senior" doesn't necessarily connote "geriatric": At many hotels, senior status kicks in at age 50.

The table on pages 194-99 summarizes the offerings of more than six dozen hotel/motel chains in the US and Canada, as of a *CRTL* report in summer 1996. (It omits chains whose discounts and restrictions depend on the policy of each member hotel.) The programs of US-based hotel chains usually apply to their overseas locations, too.

COME AND GET IT

Well over half the chains offer a senior discount chainwide to *anyone* at or over some minimum age; just show your driver's license or other ID:

- Country Side, WestCoast, and Wyndham are the most generous, with discounts of 44–50%, at least sometimes. More than a dozen other chains are runners-up; their discounts run 20–30%. But those deals are usually

"subject to availability": You'll get the discount only when the hotel doesn't expect to be full. There may also be other limitations (such as advance reservation). And the discounts may not apply to minimum-rate rooms.

- Other discounts run only a modest 10–15%, but they're usually available as long as a hotel has any vacancy at all. Budget hotels seldom give much more than that, so the senior deal is probably as good as any you'll find. With more expensive hotels, it makes sense to check around for some other, bigger sort of discount— through a half-price program, a travel agency's preferred-rate program, or a hotel broker (see chapters 14, 15, and 16). And check for weekend promotions. Take the senior deal only if you can't find anything better.

MEMBERS ONLY

Members of AARP or other senior associations enjoy a wide range of discounts:

- Country Side, Marriott, Omni, Wyndham, and West Coast are the most generous to AARP members, with discounts of 44–50%, at least some of the time. Association members can get discounts of 20–30% at sixteen other chains. AARP has official discount deals with more than two dozen major hotel chains, which are listed in the AARP *Purchase Privilege Program* directory and noted in the table. Several other chains also extend discounts to AARP members unofficially (those are noted in the table, too).

- Some chains give senior deals of 20% or better *only* to guests who belong to AARP (or other senior association). Those include Marriott, Omni, Canadian Pacific, Doubletree, Howard Johnson, and Red Lion.
- While most of the chains give discounts to seniors who aren't AARP members as well those who are, AARP membership lowers the qualifying age to 50—5–10 years younger than the minimum required by the chains' regular senior policies.
- Most subsidiaries of the Choice group

DISCOUNTS GALORE

For a rundown of senior programs in many areas, see *Unbelievably Good Deals and Great Adventures That You Absolutely Can't Get Unless You're Over 50* (1996, 8th Edition, Contemporary Books, Chicago, $9.95). For this, as well as a printout of other travel publications, contact Have Book, Will Travel, Box 576, Wilton CT 06897; 203-761-0604, fax 203-762-0148, E-mail *havebook @aol.com; AE, MC, V.*

WHAT THE CHAINS OFFER*

HOTEL CHAIN/ PROGRAM	PHONE
Admiral Benbow Inns	800-451-1986
Amerihost Inn	call local property
AmeriSuites *Suite Years*	800-833-1516
Aston *Sun Club Discount*	800-922-7866
Best Inns & Suites	800-237-8466
Senior First	
Best Western	800-603-2277
Mature Benefits	
Budgetel	800-428-3438
Canadian Pacific	800-441-1414, (c)
Candlewood	800-946-6200
Clarion Hotels	800-252-7466
ClubHouse Inns & Suites	800-258-2466
Stay Twogether	
Colony	800-777-1700
Comfort Inns & Suites	800-228-5150
Country Hearth Inns	888-443-2784
Senior Saving	
Country Inns & Suites	800-456-4000
by Carlson	
Country Side Inn & Suites	800-322-9992
Courtyard by Marriott	800-321-221
Cross Country Inns	800-621-1429
Senior Save 25%	
Crowne Plaza	800-227-6963
Days Inn	800-247-5152
September Days Club	
Doubletree	800-222-8733
Drury Inn	800-325-8300
Econo Lodge	800-553-2666
Exel Inns	800-367-3935
Fairfield Inn by Marriott	800-228-2800
Family Inns	800-251-9752
Grand Heritage	800-437-4824
Senior Rate Program	
Heartland Inns	800-334-3277
Hilton *Senior HHonors*	800-445-8667
Holiday Inn *Alumni Club*	800-465-4329
Howard Johnson	800-446-4656
Golden Years Travel Club	

WEB SITE(a)	ANY SENIOR		AARP DISC. (b)	MEMBERSHIP PROGS.	
	MINIMUM AGE	DISC.		MINIMUM AGE	DISCOUNT
	50	10-15%	10%	—	—
amerihostinn.com	50	10%	10%	—	—
	60	10%	10%	—	—
	55	25%	—	—	—
	—	—	—	50	$5-12
bestwestern.com/ best.html	55	10%	10%(b)	—	—
	55	10%	—	—	—
cphotels.ca	(c)	(c)	30%(b)	—	—
	—	—	10%	—	—
clarioninn.com	50	10%/30%(d)	10%/30%(b,d)	—	—
	65	(e)	—	—	—
	60	(c)	25%(b)	—	—
comfortinn.com	50	10%/30%(d)	10%/30%(b,d)	—	—
	50	10%	10%	—	—
	55	10%	10%	—	—
	55	50%	50%	—	—
marriott.com/trav.html	—	—	10%(b,f)	—	—
	60	25%	25%	—	—
crowneplaza.com	—	—	10%(b)	—	—
daysinn.com/daysinn.html	—	—	10%(b,g)	50	15-50%(h)
doubletreehotels.com	(c)	(c)	10-30%(b,i)	—	—
	50	10%	10%	—	—
econolodge.com	50	10%/30%(d)	10%/30%(b,d)	—	—
	55	10%	—	—	—
marriott.com/trav.html	62	10%	10%(b)	—	—
	60	10%	10%	—	—
grandheritage.com	55	10%/20%(j)	10%/20%(j)	—	—
	(c)	10%	10%	—	—
hilton.com	—	—	10-15%	60	25-50%(k)
holiday-inn.com/	55	10%	10%(b)	60	20%
travelweb.com/thisco/ hojo/common/hojo.html	—	—	15%/20%(d)	50	15-50%(l)

—Clarion, Comfort, Econo Lodge, Quality, Rodeway, and Sleep—share the basic formula of 30% off with advance reservations or 10% off anytime.

An AARP membership, at $8 a year, is a bargain. In addition to hotel discounts, it offers other services for seniors, including reduced-price prescription drugs and Medicare-supplement insurance. The Canadian Assn of Retired Persons (CARP), Catholic Golden Age, National Assn for Retired Credit Union People, and other senior organizations also offer hotel-discount programs. CARP's program offers deals at Atlific (Canada), Best Western, Choice, Howard Johnson, Marriott, Outrigger, Ramada, Sheraton, and Travelodge.

HOTEL-CHAIN "CLUBS"

A few chains run their own membership programs for senior travelers: You get discounts of 15% or more—at least at certain times—at Days Inn, Hilton, Holiday Inn, Howard Johnson, Ramada, and Walt Disney. In several of those cases, the membership discount is substantially better than the any-senior or AARP rate. Membership is the only way to get a discount at Walt Disney.

The minimum age for a hotel membership program ranges from 50 (the same as with AARP) to 60. If you don't already belong, you can usually sign up on the spot when you arrive at the hotel. (Ask about programs when you reserve by phone.)

Beyond room discounts, hotel-chain clubs that charge an enrollment fee (see *Where to Find It*, at the end of the

WHAT THE CHAINS OFFER* *(continued)*

HOTEL CHAIN/ PROGRAM	PHONE
Hyatt	
Senior Citizen Discount	800-233-1234
Innkeeper	800-822-9899
Inns of America	800-826-0778
InnSuites	800-842-4242
Kimpton	(m)
Knights Inns	800-843-5644
La Quinta	800-531-5900
MainStay Suites	800-660-6246
Marc Resorts	800-535-0085
Marriott	800-228-9290
Master Hosts Inn	800-251-1962
Masters Economy Inns	800-633-3434
Motel 6	800-466-8356
Omni	800-843-6664
Outrigger *Fifty Plus*	800-688-7444
Park Inn *Silver Citizens*	800-437-7275
Quality Inns & Suites	800-228-5151
Radisson	800-333-3333
Ramada *Best Years Club*	800-472-6232
Red Carpet Inn	800-251-1962
Red Lion	800-547-8010
Red Roof Inns	
RediCard + 60	800-843-7663
Renaissance	800-228-9898
Residence Inn	800-331-3131
by Marriott	
Rodeway Inn	800-228-2000
Scottish Inns	800-251-1962
Sheraton	800-325-3535
Shilo Inns & Resorts	800-222-2244
Shoney's Inn *Merit 50*	800-222-2222
Sierra Suites	800-474-3772
Signature Inns	800-822-5252
Sleep Inn	800-753-3746
Summerfield Suites	800-833-4353

| WEB SITE(a) | ANY SENIOR | | AARP DISC. (b) | MEMBERSHIP PROGS. | |
	MINIMUM AGE	DISC.		MINIMUM AGE	DISCOUNT
hyatt.com	65	10-15%(c)	—	—	—
	55	10%	10%	—	—
	55	10%	10%	—	—
http://mmm.arizonaguide.com/insuites	60%	10%	—	—	
	55-65(c)	$13-70(c)	$13-70(c)	—	—
travelweb.com/thisco/knight/common/knight.html	(c)	10%	10%	—	
travelweb.com/thisco/laquinta/common/laquinta.html	(c)	(c)	10%(b)	—	
	50	10%/30%(d)	—		
planet-hawaii.com/marcresorts	55	25%	25%	—	
marriott.com/trav.html	—	—	10%/50%(b,n)	—	
	(c)	(c)	10%(b)	—	
	50	$2	$2	—	
	—	—	10%(b)	—	—
	—	—	50%(b,o)	—	—
outrigger.com	50	20%(p)	25%(b,p)	—	—
	60	15%	15%	—	—
qualityinns.com	50	10%/30%(d)	10%/30%(b,d)	—	—
radisson.com	50	0-30%(c)	(c,q)	—	—
ramada.com/ramada.html	60	10-25%	15%(b)	60	25%
	(c)	(c)	10%(b)	—	—
	—	—	—	—	—
redroof.com	—	—	—	60	10%
travelweb.com/thisco/renaissa/common/renaissa.html	55	25%(c)	25%(c)	—	—
marriott.com/trav.html	—	—	15%(b)	—	—
rodeway.com	50	10%/30% (d)		—	
	(c)	(c)	10%(b)	—	—
	(c)	25%	15-25%(b)	—	—
	65	10%	10%	—	—
	50	(c)	—	—	—
sierrasuites.com	50	10%	10%	—	—
	—	—	15%	—	—
sleepinn.com	50	10%/30%(d)	10%/30%(b,d)	—	—
	50	10%	—	—	—

chapter) usually offer a few benefits that you don't find with free clubs:

- •The Days Inn, Hilton, Howard Johnson, and Walt Disney clubs offer discounts at the hotels' restaurants (or at nearby restaurants).
- •Hilton and Ramada automatically enroll senior-club members in their frequent-stay programs. Stays at a participating hotel earn credit toward free hotel stays, air tickets, and other awards.

Several chains have named their senior programs, as shown in the table. You may occasionally find it useful to refer to a program's name when you request a senior discount. However, the table doesn't note those programs as *membership* unless a paid enrollment is a requisite of getting a discount.

MAKING YOUR DEAL

Senior discounts are usually available through a chain's toll-free national reservation line. Many now also provide Web sites (see table) of varying sophistication and capability: Some accept reservations, others just provide information. Still, it's often a good idea to call each hotel's own reservation office: You may find a better choice of discount options and local promotional deals, as well as a local senior offer.

As with most discount and promotional rates, senior discounts normally can't be combined with any other reductions, such as half-price, corporate, weekend, group, or meeting rates. Even an advertised chainwide discount may not be available at all times and at all locations.

WHAT THE CHAINS OFFER* *(continued)*

HOTEL CHAIN/ PROGRAM	PHONE
Sumner Suites	800-747-8483
Super 8	800-800-8000
Susse Chalet	800-524-2538
Travelers Inns *Inn Club*	800-633-8300
Travelodge *Seniors*	
Classic Travel Club	800-578-7878
Vagabond Inn	800-522-1555
Smart Seniors	
Villager Lodge	800-328-7829
Walt Disney World *Magic*	
Kingdom Club Gold Card	800-647-7900
Wellesley Inns	800-444-8888
WestCoast	800-426-0670
Wilson Inns	800-945-7667
Wingate Inns	
Seniors Discount	800-228-1000
Wyndham	800-996-3426

* As of mid-1996; subject to change.
(a)Unless otherwise noted, all Web addresses start with *http://www.* (not required by some Internet browsers).
(b)Chains noted (b) officially affiliated with the American Assn of Retired Persons (AARP). Chains noted with only a percentage voluntarily grant discount to AARP members. Many chains also honor membership in the Canadian Assn of Retired Persons.
(c)Discounts, minimum age, membership status vary by location.
(d)No advance reservations/with advance reservations.
(e)Current discounts vary by individual locations. New chainwide program begins Jan '97: Two seniors stay at the single rate (usually $7 a night less than the double rate).
(f)15% off nonalcoholic beverages and food during lunch and dinner.

WHERE TO FIND IT

The following organizations offer travel discounts.

SENIOR GROUPS

Most are affinity groups (retired teach-

WEB SITE(a)	ANY SENIOR		AARP DISC. (b)	MEMBERSHIP PROGS.	
	MINIMUM AGE	DISC.		MINIMUM AGE	DISCOUNT
	50	10%	10%	—	—
travelweb.com/thisco/ super8/ common/super8.html	50	10%	10%(b)	—	—
	60	(r)	—	—	—
	50	10%	10%	—	—
travelweb.com/thisco/ tlodge/common/tlodge.html	50	15%	15%(b)	—	—
	55	30%(s)	—	—	—
villager.com/villager.html	—	—	10%	—	—
disneyworld.com	—	—	—	55	10-30%(t)
	60	10%	10%	—	—
	55	10-44%	10-44%	—	—
	55	10%	10-15%	—	—
wingateinns.com/wingate.html	60	15%	15%(u)	—	—
	62	50%(v)	50%(v)	—	—

(g)Card from any other senior club also honored.

(h)Also 10% off meals, beverages, and gift shop purchases, and up to 50% off admission to participating theme parks and attractions.

(i)30% off weekday rack rates, 10% off lowest weekend rate, and 10% off food and beverages.

(j)10% off weekend rates, 20% off weekday rates.

(k)Same discount applies to a second room; members also receive dining discounts.

(l)Also 10% off at participating restaurants.

(m)Each hotel has separate reservation number. Contact a travel agent or write to Kimpton, 223 Kearny St, Suite 200, San Francisco 94108.

(n)AARP members receive a minimum of 50% off regular rates with a 21-day (nonrefundable) advance purchase. 10% discount is available anytime. Anyone over 50 receives 20% off food and nonalcoholic bever-

ages and 10% off nonfood gift shop items.

(o)15% discount on food and beverages.

(p)Advance reservations required.

(q)Members of AARP, Northwest Worldperks Seniors, and United Silver Wings Plus entitled to 15% off dining with or without hotel stay.

(r)1-4 persons stay in one room at the single rate.

(s)No discount in Palm Springs.

(t)Also includes $2-10 off admissions (depending on pass type) and various dining, merchandise, and water park discounts.

(u)Also applies to members of Catholic Golden Age, Golden Buckeye Club, Natl Assn for Retired Credit Union People, Natl Council of Seniors, Natl Retired Teachers Assn, Retired Enlisted Assn, and United Airlines Silver Wings Plus.

(v)25% off rack rates at resort hotels.

ers, military, etc). Phone or write for membership requirements and fees.

American Assn of Retired Persons (AARP): Membership Processing Center, Box 729, Long Beach CA 90801; 800-424-3410 for information and application. Send $8 (or $20 for three years; $45 for 10 years), check or money order only.

Canadian Assn of Retired Persons (CARP): 27 Queen St E, Suite 1304, Toronto M5C 2M6; 416-363-8748. C$10, C$20 for non-Canadians per year. *AE, MC, V.*

Catholic Golden Age: 430 Penn Ave, Scranton PA 18503; 800-836-5699.

Golden Buckeye Card: Ohio Dept of Aging, 50 W Broad St, 9th Floor, Columbus OH 43215; 800-422-1976 in OH, 614-466-3681.

National Assn for Retired Credit Union People (NARCUP): 4W-4, Box 391, Madison WI 53701. Write for application.

National Council of Senior Citizens: 1331 F St NW, Washington DC 20004; 202-347-8800, fax 202-624-9595.

National Retired Teachers Assn: Part of AARP.

Retired Enlisted Assn: 13130 E Colfax Ave, Aurora CO 80011; 303-340-3939.

Hotel-sponsored membership programs. Join on the spot or call ahead. Except as noted, all accept *AE, Disc, MC, V.*

Days Inn: *September Days Club,* 800-241-5050. $15 for one year, $25 for two years, $33.50 for three years, $50 for five years.

Hilton: *Senior HHonors,* 800-432-3600. $50 for first year, $40 renewal, $285 lifetime. Members outside US and Puerto Rico, add $19.

Holiday Inn: *Alumni Club,* 800-258-6642. $10 fee waived first year, renewals free with five paid nights.

Howard Johnson: *Golden Years Travel Club,* 800-547-7829. $12.95 per year.

Ramada: *Best Years Club,* 800-766-2378. $15 one-time fee.

Red Roof Inn: *RediCard +60,* 800-843-7663. $10 one-time fee (includes three $5-off coupons); spouse membership, $2.

Walt Disney World Resorts: *Magic Kingdom Club Gold Card,* 800-893-4763. $50 for two years. (Does not accept Discover card.)

Airline program. Primarily a vehicle

SPECIAL ROOMS FOR SENIORS

The Econo Lodge brand of the Choice chain now offers "Choice Senior Rooms," providing brighter lighting than what's typically found in a motel room, large-button phones and TV remotes, easy-to-read alarm clocks, large-print brochures, grab bars in showers, and other features designed to appeal to senior travelers. Econo Lodge expects to convert at least 10% of its rooms to the senior standard. The move parallels earlier renovations by Rodeway Inn, another Choice brand, where 25% of the rooms are designed for seniors.

Shoney's Inns and Payless Car Rental, too, offer a special enticement for senior travelers (50 and over). Members of either Shoney's *Merit 50 Club* or Payless's *Nifty-Fifty Plus* program receive 10–15% reductions off regular room rates at 83 Shoney's Inns and reductions of $3 a day or $10 a week from regular Payless rates (rates vary depending on location). To join, call Shoney's (800-222-2222) or Payless (800-729-5377).

for special airline discounts and promotions, the following also offers some
hotel deals.

United Airlines *Silver Wings Plus:* 214-
760-0022. $75 for two years; $225 for life.

This chapter was adapted from the
Consumer Reports Travel Letter *article
"Senior Hotel Discounts" (September
1996).*

FLYING OVERSEAS

Foreign air travel poses two challenges: Getting abroad and getting around once you're there. This chapter will help you on both fronts.

LOW-FARE AIRLINES FOR TRANSATLANTIC HOPS

While domestic low-fare flights get most of the media play, a few small airlines quietly offer cheap tickets to Europe. They don't cut travelers' fare costs by as big a percentage as their domestic counterparts do, but they often provide pleasant savings nonetheless. Two of them also offer a premium option that's less than half what the major lines charge for their cheapest comfortable seats.

Here's a rundown on the four most important scheduled airlines that offer low-fare flights across the Atlantic. Fares and schedules (subject to change) are samples of what the lines were offering last year for peak-season summer travel, as listed at the time of a late-spring *CRTL* report. While the specific quotes are for midweek travel in late 1996, they give an idea of how fares compare.

ICELANDAIR

Originally called Loftleidir, Icelandair has hauled economy-minded travelers from the US to Europe since prejet days. As its first continental gateway, the airline chose Luxembourg, which had no international line to protect and so allowed Icelandair to undercut big lines' fares to their gateways in adjacent countries. Luxembourg isn't a prime destination, but it's a central starting point for an extended *Eurailpass* trip.

All Icelandair's transatlantic flights stop at Reykjavik. As a result, the line's flights to Luxembourg take about two hours longer than other lines' nonstops to nearby Amsterdam, Brussels, or Paris.

ROUTES. Icelandair flies to Reykjavik from Baltimore, Ft Lauderdale, Orlando, and New York/JFK all year, with seasonal flights from Boston and Halifax. From Reykjavik, it flies to Amsterdam, Cologne, Copenhagen, Frankfurt, Glasgow, Hamburg, London, Luxembourg,

Oslo, Paris, Salzburg, Stockholm, Vienna, and Zurich (some of those routes are summer-only; some are flown by other lines under code-sharing agreements). The through-plane New York–Reykjavik-Luxembourg flight operates daily; flights on other routes go less frequently (as seldom as once a week) and usually require a plane change.

FARES. Overall, Icelandair tries to keep its minimum US-Luxembourg Economy excursion fares below the lowest fares on major lines from the same US gateways to Amsterdam or Brussels. It also offers a cheap standby option—not available on the major lines.

Sample round-trip rates: New York–Luxembourg, $698, with seven-day advance purchase; $598 standby. Comparison round-trips on a major line: New York–Amsterdam, $828 with 21-day advance purchase, $2114 unrestricted.

PLANES/SEATING. Flights from the US to Iceland and from there to Luxembourg are on 757s, with the usual six-across seating at 33-inch pitch (a measure of legroom); the *CRTL* comfort score is 71 (see chapter 7). Icelandair flights from Iceland to most other European destinations are in a mix of 757s and 737s (31-inch pitch, comfort score 66); planes and seating on code-shared flights vary.

PREMIUM SERVICE. *Saga* Business Class is available on all 757 flights, with the equivalent of domestic First Class seats and premium cabin service. The line also claims to have Business Class on 737s, but only the fare is premium: Seating is the same tight six-across as in Economy.

Business Class fares were about the same as on major lines ($2938 round-trip New York–Luxembourg). However, Icelandair offers a year-round free-companion promotion in Business Class, effectively cutting the cost in half for a couple.

RESERVATIONS. Fares and schedules are in the computer reservation systems (CRSs) that travel agencies use; code FI. Call a travel agency or Icelandair (800-223-5500).

COMMENTS. Icelandair is a good choice whenever you're going to or near Luxembourg or the fare to there is low enough to compensate for the extra flight time and the cost and time to get to your real destination. It's also a good choice to other Northern European destinations when competing flights also require a stop. With the twofer, Business Class is a nice deal for couples, if they can schedule a 757 for the flights between Reykjavik and their final European gateway.

LTU

Quondam charter line LTU is a distant second to Lufthansa in the German airline hierarchy. Though now nominally a scheduled line, it still operates as if it were a charter: It flies most of its routes only once or twice a week, and many routes are seasonal. In addition to scheduled flights to the US, LTU also flies from Germany to the Caribbean and runs extensive charter operations to other destinations popular with German travelers.

LTU's home base and hub is at Dusseldorf—on the Rhine, about 100 miles northwest of Frankfurt, in the heart of the industrial Ruhr area. Dusseldorf is no less convenient than Frankfurt as a starting point for exploring the Rhine or Moselle valleys, but it's a bit more distant if you're heading for the Romantic Road, the Black Forest, or Bavaria.

As at Frankfurt, the Dusseldorf Airport has direct rail service. If you're heading for other parts of Germany, LTU also offers you a mix of bus and plane connections.

ROUTES. LTU flies nonstop to Dusseldorf from Florida all year and seasonally from other US gateways. In summer 1996, it operated once a week from Daytona Beach, New York/JFK, Orlando, San Francisco, and Tampa; twice a week from Ft Myers and Los Angeles; and three times a week from Miami. It also flew once a week from Miami to San Jose, Costa Rica (part of a Dusseldorf-Miami–San Jose flight).

FARES. LTU tries to keep its lowest fares below those of the big lines. Its lowest fares were capacity-controlled (seats were limited), but they required only a 48-hour advance purchase.

Sample Economy excursion round-trips to Dusseldorf: $798 from New York, $998 from San Francisco; unrestricted fares were $1238 and $1458, respectively. Connecting flights from nearby cities to US gateways and from Dusseldorf to Hamburg or Munich were available at no extra charge. Comparison fares on Lufthansa: Economy excursions were $878 from New York, $1118 from San Francisco; unrestricted round-trips were $1318 and $1558, respectively.

PLANES/SEATING. LTU uses 767s, A330s, and MD11s for transatlantic flights. Economy seats are seven-across in 767s and eight-across in A330s (both are standard), and 10-across in MD11s (charter-style tight). LTU has always featured extra legroom, with a seat pitch of 33 or 33½ inches—that's 2–3 inches more than most large lines provide in Economy. Comfort scores are 70–74, unusually high for a charter-style airline. However, LTU uses extremely narrow, charter-style seats (18 or 18½ inches wide) in all its planes, even though 767 and A330 cabins have room for seats that are at least an inch wider.

RESERVATIONS. Fares and schedules are in the CRSs that travel agencies use; code LT. Call a travel agency or LTU (800-888-0200).

COMMENTS. By virtue of its extra legroom, LTU was a good choice for routes where it competed. It was also a very good deal for travelers who couldn't reserve 21 days in advance. Its Web site (*http://www.ltu.com*) is one of the best airline pages we've seen, with detailed

CHEAP BIG-LINE TICKETS

Low-fare lines don't always undercut their giant rivals. Especially in the slow winter season, the big lines often put their Economy excursion fares on "sale" at rates that challenge low-fare lines, charters, and airfare discounters. As always, with any big-ticket travel expense, you have to check the current market to determine your best buy.

information on fares, schedules, and airplane configurations, and providing E-mail access to the US headquarters.

MARTINAIR

The self-styled "other Dutch airline," Martinair, is also a former charter line that now operates a scheduled (but charter-style) flight program to and from the US. As with LTU, its heavy schedules to and from Florida are run primarily for Europeans vacationing in the US, but seats are available for trips that originate in the US as well.

Martinair also flies from Amsterdam to other destinations popular with European vacationers. Its home base is Amsterdam's user-friendly Schiphol Airport, with direct access to the Dutch rail network.

ROUTES. Martinair flies to Amsterdam year-round from Florida and seasonally from other US gateways. In summer 1996, it flew nonstop four times a week from Miami and Orlando; three times a week from Los Angeles; twice a week from Newark, Oakland, and Seattle; and once a week from Denver and Tampa.

FARES. Martinair tries to keep its lowest fares to Amsterdam below those on the big lines. Sample minimum fares to Amsterdam: $798 from Denver, $648 from Newark, $828 from Seattle, Economy excursion (21-day advance purchase, 7–30-day stay); unrestricted round-trips were $1038, $838, and $1038, respectively. Comparison fares on KLM: $1018, $828, and $1068 for Economy excursion; $3202, $2114, and $3374 for unrestricted Economy.

PLANES/SEATING. Martinair uses 747s, 767s, and MD11s on transatlantic flights. Seats are 10-across in 747s and seven-across in 767s (both are standard) and 10-across in MD11s (charter-style tight); pitch is a tight 30–31 inches (comfort scores 64–73).

PREMIUM SERVICE. *Star Class* provides superior cabin service and roomy Business Class seating equivalent to domestic First Class, with a seat pitch of 36–39 inches.

Sample round-trip fares: $1518 from Denver, $1198 from Newark, and $1698 from the West Coast. While more than double Martinair's cheapest Economy excursions, those premium fares were less than half the price of Business Class on a major airline.

RESERVATIONS. Fares and schedules are in the CRSs; code MP. Call a travel agency or Martinair (800-627-8462).

COMMENTS. Martinair offered the only nonstops to Amsterdam from sev-

WORTH A STOPOVER

Icelandair has turned its Reykjavik stop into an advantage, with an elaborate duty-free shop for through travelers and some attractive no-extra-airfare stopover packages for travelers who want to explore Iceland for a day or two. We recommend one of those stopovers, either going or returning. Iceland's unique landscape, geothermal features, and local culture are well worth the time and effort.

eral Florida points and Seattle, and the only nonstops to the European continent from Denver. It was a clear choice for any of those routes and a good low-cost option from other gateways. *Star Class* was an outstanding deal for anyone who wanted a comfortable flight to Europe at a reasonable price.

TOWER

In addition to being a domestic money-saver (see chapter 4), Tower also operates a few low-fare flights to Europe. Tower has evolved from tour operator to charter airline to scheduled line (though it still flies quite a few charters). Its primary US base is New York/JFK, where it operates from its own terminal.

ROUTES. For summer 1996, Tower flew nonstop from New York/JFK four times a week to Paris and six times a week to Tel Aviv.

FARES. Where government regulations permit, Tower likes to sell all Economy seats at a single, low price, with no restrictions—not even a round-trip requirement. Summer 1996 fares to Paris followed that pattern, at $299 each way or $598 round-trip. That round-trip fare was substantially less than the cheapest restricted Economy excursion on a major line, at $838, and far less than the unrestricted round-trip fare of $1982.

Tower's cheapest tickets to Tel Aviv required round-trip purchase; at $1139, the summer round-trip was the same as on El Al and other big lines. However, Tower's unrestricted one-way, at $824, was about half the unrestricted fare on other lines.

PLANES/SEATING. All Tower flights are on 747s, with conventional, 10-across Economy seating at 32-inch pitch (comfort score 72).

PREMIUM SERVICE. Tower offers two premium options. Business Class, equivalent to domestic First Class, was available to Paris for $998 round-trip —less than one-third of the Business Class fare on a big line. Business Class to Tel Aviv was available at a surcharge of $750 round-trip—lower than El Al's surcharge of $1098.

Alternatively, Tower's Tel Aviv travelers had the option of sitting in the front cabin of the 747 in conventional Economy seating, but with a guarantee that the middle seat in a three-seat unit would be unoccupied. That option, which cost an additional $350 round-trip, was not available on other lines.

RESERVATIONS. Fares and schedules are in the CRSs; code FF. Call a travel agency or Tower (800-221-2500).

COMMENTS. Tower's unrestricted fare to Paris was a good deal for anyone and a great deal for travelers who wanted a one-way ticket or who couldn't reserve 21 days in advance. Tower's Business Class provided the cheapest comfortable seat to Europe on any airline.

To Tel Aviv, Tower enjoyed an advantage only for travelers who needed unrestricted tickets or wanted a premium seat. Moreover, its schedule was unattractive—westbound as well as eastbound flights were overnight red-eyes.

ALTERNATIVES

For cheap seats to Europe, the four low-fare lines aren't the only game in town. Before you buy a ticket, check out your other options:

- Charter flights are often available at about the same prices, and a few charters also offer a low-cost premium option (see chapter 6).
- Discount (consolidator) tickets on major lines are also about the same price as tickets on low-fare lines during the peak summer season, and, with a major line, you usually have far more schedule and route options (see chapter 5).
- Virgin Atlantic often runs short-term sales and promotions from various US gateways to London.

DEALS ON LOCAL AIR TRIPS OVERSEAS

If you plan to tour by air once you're at your destination, you have a lot of options. Dozens of overseas airlines offer deals on local air travel to Americans, Canadians, and other foreign visitors. Some save you money whenever you fly within the host country or region. Others make sense only for extended local travel.

Visitor airfares come in several forms:

- **Air passes** nominally let you fly as often as you like during their validity period, or at least on certain days within the validity period.
- **Visitor tickets** or coupons sold in sets at a fixed, discounted price per flight provide individual one-way flights. Some are available at more than one price, varying by distance. Most impose a minimum and maximum number of flights.
- **Visitor discounts** give foreign visitors a break from the local list prices for individual one-way or round-trip tickets.
- **Visitor itineraries** provide one or more fixed, multistop itineraries for less than the sum of the standard one-way fares.

Typically, visitor fares work out best for multiple-stop regional air trips. Travelers who need just one or two short side trips from one hub city are often better off with individual Economy excursion airline tickets (or, in Europe, the train). Always have your travel agency price individual tickets for your itinerary before you buy a pass.

THE FINE PRINT

Most visitor airfares share some limitations. You must usually buy your tickets or passes before entering the country or countries where you use them, showing proof of foreign citizenship or residence. (Any purchase conditions we list apply to residents of North America.) Many offers are limited to travelers with international air tickets —sometimes only on the line sponsoring the visitor fare—to or from the area where the visitor program is to be used. (In airline argot, you get the visitor fare "in conjunction with" an international ticket.) International travel on frequent-flier awards may not qualify. Where several airlines offer visitor fares in the same country or region, your travel is normally confined to the line that issued your ticket.

Many visitor airfares limit you to one stop in each destination city. In most cases, however, you're allowed to connect through the sponsoring line's hubs as often as required.

Visitor fares for travel in Economy Class are usually reduced for children (typically, ages 2 to 11) and infants under 2. An infant fare does not guarantee a separate seat; if the airplane is full, an adult must hold the child.

Tickets at visitor fares can ordinarily be bought through any US or Canadian travel agency or the US or Canadian office of an international airline and are valid for travel year round. If a North American office can't sell you a ticket directly, it sells you a Miscellaneous Charge Order (MCO), which you exchange for your ticket at your destination. Validity periods are measured from the date of a ticket's first use, not its purchase date.

FLYING AROUND EUROPE

European visitor tickets used to be valid only on one issuing airline. To fly between any two cities outside the issuing airline's hub, you generally had to travel via that hub. To fly from Frankfurt to Paris on the old version of a British Airways visitor ticket, for instance, you had to take separate Frankfurt-London and London-Paris flights and use a separate coupon for each leg of the trip.

More recently, several multiairline visitor tickets have been introduced, permitting far more direct travel, without the need to keep returning to

GOING TO TOWN

The handy *Airport Transit Guide* covers airport-to-town options at more than 400 airports around the world, with rates for taxis, public transit, airport coaches, and shuttle vans. It includes schedules, too. (Its biggest failing is a lack of listings for private-car or limo services.) You can buy it at travel bookstores or, for $8.95 including postage, directly from Magellan's Catalogs (800-962-4943; *AE, Disc, MC, V*).

In Paris, one such option is the Paris Airports Service, which provides direct van transportation between either Charles de Gaulle or Orly Airport and anywhere you want to go in Paris. Rates from de Gaulle are about $29 for one person, about $36 for two. (There are further price breaks for larger groups traveling together.) That's substantially less than a metered taxi, which runs about $50. From Orly, rates are about $23 for one person, about $27 for two. The vans accommodate up to eight passengers. Reservations are requested (*V* and *MC* are accepted). Of course, public transportation is considerably cheaper, but it involves a lot of bother.

You can reserve ahead by calling 011-33-1-49-62-78-78 (fax 011-33-1-49-62-78-79). If you arrive in Paris without a reservation, you can call 49-62-78-78. Paris Airports Service says its entire staff speaks English.

one airline's hub. While the permissible itineraries on those tickets are still limited, they offer a lot more flexibility than the older single-airline, single-hub tickets.

Only a few European countries are big enough to make air travel practical for trips within the country. Still, if you like to fly, you have some attractive options.

EXCURSIONS IN LATIN AMERICA

Multicountry air passes let you visit a number of South America's major cities. But you'll waste a lot of time in the air (and sometimes in layovers) because you must return to a hub city between visits to some of the more popular destinations. Individual-country passes may serve you better. They're available for several countries that are large enough to justify flying and where trains are often slow and infrequent.

AUSTRALIA AND THE PACIFIC

Flying is about the only practical way to island-hop in the South Pacific, and it's a good way to cover the vast stretches of Australia. Travelers to this region have a variety of visitor airfare options. Australia and New Zealand, in particular, offer a wide range of choices, but you'll also find visitor tickets for Papua New Guinea, the Solomon Islands, Vanuatu, and other Pacific Island destinations.

WINGING IT IN ASIA

Several of Asia's important destination countries are large enough to justify the costs of flying. Air travel also com-

mends itself because trains in those countries are slow and infrequent.

India, Indonesia, Malaysia, and Thailand are among the countries with attractive visitor tickets.

DEALS ON ONE-WAY FLIGHTS ABROAD

Buying tickets from a consolidator overseas makes particular sense when you need a short-haul ticket to close the gap in an open-jaw flight, when you need a local excursion ticket for a side trip, or when you want a one-way, long-haul ticket as part of your own spur-of-the-moment, round-the-world itinerary. You can sometimes save on a one-way ticket back to the United States, too (though that's generally possible only when the dollar is strong).

When you shop for airfare discounts abroad, deal with a consolidator that has an office in the country where you plan to buy. Especially with regional tickets, agency margins are too small to cover multiple international fax exchanges and extended phone calls.

Long term, you probably come out ahead by doing business with a good local travel agency overseas. You then won't have to deal directly with consolidators. All the agencies listed below also sell at wholesale rates to retail agencies, which resell to the public. Your retail travel agency can get those discount tickets wholesale and resell them to you at about the same price you'd pay the consolidator.

Find out the cheapest ticket you can buy at an airline's list price before you collect quotes from discounters. If the airlines are having one of their periodic price wars and if you can abide the cheap ticket's restrictions, the airline's advertised price may be your best bet.

No matter what a consolidator's price list says, get a specific quote for any individual ticket. And be prepared to buy a full-fare ticket if the deal falls through.

GETTING TICKETS ABROAD

All the consolidators listed below may apply a surcharge of up to 5% to some credit-card purchases.

•**From London.** We checked the offerings of two large discount agencies in late summer 1995:

Bridge the World Travel Centre specializes mainly in long-haul tickets. It offers a wide selection of Business Class and First Class discount options. 13 Ferdinand St, Camden Town, London NW1 8ES (tube stop Chalk Farm); 011-411-71-911-0900; fax 011-411-71-916-0900; for Europe and North America, 011-441-71-916-0990; for Business Class and First Class, 071-411-911-0800; fax 011-411-71-916-1724.

Major Travel is reportedly one of London's largest consolidators, with contracts with dozens of airlines. It offers a complete range of short- and long-haul deals. 28/34 Fortess Rd, Kentish Town, London NW5 2HB (tube stop Kentish Town); 011-441-71-482-4840; fax 011-441-71-487-2719.

•**From Germany.** *Skytours,* a German agency, often offers attractive long-haul fares to many major cities of the world from six big German cities (Dusseldorf, Frankfurt, Hamburg, Hannover, Munich, and Stuttgart) plus Copenhagen, Oslo, Stockholm, and Zürich. Skytours also sells a broad range of discounted long-haul and intra-European tickets.

Skytours GmbH: Basler Strasse 59-61 Freiburg 79100, Germany; 011-49-761-459-460; fax 011-49-761-459-4646. *AE, DC, MC, V.*

•**From Amsterdam.** Amsterdam was once Europe's hottest discount-airfare center. You can still usually find discount tickets from there to major cities in Africa, Asia, South America, the South Pacific, and the United States, and comparable fares from other big European cities to destinations in Africa, Asia, South America, and the United States. Amsterdam agents also quote low-end round-the-world fares. *Malibu Travel* is one of the most visible consolidators operating in this market.

Malibu Travel: Damrak 30, 1012 LJ Amsterdam, Netherlands; 011-3120-623-2977; fax 011-3120-638-2271. No credit cards accepted.

•**From Canada.** *Connections Travel* offers discounted airfares to Africa, the South Pacific, and Asia from western Canada.

Connections Travel: 1927 W 4th Ave, Vancouver, BC V6J 1M7; 604-738-9499; fax 011-604-738-9228. *MC, V.*

•**From Singapore.** Check *CIEE Travel* for discounts on Economy fares; it may also discount Business Class and First Class fares on a few routes.

CIEE Travel: 110D Killiney Rd, Singapore 239549; 011-65-734-0001; fax 011-65-733-7421. *MC, V.*

This chapter was adapted from the *(June 1996) and the 1996 edition of*
Consumer Reports Travel Letter *article* Consumer Reports Best Travel Deals.
"Low-Fare Transatlantic Airlines"

US AGENCY CUTS FARES WITHIN EUROPE

Looking for a discount ticket out of London? A Florida agency, Interworld Travel, sells cut-price tickets for long- and short-haul flights from London to European, African, and Asian points. Such tickets will interest travelers who get to London on a ticket that doesn't provide for multiple stops or stopovers, and those who are building their own round-the-world itineraries.

Several US agencies sell discount tickets from London. But Interworld has an unusual twist: Instead of handling just a few charter line flights, it keeps day-to-day track of hundreds of bargain fares on dozens of airlines by tapping into *Farebase*. That's a data base of consolidator airfares, maintained in London, that local discount agencies use.

For US travelers, Interworld converts the pound-based rates into US dollars at an exchange rate that's about what you'd get if you exchanged currency at a London bank. Presently, it accepts all major credit cards with a surcharge up to 4%.

Interworld won't necessarily have a better fare for any trip out of London than a London agency—you have to deal with foreign exchange and, possibly, an additional middleman's markup. The advantages to dealing with a US agency are that you can make beyond-London flight arrangements before you leave, and you can avoid having to look for a discount agency after you arrive in London and carrying the cash to pay for a ticket there. In any event, it can't hurt to ask for a quote.

Interworld also sells discount tickets from the US to Europe and South America. If you're leery about sending cash to a discount agency, Interworld will refer you to the local sales office of the airline on which it sells you the ticket, for validation that it is, in fact, an authorized agency. (For more information, contact Interworld at 800 Douglas Rd, Suite 140, Coral Gables FL 33134; 305-443-4929, fax 305-443-0351.)

FOREIGN LODGINGS FOR LESS

With today's high hotel prices overseas, it's more important than ever to get a good rate. Consider first a half-price program, available for rooms in Canada, Mexico, the Caribbean, Europe, and elsewhere. But if you're going to Asia, you'll find the offerings of half-price programs meager. In that case, ask your travel agent to find a wholesale or preferred rate for you.

When you can't get a large discount, smaller ones are often available. But failing even one of those, you can still save by comparing costs from different sources. Check directly with a hotel's reservation desk, through a travel agent's computer-reservation system, or through a US-based hotel representative. Or consider a budget hotel.

FOREIGN HOTELS AT HALF PRICE

Overseas, half-price hotel programs work as they do at home. You buy a directory of participating hotels or join a club that issues a directory. About 30 days before a trip, you call or fax the hotel (not its US representative or toll-free reservation line), identify yourself as a member, and ask if a room is available at your program's half-price rate. If the hotel expects to be no more than about 80% full, you're supposed to get a discount—though not necessarily half-price (more about that in *Half of What?*, page 215).

This section reviews six programs. Five included US and foreign locations in single, worldwide directories.

Entertainment Publications offers multiple books: To present its worldwide coverage, we included both the *National Hotel & Dining Directory*, covering the US and some other areas, and the *Entertainment Europe Hotel Directory*. The directories cost $28–81 when we checked for a 1996 report. For more information on the 1997 editions, see page 224.

HOW THEY STACKED UP

The *Worldwide Coverage* table shows the number of participating hotels in each program's directory (directories, in the case of Entertainment). The tally is by country for North America and Europe, overall for Africa, Asia, the Caribbean, Latin America, the Middle East, and the South Pacific. The more listings, the more useful the program.

However, geographical coverage was uneven. *Entertainment* and *ITC-50* included more than 100 locations in both Canada and Latin America, and a few offered a decent sampling in the Caribbean and Bermuda. Most travelers to those areas would have found enough choices to make signing up worthwhile.

Except for *ITC-50*, on the other hand, listings remained minimal in Asia and the South Pacific. Travelers there would probably have done better to search for hotel discounts through, say, a broker or a travel agency that could arrange a preferred or wholesale rate (see chapters 14 and 16).

Here's how we ranked the programs:

Entertainment took the top spot, mainly because of the big edge its *Europe Hotel Directory* had over all competitors in Europe. Among 10 major tourist destinations (see pages 216–17), it was a solid choice for Amsterdam, London, Madrid, and Paris, and it was adequate (barely) for Munich, Rome, and Zurich.

As an alternative to its regular *Europe* directory, Entertainment publishes individual city directories, in local languages, for Amsterdam, Gothenburg, London, Malmo, Paris, and Stockholm. Those directories also included a listing of hotels that was similar (but not identical) to that in the *Europe* directory. For stays of several days in any of those cities, the city directories' extensive local restaurant discounts (usually 25% off the entire food bill or a twofer price on entrees) made them a preferred buy.

For the rest of the world, the *Entertainment Hotel & Dining Directory* covered Canada and Latin America about as well as any competitor. Entertainment also publishes directories for Mexico; Melbourne, Australia; and 14 localities in Canada. But it lagged behind *Encore* and *ITC-50* in the Caribbean and the South Pacific.

ITC-50 had the most international listings in a single directory. There were substantially fewer than the two Entertainment books together offered, but the one ITC-50 directory was also cheaper. The program was strong in Canada, the Caribbean, and Latin America, and it was the top choice for Asia and the South Pacific. However, it didn't do particularly well in the 10 cities for which we compared coverage.

Encore was about on a par with ITC-50, overall. It was especially strong in the Caribbean and competitive in Canada. In our 10 test cities, it had a few attractive upmarket properties that the other programs didn't. However, many of its overseas locations offered only 20–30% off, rather than the usual 50%.

Great American Traveler ranked next, mainly because of its 203 German locations—almost 10 times as many as offered by its nearest competitor—and it was strong in Austria, France, Norway, Sweden, and Switzerland. Elsewhere in Europe, however, it trailed its bigger rivals.

In addition to offering standard half-off deals, *Great American* also referred members to *Hotel Reservations Network,* one of the largest hotel brokers, for discounts at some listed hotels. While that might be a good suggestion when you can't get a half-price rate, you needn't belong to any program to take advantage of HRN's services (see chapter 16).

Privilege Card was surprisingly big overseas, given its minor position in the US. However, at least one competitor bested it in almost every region. Among the test cities, it outdid the others in Rome and Singapore and offered a very good selection in Paris.

Carte Royale had thinner coverage than the others. In Europe, it was outstanding mainly for Italy. Among our test cities, it beat the others only in Hong Kong (but even there, it offered only three hotels).

OTHER FACTORS. Almost all the programs promised a variety of other discounts or rebates—on airfares, restaurants, car rentals, theater tickets, and such. Typically, the individual-city *Entertainment* directories offered more of those than any others: The dining discounts and dollars-off airfare certificates were of substantial value.

On the other hand, many of the various programs' extra deals were either of only marginal value or easily duplicated elsewhere. Two programs— *Encore* and *Great American Traveler* —also shared a major shortcoming: They didn't print numbers for fax, probably the most convenient way to request a half-price rate (or any other sort of information) from a hotel overseas.

A TALE OF 10 CITIES

The *Plan vs Plan* table shows the number of hotels each program listed in 10 popular tourist-destination cities. Of those, the listings were extensive only for London and Paris. (In the following examples, *Entertainment* refers to the European directory.)

- For Amsterdam, the top choice was *Entertainment,* with a good selection in the mid- to high-priced range, including the Golden Tulip Barbizon Center, the Memphis, and the Renaissance. (Nobody offered budget properties.) *Encore* had six hotels, one of them the popular Pulitzer, but most at just 20% off.
- In Auckland, *ITC-50* was the one to try, with the Airport Travelodge, Hobson Motor Inn, and Waipuna Intl.
- In Hong Kong, *Carte Royale* shone, with the two New World hotels and the Victoria.
- In London, the programs taken together offered 77 different hotels. The listings included three Tourist hotels with rack (regular) rates under $80 a night: Julius Caesar (*Entertainment),* Queensgate (20% off through *Encore),* and Regent Palace (*ITC-50, Privilege,* and 30% off through *Encore*). At the high end were several Deluxe hotels, including the Britannia Inter-Continental (*Entertainment*), Grosvenor House (30% through *Encore*), and Sheraton Park Tower (*Entertainment*). *Encore* and *Enter-*

tainment had the best selection of midpriced properties.

A few US hotels seem to have signed up with almost all the half-price programs. Not so in London, where only the Flemings Mayfair showed up on four different lists and only the Henry VIII, Regent Palace, and Westminster were on three.

- In Madrid, *Entertainment* was probably the best choice, with 11 options. However, only *Encore* had the classic Ritz (30% off).

- In Munich, *Great American Traveler* had the most listings, mainly in the Tourist category. *Entertainment's* three choices were midpriced (Arabella Bogenhausen, Hungar, and Pannonia Koenigin Elisabeth).

- The Paris numbers included 21 Tourist-class Abotels on both the *Entertainment* and *Privilege Card* lists. The two "all-suite" Home Plazza hotels (both typical family-oriented hotels, with extremely small rooms) were in three different programs. *Entertainment* also listed two budget Fimotels. In the midrange, it included the Brebant, the Garden Elysee, and the all-suite Residence du Roy. High-end offerings included the Demeure Parc Victor Hugo, Lotti, and Scribe. Runner-up *Privilege Card* featured mainly lower-priced properties. *Encore's* listing was limited, but it offered 30% off at the de la Tremoille and even at the haughty George V.

- In Rome, *Privilege Card* had the most options (six), including the two midrange Atlante properties (the expensive Lord Byron, listed in the

directory, had dropped out). *Entertainment's* four-hotel list included the popular Ambasciatori Palace and two of the midrange Jolly locations. *Carte Royale* included three Jollys.

- In Singapore, *Privilege Card* provided the best choice, from the budget Asia Pte to the upmarket Orchard. *Carte Royale's* two listings (Furama and Golden Landmark) were both upmarket.

- In Zurich, two programs gave three choices each. *Entertainment* offered the upscale Atlantis Sheraton, the midpriced Sofitel, and the lower-priced Senator. *Great American Traveler* offered three relatively expensive choices: Central Plaza, Nova Park, and Swissotel Zurich.

HALF OF WHAT?

The discounts of "half-price" programs are often less than 50% off the price other travelers pay. In mid-January '96, we requested half-price rates for mid-February from 20 European hotels listed by one or more of the programs we're reporting on here. We compared the rate quoted in the response with the rack rate listed in the most recent issue of the *Hotel & Travel Index,* an industry reference:

- Eleven of the hotels offered a room at 42–50% off the rack rate—in our view, close enough to count as compliance, given the vagaries of exchange rates and short-term price adjustments. Those were the Memphis in Amsterdam; the Auckland Airport Travelodge; the Flemings Mayfair and Westminster in London; the Miguel

Angel in Madrid; the Abotel La Concorde, Garden Elysee, and Scribe in Paris; the Furama in Singapore; and the Atlantis Sheraton and Sofitel in Zurich.

• Another five offered rates at 20–28% off rack rate—attractive discounts, though not close to 50%. Among those hotels were the New World Harbour View in Hong Kong, the Marble Arch Marriott in London, and the Ambasciatori Palace in Rome.

• The Arabella Bogenhausen in Munich responded with a disappointing offer of only 16% off. The high-end Lord Byron in Rome responded that it had dropped out of the *Privilege Card* program but offered a 10% discount anyway. The others didn't respond.

As with domestic programs, overseas half-price programs sometimes offer less than they claim. Clearly, not every hotel that signs up really gives half off the everyday asking price. Still, whatever the real discount, the "half-price" rate is often the best you'll be quoted. Compare it with the rack rate: If the price is attractive, take it. If it isn't, try another hotel—or another discount program.

WHOLESALE DEALS AT ASIAN HOTELS

ITC-50 aside, the Asian offerings of half-price programs are pretty thin. You might instead want to try a wholesale agency (basically a tour operator that guarantees suppliers a certain volume of bookings in exchange for price cuts). *Travel Interlink* and *VacationLand* are two that are probably fairly typical of the group.

A few years ago, we compared rack (regular) rates with what the wholesalers were offering for hotels in six Asian cities: Bali, Bangkok, Hong Kong, Kuala Lumpur, Singapore, and Tokyo. (Both agencies had deals in other major Asian cities as well.) The discount agents' rates on standard rooms averaged about 35% less than rack rate, but discounts at some hotels ran up to 50%, occasionally a bit more. (A later follow-up for Bangkok and Hong Kong included those two agencies plus a third, *Absolute Asia*. The results were similar.)

There was a broad choice of hotels —from Superior Tourist, just below the middle of the ratings of the *Official Hotel Guide* (a common classification system; see chapter 14), through Superior Deluxe. Individual agencies may use a different classification in their brochures, so it's useful to have some knowledge of the hotels in each city you're

PLAN VS PLAN: 10 CITIES*

CITY	CARTE ROYALE	ENCORE (a)
Amsterdam	—	6
Auckland	—	3
Hong Kong	3	1
London	4	34
Madrid	2	8
Munich	1	2
Paris	2	4
Rome	4	2
Singapore	2	1
Zurich	—	—
Totals	18	61

* As of early 1996; subject to change.

visiting, from the *OHG* or a guidebook, before you call a discount agency.

ARRANGING YOUR ROOM. Tell the agency where you're going, when, and any preferences for location or specific facilities. If you already have one or two favorite hotels, ask what deals the agency might have there. Otherwise, ask what's available in your price range.

You reserve in advance and prepay by check; neither *Travel Interlink* nor *VacationLand* accepts charge cards. The wholesale agency sends you a voucher that you present on arrival at each hotel. (In some cases, the vouchers are sent directly to the hotel.) Cancel well before your departure and you get a full refund, less a modest fee; cancel closer to departure and you forfeit the cost of one night's lodging. (Specifics vary among agencies; check for details when you book.) If you'd rather have your own travel agent make arrange-

ments for you, note that *VacationLand's* listings are commissionable.

One warning: As with any prepaid lodging, once you get past the cancellation deadline, you're locked into the deal. Book through a wholesale agency only if your travel plans are firm and you know the hotel where you'll be staying. For other situations, a preferred rate—even though not quite such a good price—may turn out to be a better overall deal.

ANY OTHER DISCOUNTS TO BE HAD?

If you can't get a 50% discount or the 35%-and-up reductions we've described above, do you have any other recourse? Try aiming for at least a 20 to 25% discount off rack rates. Here are some other options:

- Preferred rates—deeply discounted corporate rates. (See chapter 14.)

ENTERTAINMENT EUROPE HOTEL DIRECTORY	ENTERTAINMENT HOTEL & DINING DIRECTORY	GREAT AMERICAN TRAVELER	ITC-50	PRIVILEGE CARD
10	4	—	2	4
—	—	—	3	1
—	—	—	—	1
30	16	14	7	17
11	1	—	3	—
3	1	8	—	1
63	7	17	3	61
4	4	2	—	6
—	—	—	1	4
3	1	3	1	2
124	34	45	20	97

(a) Most discounts 20-40% off rack rates.

- Discount through a tour operator's package. (See chapter 2.)
- Weekend, holiday, and off-season sales promotions run by hotels and resorts.
- Senior discounts. As in the United States, hotels abroad may offer discounts for travelers of even not-so-mature years (sometimes as young as 50); ask before you book.

LIST-PRICE BARGAINS

Even dedicated discount shoppers are sometimes forced to reserve a room at rack rate. In those cases, you can still save yourself some money by comparing rates among different hotels in the same location. There are generally three ways to find out if a room is available—and what it will cost—in overseas hotels that don't have US reservation numbers:

•Reserve by computer. Many hotels abroad are listed in the computer-reservation systems that travel agents use. Rooms at those hotels can be booked in the same way you'd book a domestic hotel. For most agencies, the commission on a hotel booking for a few nights would never cover the costs of extensive comparison shopping. But once you've identified your preferred hotels, a travel agent will probably at least be willing to check the prices in a reservation computer—especially if you then book the accommodations through the agent.

•Call directly, by international telephone or fax. Phone calls can be expensive and cumbersome—especially with time-zone and language barriers. Fax messages are convenient, but they may be ignored by hotel personnel when received from an unknown individual traveler.

•Check hotel reps. Many overseas hotels are represented in the US by one or more hotel representatives, independent booking services that will sell you a room at whichever facilities they represent in the location and time period you desire.

Overseas reps are the least attractive option: You often pay more than rack rate. However, if you feel that the convenience is worth the extra cost, you may want to book your overseas lodgings that way. Many reps (see *Where to Find It* at the end of this chapter for a few) list their rates in the computer-reservation systems used by travel agents and then book overseas hotels through those systems. (A hotel is often listed more than once in a reservation system at different rates—in the hotel's own listing and through one or more representatives.)

Reps can usually issue immediate space and rate confirmations by phone. Most require a deposit (the cost of one to three nights) or a credit or charge-card number, to confirm reservations. Some require full prepayment. Some reps may charge extra for last-minute reservations (booking one day ahead, say). Most impose some limits on cancellation. You're usually charged one night for a no-show, but some reps charge for three nights. If you've booked resort accommodations during high season, the cancellation policy may be more stringent than for low season.

Payment procedures also vary: Some

WORLDWIDE COVERAGE *

REGION/ COUNTRY	CARTE ROYALE	ENCORE (a)	ENTER. EUROPE HOTEL DIREC.	ENTER. HOTEL AND DINING DIRECTORY	GREAT AMERICAN TRAVELER	ITC-50	PRIVILEGE CARD
NORTH AMERICA							
US*	468	3073	320	2893	1661	1918	1505
Canada	46	308	26	377	122	100	80
EUROPE							
Andorra	—	—	1	—	—	—	—
Austria	4	5	10	5	42	3	6
Belgium	4	5	38	9	4	6	15
Bulgaria	—	—	6	1	—	—	—
Canary Islands	—	6	4	—	—	—	3
Cyprus	2	—	2	—	—	—	—
Czech Republic	1	—	2	1	—	1	—
Denmark	3	2	20	1	18	1	8
England	7	134	117	41	18	45	93
Finland	—	—	3	—	3	—	—
France	5	4	180	8	88	30	79
Germany	4	21	14	3	203	10	23
Greece	5	—	17	3	—	3	5
Hungary	2	—	34	1	—	4	4
Iceland	—	1	—	—	—	1	1
Ireland/ Northern Ireland	—	3	11	2	—	4	4
Italy	42	11	47	24	28	17	26
Luxembourg	—	1	—	1	—	1	1
Malta	—	1	—	—	—	2	1
Monaco	—	1	—	—	—	—	—
Netherlands	2	42	35	5	1	7	9
Norway	—	—	4	1	10	2	—
Poland	—	—	8	—	—	1	—
Portugal	4	1	19	9	—	6	11
Romania	—	—	26	4	—	—	2
Russia	1	—	1	—	—	—	1
Scotland	—	8	17	5	—	12	11
Slovakia	—	—	1	—	—	2	—
Slovenia	—	—	2	—	—	1	—
Spain	10	44	82	5	3	9	49
Sweden	—	—	97	2	46	2	7
Switzerland	3	5	19	3	23	12	10
Wales	—	8	5	—	—	9	19
REST OF WORLD							
Africa	—	1	20	—	—	10	2
Asia	14	13	5	2	1	51	16

WORLDWIDE COVERAGE* *(continued)*

REGION/ COUNTRY	CARTE ROYALE	ENCORE (a)	ENTER. EUROPE HOTEL DIREC.	ENTER. HOTEL AND DINING DIRECTORY	GREAT AMERICAN TRAVELER	ITC-50	PRIVILEGE CARD
REST OF WORLD *(continued)*							
Carribbean/ Bermuda	13	69	7	19	4	38	47
Latin America(b)	31	34	2	174	60	134	50
Middle East	4	2	22	3	1	18	3
South Pacific	10	33	2	17	—	78	17
TOTALS							
Europe	99	303	826	134	487	191	388
Outside US	217	766	887	625	632	906	625
Program Total	787	397	927	3555	2586	3307	2418

*As of early 1996; subject to change.
(a) Most discounts 20-40% off rack rates.

(b) Mexico, Central America, South America.

reps accept payment directly. You either remit payment for one to three nights as a deposit or prepay the entire stay. In most cases, payment can be by cash or charge card; a few reps accept personal checks. The advantage of going through a rep who takes payment is that your deposit is refundable from a US organization in case you cancel. Also, a few reps who work that way accept the US dollar payment converted at the exchange rate in effect at the time of booking and honor that rate regardless of any subsequent currency exchange fluctuations.

Other hotel reps obtain charge-card guarantee information and forward it to the hotel. Your rate is computed and paid in foreign currency at the time you check out; any refunds due you have to come through the hotel.

YOUR PERSONAL BEST BUY

Your travel agent or your company's travel department can help you narrow your list of hotels or find the names and phone numbers of reps to call for information about hotel prices and room availability. You could also consult a copy of the *Hotel and Travel Index, Official Hotel Guide,* or *Star Service,* available in large libraries as well as at travel agencies.

Regardless of how you make the reservation, be sure to get the information you'll need: confirmation number, deposit requirements, guarantees, credit or charge cards accepted, and cancellation provisions.

BUDGET MOTELS

In Europe, budget motels are among the best deals in list-price lodgings. If you're looking for efficiency rather than charm, they're a great bargain.

In the United Kingdom, there's the *Granada Inns* chain, located next to Granada gas stations and restaurants along the motorways. Even cheaper are the *Little Chef Lodges,* which are affiliated with a UK fast-food chain.

You'll find more budget-motel chains in France, however, than in any other European country. They come in several flavors: subbudget and something a notch or two above.

There's no real US counterpart to the French subbudget hotel. At somewhere near 100 square feet, the rooms are less than half as big as those you find at even the bottom-end US chains, and they're not air-conditioned. You get one standard double bed (with, perhaps, an overhead bunk or a foldout mini-single as well). Bathrooms are tiny, with a shower down the hall. Check-in counters may be open for only a few hours in the morning and again in the evening. (At other times, guests can check themselves in automatically with a charge card.)

The rooms are spartan, but they're clean and efficient. They were generally going for under $30 a night when we priced them for a mid-1995 report.

You must go upmarket two levels and spend perhaps $50–100 a night to find something close to the US budget motel. Chains such as Climat de France and Campanile approximate what you

SOMETHING ELSE?

If a French budget motel sounds a bit dreary to you, consider these alternatives:

RURAL FRANCE

The French countryside is full of small inns where you can often find accommodations in the same price range as the subbudget chains. Very few of them are listed in guidebooks published in the US. The easiest way to find them, almost anywhere in France, is to study the current edition of the *Red Michelin Guide*. Look for two types of entry:

- Hotels listed under the *Guide's* "quite comfortable" or "modest comfort" symbols often show rates as low as the subbudgets.
- You can sometimes find even better room deals among the countryside restaurants that are noted as *restaurants avec chambres*. Those are establishments where the main business is food service.

Many city tourist offices maintain lists of *gîtes* (cottages) available for rent in the nearby countryside. Rentals are usually by the week, but you can sometimes make a deal for a shorter stay.

CITIES

In most French cities (as well as in cities throughout the rest of Europe), you'll find a hotel-booking office run by the local community or its tourist office. It's usually either in or near the main rail station. There, you can check availability and make a reservation for one of many inexpensive hotels that use the system.

find at Motel 6 or Hampton Inn. Even then, you get a smaller room than a US chain provides for less money. The bath is a bit more like what you're used to, but air-conditioning is still relatively rare.

Three big French-based hotel chains offer two or more low-end options. All the "brands" we list here publish directories that show hotel locations and rates; most also show facilities and number of rooms. They're not distributed in the US, but you can pick one up at your first stop.

- **Accor's** subbudget brand is *Formule 1,* concentrated in France but with a few locations elsewhere—mainly in Belgium and Germany. Most locations offer free parking. Formule 1 does not maintain a US reservation center. The local reservation number is (011-33) 1-43-04-10-22; you'd better speak some French to use it.

  Etap is a step up from Formule 1. Rooms are still small, but each has a private shower and toilet. For rooms equivalent to what you find in a US budget motel, you must move one more notch up the scale, to Accor's mainstream *Ibis* chain. Few are air-conditioned, however.

- **Hotels & Compagnie,** a smaller chain, offers *Nuit d'Hotel* in the subbudget range. The chain's more conventional budget brand is *Balladins,* with somewhat larger rooms and private showers. A few locations, mainly in the south, offer air-conditioned rooms. Parking is free at most locations, but there's a charge at some in central-city locations.

  At the top of the chain's budget

operations are *Climat de France* and *Relais Bleu.* As with their competitors, facilities are much closer to what you get in a US budget motel—but at roughly twice the price.

Balladins, Climat, and Relais Bleu offer similar (but separate) promotion programs: a *Carte* that entitles travelers to a 10% reduction on room rates Monday–Thursday, a 30% reduction on room rates Friday–Sunday, and a 12–20% reduction on *demipension* rates (room, breakfast, and lunch or dinner), with minor limitations and variations among the three chains. In 1995, *Cartes* cost $44–52 for ordinary tourists, $27–31 for seniors (60 years or over).

Hotels & Compagnie has no US reservation number, but you can reserve at all its chains by calling France: (011-33) 1-64-46-49-00; be prepared to speak French. In France, the toll-free numbers are 05-39-66-66 for Balladins and 05-45-22-66 for Relais Bleu (there's none for Campanile).

- **Groupe Envergure** operates the *Premiere Classe* subbudget chain. Rooms are still cramped but, unlike those of the two subbudget competitors above, include private shower. Parking is free. There's no US reservation number, nor is there a central toll-free number in France.

  Envergure's main upper-budget brand is *Campanile,* which offers considerably larger rooms, as well as facilities that more closely approach those of US budget hotels. While most Campaniles are in France, there are a scattering in Spain, Portugal, the UK, the Netherlands, and Belgium. There's no US reservation office; the French central reservation number is (011-33) 1-64-62-46-46, Internet address: *http//www.campanile.fr*.

•Other chains in the subbudget class include *Bonsai, Fasthotel,* and *Liberté.*

WHERE TO FIND IT

HALF-PRICE PROGRAMS

Except as noted, all prices are per year from date of purchase.

Carte Royale: 800-218-5862. $39.95. *MC, V.*

Encore: 800-444-9800. $49.95. *AE, Disc, MC, V.*

Entertainment Publications: 800-445-4137. International Hotel Directory, $59.95; also books in local languages: *Amsterdam, Gothenburg, London, Malmo, Melbourne, Paris, Stockholm,* $39.95; *National Hotel & Dining Directory* (hotel listings for most US states, Canada, the Carribean, Mexico, Puerto Rico, and some of Europe; also includes limited local dining discounts, $42.95, or $27.95 without dining listings). Once you buy one book, you can buy local books at reduced prices.

Books are valid for 12–18 months, depending on when you buy. *MC, V.*

Great American Traveler: 800-548-2812, 801-262-2233, fax 801-262-2311. $49.95. *AE, Disc, MC, V.*

ITC-50: 800-342-0558, 312-465-8891, fax 312-262-6159. $49. *AE, DC, MC, V.*

Privilege Card: 800-236-9732, 404-262-0222, fax 404-262-0235. $80.90. *Disc, MC, V.*

WHOLESALE AGENCIES

Absolute Asia: 180 Varick Street, 16th Floor, NYC 10014; 800-736-8187; fax 212-627-4090.

Travel Interlink: 4348 Van Nuys Blvd, Suite 206, Sherman Oaks CA 91403; 800-477-7172; fax 800-888-0191; E-mail *Travelink@aol.com*. Ask for the *Consumer Discount Travel Program*.

VacationLand: 150 Post St, Suite 680, San Francisco CA 94108; 800-245-0050, 415-788-0503; fax 415-788-0103. Ask for the *Hotemart* program.

HOTEL REPS

B and V Assoc.: 140 East 56th St, Suite 4C, New York 10022; 800-546-4777; fax 212-688-9467. *AE, MC, V.*

Edwardian Hotels of London: Carlson Hospitality Worldwide Reservation Center, 11340 Blondo St., Omaha NE 68164-3822; 800-333-3333; fax 402-498-9166. *AE, DC, MC, V* (to guarantee reservation, not to prepay).

Jamaica Reservation Service: 1320 S Dixie Hwy, Suite 1102, Coral Gables FL 33146; 800-526-2422; fax 305-667-3638. *AE, MC, V.*

Jarvinen Worldwide Hotels: 1717 N Highland Ave, Suite 1100, Los Angeles 90028; 800-876-5278 (213-462-6391 in Los Angeles); fax 213-461-7559. Charge-card acceptance depends upon individual hotel policy.

Leading Hotels of the World: 747 Third Ave, NYC 10017; 800-223-6800 (212-838-3110 in NY); fax 212-758-7367. Charge-card acceptance depends upon individual hotel policy.

Loews Representation Intl: 7500 N Dreamy Draw Dr, Suite 120, Phoenix

85020; 800-223-0888; fax 602-997-6586. Credit card acceptance depends on location.

Marketing Ahead: 433 Fifth Ave, NYC 10016; 212-686-9213; fax 212-686-0271. *AE or check*.

Preferred Hotels & Resorts Worldwide: 3115 Wacker Dr, Suite 1900, Chicago IL 60606-6628; 800-323-7500. Charge-card acceptance depends upon individual hotel policy.

ENTERTAINMENT'S BLOCKBUSTER HOTEL BOOK

Since this writing, Entertainment Publications has published a new directory called the *Ultimate Travel Savings Directory*. With more than 5500 hotels listed, this new book includes virtually all the hotels that are covered in its other publications. The *Ultimate Travel Savings Directory* is valid through the end of 1997 and costs $59.95 plus $3 shipping and handling.

Robert F. Warner, Inc.: 310 Madison Ave, Suite 1804, NYC 10017; 800-888-1199; fax 212-682-9254. Charge-card acceptance depends upon individual hotel policy.

Robert Reid Associates: 810 N 96th St, Omaha 68114; 800-223-6510. Charge-card acceptance depends upon individual hotel policy.

Steigenberger Reservation Service: 5505 S Semoran Blvd, Suite 1129, Winter Park FL 32792; 800-223-5652; fax 407-679-3361. Charge-card acceptance depends upon individual hotel policy.

Supranational Hotel Reservations: Suite 1 Grasmere, Butler's Wharf Building, 36 Shad Comes, London, GB, 5E1 2YE; 800-843-3311. Charge-card acceptance depends upon individual hotel policy.

Utell Intl: 810 N 96 St, Omaha 68114; 800-448-8355; fax 402-398-5484. Charge-card acceptance depends upon individual hotel policy.

This chapter was adapted from the Consumer Reports Travel Letter *article "Foreign Hotels at Half Price" (March 1996) and the 1996 edition of* Consumer Reports Best Travel Deals.

21

SEEING EUROPE: ROAD OR RAIL?

How you tour in Europe can make a difference of hundreds of dollars to your budget. If your decision depends on cost, the comparisons of typical car and train trips in this chapter can point you in the right direction.

In 1996, *CRTL* checked the weekly rates of companies that arrange European car rentals for US travelers. We also checked the latest prices for rail passes and individual train tickets. Using those prices, we figured the costs per person for one- and two-week trips covering 1000 and 3000 miles, by train and by car, for travel parties of various sizes. The chart *Car vs Train Costs*, page 227, presents the details, but here are some highlights:

- Solo travelers pay a big premium to drive a rental car. For parties of two or more, however, a rented car proved to be an economical and convenient way to tour Europe—if rented in a country where rates were reasonable.
- For long-term driving, a new-car purchase-repurchase "lease" in France was often the best deal.

- Rates were extremely high in Scandinavia and most of Eastern Europe. Travelers should, if possible, avoid renting a car there.
- While a car had a big edge for touring, trains would best serve travelers who stay mainly in big cities.
- Buying individual Second-Class rail tickets makes sense for short trips if you want to be able to travel every day. Otherwise, if you take the train, a pass is your best bet.
- Torn between driving and the train? You needn't choose. Several rail passes combine rail-travel and car-rental days.

When comparing driving with rail travel, don't forget some necessary extras:

- With a rented car, parking (seldom included in city hotel rates) may add $10–20 a day to your costs in big cities. And if you drive extensively in Austria, France, Greece, Italy, the Netherlands, Norway, Portugal, or Spain, motorway tolls can easily add $5–25 a day.
- With a train, you'll normally pay extra for seat reservations—an essential on long-haul express trains. If you buy

individual train tickets, also figure on supplements for express trains and other fees.

- Station-to-hotel costs may add $2–20 to each arrival or departure.

Of course, you needn't base a choice between car and train purely on cost. A rented car is a much more urbane way to explore scenic byways and enjoy Europe's rural hospitality and cuisine. In a car, you set your own itinerary, pace, and schedule—you can stop to take snapshots or detour down side roads to your heart's content.

Then again, trains have advantages of their own. They're faster for long hauls and they let you forget about traffic and parking. We cover the pros and cons of rail touring later in this chapter.

OVERSEAS RENTERS AND THEIR DEALS

Several familiar US-based names operate their own rental fleets in Europe. So, of course, do Europe-based companies, some of which are represented in the US (EuroDollar by Dollar; Europcar by National; and Kenning, Town and Country Intl, and Woods Car Rental–UK by US sales offices). A handful of independent US rental agencies (some are tour operators as well) also arrange cars through various European rental companies.

FIGURING COSTS

The type of rental company you deal with won't matter much unless you want to use a frequent-flier upgrade or have some other special reason to pre-fer one company over another. But you'll generally do better if you strike your deal before you leave.

Weekly touring rates ordinarily provide the best deals. To qualify, you may have to keep your car for at least five days. If you return it early, the company may charge you at a much higher local daily rate. Most companies prorate the weekly rate for rentals of eight days or more.

All the prices in the *Weekly Rates* table on pages 230–38 are for cars booked in the US for European driving in summer 1996. (Rates for 1997 were not available at press time.) In all but a few cases, those rates provide unlimited mileage. Rates were usually uniform at all locations in a country, but some of Europe's airports imposed extra taxes or fees.

Rates in some locations are higher in July and August than in other summer months, and rates on Greek and Spanish islands may be higher than on the mainland. Where rates varied by location, we list the rate that applied at most locations (excluding airport surcharges).

For ready comparisons, country by country and among competing companies, we adjusted the rates in our tables:

- **VAT (Value Added Tax).** We added in VAT where advertised rates didn't include it, as most didn't.

  Auto Europe had arranged for VAT refunds in Hungary and Italy, so that it could offer no-tax rates there—a unique advantage, at this writing. Also, in the Czech Republic, companies cited various VAT rates. We used 5%, a figure confirmed by the Czech

Embassy, but some companies quoted 22%. On a Czech rental, ask about the final VAT rate before you agree to a price.

- **CDW.** Most rates that we list don't include collision-damage waiver (CDW). No loss: It's overpriced (more than $20 a day in some countries) and, for most travelers, unnecessary. You can cover the risks of collision damage and theft by renting with a charge card that offers those coverages as free benefits. In a few cases, noted in the table, rentals were available only with CDW.
- **Dual rates.** Some car-rental companies

offered both a bare-bones weekly rate (excluding VAT and CDW) and a rate that included those extras. Since we don't recommend paying for CDW, we started with bare-bones rates and added just the VAT.

- **Insurance in Italy.** Separate theft insurance is mandatory in Italy: We added it to any published rate that didn't include it.

PAYMENT AND CURRENCY. Some rental companies offered the option of prepaying in full or paying at the end of a rental. The latter is your better choice when the rates are equal— there's less hassle if you have to cancel.

CAR VS TRAIN COSTS: TYPICAL TRIPS

	CAR		TRAIN	
	2 PERSONS	4 PERSONS	TRAVEL 4 DAYS OR LESS(a)	TRAVEL 7 DAYS(a)
SHORT TRIP (1 week/1000 miles)				
Europass Area(b)	$145	$109	$237	$240(c)
France	211	155	150	180(c)
Germany	144	106	134	215
Italy	224	179	132	160(c)
UK	129	104	199	235
	2 PERSONS	4 PERSONS	TRAVEL 8 DAYS OR LESS(a)	TRAVEL 14 DAYS(a)
LONG TRIP (2 weeks/3000 miles)				
Europass Area(b)	370	274	332	522(d)
France	495	363	270	440
Germany	383	280	215	290
Italy	522	411	184	208
UK	321	254	280	365

Note: All costs per person as of late March 1996; subject to change. Driving costs are for a couple in an economy car and for four people in a midsized car; rental charges, taxes, and operating expenses are included.

(a) Except as noted, using flexible rail pass (a pass that allows travel on a limited number of days in its total validity period); for Europass areas, the cheapest First

Class Europass that met trip requirements; for individual countries, a Second Class national pass; companion passes, where available, in Europass area and Germany.

(b) France, Germany, Italy, Spain, Switzerland.

(c) Second Class tickets bought separately for each train trip.

(d) Eurailpass (First Class).

However, at the time we checked, pre-paid rates were generally lower than end-of-rental rates.

Similarly, some renters gave a choice of a local-currency or US-dollar rental rate. (In a few soft-currency countries, even the local rate is in dollars or marks.) Where a rental company published both local and dollar rates, we list the lower of the two.

ONE-WAY RENTALS. You usually don't pay extra for a one-way rental between cities in a single country. But there's often a hefty surcharge for renting a car in one country and returning it in another. Check first with the car-rental companies: Some allow limited one-way rentals between adjacent countries at no additional cost. (You pay the originating country's rate and tax.)

TRYING 'EM FOR SIZE

Rental companies classify cars by letter or number, but with no great consistency. In any given country, one firm's C car may be another's D. And for any given company, the same model may be an A in one country and a B in another.

We based the prices in our *Weekly Rates* table (see pages 230–38), to the extent possible, on specific car models rather than the companies' classifications. Still, there are uncertainties. A rental company usually promises only a car in a certain group, not a specific model. You find out what's available when you arrive at the rental counter.

The smallest car we recommend for a week of touring is a size we call *standard economy*—typically, a two- or three-door car with adequate room for two adults and a modest amount of baggage. Typical of the breed are the *Austin Montego, Citroen AX, Fiat 131/ Bravo/Punto/Tipo/Uno, Ford Fiesta, Hyundai Elantra, Mitsubishi L Sedan, Nissan Micra/Sunny, Opel/Vauxhall Astra/Corsa, Peugeot 205, Renault 5/Clio, Seat Ibiza, Skoda Favorit/ Felicia, Subaru Justy, Suzuki Swift, Toyota Corolla, VW Golf/Polo,* and *Zastava.*

To satisfy dedicated budget travelers —and to snag a lowball price to feature in their brochures—some companies offer smaller, less powerful cars. We list those, where available, as the *cheapest rental.* Among the specific models are the *Austin Mini* and the *Fiat 124/ Cinquecento.* Even the companies that rent them, when they're being frank, admit that those models are useful mainly for chugging around town, not for the open highway.

For groups of three or four, we recommend a *standard midsized* car, which is usually two size groups up from standard economy. Models there include the *Alfa Romeo 155, Audi 80/100, Citroen Xantia, Fiat Croma/ Tempra, Ford Mondeo/Sierra/ Tempo, Lancia Dedra/Thema, Mazda 626, Mitsubishi Galant, Nissan Bluebird/ Primera, Opel Vectra, Peugeot 405/505, Renault 21/25/ Laguna/Safrane, Seat Toledo, Toyota Camry/Carina, Vauxhall Cavalier, VW Jetta/Passat/Vento,* and *Volvo 440.*

Rental companies may tout four-door cars between standard economy and standard midsized as adequate for three or four travelers. Specific models are *Citroen ZX, Fiat 131, Ford Escort/*

Orion, Opel Astra/Kadett, Peugeot 306, and *Subaru 1.6.* We don't recommend those models—they're too cramped for rear-seat passengers. The cheapest cars with automatic transmission are generally in that same category. In some countries, however, automatics may be available only on large, luxury cars. That's why our table shows so much variation in the price for the *cheapest automatic* rentals.

Air-conditioning adds quite a bit to the cost. You can also rent minivans and minivan-campers, but they're pricey during the summer season— often as much as you'd pay for a smaller rental car and a hotel every night. Check with the rental companies if you're interested in a camper, a minivan, or an air-conditioned car.

SAVE WITH A FRENCH LEASE?

Several rental agencies offer "leases" on brand-new, French-made cars. A lease, actually a purchase-repurchase agreement, can save you a bundle on rentals of 17 days or more. You contract to buy a brand-new car, then resell it at a fixed price at the end of the lease period.

You pay only the net cost—the difference between the buying and selling price—and the leasing company takes care of the paperwork and financing. The lease rate includes VAT and full collision insurance. You pay extra to pick up or return a car at any location other than a few cities in France.

The minimum lease period is 17 days. Typical rates for an economy *Citroen Saxo, Renault Twingo,* or

Peugeot 106 start at $515 for 17 days, $1159 for two months. For a midsized *Citroen Xantia, Peugeot 405,* or *Renault Laguna,* rates start at $1145 for 17 days, $2039 for two months.

A lease is a bit more bothersome than a regular rental. You must pay in full by cash or check (no charge cards) at least 30 days in advance. You can pick up and return the car only at a limited number of locations in France during limited hours, unless you make an extra-cost arrangement for pickup and check-in at other locations. You're also responsible for such routine maintenance items as changing oil and oil filters.

NUISANCES AND EXTRAS

Renting a car in Europe involves some of the same bother and left-field charges as at home.

INSURANCE HARD-SELL. You may be pressured overseas to buy CDW and other insurance. If you decline CDW, the rental company may slap a hold of

READING UP

Eurail Guide (Houghton-Mifflin, NYC, 1996; $14.95) offers plenty of details on train travel plus recommended scenic trips. And the latest monthly "Thomas Cook European Timetable" (Thomas Cook Publishing, Peterborough, UK) is essential if you want to plot a detailed itinerary; it's about $25 in many US travel bookstores, or $32.45 by mail from Forsyth Travel Library (see *Where to Find It*).

WEEKLY RENTAL RATES

COMPANY	CHEAPEST RENTAL	STANDARD ECONOMY	STANDARD MIDSIZED	CHEAPEST AUTOMATIC
AUSTRIA (21.2% tax incld.)				
Alamo	$215	—	$256	$570
Auto Europe	241	$253	433	469
Avis	273	273	491	491
Bon Voyage(a)	263	269	437	541
Budget	261	261	697	483
DERCar	265	298	520	520
EuroDollar	215	225	369	420
Europcar	219	274	—	505
Europe by Car	229	253	411	459
Hertz	220	264	491	520
Holiday	198	211	322	508
ITS	200	212	354	417
Kemwel	241	253	423	411
BELGIUM (21% tax incld.)				
Alamo	117	117	178	225
Auto Europe	129	129	156	226
Avis	124	124	188	237
Budget	114	114	—	192
DER Car	156	156	241	313
ECR	154	154	232	342
Europcar	116	116	185	218
Europe by Car	127	132	204	241
Hertz	119	124	188	237
ITS	122	160	214	265
Kemwel	156	156	265	338
BULGARIA (18% tax incld.)				
Auto Europe	445	445	695	—
Avis(b)	395	395	814	661
Budget	208	208	431	—
EuroDollar	190	248	380	405
Hertz	157	157	289	306
CZECH REPUBLIC (5% tax incld.)(c)				
Alamo	269	269	394	630
Auto Europe	270	270	419	—
Avis	633	633	904	—
Budget	255	255	—	—
DER Car	447	447	660	671
EuroDollar	270	270	439	—

COMPANY	CHEAPEST RENTAL	STANDARD ECONOMY	STANDARD MIDSIZED	CHEAPEST AUTOMATIC
Europcar	$271	$271	$476	—
Hertz	275	275	412	$421
Holiday	246	263	385	—
ITS	265	265	414	—
Kemwel	198	230	345	—
DENMARK (25% tax incld.)				
Auto Europe	274	274	411	624
Avis	263	263	388	940
Budget	329	455	707	746
DER Car	286	286	424	549
ECR	323	327	471	700
EuroDollar	316	316	457	697
Europcar	289	289	414	636
Europe by Car	224	269	299	431
Hertz	284	284	414	530
Holiday	278	285	434	591
ITS	238	280	475	594
Kemwel	249	299	449	686
FINLAND (22% tax incld.)				
Auto Europe	582	582	716	1170
Avis	444	444	858	1909
Budget	502	502	751	—
ECR	545	605	910	808
EuroDollar	488	488	857	—
Hertz	483	483	527	625
ITS	561	561	1303	—
Kemwel	462	487	1097	—
FRANCE (18.6% tax incld.)				
Auto Europe	248	248	331	366
Avis	259	259	400	400
Bon Voyage	229	229	363	391
Budget	247	247	478	370
DER Car	224	260	331	355
ECR	290	290	415	462
EuroDollar	232	232	369	397
Europcar	258	258	477	435
Europe by Car	212	248	366	366
Hertz	256	259	369	358
Holiday	230	230	363	403

WEEKLY RENTAL RATES *(continued)*

COMPANY		CHEAPEST RENTAL	STANDARD ECONOMY	STANDARD MIDSIZED	CHEAPEST AUTOMATIC
FRANCE (18.6% tax incld.) *(continued)*					
ITS		$251	$251	$393	$623
Kemwel		212	260	402	414
GERMANY (15% tax incld.)					
Alamo		138	153	179	312
Auto Europe		123	123	194	307
Avis		160	160	210	315
Bon Voyage(a)		255	255	351	344
Budget		109	109	556	261
DER Car		113	125	179	263
ECR		112	127	151	231
EuroDollar		109	109	184	261
Europcar		138	138	207	311
Europe by Car		132	137	183	309
Hertz		138	147	207	311
Holiday Autos		101	174	236	262
ITS		145	174	294	274
Kemwel		102	114	183	263
GREECE (18% tax incld.)					
Alamo		241	241	517	453
Auto Europe		235	282	742	445
Avis		215	240	421	388
Budget	high	310	310	—	499
	low	236	236	—	418
DER Car	high	258	270	341	542
	low	247	258	317	506
ECR	high	312	343	591	522
	low	288	312	537	474
Euro Dollar	high	210	258	—	406
	low	168	201	—	325
Europcar		266	302	—	—
Europe by Car		235	258	447	494
Hertz	high	247	289	345	463
	low	202	237	345	379
Holiday Autos	high	192	204	342	347
	low	179	183	328	334
Kemwel		199	258	—	518
HUNGARY (25% tax incld.)					
Auto Europe(a)		247	247	339	379
Avis		405	405	740	591

COMPANY		CHEAPEST RENTAL	STANDARD ECONOMY	STANDARD MIDSIZED	CHEAPEST AUTOMATIC
Budget		$341	$341	—	—
ECR		262	262	$385	$323
EuroDollar		175	175	516	368
Europcar		342	410	786	—
Hertz		424	424	674	674
Holiday		196	196	375	404
ITS		293	293	469	450
Kemwel		236	261	361	374
ICELAND (24.5% tax incld.)					
Avis(d)		808	808	—	1240
Budget(a,b)	high	940	940	—	—
	low	752	752	—	—
Hertz	high	934	934	—	1434
	low	381	381	—	789
Kemwel	high	571	571	—	—
	low	497	497	—	—
IRELAND (12.5% tax incld.)					
Alamo		289	289	417	296
Auto Europe		201	201	278	224
Avis		379	379	581	670
BonVoyage(a)	high	331	331	537	626
	shoulder	208	208	380	445
	low	193	193	365	320
Budget	high	333	333	530	619
	shoulder	211	211	317	388
	low	195	195	300	335
DER Car	high	336	336	561	674
	shoiulder(e)	235	235	415	449
	shoiulder(f)	213	213	359	303
	low	213	213	280	246
ECR	high	333	333	488	442
	low	194	194	318	302
EuroDollar	high	346	346	443	585
	shoiulder	236	236	347	422
	low	198	198	298	347
Europcar	high	505	505	682	780
	low	223	223	317	335
Europe by Car		190	190	325	359
Hertz	high	381	381	505	532
	low	246	246	353	452

WEEKLY RENTAL RATES *(continued)*

COMPANY		CHEAPEST RENTAL	STANDARD ECONOMY	STANDARD MIDSIZED	CHEAPEST AUTOMATIC
IRELAND (12.5% tax incld.) *(continued)*					
Holiday	high	$291	$291	$416	$487
	low	131	131	233	251
ITS		343	343	523	457
Kemwel	high	269	303	505	438
	low	179	201	348	303
Kenning(g)	high	357	397	540	603
	low	222	254	345	357
Payless	high	292	292	434	567
	low	186	186	319	353
Thrifty		496	496	567	665
ISRAEL (no taxes)					
Auto Europe		199	199	369	349
Avis		420	420	—	644
Budget	high	266	266	413	413
	low	161	161	308	308
EuroDollar	high	252	252	553	392
	low	161	161	462	301
Hertz		238	238	371	371
Holiday	high	246	263	323	317
	low	132	160	230	202
Kemwel	high	220	220	370	360
	low	129	129	279	269
Thrifty		245	245	567	343
ITALY (19% tax incld.)					
Auto Europe(a,h)		287	287	567	567
Avis		305	305	521	727
Bon Voyage(a,b,h)		290	305	540	—
Budget (a,b,g,h)		417	417	—	—
DER Car		298	298	—	508
ECR(b,h)		386	452	765	819
EuroDollar		297	297	494	—
Europcar(b,h)		412	484	799	755
Europe by Car(a,b,g,h)		299	319	459	579
Hertz(h)		295	295	513	539
Holiday		301	301	422	—
ITS		288	288	594	425
Kemwel(h)		224	327	431	399
Thrifty		288	319	485	695

COMPANY	CHEAPEST RENTAL	STANDARD ECONOMY	STANDARD MIDSIZED	CHEAPEST AUTOMATIC
LUXEMBOURG (15% tax incld.)				
Auto Europe	$146	$146	$261	$330
Avis	138	138	219	251
Budget	148	148	—	646
DER Car	137	137	229	298
Hertz	138	138	219	349
Kemwel	148	183	367	378
NETHERLANDS (17.5% tax incld.)				
Alamo	236	251	287	315
Auto Europe	217	217	282	316
Avis	214	214	321	288
Bon Voyage(a)	177	189	378	414
Budget	250	250	584	374
DER Car	170	195	397	281
ECR	151	173	298	251
EuroDollar	150	160	319	299
Europcar	203	203	274	314
Europe by Car	206	210	328	351
Hertz	239	239	289	317
Holiday Autos	170	208	283	309
ITS	128	147	209	254
Kemwel	152	175	328	293
Thrifty	227	227	574	—
NORWAY (23% tax incld.)				
Auto Europe	319	319	501	614
Avis	387	387	529	720
Budget	333	333	—	521
ECR	414	414	570	770
Europcar	324	324	508	579
Hertz	331	333	530	721
Kemwel	282	331	491	577
Thrifty	374	374	537	—
POLAND (22% tax incld.)				
Auto Europe	350	411	472	—
Avis	462	462	680	1273
Budget	381	381	601	—
EuroDollar	265	265	384	—
Europcar	339	450	—	—
Hertz	209	284	911	1096

WEEKLY RENTAL RATES *(continued)*

COMPANY		CHEAPEST RENTAL	STANDARD ECONOMY	STANDARD MIDSIZED	CHEAPEST AUTOMATIC
POLAND (22% tax incld.) *(continued)*					
ITS(g)		$254	$262	$366	—
Kemwel		304	304	426	—
PORTUGAL (16% tax incld.)					
Alamo		139	139	300	$451
Auto Europe		136	138	391	440
Avis		133	133	280	319
Budget	*high*	208	318	661	344
	low	178	275	572	300
DER Car	*high*	168	193	300	515
	low	138	143	184	458
EuroDollar	*high*	152	152	368	321
	low	133	133	320	279
Europcar	*high*	155	158	804	521
	low	135	136	396	441
Europe by Car		138	150	277	289
Hertz		135	135	389	397
Holiday(a,b)	*high*	219	219	584	347
	low	173	173	451	275
Kemwel	*high*	184	231	648	521
	low	150	208	498	393
Kenning	*high*	242	242	398	471
	low	123	123	263	281
Thrifty		209	209	569	—
ROMANIA (18% tax incld.)					
Auto Europe		386	386	—	—
Avis		455	455	694	904
Hertz		246	246	375	213
SLOVAKIA (25% tax incld.)					
Europcar		323	323	566	—
Hertz		481	481	1563	678
SPAIN (16% tax incld.)					
Auto Europe		174	174	614	428
Avis		174	174	362	387
Budget	*high*	259	259	534	—
	low	236	236	485	—
DER Car		173	173	277	324
ECR		246	246	488	405
EuroDollar(b)		190	190	384	392

COMPANY	CHEAPEST RENTAL	STANDARD ECONOMY	STANDARD MIDSIZED	CHEAPEST AUTOMATIC
Europcar	194	194	621	449
Europe by Car	$184	$196	$428	$544
Hertz	167	169	310	310
Holiday(a,b)	244	244	311	—
ITS	232	232	361	—
Kemwel *high*	219	219	405	509
low	196	196	347	498

SWEDEN (25% tax incld.)

Auto Europe	334	334	484	774
Avis	299	299	421	701
Bon Voyage(a)	341	341	446	604
Budget	476	476	598	—
DER Car	324	324	416	715
ECR	323	323	428	718
EuroDollar	336	336	439	594
Hertz	289	289	409	601
Holiday	320	320	471	—
ITS	296	313	400	609
Kemwel	274	324	461	599
Thrifty	292	292	387	716

SWITZERLAND (6.5% tax incld.)

Alamo	161	223	274	284
Auto Europe	169	169	286	295
Avis	187	187	294	324
Bon Voyage(a)	268	268	411	387
Budget	183	183	—	316
DER Car	137	137	212	235
ECR	158	173	232	233
EuroDollar	142	142	258	258
Europcar	170	170	299	287
Europe by Car	176	180	308	340
Hertz	152	175	280	275
Holiday	149	178	224	281
ITS	145	145	256	256
Kemwel	148	159	265	244

TURKEY (23% tax incld.)

AutoEurope	380	380	—	—
Avis	568	568	—	—
Budget *high*	376	376	—	—
low	325	325	—	—

WEEKLY RENTAL RATES *(continued)*

COMPANY		CHEAPEST RENTAL	STANDARD ECONOMY	STANDARD MIDSIZED	CHEAPEST AUTOMATIC
TURKEY (23% tax incld.) *(continued)*					
ECR	high	424	424	—	—
	low	$358	$358	—	—
EuroDollar	high	336	370	—	—
	low	293	319	—	—
Europcar		396	396	—	—
Hertz	high	501	501	$819	—
	low	454	454	819	—
Holiday	high	276	276	501	—
	shoulder	171	171	401	—
	low	157	157	403	—
Kemwel		343	343	—	—
UNITED KINGDOM (17.5% tax incld.)					
Alamo		184	243	293	$317
Auto Europe		128	128	208	290
Avis		197	197	233	357
Bon Voyage(a)		116	135	229	229
Budget		196	196		376
DER Car		116	116	187	264
ECR		155	182	332	315
Euro Dollar		171	171	270	315
Europcar		201	201	270	264
Europe by Car		128	163	234	257
Hertz		165	205	275	266
Holiday		119	134	202	204
Kemwel		140	152	257	257
Kenning		129	147	248	246
Thrifty		205	205	282	—
Town & Country		101	117	189	173
Woods(a)		171	193	300	246

Note: Prices as of spring 1996; subject to change. Unless noted, all figures are for a 1-week rental with unlimited mileage, including VAT but not including airport surtaxes (if any) or CDW. Rates established in local currency were converted at mid-March '96 exchange rates. Where a company offers both advance-payment and after-rental payment, the lower of the two options is shown; see text. Where applicable, seasonal rates are indicated by *high*, *shoulder*, and *low*; high season is generally July and August, but exact dates vary by company and country. See text for definitions of car classes and for rental limitations and conditions. All rates subject to change.

(a) Value Added Tax (VAT) included in published rates.
(b) Collision Damage Waiver (CDW) included in published rates.
(c) While VAT on a rental car should be 5%, some renters quote 22% (see text).
(d) 700 free km; 34–52 kronur each additional km, depending on model.
(e) 5/1–6/30/96; 9/1–30/96.
(f) 10/1–31/96.
(g) Published inclusive rate covers airport fee no matter where car is rented.
(h) Theft insurance (mandatory in Italy) included in published rates.

several thousand dollars on your charge card. Before you book, ask for written confirmation that you won't be forced to buy CDW abroad or to accept a huge hold on your card. (Should a US rental office balk, try another company.)

If the European rental office still demands that you buy CDW once you arrive, do so. You can then use the written statement as a basis for demanding a refund from the US office—in small-claims court, if necessary.

AIRPORT SURCHARGES. Several European airports hit rental companies with taxes and fees that they pass along to renters. The following extras, in a list supplied by Hertz, are typical (we've converted all per-rental fees to US dollars). Except where noted, the charge applies at all airports in a country: Austria, 9%; Belgium, 12% in Brussels, 9% elsewhere; Bulgaria, $8; Czech Republic, 8% in Prague, 5% elsewhere; Denmark, $18; Finland, $16; France, $10; Germany, $9; Hungary, 7%; Israel, $20; Italy, 10%; Luxembourg, 9%; Netherlands, $25; Norway, $14; Poland, $10 in Warsaw, $20–30 elsewhere; Portugal, $13; Slovakia, $12; Spain, $9; Switzerland, 11%; and UK, 10%.

Of course, you can avoid an airport charge by picking up your car at a downtown office. That's apt to be a nuisance as well as misplaced economy; the fee may be less than the cost of a taxi from the airport to downtown. But waiting a day and renting downtown might be a good idea for safety reasons: Arriving after an overnight flight, you might not be alert enough to cope immediately with foreign traffic.

HIGHWAY FEE. Any car you drive in Switzerland must have a sticker indicating payment of a 40-franc ($33) superhighway fee. Swiss-based rental cars normally have that sticker. But if

SPLURGE IN FIRST?

Quite a few American visitors travel First Class on European trains—including many who would never pay the stiff price for a Business or First Class airline ticket. If you buy *Eurailpass, Europass,* or *European East,* that decision is made for you: Adults can't buy those passes for Second Class.

Even when they have a choice, however, many travelers opt for First Class. As with airlines, you get a wide seat with ample leg room. On some train services, you even get a meal. In the peak summer season, First Class also spares you much of the crush of European vacationers, who often fill Second Class to overflowing.

Fortunately, the price premium for a roomy seat on a train is much lower than on a plane—usually no more than 50% over Second Class. For extended traveling, the extra room and comfort can be well worth the modest extra cost.

Still, in most of Europe, Second Class train travel is perfectly acceptable. It shouldn't give pause to budget-minded travelers.

you rent elsewhere and drive into Switzerland, you, not the rental company, must buy the sticker or pay a stiff fine. Rental cars based in nearby foreign cities such as Lyons and Milan sometimes already have a sticker—ask for one if you plan to drive in Switzerland.

GEOGRAPHIC LIMITS. Rental companies in some locations forbid you to drive into certain other countries—especially into Eastern European ones. When you reserve your car, tell the company where you plan to drive. If your itinerary poses a problem, try another rental company.

BOOKING AND PICKUP

If you've already chosen your European gateway city and have decided to drive a rented car, check the *Weekly Rates* table for an inkling of the best deals. Those rates are from 1996, but the relative standings of the companies will probably be much the same now.

If you're touring several countries, you may want to pick your country of arrival for good rental rates:

- Weekly rates were lowest in Belgium, Germany, and the UK, but were also reasonable in Luxembourg, Portugal, and Switzerland. Car travel was less alluring in France and Italy, where car-rental costs were high and train travel cheap.
- For long-term driving, a new-car purchase-repurchase "lease" in France was often the best deal.
- Rates were hair-curling in Scandinavia and most of Eastern Europe. Avoid renting a car there.

RAIL PASSES FOR EUROPE

REGION OR COUNTRY/ TYPE OF PASS (✔ = NEW FOR 1996)	VALIDITY(a)	
	TRAVEL(b)	TOTAL
EUROPE (17 countries): Eurailpass		
Rail/car(f)	7(4/3)	2 months
Rail	10	2 months
Rail/youth(g)	10	2 months
Rail	15	15
Rail	15	2 months
Rail/group(h)	15	15
Rail/youth(g)	15	15
Rail/youth(g)	15	2 months
Rail	21	21
Rail/group(h)	21	21
Rail	1 month	1 month
Rail/group(h)	1 month	1 month
Rail/youth(g)	1 month	1 month
Rail	2 months	2 months
Rail/youth(g)	2 months	2 months
Rail	3 months	3 months
EUROPE (3 countries): Europass		
Rail(i)	5	2 months
Rail/companion(i,j)	5	2 months
Rail(i) ✔	6	2 months
Rail/companion(i,j) ✔	6	2 months
Rail(i) ✔	7	2 months
Rail/companion(i,j) ✔	7	2 months
Rail/car(i,k)	8(5/3)	2 months
EUROPE (4 countries): Europass		
Rail/youth(g,i)	5	2 months
Rail/youth(g,i) ✔	6	2 months
Rail/youth(g,i) ✔	7	2 months
Rail(i)	8	2 months
Rail/companion(i,j)	8	2 months
Rail/youth(g,i)	8	2 months
Rail(i) ✔	9	2 months
Rail/companion(i,j) ✔	9	2 months
Rail/youth(g,i) ✔	9	2 months
Rail(i) ✔	10	2 months
Rail/companion(i,j) ✔	10	2 months
Rail/youth(g,i) ✔	10	2 months

(MULTINATIONAL)

| FIRST CLASS | | | | SECOND CLASS | | | |
PRICE(c)	COST PER DAY(d)	BREAKEVEN MILES(e) TOTAL	PER DAY	PRICE(c)	COST PER DAY(d)	BREAKEVEN MILES(e) TOTAL	PER DAY
$339	$48	—	—	—	—	—	—
616	62	1925	193	—	—	—	—
—	—	—	—	$438	$44	2086	209
522	35	1631	109	—	—	—	—
812	54	2538	169	—	—	—	—
452	30	1413	94	—	—	—	—
—	—	—	—	418	28	1990	133
—	—	—	—	588	39	2800	187
678	32	2119	101	—	—	—	—
578	28	1806	86	—	—	—	—
838	28	2619	87	—	—	—	—
712	24	2225	74	—	—	—	—
—	—	—	—	598	20	2848	95
1148	19	3588	59	—	—	—	—
—	—	—	—	798	13	3800	62
1468	16	4588	50	—	—	—	—
316	63	832	166	—	—	—	—
237	47	624	125	—	—	—	—
358	60	942	157	—	—	—	—
269	45	707	118	—	—	—	—
400	57	1053	150	—	—	—	—
300	43	789	113	—	—	—	—
305	38	—	—	—	—	—	—
—	—	—	—	210	42	875	175
—	—	—	—	239	40	996	166
—	—	—	—	268	38	1117	160
442	55	1163	145	—	—	—	—
332	41	872	109	—	—	—	—
—	—	—	—	297	37	1238	155
484	54	1274	142	—	—	—	—
363	40	955	106	—	—	—	—
—	—	—	—	326	36	1358	151
526	53	1384	138	—	—	—	—
395	39	1038	104	—	—	—	—
—	—	—	—	355	36	1479	148

To choose between car and train travel, pick the sample trip in our *Car vs Train Costs* table, page 227, that most closely matches your plans and compare the cost figures.

All the companies listed in *Where to Find It,* at the end of this chapter, rent cars at weekly touring rates or lease them. Whether you rent directly or through a travel agency, the cost is the same.

If you wait until you arrive in Europe to rent a car, chances are that any rental company will quote a rate that's higher than the weekly touring rate, possibly with a mileage cap. To avoid overpaying, check with some of the independent local renters that advertise in classified phone directories or tourist brochures—they may have rates that beat the big chains' local rates. Or you may be able to reserve from one of the US-based firms at the touring rate by calling the US office from Europe (or stopping into an office of a US airline and arranging a rental through the airline's reservation computer).

Minimum and maximum age limits for renting a car vary by country and company. Check the specifics if any driver in your party is under 25 or over 70. Check as well for any other hidden extras, such as an additional-driver charge.

The big car-rental companies maintain counters at most European airports: Follow the signs in the arrivals area to the rental-car desks. (Look up a city address in a local phone book.) Rental agencies give you a voucher that shows the name and location of the rental

RAIL PASSES FOR EUROPE (MULTINATIONAL) *(cont'd)*

REGION OR COUNTRY/ TYPE OF PASS (✔ = NEW FOR 1996)	VALIDITY(a) TRAVEL(b)	TOTAL
EUROPE (5 countries): Europass		
Rail(i)	11	2 months
Rail/companion(i,j)	11	2 months
Rail/youth(g,i)	11	2 months
Rail(i) ✔✔	12	2 months
Rail/companion(i,j) ✔	12	2 months
Rail/youth(g,i) ✔	12	2 months
Rail(i) ✔	13	2 months
Rail/companion(i,j) ✔	13	2 months
Rail/youth(g,i) ✔	13	2 months
Rail(i) ✔	14	2 months
Rail/companion(i,j) ✔	14	2 months
Rail/youth(g,i) ✔	14	2 months
Rail(i) ✔	15	2 months
Rail/companion(i,j) ✔	15	2 months
Rail/youth(g,i) ✔	15	2 months
EASTERN EUROPE (Austria, Czech Republic,		
Rail	5	15
Rail	10	1 month
BENELUX (Belgium, Luxembourg, Netherlands):		
Rail	5	1 month
Rail/companion(j) ✔	5	1 month
Rail/youth(g)	5	1 month
BRITAIN/FRANCE: UKFrance Sampler		
Rail/car(l) ✔	6(3/3)	1 month
BRITAIN/IRELAND: BritRail Pass Ireland		
Rail(m)	5	1 month
Rail(m)	10	1 month
SCANDINAVIA (Denmark, Finland, Norway,		
Rail	5	15
Rail/senior(n) ✔	5	15
Rail/youth(g)	5	15
Rail/car(o,p)	8(5/3)	15
Rail	10	1 month
Rail/senior(n)	10	1 month
Rail/youth(g)	10	1 month

FIRST CLASS				SECOND CLASS			
PRICE(c)	COST PER DAY(d)	BREAKEVEN MILES(e) TOTAL	PER DAY	PRICE(c)	COST PER DAY(d)	BREAKEVEN MILES(e) TOTAL	PER DAY
$568	$52	1495	136	—	—	—	—
426	39	1121	102	—	—	—	—
—	—	—	—	$384	$35	1600	145
610	51	1605	134	—	—	—	—
458	38	1204	100	—	—	—	—
—	—	—	—	413	34	1721	143
652	50	1716	132	—	—	—	—
489	38	1287	99	—	—	—	—
—	—	—	—	442	34	1842	142
694	50	1826	130	—	—	—	—
521	37	1370	98	—	—	—	—
—	—	—	—	471	34	1963	140
736	49	1937	129	—	—	—	—
552	37	1453	97	—	—	—	—
—	—	—	—	500	33	2083	139

Hungary, Poland, Slovakia): European East Pass

195	39	848	170	—	—	—	—
299	30	1300	130	—	—	—	—

Benelux Tourrail Pass

217	43	620	124	155	31	674	135
163	33	466	93	117	23	507	101
—	—	—	—	104	21	452	90

305	51	—	—	241	40	—	—

405	81	764	153	299	60	808	162
599	60	1130	113	429	43	1159	116

Sweden): Scanrail Pass

222	44	740	148	176	35	926	185
193	39	643	129	153	31	805	161
167	33	557	111	132	26	695	139
289	36	—	—	249	31	—	—
346	35	1153	115	278	28	1463	146
301	30	1003	100	242	24	1274	127
260	26	867	87	209	21	1100	110

company that actually provides your car. If there's a chance that you'll make a last-minute decision to leave off the car in another country, get a list of the rental company's foreign affiliates— they may go by different names in different countries.

At the counter, all you need to get into your car is a reservation confirmation or voucher, a valid US driver's license, a charge card, and your passport. European car-rental agents usually speak enough English to handle the transaction.

An International Driving Permit (obtained through local American Automobile Assn offices) is not a legal requirement to rent a car in Europe. But police in some countries are fussy about a requirement that you have a license they can read—and the IDP satisfies that requirement. Driving authorities tell us that the IDP is not needed in countries where English is widely spoken, but that it's a good idea if you'll be driving in Austria, Germany, Italy, Eastern Europe, or the Middle East.

TRAINS: YOUR BEST BET FOR INTERCITY TRAVEL

Though cars are good bets for touring the countryside, they do have their downside—you have to cope with parking, traffic, and foreign road signs. Rail makes more sense if you travel alone, stay mainly in big-city centers, or plan to pile up a lot of intercity mileage. Your main question is then whether to buy a separate ticket for each trip or an unlimited-travel pass.

Rail passes are hyped heavily. But

it's often cheaper to buy a separate ticket for each trip—especially if you're eligible for a senior discount or if you decide to travel in Second Class. To find your best buy, decide on an itinerary and figure the total rail miles you're likely to cover. (A rough estimate based on a highway map should be close enough.) Then check the tables on pages 240–45 and 246–253, *Rail Passes for Europe,* for the cheapest pass that covers your needs. (The table is based on prices for summer 1996; 1997 prices weren't available at this writing.)

RAIL PASSES FOR EUROPE (MULTINATIONAL) *(cont'd)*

REGION OR COUNTRY/ TYPE OF PASS (✔ = NEW FOR 1996)	VALIDITY(a)	
	TRAVEL(b)	TOTAL
SCANDINAVIA (*Denmark, Finland, Norway,*		
Rail	1 month	1 month
Rail/senior(n)	1 month	1 month
Rail/youth(g)	1 month	1 month

Note: Breakeven-miles entries for the 17-country Eurail area based on an average individual-ticket price of about 32¢ per mile in First Class, 21¢ in Second; for national and regional passes, based on average per-mile price of individual local tickets. Prices as of January 1996; contact rail companies for 1997 rates.

(a) In days, except as noted.
(b) Days in the total validity period on which pass can be used for travel. In rail/car and rail/air passes, the first number in parentheses is the number of rail-travel days, the second is the number of car rental or air travel days. In rail/car/air pass, the third number is the number of air-travel days.
(c) Prices that include rental car are per person, based on 2 persons sharing subcompact car; larger cars available at extra cost; car taxes and insurance not included.
(d) Cost of pass divided by number of travel days.
(e) The number of miles (or miles per day) at which cost of separate tickets equals cost of pass (see text). Breakeven not calculated for passes including car or air travel. In regions/countries where Second Class passes aren't available, breakeven for Second Class

If your planned mileage comes within 90% or so of the table's *breakeven-mileage* entry for that pass, the pass is your better bet. If it's lower, you're better off with individual tickets.

Say that you plan to travel through France, Germany, and Switzerland, covering about 1000 intercity miles, and that your long-haul trips will be on six different days. The cheapest pass you can use is the six-day, three-country *EuroPass*, at $358 in First Class. The breakeven mileage for that pass is 942 miles, so it would cost less than individual tickets.

Now, let's say you're planning to visit Germany for two weeks, staying mainly in and around the Mosel and Rhine valleys. You plan to cover only 600 miles but to move your base city every day or two. You'd need a 10-day pass, at $286 in Second Class. Since the breakeven for that pass is 841 miles, you'd be better off buying separate tickets for each train trip.

Some travelers may find it easier to evaluate a pass on a per-day basis rather than for an entire trip. The *Breakeven Miles per Day* data show, for each pass, the average number of miles you'd have

FIRST CLASS				SECOND CLASS			
	COST PER	BREAKEVEN MILES(e)			COST PER	BREAKEVEN MILES(e)	
PRICE(c)	DAY(d)	TOTAL	PER DAY	PRICE(c)	DAY(d)	TOTAL	PER DAY
Sweden): Scanrail Pass(cont'd)							
$504	$17	1680	56	$404	$13	2126	71
438	15	1460	49	351	12	1847	62
378	13	1260	42	303	10	1595	53

travel based on costs of First Class pass and individual Second Class tickets.

(f) Extra rail days (5 max) $55/day; extra car days (no limit) $55/day.

(g) Must be 25 or under on first day of travel.

(h) Price per person; requires 3 traveling together 4/1-9/30/96; 2 at other times.

(i) Supplement for travel in Associate Countries (adult/youth): Austria $45/32, Benelux $42/28, Greece $90/70 (includes access to the Brindisi-Patras ferry), and Portugal $29/22.

(j) Price per person, 2 traveling together.

(k) Extra rail days (15 max) $31.50/day; extra car days (no max) $55/day.

(l) Includes one Eurostar round-trip ticket in Standard class.

(m) Includes round-trip Stena Line ferry between Holyhead and Dun Laoghaire, Fishguard and Rosslare, or Stranraer and Belfast via ship, HSS, or Stena Lynx catamaran.

(n) Minimum age 55; proof may be required.

(o) Extra car days (no max) $55/day.

(p) Car rental in Finland, $59/day supplement.

(q) Minimum age 60.

(r) Extra rail days (8 max) $30/day any class.

(s) Extra rail days (6 max) $30/day any class; extra one-way air ticket (no max) $99.

(t) Extra car days (no max) $44/day.

(u) Additional flight coupons (no max) adult $63; 2-10 $32; under 2 $6.30.

(v) Includes DART and Suburban Rail services in Dublin.

(w) Includes local rail services in Dublin and city bus services in Cork, Limerick, Galway, and Waterford.

(x) Irish rail plus Northern Ireland Rail, DART, and Suburban Rail services in Dublin and suburban services in Northern Ireland.

(y) Irish Rail plus Northern Ireland Rail, Irish Bus, Ulsterbus, DART, Dublin Suburban Rail, and city bus services in Dublin, Belfast, Cork, Limerick, Galway, and Waterford.

(z) Supplement required for upgraded services on the Flam Line during high season.

(aa) Extra rail days (no max) $40/day 1st class, $32/day 2nd class.

(bb) Extra car days (no max) $49/day.

(cc) Valid 5/1-10/31/96.

(dd) Valid 11/1/96-4/30/96.

to ride the train each day to break even.

TYPES OF PASS

You can also save by making a judicious choice of the kind of pass you buy:

- **Full-time** rail passes let you travel as much as you like anytime, for as long as a pass is valid. They're good mainly for extensive city-hopping. Some are also valid on national (but not private) bus lines—useful in the few areas where rail coverage is sparse.

- **Flexible** passes provide unlimited train travel, but only on certain days in their validity period. (The travel days needn't be consecutive.) With a 5/15-day pass, say, you can travel on any five out of 15 days. Such passes are cheaper than full-time ones, so you aren't paying for train travel on the days you're exploring a city.

- **Rail/car** passes combine rail and rental-car days, a fixed number of each. (A few passes even include air-travel days.) Those passes can be matched especially closely to your itinerary: a train (or plane) for long-haul intercity segments, a car to explore the cities or their environs. At the regular daily rates, such one-shot car rentals would be very expensive.

    But what if you plan to use a car for four or more consecutive days in the same area? Then you're better off arranging a separate weekly car rental before you leave the US.

- **Companion** passes give a price break to two travelers who travel together; **Group** passes give a break to parties of three or more traveling on the same itinerary. (The **Eurail Saverpass**

RAIL PASSES FOR EUROPE

REGION OR COUNTRY/ TYPE OF PASS (✔ = NEW FOR 1996)	VALIDITY(a)	
	TRAVEL(b)	TOTAL
AUSTRIA: *Austrian Railpass*		
Rail	4	10
BRITAIN: *BritRail Pass*		
Rail	4	1 month
Rail/senior(q) ✔	4	1 month
Rail/youth(g)	4	1 month
Rail/car	6 (3/3)	1 month
Rail/car/senior(q)	6 (3/3)	1 month
Rail	8	8
Rail/senior(q)	8	8
Rail/youth(g)	8	8
Rail	8	1 month
Rail/senior(q)	8	1 month
Rail/youth(g)	8	1 month
Rail/car	13 (6/7)	1 month
Rail/car/senior(q)	13 (6/7)	1 month
Rail	15	15
Rail/senior(q)	15	15
Rail/youth(g)	15	15
Rail	15	1 month
Rail/senior(q)	15	1 month
Rail/youth(g)	15	2 months
Rail	22	22
Rail/senior(q)	22	22
Rail/youth(g)	22	22
Rail	1 month	1 month
Rail/senior(q)	1 month	1 month
Rail/youth(g)	1 month	1 month
BRITAIN: *BritRail Southeast Pass*		
Rail	3	8
Rail	4	8
Rail	7	15
BRITAIN: *BritRail Pass Eurostar*		
Rail(l) ✔	4	3 months
Rail(l) ✔	8	3 months
BRITAIN: *Freedom of Scotland Travelpass*		
Rail	8	8

(NATIONAL)

	FIRST CLASS				SECOND CLASS		
		BREAKEVEN MILES(e)				**BREAKEVEN MILES(e)**	
PRICE(c)	**COST PER DAY(d)**	**TOTAL**	**PER DAY**	**PRICE(c)**	**COST PER DAY(d)**	**TOTAL**	**PER DAY**
$165	$41	611	153	$111	$28	617	154
289	72	545	136	199	50	538	134
245	61	462	116	—	—	—	—
—	—	—	—	160	40	432	108
269	45	—	—	207	35	—	—
237	40	—	—	—	—	—	—
325	41	613	77	235	29	635	79
275	34	519	65	—	—	—	—
—	—	—	—	189	24	511	64
399	50	753	94	280	35	757	95
339	42	640	80	—	—	—	—
—	—	—	—	225	28	608	76
427	33	—	—	350	27	—	—
383	29	—	—	—	—	—	—
525	35	991	66	365	24	—	—
445	30	840	56	—	—	—	—
—	—	—	—	289	19	781	52
615	41	1160	77	425	28	1149	77
490	33	925	62	—	—	—	—
—	—	—	—	340	23	919	61
665	30	1255	57	465	21	1257	57
565	26	1066	48	—	—	—	—
—	—	—	—	359	16	970	44
765	26	1443	48	545	18	1473	49
650	22	1226	41	—	—	—	—
—	—	—	—	435	15	1176	39
90	30	170	57	69	23	186	62
120	30	226	57	89	22	241	60
169	24	319	46	119	17	322	46
439	110	828	207	383	96	1035	259
559	70	1055	132	445	56	1203	150
—	—	—	—	159	20	430	54

requires a minimum of three travelers in the summer but only two in the winter.)

- **Senior** and **Youth** passes offer reductions for special age groups (see *Seniors, Couples, Youth,* page 253).

Of whatever type, most passes cover at least some supplemental charges for the top express trains. But you must usually pay extra for seat reservations, overnight sleeper accommodations, or a cabin on overnight ferries.

LARGE AND SMALL

Passes vary widely in their geographical coverage, offering another possibility for a saving.

Multinational passes are valid in more than one country:

- **Eurailpass** has the widest reach—it's good in Hungary and for all the major national railways of Western Europe except Britain's. It also entitles you to free or discounted travel on some suburban trains (but not city transit systems), some private railways, national buses, and some ferries and excursion boats. Unfortunately, *Eurailpass* is now so expensive that it probably makes sense for only a few travelers. Adult passes are sold only for First Class, youth passes only for Second.
- **EuroPass,** less expensive than *Eurailpass,* is a possibility if you're traveling mainly in France, Germany, Italy, Spain, and Switzerland. It's available in combinations of three, four, or five of the participating countries (all the countries you select must be contiguous). You can also add a

RAIL PASSES FOR EUROPE (NATIONAL) *(cont'd)*

REGION OR COUNTRY/ TYPE OF PASS (✔ = NEW FOR 1996)	VALIDITY(a)	
	TRAVEL(b)	TOTAL
BRITAIN: *Freedom of Scotland Travelpass (cont'd)*		
Rail	8	15
Rail	15	15
Rail	22	22
BULGARIA: *Bulgarian Flexipass*		
Rail	3	1 month
CZECH REPUBLIC: *Czech Flexipass*		
Rail	5	15
FINLAND: *Finnrail Pass*		
Rail	3	1 month
Rail ✔	5	1 month
Rail ✔	10	1 month
FRANCE: *France Railpass*		
Rail(r)	3	1 month
Rail/companion(j,r)	3	1 month
Rail/air(j,s)	4 (3/1)	1 month
Rail/car(j,r,t)	5 (3/2)	1 month
Rail/car/air(j,s,t)	6 (3/2/1)	1 month
GERMANY: *German Railpass*		
Rail	5	1 month
Rail/youth(g)	5	1 month
Rail/companion(j)	5	1 month
Rail	10	1 month
Rail/youth(g)	10	1 month
Rail/companion(j)	10	1 month
Rail	15	1 month
Rail/youth(g)	15	1 month
Rail/companion(j)	15	1 month
GREECE: *Greek Flexipass*		
Rail	3	1 month
Rail/air(u)	4 (3/1)	1 month
Rail	5	1 month
HUNGARY: *Hungarian Flexipass*		
Rail	5	15
Rail	10	1 month

| FIRST CLASS | | | | SECOND CLASS | | | |
PRICE(c)	COST PER DAY(d)	BREAKEVEN MILES(e) TOTAL	PER DAY	PRICE(c)	COST PER DAY(d)	BREAKEVEN MILES(e) TOTAL	PER DAY
—	—	—	—	185	23	500	63
—	—	—	—	220	15	595	40
—	—	—	—	269	12	727	33
70	23	389	130	—	—	—	—
69	14	329	66	—	—	—	—
179	60	778	259	119	40	793	264
249	50	1083	217	169	34	1127	225
339	34	1474	147	229	23	1527	153
198	66	683	228	160	53	889	296
149	50	512	171	120	40	667	222
245	61	—	—	215	54	—	—
189	38	—	—	159	32	—	—
289	48	—	—	259	43	—	—
260	52	510	102	178	36	524	105
—	—	—	—	138	28	406	81
195	78	765	153	134	53	785	157
410	41	804	80	286	29	841	84
—	—	—	—	188	19	553	55
508	62	1206	121	215	43	1262	126
530	35	1039	69	386	26	1135	76
—	—	—	—	238	16	700	47
398	53	1559	104	290	39	1703	114
86	29	344	115	—	—	—	—
163	41	—	—	142	36	—	—
120	24	480	96	—	—	—	—
55	11	196	39	—	—	—	—
69	7	246	25	—	—	—	—

few adjacent countries to some *EuroPasses* by paying extra: $45 for Austria, $42 for Benelux, $90 for Greece, $29 for Portugal; youth add-ons are cheaper.

• The **Benelux** (Belgium, the Netherlands, and Luxembourg) and **Scanrail** (Denmark, Finland, Norway, and Sweden) passes are also cheaper than *Eurailpass*. Adults can buy them in Second Class versions—and clip another 20% or so off the local transport budget without much sacrifice.

• In Eastern Europe, there's the **European East Pass**. It covers Austria, the Czech Republic, Hungary, Poland, and Slovakia.

NATIONAL PASSES. Whenever your trip is confined to a single country, chances are that a national pass for that country—especially in Second Class—will be much cheaper than a *Eurailpass* or *EuroPass* of comparable duration. Those one-country passes are especially attractive in Germany, France, Italy, and some small countries.

Some one-country passes don't cover ferry travel or exempt you from surcharges, as *Eurailpass* does. On the other hand, others provide special extras: The Swiss national pass, for example, provides free or discounted travel on important private railroads that *Eurailpass* excludes. (If you're unsure if *Eurailpass* covers any given trip, check with Rail Europe, the official *Eurailpass* representative in the US; see *Where to Find It*, at the end of this chapter, for address and phone.)

VE Tours (800-222-8383) can now make seat reservations on Spanish trains

RAIL PASSES FOR EUROPE (NATIONAL) *(cont'd)*

REGION OR COUNTRY/ TYPE OF PASS (✔ = NEW FOR 1996)	VALIDITY(a)	
	TRAVEL(b)	TOTAL
IRELAND (Republic only): Irish Explorer		
Rail(v)	5	15
Rail/bus(w)	8	15
IRELAND (Republic and Northern Ireland):		
Rail(x)	5	15
Rail/bus(y)	8	15
Rail/bus(y)	15	30
ITALY: Italian Rail Card, Italian Flexi Card		
Rail	4	1 month
Rail	8	8
Rail	8	1 month
Rail	12	1 month
Rail	15	15
Rail	21	21
Rail	30	30
NETHERLANDS: Holland Railpass		
Rail	3	1 month
Rail/youth(g)	3	1 month
Rail	5	1 month
Rail/youth(g)	5	1 month
Rail	10	1 month
Rail/youth(g)	10	1 month
NORWAY (high season, May-Sep): Norway Railpass		
Rail(z)	3	1 month
Rail(z)	7	7
Rail(z)	14	14
NORWAY (low season, Oct-Apr): Norway Railpass		
Rail	3	1 month
Rail	7	7
Rail	14	14
POLAND: Polrail Pass		
Rail	8	8
Rail/youth(g)	8	8
Rail	15	15
Rail/youth(g) ✔	15	15
Rail	21	21
Rail/youth(g)	21	21

FIRST CLASS				SECOND CLASS			
PRICE(c)	COST PER DAY(d)	BREAKEVEN MILES(e) TOTAL	PER DAY	PRICE(c)	COST PER DAY(d)	BREAKEVEN MILES(e) TOTAL	PER DAY
—	—	—	—	100	20	286	57
—	—	—	—	150	19	—	—

Emerald Card, IrishRover

FIRST CLASS				SECOND CLASS			
—	—	—	—	124	25	354	71
—	—	—	—	174	22	—	—
—	—	—	—	300	20	—	—
194	49	719	180	132	33	825	206
248	31	919	115	168	21	1050	131
284	36	1052	131	184	23	1150	144
356	30	1319	110	238	20	1488	124
312	21	1156	77	208	14	1300	87
362	17	1341	64	242	12	1513	72
436	15	1615	54	290	10	1813	60
88	29	220	73	68	23	252	84
—	—	—	—	56	19	207	69
140	28	350	70	104	21	385	77
—	—	—	—	79	16	293	59
260	26	650	65	184	18	681	68
—	—	—	—	130	13	481	48
190	63	528	176	135	45	563	188
250	36	694	99	190	27	792	113
330	24	917	65	255	18	1063	76
170	57	472	157	120	40	500	167
200	29	556	79	150	21	625	89
265	19	736	53	205	15	854	61
70	9	500	63	50	6	556	69
49	6	350	44	35	4	389	49
90	6	643	43	60	4	667	44
63	4	450	30	42	3	467	31
100	5	714	34	70	3	778	37
70	3	500	24	49	2	544	26

via a direct computer link. There's no extra fee when you buy tickets or a rail pass through VE Tours.

A few countries offer regional passes, which cost less than the national pass and cover less territory. Our table lists the two most attractive British regional options: one covering all of Scotland, the other a southeastern region that includes most of the important visitor destinations—Cambridge, Canterbury, Exeter, and Oxford (but not Stratford) —that you can reach from London on day trips.

Your travel agency can now issue point-to-point *BritRail* tickets through the Apollo computer reservation system. Be warned, however, that *BritRail* sells only full-fare tickets in the US. If you want to take advantage of the many excursion and other promotional fares, you must buy your tickets in England. If you want to buy them before you leave, call a travel agency in Britain—the American Express office in The Haymarket, for example.

PACKAGES, TOO. Many European railways bundle their rail passes with hotel accommodations, sightseeing, and other features into tour packages. If you prefer to buy your travel that way, ask the US office of the rail system where you plan to travel for rail-tour brochures (see *Where to Find It*).

SENIORS, COUPLES, YOUTH

European railroads typically offer far too many special fares—group, family, student, mileage-based, and such—to list in the table. While they're designed for residents, some are attractive for visitors:

• In many countries, seniors can buy individual tickets at discounted rates (though travel may be blacked out on peak days or at peak times). You need to prove your age (a passport will do) in *Denmark* (age 65, discount varies), *Finland* (age 65, 50% off), *Luxembourg* (age 65, 50% off), *Norway* (age 67, 50% off), and *Portugal* (age 60, 30% off).

You need an official senior ID in

RAIL PASSES FOR EUROPE (NATIONAL) *(cont'd)*

REGION OR COUNTRY/ TYPE OF PASS (✔ = NEW FOR 1996)	VALIDITY(a)	
	TRAVEL(b)	TOTAL
POLAND: *Polrail Pass (cont'd)*		
Rail	1 month	1 month
Rail/youth(g)	1 month	1 month
PORTUGAL: *Portugese Railpass*		
Rail	4	15
ROMANIA: *RomanianPass*		
Rail	3	15
SPAIN: *Spain Flexipass*		
Rail(aa) ✔	3	2 months
Rail/car(aa,bb)	6 (3/3)	2 months
SWITZERLAND: *Swiss Flexipass, Swiss Pass*		
Rail	3	15
Rail/companion(j,cc) ✔	3	15
Rail	4	4
Rail/companion(j,cc) ✔	4	4
Rail/car(o,cc)	6 (3/3)	15
Rail/car(o,dd)	6 (3/3)	15
Rail	8	8
Rail/companion(j,cc) ✔	8	8
Rail	15	15
Rail/companion(j,cc) ✔	15	15
Rail	1 month	1 month
Rail/companion(j,cc) ✔	1 month	1 month

See pages 244–45 for footnotes.

Austria (card $27, age 60 for women, 65 for men, 50% off), *France* (card $28 for four trips, $52 for unlimited travel, age 60, generally 50% off), *Germany* (card $149 in First Class, $75 in Second, age 60, 50% off), *Greece* (card $24 in First Class, $16 in Second Class, age 60, five free trips, 50% off for additional trips), and *Sweden* (card $6, age 65, off-peak days, 25% off). Austrian cards are available in advance by mail (see *Where to Find It*). Otherwise, you can have a card issued on the spot at main rail stations within a country.

- In France, a *couple* traveling together enjoys 25% reductions on individual ticket prices. Each couple needs a single *carte au couple* ID (free at a main station, but bring passport-type photos).

- *Youth/student* ticket discounts are

FIRST CLASS				SECOND CLASS			
PRICE(c)	COST PER DAY(d)	BREAKEVEN MILES(e) TOTAL	PER DAY	PRICE(c)	COST PER DAY(d)	BREAKEVEN MILES(e) TOTAL	PER DAY
130	4	929	31	90	3	1000	33
91	3	650	22	63	2	700	23
99	25	707	177	—	—	—	—
60	20	207	69	—	—	—	—
180	60	1059	353	144	48	1309	436
249	42	—	—	219	37	—	—
264	88	394	131	176	59	440	147
198	66	296	99	132	44	330	110
264	66	394	99	178	45	445	111
198	50	296	74	132	33	330	83
275	46	—	—	205	34	—	—
325	54	—	—	245	41	—	—
316	40	472	59	220	28	550	69
237	30	354	44	165	21	413	52
368	25	549	37	256	17	640	43
276	18	412	27	192	13	480	32
508	17	758	25	350	12	875	29
381	13	569	19	263	9	656	22

available in many countries, and reduced-price youth options are available on many passes. Check a student travel agency or a youth-travel guidebook for specifics.

All breakeven figures in the table are based on the average cost of full-fare tickets. Seniors, couples, and youth who qualify for discounts on individual tickets should adjust those breakeven mileages: If the discount on individual tickets is 50%, the breakeven mileage is double the figure shown.

WHERE TO FIND IT

CAR-RENTAL COMPANIES

A indicates a US-based, multinational rental company; *B*, an independent rental agency; *C*, a leasing company; *D*, a European renter with a US sales office; *E*, a European rental company represented in the US by an affiliated US rental company.

Alamo: 800-522-9696; 800-327-9633 in Canada; Web site *http://www.freeways. com/; or www.goalamo.com. (A)*

Auto Europe: 800-223-5555; Web site *http://www.wrld. com/ae/. (B)*

Avis: 800-331-1084; 800-879-2847 in Canada; Web site *http://www.avis.com/. (A)*

Bon Voyage by Car: 800-272-3299, 818-786-1960; Web site *http://www. pcmvisual.com/bonvoyage/. (B,C)*

Budget: 800-472-3325; 800-268-8900 in Canada. *(A)*

DER Car: 800-782-2424, or contact travel agent. *(B)*

EuroDollar (Dollar in the US): 800-800-6000; fax-back 918-669-3143. *(E)*

Europcar (National InterRent in the US): 800-227-3876; 800-227-7368 in Canada; Web site *http://www.nationalcar. com/. (E)*

European Car Reservations (ECR**):** 800-535-3303. *(B)*

Europe by Car: 800-223-1516; 800-252-9401 in CA; Web site *http://www. europebycar.com/. (B,C)*

Hertz: 800-654-3001; 800-263-0600 in Canada. *(A)*

Holiday Autos: 800-422-7737; Web site *http://www.holauto.com/holiday/. (B)*

Intl Travel Services (ITS): 800-521-0643. *(B)*

Kemwel: 800-678-0678. *(B,C)*

Kenning: 800-227-8990. *(D)*

Payless: 800-237-2804. *(A)*

Renault Eurodrive: 800-221-1052 to 5 P.M. Eastern time, 800-477-7116 to 5 P.M. Pacific time. *(C)*

Thrifty: 800-331-9111. *(A)*

Town and Country Intl: 800-248-4350. *(D)*

Woods Car Rental UK/British Network: 800-274-8583.*(D)*

RAIL PASSES

All rail passes below can be bought in the US from any travel agency. For many passes, expect to pay a handling or mailing fee. Agencies noted *Eurail* sell both *Eurailpass* and *EuroPass.* Most passes, but not *Eurailpass,* can be bought in Europe, too. Some national passes must also be purchased outside the country of validity. Proof of non-resident status (usually a passport) may be required.

Austrian Senior Citizen Railway Card: Send a check for US$27 with photocopy of passport showing age and a passport-sized photo to OeBB, Verkehrseinnahmen-und-Reklamationsstelle, Mariannengasse 20, A-1090 Vienna, Austria. Or buy at central rail stations in Austria or main train stations in major German cities.

BritRail Travel Intl: 1500 Broadway, NYC 10036; 212-575-2667. Britain. *AE, MC, V.*

CIE Tours Intl: 100 Hanover Ave, Box 501, Cedar Knolls NJ 07927; 800-243-8687, 201-292-3438, fax 201-292-0463. Ireland. *AE, Disc, MC, V.*

CIT Tours: 342 Madison Ave, Suite 207, NYC 10173; 800-223-7987, 212-697-2100, fax 212-697-1394. *Eurail, Germany, Italy. MC, V.*

DER Tours/GermanRail: 9501 W Devon Ave, Suite 400, Rosemont IL 60018; 800-421-2929, fax 800-282-7474. *Eurail, Benelux, Scanrail,* Austria, Germany, Greece, Italy, Netherlands, Norway, Spain, Sweden. *AE, Disc, MC, V.*

Forsyth Travel Library: Box 480800, Kansas MO 64148; 800-367-7984, fax 816-942-6969. All listed passes. *Disc, MC, V.*

Netherlands Service Center for Tourism: 225 N Michigan Ave, Suite 1854, Chicago 60601; 800-598-8501. *Benelux,* Netherlands. *AE, MC, V.*

Orbis Polish Travel Bureau: 342 Madison Ave, Suite 1512, NYC 10173; 800-223-6037, 212-867-5011, fax 212-682-4715. Poland. *AE, Disc, MC, V.*

Rail Europe: 226-230 Westchester Ave, White Plains NY 10604; 800-438-7245, fax 800-432-1329. *Eurail, Benelux, European East, Scanrail,* Austria, Bulgaria, Czech Republic, Finland, France, Hungary, Norway, Portugal, Romania, Spain, Switzerland. *AE, DC, MC, V.*

Scandinavian American World Tours (Scanam): 933 Highway 23, Pompton Plains NJ 07444; 800-545-2204, 201-835-7070, fax 201-835-3030. *Scanrail,* Denmark, Finland, Norway, Sweden. *MC, V.*

Scantours: 3439 Wade, Los Angeles CA 90066; 800-223-7226, fax 310-390-0493. *Benelux, Eurail, Euro East, Scanrail,* Austria, Bulgaria, Czech Republic, Finland, France, Germany, Hungary, Italy, Norway, Portugal, Romania, Spain, Switzerland. No charge cards.

This chapter was adapted from the Consumer Reports Travel Letter *articles "By Car Through Europe: Rental Rates Still Down" (May 1996) and "By Train Through Europe: Separate Tickets? A Pass?" (March 1996).*

22

RAIL PASSES: ASIA AND THE SOUTH PACIFIC

O nly a few countries outside Europe operate passenger rail systems that are efficient—that is, that can compete with other transport in speed, frequency of service, and comfort. Chief among those are Japan, South Korea, and Taiwan (and a few places in Canada and the US). Elsewhere, travelers who want to get around inside a country efficiently must fly, take a bus, or drive a rented car.

Of course, efficiency isn't everything. Some people just like to ride trains, slow and infrequent or not. And in most countries, trains are usually cheaper than airlines—especially for a series of short trips.

Many readers are probably familiar with *Eurailpass* and the other European passes (see chapter 21). But some may not know that similar passes can provide comfortable local transportation elsewhere in the world.

THE MECHANICS OF PASSES

Rail passes are similar the world over: You pay a fixed price and get unlimited train (and sometimes bus and ferry) travel within a specified time. *Full-time* passes let you travel on any day on which the pass is valid. *Flexible* passes are good for travel on a set number of days anytime during the pass's validity period.

The pass usually gets you just a daytime seat, with overnight sleeping accommodations, private compartments, meals, and such extra. There's also sometimes a supplementary charge for some premium trains.

Some countries offer rail passes in more than one class. Travelers used to Second Class in Europe may want to consider First Class (or its equivalent) in other parts of the world. Cheaper classes may also be jam-packed.

You or your travel agent may be able to book seats, compartments, and the like before you leave. If you do, recheck your arrangements as soon as you get to your destination. If you expect to make arrangements when you arrive, allow plenty of time. Where a country limits rail passes to nonresidents, you may have to prove you're a foreigner by showing your passport, birth certificate, or driver's license when you buy the pass and, perhaps, again when you use it.

This chapter presents an overview of what's available in Asia and the South Pacific, based on a *CRTL* report in early 1996. The prices in the listings that follow are in US dollars as of that year, converted where necessary at late-February '96 exchange rates (1997 prices weren't available at this writing). Unless noted, infants traveled free and older children paid the adult fare. Average rail speeds are based on scheduled station-to-station times (not top running speed).

INDIA

India's extensive railway system is the primary way locals get around that huge country. The *Indrail Pass,* for foreign visitors, provided unlimited travel on Indian Railways. Price: one day, $86 Air-Conditioned First Class/$39 Regular First Class/$17 Second Class; seven days, $300/$160/$80; 15 days, $370/$185/$90; 21 days, $440/$220/$100; 30 days, $550/$275/$125; and 60 days, $800/$400/$185; children paid half. Air-Conditioned First Class provides a better selection of sleeping accommodations than Regular First Class, but wasn't available on all trains. Second Class is apt to be very basic and very crowded.

Rail trips between Bombay, Calcutta, Delhi, and Madras all require at least one night on a relatively slow (about 52 mph) train. Bombay-Delhi, for example, requires more than 16 hours.

Travelers interested in covering more than just one region of India should consider the *Discover India* air pass. At $500, it provided unlimited air travel for 21 days, with one stopover allowed at each destination. (Children 2–12 paid $250.) Still, rail buffs can find a vast selection of scenic routes in India, and rail travel is popular with visitors.

If you plan just one or two train trips, individual tickets may be cheaper —a First Class ticket from Bombay to Delhi cost just $21. However, some authorities recommend a pass even when it's more expensive than individual tickets, since passholders find it easier to get seat and sleeping-berth reservations. You can buy a pass through any US or Canadian travel agency.

JAPAN

Japan is the only country outside Europe with a system of fast, frequent, comfortable trains for which you can buy a pass. Superfast bullet trains run frequently on three main trunk routes and connect with numerous regular rail lines. That combination reaches virtually every important visitor center. Top main-line trains are air-conditioned in both Ordinary and Green Car Classes.

The *Japan Rail Pass* provided foreign visitors with unlimited travel on most Japan Railways trains. The most important exception was the super-express *Nozomi* bullet trains (but the pass did cover the *Hikari* trains, which are almost as fast). Passes were available in both Green (First) and Ordinary (Coach) classes. Price: 7 days, $346 Green/$260 Ordinary; 14 days, $561/

$414; 21 days, $730/$529. Children 6–11 paid 50%. Sleepers were available at extra cost (but weren't used on the bullet trains, which ran during the day).

For most foreign visitors, the most popular train ride is probably the trip between Tokyo and Kyoto. That's on the main bullet-train line, where the fastest trains average 142 mph. Bullet trains also cross Honshu to Niigata, on the shore opposite Tokyo, and they go as far north as Morioka.

If your local travel is limited to a few day excursions—Tokyo to Nikko, say, or Kyoto to Nara—you may be better off with individual tickets, especially since the best service for some of those trips is on private railways the pass doesn't cover. Otherwise, the *Japan Rail Pass* was an excellent buy: The seven-day version paid for itself after just one round trip between Tokyo and Osaka. Furthermore, the train handles relatively short domestic trips with much less bother than an airplane.

You buy an exchange order from a US travel agency and exchange it for a pass at a Japan Railway Travel Service Center (at an airport or big-city rail station) after you arrive in Japan. If you fly to Japan on Japan Airlines (JAL), you can also buy an exchange order at a JAL office in the US. You must specify the date on which you'll start using the pass.

MALAYSIA

Malaysia's rail system runs the length of peninsular Malaysia; it also carries some through trains that run from Singapore to Bangkok. The *Malayan Railway Pass,* for foreign visitors, provides unlimited travel on the Malayan Railway, including a trip to Singapore. Price for travel in any class where seats are available: 10 days, $55; 30 days, $120. Children 4–12 paid 50%. Sleeping accommodations were extra. Only a few of the top trains are air-conditioned,

ESSENTIAL REFERENCES

Anyone planning extended rail travel overseas should have the latest issue of the *Thomas Cook Overseas Timetable,* a compilation published every two months of rail schedules throughout the world (except for Europe, which has its own timetable). Thomas Cook Publishing, Peterborough UK, about $25 at US travel bookstores or by phone from Forsyth Travel Library (800-367-7984, fax 913-384-3553; $28.95; *MC, V*).

The *Eurail Guide to World Train Travel,* updated annually, covers recommended schedules, routes, and itineraries worldwide. However, it has slipped a bit since the founding authors retired. The most glaring weakness is that it doesn't identify which recommended trips are covered by the local rail passes and which aren't. It also contains information on routes that have long since been abandoned. Houghton Mifflin; 1996 edition, $18.95 at bookstores.

but the pass allowed travelers to ride in air-conditioned cars whenever they were available.

Malaysia's top train, the *Rakyat Ekspres,* runs between Singapore and Butterworth, mostly by day, at a pokey 35 mph—a good sightseeing option, especially if you break your trip in Kuala Lumpur. Train buffs can connect at Butterworth (with an overnight layover) to an overnight train to Bangkok, not covered by the Malaysian pass. (A very expensive luxury excursion train, not covered by any rail pass, also runs over that route.)

Travelers interested in traveling to outlying Malaysian islands have no choice but to fly—the *Discover Malaysia Pass* visitor ticket provided five flights anywhere within Malaysia for $199. But train travel in the corridor between Singapore and Butterworth or Bangkok is another of those rides that rail buffs favor.

If you're just doing a short leg, such as Kuala Lumpur–Butterworth, you can buy a separate First Class ticket for $26. But for more extended travel, a pass is attractive. You can buy it after you arrive (show foreign ID).

THAILAND

The Thai rail system operates to some of the country's most important outlying visitor centers. However, trains are slow and infrequent.

The *Visit Thailand Rail Pass* provided unlimited Second or Third Class travel for foreign visitors on the State Railway of Thailand. Price: 20 days, $79 including sleeping accommodations and air-conditioning; children 4–12 paid 50%. Only a few trains are air-conditioned, but the pass allowed travelers to ride in air-conditioned cars whenever they were available. You can buy a pass after you arrive in Thailand.

The train lets you travel by day in either direction between Bangkok and Chiang Mai, Thailand's most important outlying visitor center, at a modest 44 mph, on average. A special weekend tourist train gets you from Bangkok to Nam Tok (River Khwae Bridge) and back as a day trip.

The rail pass was much cheaper than an airline visitor ticket, at $259 for four flights. If you don't mind a limited choice of schedules and destinations, train travel can be a nice way to pass through the countryside. However, unless you plan a lot of travel, individual tickets are probably an even better bet: The round-trip from Bangkok to Chiang Mai, for example, was just $20.

AUSTRALIA

As in the US and Canada, long-haul Australian trains are primarily land cruisers—slow, infrequent, and of interest mainly to rail enthusiasts. Australia offers two national passes for foreign visitors. You can buy them through any US or Canadian travel agency before you leave:

- The *Austrailpass* provided unlimited travel, in either First Class or Economy, throughout the country on Railways of Australia (ROA) and on ROA-run suburban trains and buses. Price: 14 days, $592 First/$349 Economy; 21 days, $748/$452; 30 days,

$919/$547. Pass prices included seat-reservation charges, but sleeping accommodations and meals were extra.

- The *Austrail Flexi-Pass* provided travel on a limited number of days during a six-month period: eight days, $494 First/$289 Economy; 15 days, $695/$418, 22 days, $965/$585; or 29 days, $1230/$756. The eight-day pass was not valid for travel on the *Indian Pacific* or the *Ghan* (see *For Rail Buffs*, page 261).

There were also three rail passes good only for travel within one of Australia's states. Except as noted, they weren't limited to foreign tourists; anyone could buy one, either from a US travel agency or after arrival in Australia:

- **Queensland.** The *Sunshine Rail Pass* provided unlimited travel on Queensland Railways, suburban services in Brisbane, and the Cairns-Kuranda scenic railway. Price: 14 days, $295 First/$203 Economy; 21 days, $362/$235; 30 days, $442/$295. Children 4–16 and students holding Australian student ID issued by ROA paid 50%.
- **Victoria.** The *Victoria Pass* provided unlimited First Class travel on V-Line trains and buses. Price: 14 days, $99; children 4–16 paid 50%. A seven-day version was available for $57 to foreign visitors only (if they bought in Australia and showed their passport and a return air ticket).
- **Western Australia.** The *Westrail Premier Discovery Pass* provided unlimited travel on all Western Australia Government Railways trains and buses. Price: 21 days, $144.

Australia's major visitor centers are so far apart that most visitors will find one of the many airline visitor tickets a more practical way to get around in extended touring. And individual tickets are a better bet for suburban services around Brisbane, Melbourne, and Sydney. But if you want to try one or more of the top long-haul runs, consider a pass. For comparison, a one-way Sydney-Perth trip in Holiday Class (sleeper but no meals) cost $522-582, depending on season.

NEW ZEALAND

New Zealand's railways run trunk-line services on both islands, which extend to most of the country's main visitor centers. Travelers who want to see a lot of the country in a hurry are probably better off with one of the many airline visitor tickets. However, New Zealand's rail system is well organized for daytime sightseeing, and the train is a practical alternative for travelers who would prefer not to drive a car in a strange environment.

The *New Zealand Travelpass* provided unlimited travel on New Zealand Rail's trains, buses, and interisland ferries. Price: any 8 out of 21 days, $296; 15 out of 35 days, $372; 22 out of 56 days, $435; children paid ⅔.

For limited travel, individual tickets may be better: A round-trip from Auckland to Wellington cost $174. But if you plan to go much farther than that, the pass was a good deal. You can buy rail passes from a US or Canadian travel agency or in New Zealand after you arrive.

Long-distance trains cover the main routes, but only once or twice daily. You can travel either way between Auckland and Wellington as a day trip (averaging about 39 mph), and you can get to Rotorua and back as a day trip from Auckland. On the South Island, you can do the main runs from Picton to Invercargill by day (if you stop overnight at Christchurch). You can also do the scenic route from Christchurch to Greymouth and back as a day trip.

This chapter was adapted from the Consumer Reports Travel Letter *article "Rail Passes: North America, Asia, and the South Pacific" (April 1996).*

FOR RAIL BUFFS

Several Australian routes are of special interest to visiting rail fans:

- The *Indian Pacific* crosses the continent from Sydney to Perth in 64 hours (three nights on board), at an average 42 mph.
- The *Ghan* runs from Adelaide to Alice Springs—the primary center for tours to the outback and Ayers Rock.
- A number of trains go north from Brisbane to Cairns, passing through several points from which you can get to the Great Barrier Reef.
- You can also do some shorter trips as all-daytime rides, including Brisbane-Sydney, Brisbane-Rockhampton, Cairns-Townsville, Canberra-Sydney, and Melbourne-Sydney.

THE TRAVEL STRATEGIST

Interested in a smooth trip abroad? Take a few preparatory steps: Check State Department advisories for any cautionary information on the region you're visiting. Make arrangements for access to cash overseas. For ready cash, always carry some traveler's checks, perhaps in the currencies of the places you plan to visit. Consider whether it's worthwhile to go after tax refunds of your foreign purchases. And check out some phone services that make US-bound and intercountry calls easy.

AVOIDING TROUBLE ABROAD

The US State Department alerts traveling Americans of possible risks abroad with information in two categories:

TRAVEL WARNINGS. Those are issued when the State Department decides to recommend that Americans avoid travel to a given country. The basis for such a recommendation includes unusual security and/or travel conditions—for instance, the potential for unexpected detention, unstable political conditions, or serious health problems.

CONSULAR INFORMATION SHEETS. Available for every country of the world, these include such information as the location of the US embassy or consulate, unusual immigration practices, health conditions, minor political disturbances, unusual currency and entry regulations, crime and security information, and drug penalties.

Any instabilities in a country that aren't severe enough to warrant a warning may be included in an optional section called Areas of Instability. Once in a while, that section will also restate any embassy advice given to official employees. Otherwise, consular information sheets generally don't include advice.

State Department policy requires that any information that is *routinely* made available to embassy employees must be made available to the traveling public. But, in response to criticism from the travel industry and the General Accounting Office in 1991, Consular Affairs took steps to specify whether an advisory concerns a threat to the general traveling public or just to diplomatic personnel. It has also made consular information and warnings more accessible: You can now get the information by fax or on a free electronic bulletin board instead of phoning, writing, or asking a travel agent to get it for you. (See *Where to Find It,* page 273.)

Travel agents can get the full text (and for some services, an index) of the consular information sheets and travel warnings through all the major computer- reservation systems.

Check the announcements for any location you're considering visiting, or ask a travel agent to do so. (Each month, *Consumer Reports Travel Letter—CRTL* —publishes a list of countries for which some sort of warning is in effect.)

If your trip is already booked and you cancel because of a travel advisory that you feel is serious, you risk losing any deposits and being liable for any cancellation fees. Your ability to recoup losses often depends on the policies of the carriers with which you've booked your trip. And trip cancellation insurance may not reimburse you if you cancel because of a travel advisory. (See chapter 24.)

MONEY MATTERS

Developing a foreign-currency strategy is an important part of trip planning. Here's how to minimize exchange costs:

- Put big expenditures—tickets, hotels, car rentals, and the like—on your credit card or charge card. (For instance, the German railroads— Deutsche Bundesbahn and Deutsche Reichsbahn—accept *Visa* cards at many major rail stations within Germany.) You thus save the percentage point or two of the price that you'd otherwise lose in currency conversion. You also get the protection of the card's chargeback provisions and (with some cards) an extra guarantee on your purchases.
- Use an automatic teller machine (ATM) card for incidental cash whenever you can (see below).
- Carry a small amount of money in traveler's checks as a backup.

ATM CARDS. If your ATM card works in the Cirrus or Plus network at home, you may be able to withdraw cash from foreign bank ATMs that belong to the same network. Your withdrawal will be converted at the interbank exchange rate —the "wholesale" rate that banks use for large-scale financial transactions.

That's quite an advantage. If you exchange currency or traveler's checks at a bank exchange counter, you get a retail rate that's often 3–5% less favorable. At many banks, an additional fee—per transaction, per check, or a percentage of the transaction—can add another 2–5% to your cost.

The expense can be even worse if you exchange at hotels and nonbank exchange counters when banks are closed. And foreign cash advances on credit cards or charge cards typically incur interest (charged from the date of cash advance until you pay your bill, regardless of any grace period on purchases), a per-transaction fee, or a percentage of the advance (up to 3%).

Overseas, Cirrus and Plus work exactly as ATMs work at home: You punch in your personal identification number (PIN) and the amount of withdrawal (in local currency). The machine issues the currency, and your home account is debited automatically. The foreign bank imposes no fees. The only possible extra is a per-use fee your bank may impose for using an ATM elsewhere on the network (usually $2–3 per transaction, $5 at a few banks). Those fees can add up, though, so plan ahead to minimize the number of transactions you make.

Some tips:

- ATMs outside North America often do not accept PINs longer than four digits. If your PIN is longer, ask your bank for a different number.
- Keypads on many foreign ATMs have numbers only. If your PIN contains letters, use the standard letter-number correspondences from US phones to convert.
- Don't worry about a language problem —most foreign ATMs affiliated with Cirrus or Plus provide instructions in English.
- Overseas ATMs may not give you a choice of accounts to tap. If you want to withdraw overseas, make sure funds are available in your primary checking account.

Finding an overseas ATM that will accept your ATM debit card can be a problem. Banks in a few important tourist countries still aren't set up to handle ATM debit withdrawals—travelers from the US can get cash only by using a credit card (and paying interest on the withdrawal as a cash advance). But the situation is getting better, as both Cirrus (*MasterCard*) and Plus (*Visa*) extend their ATM networks. Both systems now publish directories of overseas locations, which should be available from the issuing bank.

According to both Visa International (which owns the Plus name overseas) and Cirrus System, Inc., you must rely on the bank that issued you the ATM card to give you exact overseas locations. Cirrus prints a directory twice a year that is available from the issuing bank.

Caution is usually still the watchword with foreign ATM technology. Finding a participating ATM may be difficult, and your card may not work at all locations. Don't rely solely on ATMs to replenish your cash supply while you're traveling, unless you're sure (from a prior trip) that your card will work.

TRAVELER'S CHECKS (US$). Widely accepted in hard-currency countries, traveler's checks offer protection against loss or theft. Most provide worldwide refunds and emergency services if checks are lost or stolen.

You can purchase traveler's checks at a bank or thrift, credit union, AAA office (free to members), American Express Travel Service Office, or currency exchange service, such as Thomas Cook or Ruesch Intl. Fees vary, but average 1–2% of your check purchase. (Two-thirds of American Express offices don't charge for traveler's checks.)

American Express and *Visa* also offer two-signature traveler's checks. When a couple buys, both sign. Then, the check can be cashed by either person. Two-signature checks are handy: A couple needn't decide ahead of time how many checks each person is likely to need.

AmEx charges more for its two-signature checks than for regular checks. Visa says it charges member banks the same price for its two-signature as for regular checks, but that it can't control what the banks charge their customers.

PLASTIC CHECKS. *Visa's Travel-Money* card, available at US banks, is meant to compete with travelers' checks: You prepay the selling bank as much as you want, plus a 2% fee, then use the card as you would an ordinary debit card at *Visa/Plus* ATMs throughout the world. As with ATM withdrawals, you get a good exchange rate.

The 2% fee is more than you typically pay for traveler's checks, often free and seldom sold at a fee of more than 1%. Then again, with *TravelMoney* you get a much better exchange rate than you do with paper checks. Overall, you probably come out a bit ahead. You can also cut your chance of losses by buying two or more cards, so that if one is lost or stolen, the others are still valid.

What the advantage might be over ordinary ATM cards or charge cards is a tougher question. Visa apparently thinks that some travelers will like the idea of limiting what they can spend to the money tied up in the card, rather than dipping into their bank accounts with an ATM or building up charge-card debt through cash advances.

TRAVELER'S CHECKS (FOREIGN CURRENCY). If you have to cash a US$ traveler's check overseas at a hotel, restaurant, store, or nonbank exchange office, you can lose 10–20% on the exchange rate and fees. That's why many savvy travelers buy some of their traveler's checks in foreign currency.

It pays to shop around. Three channels handle foreign-currency transactions: banks with foreign exchange offices, foreign-currency exchange services, and travel agents. Among several foreign exchanges *CRTL* has surveyed, two cater to leisure travelers and conduct transactions by mail.

• **Thomas Cook Currency Services** issues both US dollars and foreign-currency traveler's checks; there is a fee of 1% for purchasing US dollar checks. Foreign checks are free. You can buy either directly through Thomas Cook or through a travel agent.

Orders can be made by phone, fax or mail, and overnight delivery is available.

• **Ruesch Intl** offers foreign-currency traveler's checks in seven currencies. The minimum order quantity is $100 per country. The checks are commission-free when purchased over-the-counter, but there's a $2 charge per currency per person. When purchased by mail there's no fee but there's a $10 shipping charge.

Foreign-currency checks are a good idea if:

• You know you'll arrive in a foreign country at a time when exchange offices are closed.

• You don't want to carry a lot of foreign cash, don't want the bother of exchanging US$ traveler's checks at a bank every day or so, and don't want to charge purchases.

• You want to lock in the exchange rate at the time you buy checks. But don't overbuy—you're apt to lose a bit of money when you change left-over checks back into US dollars when you return home.

Be aware that foreign-currency checks don't let you avoid exchange losses. You still take a hit; the only change is in where you take it: When you buy foreign-currency checks from a US source, you lose about as much as when you exchange dollar checks overseas. There's another problem, too. Overseas hotels, restaurants, and even local banks occasionally refuse to accept local-currency traveler's checks.

HOTEL MONEY EXCHANGE. Holders of *Diners Club* cards can exchange up to $1000 per week for local currency at 65 participating Inter-Continental hotels around the world. You get the bank rate, less a service charge of 4%. That's only a bit worse than you get at a bank, and it's a much better deal than you usually get at a hotel desk. The service is handy and relatively inexpensive if you're in a country where you can't use an ATM or if you need to pick up some foreign currency when banks are closed.

OTHER CURRENCY SERVICES. Foreign payment services are also available through large banks, exchange services, and travel agents. Upon receipt of your US payment in check or money order, a bank draft or wire transfer is issued in local currency to the foreign hotel, air, rail, or other travel company you specify. (By making your deposit or even prepaying the full amount in the

local currency, you may be able to save yourself some money if the dollar's exchange rate weakens by the time the bills are rendered.) Ruesch Intl and Thomas Cook both offer check and wire-transfer services at modest fees.

It's also a good idea to carry a small amount of the local currency with you for transportation, phone calls, and incidentals upon arrival. Most airports abroad have exchange booths, but you may not get the best exchange rate. US exchange offices can also sell you foreign currency before your trip.

VAT REFUNDS—MAYBE

Travelers who shop abroad are supposed to be able to get a refund of the value-added tax (VAT) that's added to the retail price of merchandise in most European countries. You can save a good deal—VAT accounts for as much as one-fourth of an item's retail selling price. But there are stiff minimum-purchase requirements.

The Europe Tax-Free Shopping system (ETS), run by Europe's largest tax-refund specialist, seems to have become the preferred refund mechanism. You shop at stores displaying a blue and silver *Tax Free for Tourists* sign or sticker (in English) in the window or on the door. At the end of your shopping in each store, you ask for a Tax-Free Shopping Cheque for the amount of the tax refund.

For countries within the European Economic Community, you get your refund at an ETS desk after you've passed through departure customs in the last country you visit before you leave for the United States. In non-EEC countries, you get your refund when you leave each country; ask about local procedures. Either way, you must show your purchases to a customs official, so keep them handy in your carry-on baggage.

ETS maintains refund desks in the departure areas of most of Europe's international airports and seaports. In most cases, you can request the refund in the form of local currency, US dollars, or a credit to your charge card.

Take note of three pitfalls:

- In each country, you must make some minimum purchase to qualify for a refund. Typically, the minimum applies to all the goods you buy during one shopping session (one visit to one store). In Italy and Luxembourg, however, it applies per individual item. If you go to more than one store or revisit a store more than once, the minimum applies separately to each shopping session.

  The minimum is under $100 in most countries, but it's well over that in Belgium, Greece, the Netherlands, Italy, Hungary, France, and Switzerland.

- ETS deducts as much as 20% of the refund as a handling fee (the percentage may go down on large refunds).

- Many of the goods you might be tempted to buy in Europe are cheaper in the United States.

Any visitors to Europe can take advantage of value-added-tax refunds on merchandise they buy. But tourists aren't eligible for VAT refunds on the travel *services* they use while vacationing.

People who travel on business, on the other hand, can get refunds of the VAT charged on hotel, restaurant, and rental-car bills in some countries. As of our latest report (summer 1996), corporate refunds were available in Austria (10% on hotels and meals), Finland (6% on hotels, 22% on car rentals), Germany (15% on hotels, entertainment, and car rentals), the Netherlands (17.5% on car rentals), Sweden (12% on hotels, 25% on meals and car rentals), Switzerland (6.5% on all three), and the UK (17.5% on all three).

The paperwork for refunds is complex and exacting. Even big companies generally rely on a few VAT-refund specialists, which typically handle all the details in exchange for a 20–30% cut of the refunds. Six US-based VAT-processing specialists are Euro VAT Refund (310-204-0805), Intl Sales Tax Refund (716-284-6287), Intl VAT Consulting Group (703-478-2220), Meridian VAT Reclaim (212-554-6600), Universal VAT Services (800-627-1002),and VAT America (609-924-3646). To take advantage of refunds, business travelers should require that hotel bills and car-rental contracts specifically list the VAT on the face of the documentation.

If you spend just a few hundred dollars a year abroad, the rebate probably isn't worth the hassle, either to you or to a VAT-refund specialist. But if you spend several thousands of dollars a year, a refund should repay the effort.

BAGGAGE LIABILITY

If an airline loses or damages your checked or carry-on baggage on a domestic trip, its liability to you is limited to $1250 per person. The limit applies to flights on a plane seating more than 60 and to flights on a smaller plane included on the same ticket with a flight on a larger plane. On international trips, maximum baggage compensation is set by treaty at $20 a kilogram of checked baggage weight (about $9 a pound). The airline is liable only for depreciated value, not replacement value or original purchase price.

The US limit of $1250 in depreciated value will probably cover most ordinary baggage containing clothing and personal-care items. The international limit, however, is grossly inadequate: With a typical 20-pound suitcase, for example, the claim allowance of $180 would hardly begin to cover the possessions in most travelers' baggage. But the DOT says that claims are seldom based on actual weight. Most carriers serving the United States have filed tariffs stating that rather than weighing every bag at check-in, they will assume that every lost or damaged bag weighed the maximum that they will accept, usually 32 kilos (around 70

BAGGAGE ALLOWANCES AND CHARGES

AIRLINE	CHECKED BAGGAGE			CARRY-ON BAGGAGE			ADDT'L PIECE	BICYCLE (One-Way)	FARE FOR ITEM Occupying Seat (b)
	NO.	SIZE (a) (in)	WEIGHT (lb)	NO.	SIZE (a) (in)	WEIGHT (lb)			
Alaska	2	62	70	2	50	—	$45(c)	$45	100% applicable fare
America West	2	62(d)	70	2	45	—	45(c)	45	50% full Coach or 100% excursion
American	3(e)	62(d)	70	2	45	70	45(c)	45	100% applicable fare
Continental	3(e)	62(d)	70	2	45	25	45(c)	45	100% applicable fare
Delta	3(e)	62(d)	70	2	45	40	45(c)	45	100% applicable fare
Hawaiian	2	62	70	2	41	10	45(c)	45	50% applicable fare
Midwest Express	3(e)	62(d)	70	1	45	69	25(c)	25	100% applicable fare
Northwest	3(e)	62	70	2	40	—	45(c)	45	100% applicable fare
Southwest	3	62	70	2	50	—	20(f)	25	Applicable child's fare
TWA	3(e)	62(d)	70	2(g)	45	70	45(c)	45	50% full Coach or 100% excursion
United	3(e)	62(d)	70	2	45	50	45(c)	45	100% applicable fare
USAir	3(e)	62(d)	70	2	45	40	45(c)	45	100% applicable fare

Note: Data apply to domestic flights as of summer 1994 and are subject to change; contact airline for requirements on intl flights. Piece and weight limits apply to major airlines; limits may be higher on some planes; limits may be substantially lower on some commuter lines.

(a) Combined length plus width plus height; comparable limits for garment bags.

(b) Where 2 options are shown, the lower-cost option for your route applies.

(c) Per piece for first 3 additional pieces; higher rates for additional pieces.

(d) For first (largest) piece; lower limits for additional pieces

(e) Limit for total number of checked and carry-on pieces.

(f) Per piece for first 2 additional pieces; higher rates for additional pieces.

(g) Check 2 and carry 1, or check 1 and carry 2.

pounds). Thus, the international liability limit for most airlines serving the United States (both US and foreign carriers) is a flat $640 per bag (32 kilos times $20), regardless of what a bag weighed.

To protect yourself, cover the difference between the value of your personal effects and the maximum airline payment with insurance. Possibilities include a year-round personal property policy, insurance purchased as a policy or offered by your credit card or charge card, or excess valuation coverage bought from the airline.

Note, by the way, that DOT has no authority to force airlines to pony up for lost baggage. The law states the liability limit, but it doesn't provide for enforcement. Most airlines voluntarily accept valid claims up to the maximum amount; when an airline refuses, the best recourse is probably small-claims court.

Baggage is delayed far more often than lost. Though the airlines aren't required to give you anything if that happens, some offer free kits of supplies to tide you over. (As insurance, pack what you need for 48 hours, including small valuables, keys, travel documents, and medicines, in your carry-on luggage.) An airline may also offer to reimburse you for the cost of personal-care products plus a few basic clothing items (shirts, underwear). But if you expect reimbursement, don't buy anything without prior authorization from the airline and save all your receipts. If the delay drags on a day or more, ask the airline to authorize additional purchases.

Always negotiate your baggage problems with the airline on which you arrived. If another airline is involved—either in tracing the baggage or paying for it—the airline on which you arrived will initiate the necessary procedures.

WHEN DUTY CALLS

Some customs hints for overseas travelers:

- If you've been abroad for at least 48 hours and are returning to the United States, you may bring $400 worth of personal or household articles with you duty-free ($800 if you're coming from American Samoa, Guam, or the US Virgin Islands; there is no time limitation if returning from Mexico or the Virgin Islands). Beyond that, you must pay a flat 10% duty on the next $1000 worth (5% from US possessions), and various duty rates for any additional items.

- The duty-free goods can't include more than 100 cigars (non-Cuban), 200 cigarettes (one carton), and one liter of wine, beer, or liquor (none if you are under 21; some states have other restrictions). Items that may require a permit or license, or that may be restricted, include food, drugs, and certain items not approved by the US Food and Drug Administration; fruits, plants, vegetables and their by-products; meat and poultry; pets and wildlife; trademarked items (certain cameras, watches, perfumes); lottery tickets; firearms; ammunition; and hazardous materials.

- Keep receipts for anything you purchase: If you've spent more than

$1400, you must list in writing all articles acquired on your trip and what you paid for them. It's also wise to carry receipts for any foreign-made articles you take on your trip, to prove that you didn't buy them abroad on the present trip.

- Gifts under $200, except perfume and tobacco, may be mailed duty-free to friends or relatives (the limit is $200 from US possessions). Postal laws, however, don't allow you to ship alcoholic beverages.
- If you take out of or bring into the United States more than $10,000 in currency, you must file a form with US Customs.
- Items designed for personal use can be brought duty-free into most foreign countries, including souvenirs purchased in other countries (a verbal declaration may be required). Other items may be restricted or prohibited; check with the appropriate consulate before you go if you have questions.

For more information, write the Department of the Treasury, US Customs Service, P.O. Box 7407, Washington, DC 20044 and ask for the booklet "Know Before You Go." Regulations for Canada are similar; for details, write to Canada Customs, Inquiries Unit, First Floor, 333 Dunsmuir Street, Vancouver, BC Canada V6B 5R4, and ask for the booklet "I Declare."

PHONING HOME

In most countries, the cheapest way to call home is to use a public phone. It's

VACATION COMMUNICATIONS

Travelers who can't bear being unreachable can rent portable cellular phones for use while they're traveling overseas. (US cellular phones don't work abroad.) Before you leave, you arrange through a US office for your phone and are assigned your own individual phone number for the duration of the rental. That number won't change, even if you travel in more than one country.

Destination Europe (a division of Auto Europe) rents cellular phones for use in Europe. Rates (as of a *CRTL* report in January 1996) were $40 for up to three days or $80 for a week; a delivery charge of $30 at each end of the trip was waived if you rented for 14 days or more. You had to reserve at least three business days in advance. Call a travel agency or Destination Europe (800-223-5555).

We also looked at the rental rates of two companies in summer 1996:

- Parker Company (800-280-2811) charged $9.50 a day, $56 a week, and $155 a month in most European countries. You could have the phone delivered to you in the US before you leave or to an overseas address (including your hotel). You could also pick it up at a few locations in the UK and Italy. Next-day delivery was free on rentals of two weeks or longer.

easy in countries with phones that can accept prepaid cards. (You buy a card with a specified value encoded on a magnetic strip, and the phone automatically deducts the cost of each call. Cards can be used for both local and international calls.) Where you can't use a card, you must stuff coins into a slot; in some countries, you can also place calls from a central office and pay an attendant.

Dialing direct from your hotel room is the most convenient way to call home. Unfortunately, some years ago, many overseas hotels hit upon the idea of adding huge surcharges to the standard telephone rates from any calls placed from a room—even charge-card or collect calls. Although a few hotels have stopped gouging guests for phone

calls, an excessive charge is still the norm.

That's the main reason why the three big US long-distance carriers—AT&T, MCI, and Sprint—all offer their own "home-direct" programs. You can call the United States from dozens of countries, and from some you can call other foreign countries as well. They all work in about the same way.

You dial an access number from any telephone. (Before you leave, contact your preferred carrier for an access code listing. See *Where to Find It,* page 273.) A US operator of the carrier you're using answers in English. You indicate which number you want to call and the manner in which the call will be charged. (Choices include charging to a calling card and billing

---

Having the phone delivered before you leave is easiest, but you pay for an extra two days and have to fit the phone into your baggage.

•Global Cellular Rental (800-999-3636) charged about $15 a day, $97 a week, and $246 a month (subject to the exchange rate). It also required a minimum of $75 in phone charges, regardless of rental length. You received and returned the phone by express delivery—free in the US, $25 each way overseas.

SHORE TO SHIP
If you're one of those travelers who absolutely has to stay in touch with your home or office even on a cruise vacation, consider Princess. Four Princess ships now provide a direct radiotelephone service (AT&T supplies it) that bypasses marine operators and all the hassle of shore-to-ship calls.

Someone trying to reach you need only call 900-225-5744, follow the recorded instructions to punch in a number for the ship you're on, and ask the ship operator for your stateroom. The fee for the 900 call, billed to the caller's phone, is steep ($8.95 a minute, in summer '96) but still below the usual maritime-call rates.

as a collect or third-party call.)

In many countries, calling the access number is free: You can place the call from a public telephone, often without inserting coins, or dial the access number from your hotel room without being charged on your room bill. (Some hotels block access to home-direct services, however; see below.)

With some phones in some countries, you must insert coins in order to reach the access number. The coins may or may not be returned to you at the end of the call. In any event, the total cost (coins plus AT&T, MCI, or Sprint bill) will probably be far cheaper than calling the United States from a hotel room without the service.

In a few places, you must go to a specially marked, "dedicated" telephone to use a home-direct service. Those telephones are usually in places where Americans tend to congregate—cruise ship piers, the better hotels, US military bases, and airports.

BYPASSING HOTEL GOUGES. If you're trying to use a home-direct service to call the US from your hotel room, you may find that the hotel blocks access. You dial the home-direct number and nothing happens, or you get connected to the hotel operator.

AT&T addresses that problem by signing up hotel chains to its *International Hotel Program*. Partner hotels agree to offer guests easy access to *AT&T Direct* services, which include *AT&T USADirect Service* and *AT&T World Connect Service*. Those services make it easier to use an *AT&T Calling Card* or an *AT&T Universal Card* to place calls to the United States and other countries.

CALLBACK SERVICES. These provide another route to telephone savings. They're designed to help consumers and businesses based overseas, and frequent business travelers, cut the costs of making calls from overseas to the US or to a third country. Unfortunately, none of the callback providers we contacted for an early-1996 report offered a package geared to short-term vacationers. However, even vacationers—if they make a lot of calls—might consider signing up.

When you first enroll, the callback service assigns you a unique US number, and you specify an overseas callback number (which you can change as you move). To call from abroad, you dial your US number from a touchtone phone, ring once, and hang up. The service's specialized computer ("switch," in telephonese) automatically calls you back and gives you a dial tone (in some cases, preceded by a recorded message). You can use that tone to place as many calls as you want, using the pound key to signal a new call.

Several services can even access you in a hotel room: A synthesized voice asks for you by name and room number (you may even have multiple language options). Callback services can also handle fax and data transmissions.

Callback services claim that they combine the low costs of US-based calling with full flexibility. Rates, they say, are 20–60% lower than you'd pay using pay phones or call-home services—even cheaper compared with inflated hotel rates. Also, most callback services time calls in intervals from 30 down to 6 seconds, rather than round up to the nearest minute as the call-home services do, shaving a few more cents off each call.

You can also cut the costs of calling from one foreign country to another. Some callback services have switches overseas; others route all your calls through the US, including those to a third country. In either case, you pay for the calls at very low US bulk rates—almost always a good bit less than you'd pay with the local phone utility or with a call-home service, even on third-country calls.

Here are the callback services available from five representative suppliers, listed alphabetically. You normally sign an open-ended contract, for a minimum of at least 30 days. You receive a monthly bill with an itemized list of calls, and all services can bill through *AE, MC,* or *V.* Several offer additional business features—voice mail, teleconferencing, videoconferencing, and such. Unless noted, all services can allow you to change your overseas call-back number, whenever you want, from a remote location; rates are as of a *CRTL* report in March 1966 and are subject to change:

- **America Tele-fone** (800-321-5817). Sample per-minute rates to the US: 55¢ from Australia, 62¢ from Hong Kong, and 34¢ from the UK, with no access charge. No activation fee; minimum billing is $10 a month. A $100 deposit is required and is returned when service is cancelled.

- **Globaltel** (770-449-1295). Sample per-minute rates to the US: 41¢ from Australia, 44¢ from Hong Kong, and 24¢ from the UK. No activation fee; minimum billing is $25 a month.

- **Intl Telephone** (ITC; 800-638-5558). Sample per-minute rates to the US: 36¢ from Australia, 53¢ from Hong Kong, and 29¢ from the UK. No activation fee or minimum billing.

- **Prime Call** (800-698-1232). Sample per-minute rates to the US: 39¢ from Australia, 55¢ from Hong Kong, and 32¢ from the UK. The system can't ask for you by name or room number. The $50 activation fee was being waived at the time of our inquiry; $3 monthly fee for unlimited changes in callback number, minimum billing $20 a month.

- **Telegroup** (800-338-0225). Sample per-minute rates to the US: 26¢ from Australia, 47¢ from Hong Kong, and 20¢ from the UK. No activation fee; minimum billing is $25 a month.

Telegroup also offers a "Global Access Telecard" option for low-volume users, with no activation fee or minimum billing. Sample per-minute rates to the US: 89¢ from Australia, $1.29 from Hong Kong, and 59¢ from the UK, plus an additional access fee of $2 per call from overseas phones. That's a bit cheaper than the call-home services, but much higher than other callback services.

WHERE TO FIND IT

TRAVEL ADVISORIES

Citizens Emergency Center: Bureau of Consular Affairs, 2201 C St NW, Room

4811, US Dept of State, Washington DC 20520 (send written requests with self-addressed, stamped envelope); 202-647-5225. Free prerecorded information available to callers with touch-tone phone, and prerecorded instructions for accessing full-text advisories by free electronic bulletin board (202-647-9225, modem number), by fax (202-647-3000), or by mail. (If a relative abroad is missing or in trouble, you can reach a live operator at 202-647-5225.)

Consumer Reports Travel Letter (CRTL) (800-234-1970). A reliable source for monthly updates on State Department travel information. Complete written copies of travel advisories are available free at any of the US regional passport agencies and at field offices of the US Dept of Commerce. Abroad, they're available at any US embassy or consulate.

Infosys America Inc: 314-625-4054 (modem number). Full text through Travel On-line BBS on the SmartNet International Computer Network in the United States, Canada, and overseas.

OAG Electronic Edition Travel Service: 800-323-4000. Full text of consular information sheets and travel warnings available to subscribers to CompuServe, Dialog, GEnie, and other computer services.

MONEY SERVICES

American Express Traveler's Checks: Contact your local bank or check phone directory for a local American Express Travel Service office.

Ruesch Intl: 700 11th St NW, Suite 400, Washington DC 20001; 800-424-2923, 202-408-1200; fax 202-408-1211.

Thomas Cook Currency Services, Inc: 1271 Broadway, 32nd Street, NYC 10001; 800-CURRENCY (800-287-7362). Local offices in the white pages and under Foreign Currency Exchange in the classified pages.

HOME-DIRECT SERVICES

AT&T: *AT&T USADirect Service, AT&T World Connect Service,* 800-222-0300 (for residential service), 800-222-0400 (for business service). No charge for a list of USA-direct access codes. Calls billed collect or to your *AT&T Calling Card* or *AT&T Universal Card.*

MCI: *CALL USA,* or World Phone Access, 800-283-9977. No charge for listing of home-direct access codes. Calls billed collect or to your MCI card or to a Bell-operated company card.

Sprint: *Sprint Express,* 800-877-4646. No charge for a list of home-direct access codes. Calls billed collect or to your *Sprint FONCARD* or local telephone company calling card.

This chapter was adapted from the Consumer Reports Travel Letter *article "Callback Phone Services" (March 1996) and the 1996 edition of* Consumer Reports Best Travel Deals.

Should You Insure Your Trip?

Insurance is probably the most grossly overpriced of all travel services. Nevertheless, there are two big-ticket risks you should consider covering: trip cancellation or interruption (TCI) and emergency medical evacuation (EME).

Most travelers can forget about the other types of travel insurance—accident and medical, for instance, with their inflated prices and, often, coverage that you already have through some other policy. (You don't even need TCI if you can accept the occasional forfeit of a modest deposit or prepayment.) And don't buy expensive bundles of coverages to protect against niggling, minor risks—say, having to buy a few extra pieces of clothing or personal-care items if your baggage is lost. This chapter covers such coverages only where they're included in TCI or EME policies at no extra cost.

You have to prepay in full for a package tour, a cruise, or an airline ticket—often many months ahead. Once you've paid, the fine print in a tour or cruise agreement often requires you to forfeit your whole payment if you cancel within a month or less of departure. And some airline tickets are neither refundable nor exchangeable: You get back nothing if you don't take the flights as originally ticketed.

But anything from a death in the family to a summons to jury duty to an act of terrorism at your destination could prevent you from leaving on schedule. Even after you've started out, your own illness or a problem back home could force you to break off your journey. You may then face a stiff penalty to change the return flight of a round-trip airline ticket. If you're forced to quit a cruise midway, a one-way flight home can be expensive. If you suffer a severe accident or illness in a remote area, you may have to be evacuated to a distant medical facility.

POLICY TYPES

Travel insurance comes in several versions:

•Standard **retail** policies are issued by

major insurance carriers, either under their own corporate name or under a special one they use to market travel insurance. The policies are sold by travel agents, by some tour operators and cruise lines, and directly by the issuing insurance company.

Retail policies have two variations. **Custom** policies let individual travelers choose their own mix of coverages from a set of options (some issuers also offer an inclusive option that bundles all the coverages). The TCI component of a custom policy (without other bundled coverages) costs $5–6 per $100 of the value of the trip, regardless of its length; EME prices are usually based on a trip's duration. For a given level of protection, custom policies are generally more expensive than alternative options.

Some companies sell a retail variant called a cruise/tour policy (or something like that). Typically, the policy is a bundle of popular coverages, at a per-person price based on total trip cost.

The cruise/tour policies we looked at for this report were generally better buys than the custom policies. We found few significant differences in eligibility, coverages, key benefits, or exclusions to account for the price variation. According to industry sources, cruise/tour policies are cheaper because they're standardized and because they carry smaller markups and commissions than custom policies.

•**Wholesale** policies are sold by tour operators and cruise lines under their own names (although the actual policy is usually provided by a big insurance company). They're typically a bit cheaper than retail policies, but not always—the cruise line or tour operator, not the insurance company, sets the selling price. Unfortunately, they don't cover some important risks—notably operator or cruise-line failure. Risk of tour-operator failure has been a long-standing problem in the industry. And, these days, some cruise lines are wobbly as well.

True, some cruise-line wholesale policies have an advantage over retail policies. If the insurance company that underwrites the policy rejects a claim for an aborted trip as arising from a preexisting medical condition, the line offers partial compensation in the form of a substantial discount on a future cruise. That's not a bad tradeoff if you're reasonably confident of your cruise line's financial stability.

•**Cancellation waivers** are the cheapest form of trip-cancellation coverage, and by far the weakest. They're not really insurance: For a fee, the tour operator or cruise line waives its cancellation penalties under certain circumstances. Waivers typically cover only limited predeparture contingencies, may not cover cancellations within 24 hours of departure, and don't cover midtrip interruption at all. Furthermore, you won't recover anything if the tour operator or cruise line fails.

DECODING THE COVERAGE

All the policies in the table on pages 278-79 cover TCI. However, there are some differences in their breadth of coverage. Here's how to interpret what each offers.

ILLNESS/INJURY/DEATH coverage protects you (or your heirs) against losses caused by personal mishaps:

- All the TCI policies we list cover an insured traveler's costs incurred because of mishaps suffered either by the insured traveler or by one or more of the insured's traveling companions. (They do not, however, cover costs incurred by the companion unless the companion also buys insurance.) All also cover cancellation or interruption of a trip because of the illness, injury, or death of a close family member at home.
- As with health insurance, *preexisting conditions* are the most contentious element of TCI. All listed policies exclude compensation if your trip is canceled or interrupted by a medical problem that arose within 60 days prior to the date you bought the policy. However, all the listed policies accept a preexisting condition that is controlled by medication. Moreover, all listed policies waive the limitation on preexisting conditions entirely, at no extra cost, if you buy TCI for the full value of the trip immediately after you make your first deposit. Some policies give you just one business day to do that, others allow up to seven days.

Not all policies are as lenient as

PRICEY COME-ONS

You can buy a variety of coverages other than TCI and EME. But they make little sense for most travelers:

- **Medical.** Many travelers are covered by their own health insurance or HMO for medical costs incurred overseas. While Medicare doesn't cover overseas costs, many Medicare supplements do. If you aren't covered, however, supplementary insurance is a good idea.
- **Accident.** If you really need accident insurance, you need it year-round, not just when you travel.
- **Theft.** Chances are that your homeowner's or tenant's policy covers your personal effects, even when you travel. Some travelers—especially those on cruises—bring along valuables that may not be covered. But even those folks are probably better off with a year-round floater policy than with by-the-trip baggage insurance.
- **Delays, overbookings.** Travelers can usually afford to take a chance on such small risks as flight delays and hotel overbookings.
- **Airline flight insurance.** That coverage cynically plays on an irrational fear of flying. Statistically, you're more likely to die of a bee sting than in an airplane crash.

Coverage, Benefits, and Costs

	ACCESS AMERICA INTERNATIONAL	CUSTOM POLICIES	
		AMERICAN EXPRESS	BERKELEY ARM CAREFREE
TRIP CANCELLATION/INTERRUPTION (TCI)			
Cost per $100 coverage(a)	$6	$5.50	$5.50(b)
Illness/injury/death	✔	✔	✔
Preexisting conditions(c)	60 days	60 days	60 days
Waiver(d)	1 day	7 days	1 day
Operator failure	✔	✔	✔
Home problems	✔	✔	✔
Destination calamities	✔	✔	—
BUNDLED WITH TCI (PER PERSON)			
Accident	—	—	—
Baggage Loss	—	—	—
CDW (primary)	—	—	—
Delay(e)	—	$400(f)	$100(f)
Evacuation	—	—	—
Hotel overbooking	—	—	—
Medical/health	—	—	—
Any-reason cancellation	—	—	—
EMERGENCY MEDICAL EVACUATION (EME, PER PERSON)			
Coverage	$50,000	$25,000	$10,000
Cost (minimum)	$42/4 days	(j)	$39/4 days
Cost (two weeks)	$62	(j)	$65
BUNDLED WITH EME (PER PERSON)			
Accident	—	$25,000	$25,000
Baggage	—	$1000	$500
Basic TCI	—	(j)	$300
Medical expense	$10,000	$10,000	$1000
STANDARD TRIP: TWO PEOPLE, 14 DAYS; $2500 TCI, 000 EME PER PERSON			
Cost	$418	$306	$339

Note: As of mid-1996; subject to change.
Some policies may not be available in all states.
(a) Range indicates that cost per $100 varies with the total amount purchased.
(b) $4.75 per $100, if you buy policy including EME.
(c) Period prior to purchase of insurance during which preexisting conditions are excluded (in absence of waiver).
(d) Maximum number of business days after purchase of ticket within which buyer must buy TCI insurance in order to qualify for no-cost waiver accepting preexisting conditions (see text).
(e) Combined maximum value of travel-delay and baggage-delay compensation, if any, may be subject to

| | | CRUISE/TOUR POLICIES | | |
TRAVEL GUARD GOLD	TRAVELERS	ACCESS AMERICA	CSA PLAN A129	TRAVEL GUARD
$8	$5.50	$3.94-6.80	$4.74-6.60	$6-6.78
✔	✔	✔	✔	✔
60 days	60 days	60 days	60 days	60 days
7 days	7 days	1 day	7days	7 days
✔	✔	✔	✔	✔
✔	✔	✔	✔	✔
✔	—	✔	✔	✔
$25,000	—	—		$25,000
$1500	—	$500	$750	$1000
$25,000	—	—	$25,000	—
$600	$250	$250	$1750	$600
$20,000	10 times TCI(g)	$20,000	$10,000(h)	$20,000
$100	—	—		—
$10,000	—	$10,000	$10,000(h)	$10,000
$400(i)	—	—		—
Incl with TCI	Incl with TCI	Incl with TCI	Incl with TCI	Incl with TCI
—	—	—	—	—
—	—	—	—	—
—	—	—	—	—
—	—	—	—	—
—	—	—	—	—
—	—	—	—	—
$400	$275	$218	$237	$296

lower daily limit.
(f) Bundled with policy that provides EME coverage.
(g) Pays up to 10 times the TCI limit, to a maximum of $25,000.
(h) Combined maximum value of medical/health and EME coverage.
(i) Pays half the penalty, up to $400, on cancellation for any reason.
(j) Cost of EME component included in price of bundled policy that provides TCI (which is based on amount of TCI purchased).

those we've listed. We've seen several that won't cover any preexisting condition, controlled or not, for which the insured person received medical treatment or advice within 90–180 days of buying the policy. If a policy doesn't offer a waiver, a claim could theoretically be denied if you so much as took an aspirin on a doctor's advice.

Usually, a policy's limitations on preexisting conditions apply to anybody—the insured traveler, a traveling companion (insured or not), or a family member at home—whose medical condition causes a trip to be canceled or interrupted.

- TCI policies usually include a long list of other exclusions. For instance, the policy won't pay if a trip is spoiled by self-inflicted injuries, injuries resulting from a hazardous activity (including many active sports) or use of illegal drugs, or war injuries.
- In case of severe accident or illness, some TCI policies cover the expenses of emergency evacuation. (See "International 911," below.)

OPERATOR FAILURE. Despite federal and state safety nets, it seems that every year or so at least one tour operator fails, leaving thousands of travelers holding worthless air tickets and prepaid hotel vouchers. Some may even be stranded abroad without return transportation. TCI can protect you against the costs arising from those contingencies:

- All listed policies pay off in case an operator "fails," "defaults," or "ceases operations," but we've seen some

"INTERNATIONAL 911"

All the retail trip-cancellation policies we're reporting on cover emergency medical evacuation, bundled either with TCI or some other coverages. But if you travel for extended periods, especially into high-risk areas, you may want to consider buying separate EME insurance—either on a per-trip or an annual basis—from a company that specializes in it.

Several companies sell comprehensive policies that combine medical insurance with EME and give access to a worldwide network of local representatives who make arrangements and provide assistance to travelers in difficulty. Among them are Global Emergency Medical Services, Health Care Abroad, Intl SOS Assistance, Travel Insurance Service, and Worldwide Assistance. Some of those companies operate their own overseas assistance networks; others subcontract that part of their coverage. (When you buy EME as part of a bundled retail policy, chances are that one of the specialist companies actually provides the EME service as a subcontractor.)

If an illness or injury prevents a traveler from returning home as an ordinary airline passenger, EME insurance pays for whatever special transportation is

that protect only against "bankruptcy." There's a big difference: Tour operators often fail and disappear without ever filing for bankruptcy.

- TCI policies typically exclude failure of the company that sells the insurance. Thus, if you buy TCI from a tour operator, the insurance won't protect you if the tour operator fails.

TCI isn't the only way to protect against operator failure. If you buy a tour or cruise with a charge card, you can get the charge removed from your account if the supplier fails to provide the service. But, of course, the charge card doesn't protect you against any other TCI risks.

HOME PROBLEMS. TCI can cover you against a laundry list of misfortunes and surprises at home that might cause you to cancel or interrupt a trip. Among them: a fire or flood at your house, a call to jury duty, or an accident that makes you miss a flight or a sailing.

DESTINATION CALAMITIES. TCI can also cover you against unexpected problems at your destination. Among those: an airplane hijack, a natural disaster (fire, flood, earthquake, or epidemic), terrorism, or an unannounced strike.

HOW TCI PAYS OFF

When a problem arises, here's how TCI soothes the financial pain.

CANCELLATION. If you cancel before you leave, TCI covers whatever fraction of prepayments or deposits you can't recover from the supplier, plus any additional costs.

If you get sick, you must first ask

required. However, that transportation is subject to the review of some designated authority—a source of a major disagreement we've heard about from a reader. Also, the insurance company, not the traveler, decides on the means of transportation.

Several EME policies offer TCI as an extra-cost option, at rates comparable with those of the retail policies (and often provided on subcontract by one of the TCI companies). However, in some cases, the TCI coverage bundled with an EME policy isn't as good as that of the retail policies. The exclusions for preexisting conditions may be much more restrictive—up to five years, in one case—and preexisting conditions may not be covered, even if controlled by medication. Moreover, some of those companies' TCI applies only to trips canceled or interrupted for medical reasons—operator failure, home misfortunes, and destination disasters aren't covered.

EME is a tough coverage to evaluate. The odds on needing a medical evacuation are minuscule. But if you do need it, the price tag can be astronomical. Some travelers want special EME insurance as a hedge, but the evacuation coverage included in a standard TCI or bundled policy is probably enough for most travelers.

the tour operator, cruise line, or airline for any refund it normally provides in such cases: TCI pays the difference between what you paid and what you can recover. If you pay for a tour or cruise at a double-occupancy rate and your traveling companion suddenly can't go, TCI typically pays the single supplement so that you can complete the trip alone.

INTERRUPTION. TCI also picks up extra costs if you have to cut off a trip and return home. If you have to change your return air ticket, you first find the best deal the airline can give you, then apply for TCI to pay for any reissue fee or additional fare. If you have to leave a tour or cruise in midtrip and buy a replacement ticket home, TCI reimburses you for "unscheduled return." If a traveling companion must return early, TCI pays single supplements so that you can complete your trip alone. If necessary, some TCI insurance arranges (and pays for) emergency medical evacuation.

DELAY. If you merely delay your departure (for a reason covered by the policy's cancellation provisions), TCI pays the extra costs of alternative transportation to join your trip—an airfare to your cruise's first port of call, say, or the penalty to switch your air ticket to a later flight.

WHICH POLICY FOR YOU?

Our table shows the key features of eight retail policies. Five are custom, three are cruise/tour. (When we prepared this report in summer 1996, Mutual of Omaha, a long-term major player both

as *Travel Assure* and under its own name in the travel-insurance market, was redesigning its policies. The new ones weren't available to us for evaluation, and the old ones are obsolete.)

All the policies we list cover the basic needs. They will reimburse you for a health problem even if a preexisting medical condition flares up, provided you adhere to the conditions of the waiver. All the policies cover injury/ death, operator failure, and home misfortunes, and most include destination disasters. Berkeley Care even extends illness/injury/ death coverage to a business partner at home.

Various policies bundle individual features in different ways and at different prices. For that reason, we developed a yardstick for comparing them. The "standard trip cost" in the table shows what a couple would have to pay for $2500 in TCI plus $10,000 in EME, per person, for a 14-day trip. (In some cases, the cheapest TCI option provides more than the standard EME.) If a company offers more than one bundled policy, we list the cheapest one that provides the specified TCI and EME (except for Travel Guard Gold, which we listed to illustrate the most comprehensive option available). Depending on the policy, the standard-trip cost may include other, unimportant coverages:

- The *Access America* cruise/tour policy covers the standard trip for less than any other company. But the *CSA A129* cruise/tour policy provides similar coverage plus more generous delay and collision-damage benefits for just a bit more. Either of those policies is your best choice.

- Of the custom policies, *Travelers* covers the sample trip at substantially lower cost than its competitors—mainly because EME is bundled with TCI at the standard TCI rate. It's your best choice among the custom policies.

- *Travel Guard Gold* is the most comprehensive custom policy, covering just about any imaginable contingency—including primary collision-damage coverage for a rented car and recovery of half your prepayments if you cancel for any reason.

- Don't overbuy TCI: You can't recover more than your actual loss, so insuring for an amount beyond what's at risk is pointless.

- Beware of pricing gimmicks. Some insurance companies offer virtually identical policies at different prices, depending on who's selling them. In addition to its excellent *Plan A129*, for example, CSA offers *Plan B109* with similar coverage—and a higher price, due mainly to a higher travel-agency markup.

- The safest way to buy TCI is directly from the insurance company. That way, you're protected in case your tour operator, cruise line, or retail travel agency fails.

WHERE TO FIND IT

The following companies provide travel insurance to travelers who live in the US. (Because of varying insurance regulations, Canadian policies differ.)

Access America Intl: 800-284-8300. *MC, V.*

American Express: 800-756-2639. *AE, MC, V.*

Berkeley Carefree: 800-323-3149. *AE, MC, V.*

CSA: 800-348-9505. *AE, Disc, MC, V.*

Global Emergency Medical Services: 800-249-2533. *AE, MC, V.*

Health Care Abroad: 800-237-6615, 540-687-3166. *AE, MC, V.*

Intl SOS Assistance: 800-523-8930. *AE, MC, V.*

Travel Guard: 800-826-1300. *AE, Disc, MC, V.*

Travel Insurance Service: 800-937-1387. *MC, V.*

The Travelers: 800-243-3174. *MC, V.*

Worldwide Assistance: 800-821-2828. *AE, Disc, MC, V.*

This chapter was adapted from the Consumer Reports Travel Letter *article "Travel Insurance: Cover Two Key Risks" (July 1996).*

Keeping Healthy Abroad

S ince illness can wreck a trip, wise travelers prepare for health risks before they pack. This chapter outlines basic trip preparations, as well as the precautions to take once you arrive. The information here isn't a substitute for professional medical advice. We urge readers, particularly those with special health problems or needs (including pregnant or breast-feeding women, older people, people with lowered immunity, people with chronic diseases, and people accompanying infants and young children), to consult physicians or other professionals for specific advice or treatment.

STEPS TO TAKE BEFORE YOU GO

Most American tourists traveling abroad don't need to be too anxious about their health. In the larger European cities, health conditions are much like those here at home. However, if your itinerary takes you off the beaten path, you may need special health-protection measures.

DOCTOR VISITS

A month or two before your trip, ask your doctor to review your immunization status, to help you plan the full course of vaccinations you'll need, and to see that they are appropriately spaced and on time. Allow at least one or two weeks before departure for possible reactions to subside. You may need even more time because of the need to space certain combinations of vaccines.

If a routine physical exam is in the offing, you may wish to move up the date, or at least get a cursory checkup, before undertaking a long journey. If you suffer from a chronic disease or are on long-term medication, a more complete checkup is essential. It's a good idea to carry with you a brief medical summary (see the sample *Emergency Medical Record* on page 298), copies of any prescriptions you may be on, and, if pertinent, a copy of your most recent electrocardiogram.

Before an extended trip, see your dentist far enough in advance to allow time for any necessary work. Have your eyes checked. If you wear corrective lenses, take along an extra pair and a copy of your lens prescription, just in case.

IMMUNIZATIONS

You may need certain immunizations before you can enter some countries. For current information about countries you plan to visit, call your county or state health department or contact the US Public Health Service's Centers for Disease Control and Prevention (CDC), in Atlanta (see *Where to Find It*). The CDC's Intl Travelers' hot line presents programmed responses to questions 24 hours a day, for users of touch-tone telephones. Operator assistance is available from 8:00 AM to 4:30 PM Eastern Time, Monday through Friday. (Information is also available through the CDC Web site and in fax-back form.) If you plan to be abroad for more than a month, particularly in a rural area, check with those agencies about any special precautions that may be recommended for that region.

Travelers' health information and international vaccination requirements and recommendations may also be obtained by contacting the US Public Health Service Quarantine Station in your area. (See the listing in *Where to Find It*, page 296.)

If any vaccinations are required, you'll need an Intl Certificate of Vaccination (Form PHS-731), available from many travel agencies and transportation companies, from your local and state health departments or, at $2 a copy, from the Superintendent of Documents, US Govt Printing Office (stock #017-001-004405). Some physicians keep a supply of the forms on hand.

All vaccines except yellow fever can be given, and the vaccination recorded on your certificate, by any licensed physician. Yellow-fever vaccine and certification of yellow-fever vaccination must be obtained at an officially designated Yellow Fever Vaccination Center, where the certificate is validated by the authorized physician or health department. Boosters are given every 10 years.

Some African countries require a certificate of yellow-fever vaccination from all travelers who enter; other countries in Africa, and some in South America and Asia, require evidence of vaccination from travelers coming from or traveling through areas where yellow fever is endemic. For the location of the nearest approved center, contact your county or state health department or Public Health Service office (see *Where to Find It*).

If your physician advises you to omit a required immunization for medical reasons, be sure that he or she records the omission on your certificate and attaches a signed and dated statement on letterhead stationery specifying the reasons.

Infants are often exempt from the vaccination requirements for foreign countries; some countries do not require certificates for very young children. Check with the foreign embassy or consulate for exemption requirements before traveling.

Keep your completed vaccination certificate with your passport and use a separate certificate for each traveler in your party.

RECOMMENDED SHOTS. When your destination country doesn't require immunizations, your physician can help you decide which vaccinations to have, taking into consideration your destination, the time of year and duration of your trip, your living arrangements and anticipated lifestyle in the host country, and personal risk factors such as your age, your state of health, and your current immunization status.

No vaccine is 100 percent protective. You should still exercise all the appropriate precautions against disease discussed in this chapter.

ROUTINE IMMUNIZATIONS are those that everyone should have, whether traveling or not, to protect against common illnesses such as measles and mumps. They're typically administered in early childhood. But adults who don't have an adequate vaccination history should discuss with their doctor the safest immunization strategy for their age, medical condition, and travel plans. The *Routine Immunizations* table lists common illnesses and the approximate length of time required for the vaccine to take full effect.

TRAVELER'S IMMUNIZATIONS are typically given to protect against specific diseases. Few if any travelers would need all of them. The following is an overview of eight immunizations and one preventive drug treatment (for malaria). Ask your physician if you fall into a high-risk group (infants, pregnant women, and people with lowered immunity), for whom the risk from the vaccine may be greater than the health risks of the disease itself.

- **Cholera** still occurs in parts of Asia, Africa, and Latin America. The disease causes intestinal cramps and diarrhea. In severe cases, dehydration can be fatal unless vigorously treated with intravenous fluid and salt replacement. Antibiotics can also help.

  Since the risk of cholera to tourists is now very low, the CDC advises that use of the vaccine is questionable. At this writing, no country officially requires you to be vaccinated against it (though local authorities may occasionally require documentation of cholera vaccination). In any event, the cholera vaccine can cause reactions and is effective less than half the time it's administered, so the best precaution is to avoid potentially contaminated food and drink (see *Safe Food* on page 291 and *Safe Water Supplies* on 290).

- **Hepatitis A** is also transmitted by contaminated food and drink or by human carriers of hepatitis A virus (HAV). Consider immunization if you're traveling anywhere but to Japan, Australia, New Zealand, Northern and Western Europe, Canada, or the US.

  Hepatitis A vaccine has replaced gamma globulin as the preferred Hepatitis A preventative. (*Havrix* vaccine is already in use; *Vaqta* should also be available by the time this book reaches readers.) However, either vaccine needs two weeks to take effect; if more immediate protection is needed, immune globulin (also recommended for travelers under 2) can be used.

One injection of the vaccine confers over 90% protection, and a booster 6–12 months later increases protection to about 99%. Immunity may last as long as 20 years.

•**Hepatitis B** is transmitted by contaminated blood or sexual contact with carriers of hepatitis B virus (HBV). Consider immunization (three injections over a six-month period) well in advance if you're planning to travel to areas where the disease is endemic. Those include sub-Saharan Africa, southeast Asia, South Pacific islands, and parts of the Caribbean—but also other regions of Africa and Asia, as well as Japan, eastern and southern Europe, the Commonwealth of Independent States, and most of Central and South America. The shots should be given in the arm, not the buttocks.

The risk of hepatitis B infection is generally low for most travelers. But it rises dramatically for those who have sexual contact with residents of infected areas (or come into contact with their blood). Condoms can lessen the chance of infection (see *Sexually Transmitted Diseases,* page 293).

•**Japanese encephalitis.** Persons who intend to travel or live for extended periods in rural parts of Asia should consider this vaccine. (The specific areas that pose risk include Bangladesh, Cambodia, China, India, Indonesia, Korea, Laos, Malaysia, Myanmar (Burma), Nepal, Pakistan, the Philippines, Singapore, Sri Lanka, Taiwan, Thailand, Vietnam, and eastern parts of Russia.) But the risk for short-term travelers is low.

•**Malaria** is transmitted by the female anopheles mosquito. Consider preventive treatment if you're traveling to areas where malaria is known to exist, generally in Central and South America, Haiti, sub-Saharan Africa, south and southeast Asia, the Middle East, and a few South Pacific island nations. In addition to a drug regimen, travelers to those regions should take precautions against being bitten by mosquitoes (see *Insects* in the section *Once You Arrive* on page 290).

Antimalarial drugs help prevent or suppress malaria, but they don't immunize against the disease. If high, spiking fevers develop (that can happen as early as a week after you arrive in a malarial area, or as long as six months after you return home), seek medical help immediately.

Preventive drug treatment should begin as early as two weeks before you enter a malarial area and continue for 4–6 weeks after you leave. Doses are taken weekly; missing even a single dose will reduce protection.

One 500-mg tablet of chloroquine *(Aralen)* taken once a week is a commonly prescribed antimalarial drug regimen. Children's dosages are determined by body weight: The carefully calculated amount can be ground up and put in gelatin capsules, to be mixed with food or drink each week.

Resistant strains of the malaria parasite are now common. Mefloquine (*Lariam*) is increasingly recommended as the antimalarial suppressant in areas infested with chloroquine-resistant malaria (all malarial areas except for parts of Central America and the Middle East, Haiti, and the Dominican Republic). One 250-mg capsule is taken starting one week before departure and continuing weekly until four weeks after return. Mefloquine shouldn't be taken by people taking beta-blockers—propranolol (*Inderal*), atenolol (*Tenormin*), etc.—by children under 30 pounds, or in areas where chloroquine is still effective.

If you intend to travel in isolated malarial areas, ask your doctor to consider prescribing three *Fansidar* tablets to take along, strictly as a backup. (But *Fansidar* should be avoided by persons with a history of sensitivity to sulfa drugs and by infants under 2 months.) That drug contains pyrimethamine and sulfadoxine; it should be taken only if you begin to have malarialike symptoms (high fever, chills, sweating, headache, and muscle ache) and you can't get medical help. Take the pills, but get to a medical facility as soon as possible.

Bring along enough of the prescribed drug(s) to cover 4–6 weeks *after* your stay in malarial areas. (Warning: Overdoses of antimalarial drugs can be fatal; observe the prescribed dosages carefully and store out of reach of children.)

In all malarious areas, it's also a good idea to protect yourself against mosquito bites. See *Insects,* page 292, for the measures to take.

- **Plague.** Vaccination against plague is recommended only for travelers to rural or highland areas of Africa, Asia, and South America who may be unable to avoid contact with infected rodents, rabbits, and fleas. It isn't needed by travelers to urban areas with modern accommodations.

- **Poliomyelitis** is transmitted by water and food contaminated by feces of human carriers of the polio virus. Consider having an additional single dose of vaccine (beyond the immunization you probably received in childhood) if you're traveling to tropical or developing countries or to most states of the former Soviet Union. That additional dose (we recommend eIPV, or Enhanced Inactivated Polio Vaccine, given by injection) should be taken only once during the adult years.

- **Spinal meningitis.** Transmitted by contaminated food and drink and by human carriers, meningitis is a frequently fatal disease caused by a bacterium called meningococcus. We recommend it if you're going to sub-Saharan Africa, Nepal, or northern India, especially if you'll be in close contact with locals or if you'll be there during the dry season (December—June). The vaccine is expensive but fairly effective; immunity typically lasts for three years.

- **Typhoid fever** is also transmitted by contaminated food and water. Consider immunization if you're traveling to Africa, Asia, or Central and South America—especially rural and tropical areas—and will spend at least six weeks there. An oral typhoid vaccine, *Vivotif Berna* (one capsule every other day for four doses), is just as effective as injectable vaccine, with fewer if any side effects. Even with vaccination, however, take strict precautions against contaminated food and water (see *Safe Food* and *Safe Water Supplies* in the section *Once You Arrive,* page 290).

- **Yellow fever**. Transmitted by mosquitoes, yellow fever is reported in Africa, South America, and south and southeast Asia—especially rural or forest areas within about 15 degrees of the equator. Consider immunization if you're traveling to those areas.

Many countries affected or threatened by the disease require evidence of vaccination if you've passed through regions known or thought to have yellow fever present. Some African countries require proof of vaccination from all entering travelers.

Vaccination isn't required to reenter the United States, but the Public Health Service still strongly recommends it for those traveling to yellow-fever areas. Even with vaccination, travelers should guard against mosquito bites in yellow-fever areas (see *Insects,* page 292).

- **Miscellaneous**. Adult travelers should be sure they've had a tetanus-diphtheria shot within the past 10 years. If they're over 65, they should also consider getting a flu shot and perhaps a pneumonia shot as well.

Travelers born in or after 1957 should consider getting a second dose of measles vaccine before going abroad.

INSURANCE COVERAGE

No matter where you travel, some emergency services may already be covered by your existing health insurance (a point to check with your carrier before a trip). Beyond that, medical-emergency coverage is available to pay for services to travelers who become ill or suffer a serious accident anywhere in the world. For more information on medical-emergency insurance, see chapter 24.

MAKE A MEDICAL RECORD

Consider carrying a brief medical record to provide information a physician might need in an emergency. Your physician can help you create a form, or you can photocopy the sample on page 298.

If you have a medical condition that could endanger your life in an emergency, you may also want to *wear* a warning for emergency personnel. For a one-time, $35 membership fee (annual renewals are $15), the nonprofit Medic Alert Foundation Intl provides a special necklace or bracelet engraved with your medical condition and a 24-hour toll-free telephone number for access to your medical history and the names of your physicians and close relatives.

PACKING A MEDICAL KIT

It can be risky to buy unfamiliar drugs abroad, where the safety standards for pharmaceutical products may not be as rigorous as American ones. In many countries, medicines sold over the counter—including some that are available only by prescription in the United States—may have serious side effects.

Refuse any unfamiliar remedies that friends or pharmacists urge on you during your travels. Instead, bring your own medications and supplies, as listed on page 299.

TRAVEL ADVISORY SERVICE

Another resource for planning a health-conscious trip is the US Department of State's travel-advisory service. It identifies countries and areas where war, civil strife, health alerts, or other problems might affect travel plans. For more information, see chapter 23.

ONCE YOU ARRIVE: A COMMON-SENSE GUIDE

Immunization can protect you from typhoid fever, but it's more difficult to protect against other intestinal diseases—several of which can result in diarrhea or worse. In each case, the best defense is to avoid food and drink that might be contaminated.

The main culprits are untreated water, unpasteurized dairy products, unpeeled raw fruits and vegetables, uncooked foods, and cooked foods that are improperly handled (by unclean hands, contaminated utensils, or inadequate cooking, storing, or serving). Good personal hygiene, including frequent hand-washing, is essential.

Health hazards vary with the territory. The US Public Health Service considers most developing countries of Africa, Asia, Latin America, and the Middle East to be high-risk areas, and most of southern Europe and a few Caribbean islands to pose intermediate risks.

SAFE WATER SUPPLIES

Since contaminated water is a prime source of infection, prudent travelers will pay close attention to the water they take in, whether as a liquid, as ice cubes, or as an aid to brushing their teeth—and even the water they bathe in.

FOR DRINKING. The drinking water is usually safe in large cities. But in rural regions, it may be contaminated by bacteria, viruses, or parasites. If chlorinated tap water is not available, or if local conditions are questionable, stick to other beverages or purify the water yourself.

Generally, carbonated drinks (canned or bottled), beer, and wine are safe. So are citrus fruit juices, either bottled or made from frozen concentrate with purified water (water that has been boiled or treated; see below). Glasses and cups, however, may be contaminated, so drink from disposable paper containers or directly from the can or bottle, after wiping it clean. Non-carbonated, bottled fluids aren't necessarily safe; it depends on how and where the drink was bottled. Use ice cubes only if they're made from purified water.

If you must drink or brush your teeth with suspect water, treat it first. Boil the water for one minute (three minutes at altitudes above 6500 feet) and let it cool. Or treat the water chemically with iodine or tetraglycine hydroperiodide tablets (*Globaline, Potable-Agua*), both available at pharmacies and camping stores. (Chlorine may be used as well, though it's less reliable than the two other chemicals.) While chemical treatment may prove more convenient and practical than boiling, however, it's less reliable. *Be especially wary of cloudy water:* If possible, boil it.

FOR SWIMMING. Swimming or bathing in contaminated water can lead to skin, eye, ear, and intestinal infections. Fresh water—particularly warm, dirty water—is most hazardous, especially in the tropics. Chlorinated pools are usually safe. So is salt water, though some beaches are contaminated by streams, sewage outlets, or animal feces. Inquire locally before you test the waters.

- **Schistosomiasis** is a disease that occurs sporadically throughout the tropics. It's acquired by swimming or bathing in freshwater streams, ponds, or lakes containing snails that harbor the infectious form (called *cercariae*) of the schistosoma parasite. The cercariae can penetrate intact skin and cause an itchy eruption known as swimmer's itch. They then enter the bloodstream and can lodge in the liver or other organs, where they become adult worms, inflicting serious damage on the liver, intestines, or urinary tract.

  While schistosomiasis can be treated with drugs, it's obviously better to avoid swimming in suspect water. If you do come in contact with contaminated or doubtful water, strip immediately and towel off vigorously to prevent the cercariae from penetrating the skin as the water evaporates.

SAFE FOOD

Where hygiene and sanitation are poor, view every food source with suspicion.

MEAT, FRUIT, AND VEGETABLES. If you think food handling may be questionable or refrigeration lacking, avoid cold cuts and potato or egg salads. Order any meat, poultry, fish, or shellfish dishes thoroughly cooked and preferably piping hot.

In tropical areas, don't eat raw fruit unless it has an unbroken skin that you can peel yourself (after washing it with purified water). Otherwise, only freshly prepared, thoroughly cooked foods are safe. Be especially wary of salads and leafy vegetables.

MILK AND DAIRY PRODUCTS. In large European cities, milk and other dairy products labeled as pasteurized can usually be considered safe. Outside the urban centers, however, dairy hygiene may not be as strict as in the US or Canada. Where sanitation, food handling, or refrigeration is a problem, avoid raw egg mixtures, cream, milk (even if pasteurized), and milk-containing foods such as cream sauces and certain pastries. Avoid ice cream, frozen desserts, whipped-cream confections, and other dairy products.

In risky regions, canned, evaporated, or condensed milk is safe only if used straight or reconstituted with boiled water. Consider bringing powdered milk to mix with boiled water.

To be free of contamination, cheese must be either made from pasteurized milk or cured for at least 60 days. In Europe, most cheeses are cured for at least that long to improve flavor. Fresh and special native cheeses similar to our cream cheese, which are not cured, are best avoided unless you're sure they came from pasteurized milk.

For infants who aren't being breast-fed, the safest and most practical food is formula prepared from commercial powder and boiled water.

TRAVELER'S DIARRHEA

Of the millions of people who travel to developing countries, about one-third get traveler's diarrhea at least once during their stay. It's usually caused by a pathogenic variant of a common bacterium that normally lives in the intestine. You can help prevent travelers' diarrhea by scrupulously observing the precautions against contaminated food and drink discussed previously.

Symptoms of traveler's diarrhea include frequent watery bowel movements and abdominal cramps, sometimes accompanied by weakness, muscle aches, dizziness, and loss of, appetite. Severe chills, high fever, nausea, vomiting, bloody stools, and dehydration usually indicate something more serious. In that case, seek medical care promptly. (Infants, toddlers, and older people in particular may become dehydrated rapidly.)

Prevent dehydration by drinking lots of fluids. Canned soup and fruit juices help offset losses of sodium and potassium in the stool. Avoid alcohol and caffeine.

As uncomfortable as it is, travelers diarrhea is rarely life-threatening. Most cases last only 1–3 days. But recurrences are possible, so before heading to a high- or intermediate-risk area, ask your doctor to prescribe an antidiarrheal product (loperamide or *Imodium A-D*, say) for mild travelers' diarrhea—and an antibiotic, in case a more severe case develops.

Bismuth subsalycilate (for instance, *Pepto-Bismol)* can prevent diarrhea in travelers who take two tablets four times a day. It does, however, turn the tongue and stools black, and it can cause mild ringing in the ears. No one should take it for more than three weeks; people who are allergic to aspirin or who take anticlotting drugs (Coumadin, Ticlid, aspirin) or who have diabetes or gout should check with their physician before using it.

INSECTS

Insects are most numerous—and most dangerous—in tropical climates. Malaria is the most common insect-borne disease, but there are also yellow fever, dengue fever, Lyme disease, and others.

A country-by-country report on the risk of malaria and other insect-borne diseases can be found in the latest edition of the Centers for Disease Control and Prevention's *Health Information for Intl Travel,* published annually (publication stock #017-023-00195-7). That comprehensive health guide can be purchased for $14 from the Superintendent of Documents, US Govt Printing Office, but it's also available via the Internet (see *Where to Find It*). Travelers can also purchase from the World Health Organization Publications

Center a copy of *Intl Travel and Health —Vaccination Requirements and Health Advice*, $13.50 plus $3 postage and handling.

To protect against mosquitoes, flies, fleas, ticks, mites, and other pests, follow these precautions:

- Sleep in an air-conditioned or well-screened bedroom, or under mosquito netting.
- Avoid insect territory from dusk to dawn.
- When you go out, cover your skin, including your feet. Avoid dark colors, which attract some insects. Wear long pants and tuck them into your boots.
- Don't use scented toiletries in insect-infested areas.
- Apply insect repellent to clothing and exposed skin. The most effective insect repellents contain "deet" (diethyltoluamide, or N,N-diethyl-meta-toluamide). However, Consumers Union's medical consultants advise against using deet-based repellents on children under 6.

  For older children, adolescents, and adults, it's usually unnecessary to use any product that contains more than 30% deet on the skin; if needed, higher concentrations can be used on clothing. Spraying clothing with permethrin *(Duranon, Permanone)* and using permethrin-impregnated mosquito netting can also be helpful.
- Shower at least daily and check for lice and ticks.
- Store food in insect-proof containers. Dispose of garbage promptly.

SEXUALLY TRANSMITTED DISEASES

With the increased prevalence worldwide of many sexually transmitted diseases (STDs), choosing a new sexual partner while traveling can be risky.

Before AIDS (acquired immune-deficiency syndrome) appeared, techniques for preventing STDs were not often discussed openly, and public awareness of the risks was low. Things have changed. Because there is not yet a cure or a vaccine for AIDS, prevention is the only way to control its spread. Other types of STDs can be successfully treated if detected early, but prevention is always better than treatment. By observing the safe-sex practices described below, one can reduce the risk of contracting any STD—including syphilis, gonorrhea, chlamydia, herpes simplex II, venereal warts, and hepatitis B, as well as infection with the human immunodeficiency virus (HIV), which causes AIDS.

- Avoid multiple, casual, or anonymous partners, prostitutes, and others who may have had multiple sex partners.
- Avoid sexual contact with a person who has genital warts, discharge, or sores.
- During intercourse (including oral-genital and anal-genital), use *latex* condoms and a spermicide. Use a water-based lubricant—not petroleum jelly—as a lubricant for the condom. Don't trust contraceptive products available abroad; bring your own.
- Consider vaccination against the hepatitis B virus (see immunization information on page 287) if you're

traveling to an area where it's endemic and you anticipate having sexual contact with residents there.

•If you engage in any high-risk sexual behavior, seek prompt medical advice.

COPING WITH CLIMATE

It doesn't have to rain every day to spoil your vacation; you could ruin it yourself with one long day in the sun. Be prepared to deal with weather extremes.

TOLERATING THE HEAT. The cardinal rule for tolerating oppressive heat is *take it easy*. Overexertion can lead to heat exhaustion or heatstroke.

The warning signs of heat exhaustion include headache, weakness, dizziness, blurred vision, cramps, and sometimes nausea and vomiting. Stop activities, get out of the sun, sip cool water, and lie down with your feet elevated until the symptoms subside; if they don't, get professional help.

Heatstroke shares many of those symptoms, but is also marked by hot, dry, flushed skin; disorientation; racing pulse; rapid breathing; and high fever. Have the victim lie down in the shade, and place cold, wet towels on the body. Seek medical care immediately.

To help shrug off the heat:

•Don't exercise during peak heat hours (generally 10 am-3 pm). Avoid the hot sun.

•Wear a broad-brimmed hat and lightweight, light-colored, loose-fitting clothing. Cotton and linen are preferable to synthetics.

•Wear cotton socks and lightweight shoes or open sandals.

•Drink plenty of fluids (but none that contain caffeine or alcohol, which can promote dehydration).

•Shower once or even several times a day (but not in very cold or hot water).

SUNBURN AND CANCER. About 90% of all skin cancers are linked to sun exposure. Fair-skinned people are the most vulnerable. Ultraviolet (UV) rays can also cause skin reactions in people taking certain drugs, including some antibiotics, diuretics, and antihypertension medication. The sun's rays—and dangers—are strongest in tropical zones and at high altitudes. But you can overdo it almost anywhere.

Sunscreens are the best defense against UV radiation. They contain one or more chemicals that absorb UV radiation before it can harm the skin. Each sunscreen carries a "Sun Protection Factor," or SPF number, which indicates the degree of protection from UV light. An SPF of 15–30 effectively blocks most UV rays.

Treat sunburn as you would other burns. First-degree sunburn can be soothed by cloths dipped in cool water, or by a cool bath with baking soda. Hydrocortisone creams and ointments may help decrease the inflammation; moisturizing lotions may also be helpful. Ibuprofen by mouth can be used for pain relief. A severe sunburn can cause fever, chills, and blistering, and usually warrants professional care.

COLD WEATHER TIPS. Extreme cold presents the twin dangers of frostbite and hypothermia (abnormally low body temperature). Anyone who is underdressed and inadequately prepared for the cold is vulnerable. Older people are especially at risk.

Frostbite results from exposure to subfreezing temperatures; the colder the temperature, the quicker and more severe the frostbite. Frostbitten skin progresses from painful to numb, turns white or bluish, and becomes firm and stiff. Do not rub the skin or thaw it with intense heat. Follow these first-aid measures:

- Gently wrap the frostbitten areas in a blanket, clothing, or newspaper.
- Find shelter immediately, preferably in a hospital. Otherwise, go indoors and start thawing immediately by immersing the frostbitten parts in warm water for up to one hour. Function, feeling, and color should return gradually. Do not touch any blisters that may appear during the warming process.
- Give acetaminophen, aspirin, or ibuprofen for pain. A hot, nonalcoholic beverage may also be useful if the victim is awake.
- After that initial thawing treatment, cover the affected skin with sterile gauze and bring the victim to a hospital.

Hypothermia is a life-threatening condition. It can result from overexposure to cold alone, and not necessarily to below-freezing temperatures. The combination of cold and wet can drastically hasten its onset.

Mental confusion is one of the most ominous symptoms of hypothermia. At the first signs—violent shivering, difficulty in walking, slurred speech—seek warmth and shelter. In a more advanced state, marked by progressive disorientation or even unconsciousness, the victim requires immediate medical help.

To avoid frostbite and hypothermia, dress warmly and stay within reach of shelter in case of emergency. Garments should be layered and loose-fitting to trap insulating pockets of air.

To protect extremities, wear thin glove liners under fur-lined or down- or synthetic-filled mittens. Shoes or boots should be loose enough to accommodate wool socks over cotton socks with a little room to spare. Wear a hat that covers the ears, a scarf, or even a face mask.

Snow presents two additional risks. Sunlight reflected off snow can burn you even more quickly than at a beach, so use sunscreen. Dark sunglasses can prevent snow blindness.

ALTITUDE PROBLEMS. Until you become acclimated to high altitudes, you may experience "mountain sickness." Symptoms include headache, nausea, shortness of breath, insomnia, fatigue, poor appetite, and mental confusion.

Acelazolamide *(Aramox)*, a prescription drug, can be used to prevent mountain sickness, though people with allergies to sulfa drugs should avoid it. Anyone with a history of heart or lung problems should consult a doctor before traveling to altitudes over 5,000 feet. Above that point, the air's oxygen content may be dangerously low for them.

FINDING MEDICAL CARE

Well-trained physicians and well-equipped hospitals can be found in most large cities worldwide, even in some of the economically underdeveloped countries of Africa, Asia, and Latin America.

The following suggestions can help you locate medical care abroad:

- In a real emergency, when minutes count, go to the nearest hospital. Transfer is always possible once an acute situation has stabilized.
- When time is less critical, find a reliable physician by checking with a hospital affiliated with a medical school or operated by the government. Medical specialty societies (French Diabetes Assn, for example) may also be able to help.
- In areas where physicians aren't connected with community or medical-school hospitals (as in Great Britain), your hotel manager may be able to direct you to a group-practice medical center or, in more remote areas, a general practitioner. If you need a specialist, those physicians can refer you to a qualified (usually hospital-based) consultant.
- If you're sick enough to require a house call, ask your hotel manager for help. Many hotels keep lists of English-speaking physicians willing to make a hotel-room call.
- If you're in a major city, contact the US embassy or consulate. Embassy personnel can refer you to English-speaking physicians who provide service for their staff.
- If there's an American military base nearby, you may be able to get reliable medical care or advice from the physicians assigned there.
- If Peace Corps representatives are nearby, check with them.

- In a remote small town or village, medical facilities may be either scarce or rudimentary, and a sick traveler may be at a loss. The hotel concierge or local police may be able to recommend a qualified practitioner.
- Consider joining the Intl Assn for Medical Assistance to Travelers (IAMAT) before you leave home. That nonprofit organization provides members with a worldwide directory of English-speaking physicians who have agreed to a set fee schedule. IAMAT also distributes a variety of helpful charts and publications on immunizations, tropical diseases, worldwide climatic and sanitary conditions, and many other travel-related health topics.

RETURNING HOME

Fever or intestinal problems that develop after you return home—even weeks or months later—may have had origins abroad. Delayed-onset illness can be caused by malaria, schistosomiasis, typhoid fever, hepatitis, sexually transmitted diseases, and certain parasitic infections. Any symptoms that occur up to six months after your return should alert you to the possibility of a travel-related illness.

WHERE TO FIND IT

The Intl Assn for Medical Assistance to Travelers (IAMAT): 417 Center St, Lewiston, NY 14092; 716-754-4883, fax 519-836-3412. Membership is free; donations are appreciated.

Medic Alert Foundation Intl: Box

1009, Turlock CA 95381; 800-763-3428 or 800-344- 3226, 209-668-3333 in CA, fax 209-669-2450. *Disc, MC, V,* money order or personal check.

US Dept of State: Travel Advisory Service, 202-647-5225.

US Govt Printing Office: Superintendent of Documents, Washington DC 20402; 202-512-1800. Have your *Visa* or *MasterCard* handy and be prepared to give the stock number of the item you're looking for.

US Public Health Service Centers for Disease Control and Prevention (CDC): Natl Center for Infectious Diseases, M/S E-03, Atlanta 30333. **CDC Intl Travelers' Hot Line:** 404-332-4559, 8:00 AM–4:30 PM, Mon-Fri. (If you have a touch-tone phone, information is available 24 hours a day.) Alternatively, access the CDC Web site at *http://www.cdc.gov/*; select the *Travelers' Health* menu, then the *Blue Sheet* option. For a fax-back copy of a current cholera, plague, and yellow-fever list, call (don't fax) 404-332-4565 and ask for *Document 220022.*

World Health Organization Publications Center: 49 Sheridan Ave, Albany NY 12210; 518-436-9686.

ROUTINE IMMUNIZATIONS

DISEASE	IMMUNIZATION TYPE	TIME REQUIRED BEFORE DEPARTURE
Tetanus, diphtheria(a)	Routine	4–6 weeks(b)
Measles(c,d)	Routine	2 weeks
Mumps(c)	Routine	2 weeks
Rubella(c)	Routine	2 weeks
Influenza(e)	Routine (for those at risk from Infection)	2 weeks
Pneumonia(f)	Routine (for those at risk from Infection)	2 weeks

(a) Combined vaccine.
(b) If time permits, consider undergoing complete basic immunization—a series of 3 injections over an 8–14-month period.
(c) Available as combined vaccine (MMR).
(d) Many parts of the US, particularly lower-income areas, experience deadly outbreaks of measles. Infants and young children are particularly vulnerable, as are unimmunized or inadequately immunized adults and those with weakened immune systems. Measles is endemic to many other parts of the world.
(e) Annual revaccination is necessary.
(f) Usually one time only, but people at high risk should be revaccinated after six years.

EMERGENCY MEDICAL RECORD

Name _____

Address _____

Blood Type _____ Rh Factor _____ Date of Birth _____

Tetanus and Diphtheria Immunization:

              Primary Series _____

                         (Date)

              Last Booster Dose _____

                         (Date)

I have these medical conditions: _____

_____

_____

I am allergic to: _____

_____

I take these drugs: Generic Name   US Trade Name   Dosage Schedule

                    _____   _____   _____

                    _____   _____   _____

                    _____   _____   _____

My medical insurance plan is: _____

My doctor is: _____

Address: _____

Phone: _____

In emergency please notify:

Address: _____

_____

Phone: _____

This Emergency Medical Record is a supplement to, and not a replacement for, the Intl Certificate of Vaccination, which may be required for entrance into certain countries (see page 285).

PACKING YOUR MEDICAL KIT: DRUGS AND SUPPLIES

The more remote your destination and the longer you'll be there, the more medications and supplies you'll want to take along. Pack all drugs safely away from heat, light, moisture—and children.

Should you need to take any prescription drugs, have your doctor prescribe or record them by their generic names, since brand names vary from country to country, and make sure that the name and strength of each medication are clearly identified on the pharmacy's original label. (Over-the-counter drugs should travel in their original containers.) If you travel with a prescription drug containing a narcotic (such as codeine), carry a copy of the prescription to satisfy customs officials.

Here are some candidates for your traveling medical kit (not all applicable for every person and destination):

Medications
Pain medication
Altitude-sickness medication
Motion-sickness preparations
Antacid
Multipurpose antibiotic
Cold remedies

Diarrhea remedies
Hydrocortisone cream
Laxative
Nausea remedies
Sedatives
Fungicidal preparations

Supplies
Adhesive bandages and tape
Alcohol
Clinical thermometer
Corn pads
Scissors
Tweezers and needle
Facial tissues, packaged moist
   towelettes

Flashlight
Condoms/contraceptives
Menstrual pads/tampons
Water heater/electric immersion*
Water purification solutions or tablets
Paper coffee filters*
Insect repellent
Snakebite kit
Sunblock

*To aid in purifying water

Directory of Toll-Free Reservation Numbers

Airlines/Tour Operators: Charter

Adventure Tours: 800-999-9046.

Ah Wee World Travel: 718-584-2100.

Airhitch: 212-864-2000 in NYC, 310-394-0550 in Santa Monica CA, 011-33-1-4700-1630 in Paris.

Amber Tours: 800-262-3701.

Char-Tours: 800-323-4444.

Club Vacations: 800-234-1700.

Council Charter: 800-800-8222, 212-661-0311.

DER Tours: 800-782-2424.

Euram Flight Center: 800-848-6789.

Fantasy Holidays: 800-645-2555, 516-935-8500.

France Vacations: 800-332-5332.

Funway Holidays Funjet: 800-558-3050.

GWV Intl: 800-225-5498.

Homeric Tours: 800-223-5570.

Hot Spot Tours: 800-433-0075; in NY area, 212-421-9090.

LTU Intl Airways: 800-888-0200.

Marcus Travel: 800-524-0821 (201-731-7600 in NJ).

Martinair Holland: 800-366-4655.

New Frontiers: 800-677-0720, 310-670-7318.

Pleasant Holidays: 800-242-9244.

Rebel Tours: 800-732-3588.

Sceptre Charters: 800-221-0924 (except NY), 718-738-9400.

Skytours: 800-246-8687 (from locations other than East Coast), 415-777-3544.

SunTrips: 800-786-8747 (CA only), 408-432-1101.

Wings of the World: 800-835-9969, 800-634-9464 (310-410-0838 in CA, 212-686-6118 in NY).

Airlines: Domestic

Air 21: 800-359-2472.

Air Canada: 800-776-3000.

Air South: 800-247-7688.

AirTran Airways: 800-247-8726.

Alaska: 800-426-0333.

Aloha: 800-367-5250.

American: 800-433-7300.

American Trans Air: 800-225-2995.

America West: 800-247-5692.

Canadian Intl: 800-426-7000.

Carnival: 800-437-2110.

Continental: 800-525-0280.

Delta: 800-221-1212.

Eastwind: 800-644-3592.

Frontier: 800-432-1359.

Hawaiian: 800-367-5320.

Horizon Air: 800-547-9308.

Jet Express: 800-386-2786.

Kiwi: 800-538-5494. (As of press time, Kiwi was closed for business; use this number for refunds.)

Laker: 888-525-3724.

Midway: 800-446-4392.

Midwest Express: 800-452-2022.

Nations Air: 800-248-9538.

Northwest: 800-225-2525.

Reno Air: 800-736-6247.

Southwest: 800-435-9792.

Spirit: 800-772-7117.

Sunair: 800-786-2476.

Sunjet Intl: 800-478-6538.

Tower: 800-221-2500, 800-348-6937 (national), 800-452-5531 (in New York).

Tristar: 800-218-8777.

TWA: 800-221-2000.

United: 800-241-6522 (national), 800-

538-2929 (international)
USAir: 800-428-4322.
ValuJet: 800-825-8538.
Vanguard: 800-826-4827.
Western Pacific: 800-930-3030.
World Airways: 800-967-5350.

AIRLINES: FOREIGN

ACES: 800-846-2237.
Aer Lingus: 800-223-6537.
Aeroflot: 800-995-5555.
Aerolineas Argentinas: 800-333-0276.
Aeromexico: 800-237-6639.
AeroPeru: 800-777-7717.
Air Caledonie/Solomon: Call APS (800-677-4277).
Air France: 800-237-2747.
Air India: 800-442-4455.
Air Inter: Call Air France (800-237-2747).
Air Jamaica: 800-523-5585.
Air Littoral: Call Air France (800-237-2747).
Air New Zealand: 800-262-1234.
Air Niugini: No toll-free number; 714-752-5440.
Air Pacific: 800-227-4446.
Air Vanuatu: Call APS (800-677-4277).
Alitalia: 800-223-5730.
Ana-All Nippon: 800-235-9262.
Ansett Australian: 800-366-1300.
Asiana: 800-227-4262.
Australian: No U.S. office.
Austrian: 800-843-0002.
Avensa: 800-428-3672.
Avianca: 800-284-2622.
Braathens SAFE: No U.S. office.
British Airways: 800-247-9297.
British Midland: 800-788-0555.
Cathay Pacific: 800-233-2742.
China (Taiwan): 800-227-5118.
Condor: 800-524-6975.

El Al: 800-223-6700.
EVA: 800-695-1188.
Faucett: 800-334-3356
Finnair: 800-950-5000.
Garuda Indonesia: 800-342-7832.
Gulfstream Intl: 800-992-8532.
Iberia: 800-772-4642.
Icelandair: 800-223-5500.
Indian: No U.S. office. (Call Air India.)
Japan (JAL): 800-525-3663.
Kenya: 800-343-2506.
KLM: 800-374-7747.
Korean: 800-438-5000.
Kuwait: 800-458-9248.
Ladeco: 800-432-2799.
LanChile: 800-735-5526.
Lloyd Aereo Boliviano: 800-327-7407.
LOT Polish: 800-223-0593.
Lufthansa: 800-581-6400.
Malaysia: 800-421-8641.
Malev: 800-262-5380.
Mexicana: 800-531-7921.
Mount Cook Airline: 800-468-2665.
Olympic: 800-223-1226.
Pakistan: 800-221-2552.
Philippine: 800-435-9725.
Polynesian: 800-592-7100.
Qantas Airways: 800-227-4500.
Royal Jordanian: 800-223-0470.
Sabena: 800-955-2000.
SAS: 800-221-2350.
Saudi: 800-472-8342.
Singapore: 800-742-3333.
Solomon/Air Caledonie: Call APS (800-677-4277).
South Africa: 800-722-9675.
Swissair: 800-221-4750.
TAP Air Portugal: 800-221-7370.
Thai Airways: 800-426-5204.
Transbrasil: 800-872-3153.
Varig Brazilian: 800-262-1706.

VASP: 800-732-8277.
Viasa: 800-892-8898.
Virgin Atlantic: 800-862-8621.

CRUISE LINES

American Canadian Caribbean Line: 800-556-7450.
American Hawaii Cruises: 800-765-7000.
Carnival Cruise Lines: 800-327-9501.
Chandris Celebrity and Fantasy Cruises: 800-437-3111.
Clipper Cruise: 800-325-0010 (314-727-2929 in MO).
Costa Cruises: 800-462-6782 (800-268-9037 in Canada).
Crystal Cruises: 800-446-6620.
Cunard Line: 800-528-6273.
Delta Queen Steamboat Co: 800-458-6789.
Discovery: 800-937-4477.
Dolphin Cruise Line: 800-222-1003.
Epirotiki Lines: 800-221-2470
Holland America Line Westours: 800-426-0327.
Norwegian: 800-262-4625.
Premier Cruise Lines: 800-327-7113.
Princess Cruises: 800-421-0522.
Renaissance Cruises: 800-525-5350.
Royal: 800-622-0538.
Royal Caribbean Cruise Line: 800-327-6700.
Royal Viking Line: 800-422-8000.
Seabourn: 800-929-9595 (individual reservations), 800-929-9696 group reservations).
Sunline: 800-872-6400.
Windjammer Barefoot: 800-327-2601.
Windstar Cruises: 800-258-7245.
World Explorer Cruises: 800-854-3835.

HOTELS/MOTELS

Admiral Benbow Inns: 800-451-1986.

AmeriSuites: 800-833-1516.
Anaheim Intl Inns & Suites: 800-251-2345.
Arborgate: 800-843-5644.
Aston: 800-922-7866.
Best Inns & Suites: 800-237-8466.
Best Western: 800-528-1234.
Budgetel Inn: 800-428-3438.
Budget Host Inns: 800-283-4678.
Canadian Pacific: 800-441-1414.
Candlewood Hotels: 800-946-6200.
Circus Circus: 800-634-3450.
Clarion: 800-424-6423.
ClubHouse Inns & Suites: 800-258-2466.
Colony: 800-777-1700.
Comfort Inns & Suites: 800-424-6423.
Concorde: 800-435-5220.
Country Hearth Inns: 888-443-2784.
Country Lodging by Carlson, Country Inns & Suites: 800-456-4000.
Country Side Inn & Suites: 800-322-9992.
Courtyard by Marriott: 800-321-2211.
Cross Country Inn: 800-621-1429.
Crowne Plaza: 800-227-6963.
Crown Sterling Suites: 800-433-4600.
Days Inns: 800-329-7466.
Doral: 800-223-6725.
Doubletree: 800-222-8733 (individual reservations), 800-233-6161 (group reservations).
Drury Inns: 800-325-8300.
Econo Lodge: 800-424-6423.
Economy Inns of America: 800-826-0778.
Embassy Suites: 800-362-2779, 800-458-4708 (hearing impaired).
Exel Inns: 800-356-8013.
Extended Stay America: 800-398-7829.
Fairfield Inn by Marriott: 800-228-2800.
Family Inns: 800-362-1188.
Forte: 800-225-5843.

Four Seasons: 800-332-3442.
Friendship Inn: 800-424-6423.
Grand Heritage: 800-437-4824.
Guest Quarters Suites by Doubletree: 800-424-2900; 800-441-1414 in Canada.
Hampton Inns & Suites: 800-426-7866.
Harley: 800-321-2323.
Harrah's: 800-447-8700.
Hawthorn Suites: 800-527-1133.
Heartland Inns: 800-334-3277.
Hilton (Intl, US, & Suites): 800-445-8667.
Holiday Inn: 800-465-4329.
Homewood Suites: 800-225-5466.
Howard Johnson/HoJo Inn: 800-446-4656.
Hyatt Hotels and Resorts: 800-233-1234.
Innkeeper: 800-466-5337.
Inns of America: 800-826-0778.
InnSuites: 800-842-4242.
Inter-Continental: 800-327-0200.
ITT Sheraton: 800-325-3535.
Knights Inns/Courts: 800-843-5644.
La Quinta: 800-531-5900.
Lexington Suites: 800-537-8483.
Loews: 800-235-6397.
MainStay Suites: 800-660-6246.
Manhattan East Suite Hotels: 800-637-8483.
Marc Resorts: 800-535-0085.
Marriott: 800-228-9290.
Masters Economy Inns: 800-633-3434.
Master Hosts Inn: 800-251-1962.
Meridien: 800-543-4300.
Motel 6: 800-466-8356.
National 9 Inns: 800-524-9999.
Nendels Inns: 800-547-0106.
Nikko: 800-645-5687.
Omni: 800-843-6664.
Outrigger: 800-462-6262.
Pan Pacific: 800-538-4040.

Park Inn: 800-437-7275.
Passport Inn: 800-251-1962.
Presidente: 800-472-2427.
Prince: 800-542-8686.
Quality Inns Hotels & Suites: 800-424-6423.
Queens Moat Houses: 800-641-0300.
Radisson: 800-333-3333.
Ramada: 800-722-9467; Ramada Limited (budget): 800-272-6232; Ramada Suites: 800-272-6232.
Red Carpet Inn: 800-251-1962.
Red Lion: 800-547-8010 (individual reservations), 800-733-5466 (group reservations).
Red Roof Inns: 800-843-7663.
Renaissance: 800-468-3571.
Residence Inn by Marriott: 800-331-3131.
Ritz-Carlton: 800-241-3333.
Rodeway Inn: 800-424-6423
Scottish Inns: 800-251-1962.
Sheraton Suites: 800-325-3535.
Shilo Inns: 800-222-2244 (800-228-4489 in British Columbia, and Alberta, Canada).
Shoney's Inn: 800-222-2222.
Sierra Suites: 800-474-3772.
Signature Inns: 800-822-5252.
Sleep Inn: 800-424-6423.
Sofitel: 800-763-4835.
Stouffer: 800-468-3571.
Studio Plus: 800-646-8000.
Summerfield Suites: 800-833-4353.
Super 8: 800-800-8000.
Susse Chalet: 800-524-2538.
Thistle and Mt Charlotte Hotels: 800-868-7285.
Thriftlodge/Travelodge: 800-578-7878.
Tokyu: 800-428-6598.
Travelers Inns: 800-633-8300.
Vagabond Inns: 800-522-1555.

Villager Lodge: 800-328-7829.
Viscount: 800-527-9666.
Vista: 800-445-8667.
Walt Disney World: 407-934-7639.
Wellesley Inns: 800-444-8888.
WestCoast: 800-426-0670.
Westin: 800-228-3000.
Wilson Inns: 800-945-7667.
Wingate Inns: 800-228-1000.
Woodfield Suites: 800-338-0008.
Woodfin Suites: 800-237-8811.
Wyndham: 800-996-3426.

RENTAL-CAR COMPANIES

A indicates a multinational rental company; *B*, an agency for European rentals; *C*, a company that handles European leases; *D*, a European renter with a US sales office; *E*, domestic rentals only. (I) = Intl reservations.

Alamo: 800-327-9633.(A)
Auto Europe: 800-223-5555. (A, B)
Avis: 800-331-1212 (US); (I) 800-331-1084. (A,C)
Bon Voyage by Car: 800-253-3876. (C)
Budget: 800-527-0700; (I) 800-472-3325. (A)
DER Tours: 800-782-2424 (B), or contact travel agent.
Dollar: 800-800-4000 (A); (I) 800-800-6000.
Enterprise: 800-325-8007. (E)
EuroDollar (Dollar in the United States): 800-800-6000. (A)

Europcar (National in the United States): 800-227-3876, 800-227-7368 in Canada. (A)
European Car Reservations (ECR): 800- 535-3303. (A,C)
Europe by Car: 800-223-1516 (800-252-9401 in MA, PA, IL, or 213-272-0424 in CA, 212-245-1713 in NY). (B,C)
Foremost Euro-Car: 800-272-3299 (800-253-3876 in Canada). (B,C)
Hertz: 800-654-3131 (national); 800-654-300 (international). (A)
Holiday Autos: 800-422-7737. (A,B,C,D)
Intl Travel Services (ITS): 800-521-0643. (B)
Kemwel: 800-678-0678. (A,B,C,D)
Kenning: 800-227-8990. (D)
National: 800-227-7368; (I) 800-227-3876. (A)
Payless: 800-237-2804. (A)
Renault Eurodrive: 800-221-1052 (800-477-7116 in the West). (C)
Thrifty: 800-367-2277. (A,C)
Town and Country Intl: 800-248-4350. (D) (England, Scotland, Wales)
Ugly Duckling: 800-843-3825. (E)
U-Save: 800-438-2300. (E)
Value: 800-327-2501, 800-468-2583, 800-327-6459 (customer relations). (E)
Woods Car Rental UK/British Network: 800-826-6245. (D)(UK only)

INDEX

AARP. *See* American Association of Retired Persons (AARP)

Access America, 278–79, 282–83

Access America International, 283

Accommodation Express, 175

Accommodations
condominium/villa rentals, 10
foreign discount lodgings.
See Foreign discount lodgings
hotels. *See* Hotels
motels. *See* Motels
timeshares, 5, 164–65

Accor's, 222

ACES, 57

Admiral Benbow Inns, 194–95

Aer Lingus, 79, 87, 91

Aeroflot, 80

Aerolineas Argentinas, 86, 87

AeroMexico, 80

AeroPeru, 80

Air Canada, 80, 87, 94–95, 100, 102–103, 107, 108, 116–17, 118, 120, 122, 124

Airfares, 1–2, 43–57
back-to-back tickets, 49
charge cards, miles earned through
See Travel cards
charter flights, 46–47, 73–75
club discounts, 14
compassionate, 48–49, 94–95
consolidator tickets. *See* Consolidators
courier travel, 51–52
discount coupons, 47–48
discounters of. *See* Discounters of airline tickets
frequent-flier coupons, 50
frequent-flier programs. *See* Frequent-flier programs
hidden-city ploys, 49–50
hubbing reductions, 47
low-fare airlines, 44–46
1997 outlook, 2–3, 5
overseas, 202–11
premium seats, 50–54
rebates, 48

recognizing bargains, 43
sales fares, 43–44
for seniors, 48, 90–97
standby, 53, 55–56
status airfares, 48–49, 90–97
twofers, 48, 57

Air France, 79, 83, 86, 87

Airhitch, 55–56

Air India, 52, 80, 87, 91, 99

Air Jamaica, 79

Air New Zealand, 80, 86, 87

Air Pacific, 87

Airport hub survival guide, 122, 124–26

Airport lounge clubs, 113–26
benefits of, 113–15
cost of, 116–17
locations, 117–25
Priority Pass program, 114
value to you, determining, 117, 122

Airport shuttles, 127–45
arranging your trip, 129
cautions, 128
fares, 128–29
how they work, 127–28
listings by airport, 132–41
listings by city, 129–45
tipping, 128

Airport Transit Guide, 208

Air South, 45, 57, 112

AirTran Airways, 45, 57, 79

Air travel
airfares. *See* Airfares
comfortable seating, 50–54
Business or First Class, 52–53, 85–89
on charters, 56–57, 84
in coach, 51, 76, 77–85
empty seats, next to, 84–85
frequent-flier miles for free premium seats, 53–54
mileage upgrades, 54, 104, 106
by plane model, 83–84
premium Economy cabins, 51–52
purchased upgrades, 54

seats to try for, 77–78
twofers, 57
very frequent flier upgrades, 54–56
yardsticks of comfort, 76–77
empty seats, seating near, 84–85
frail elderly, 97
hub survival guide, 122, 124–26
lounges. *See* Airport lounge clubs
off-season, 15
overseas, 202–11
toll-free reservation numbers, 300–304
unaccompanied minors, 96–97
Air 21, 45, 57
Alamo, 112, 150, 153, 230, 232, 233, 235, 236, 237, 238, 254
Alaska Airlines, 40, 79, 94–95, 97, 100, 101, 103, 107, 108, 115, 116–17
Alitalia, 79, 86, 87
All Nippon, 80, 87
Aloha Airlines, 80, 116–17
Altitude problems, coping with, 295
American Airlines, 40, 79, 80, 91, 94–95, 99, 100, 103, 107, 108, 116–17, 118, 120, 123,125
American Association of Retired Persons (AARP), 16, 160
hotel discounts through, 193–99
American Automobile Association (AAA), 160, 244, 264
American Express, 148–49, 150
mileage and hotel credits earned with charge card, 32–34, 103
traveler's checks, 264–65, 274
travel insurance, 278, 283
American Society of Travel Agents (ASTA), 25, 28
American Trans Air, 45, 57, 80, 83, 92, 94–95
America Tele-fone, 273
America West, 80, 91, 94–95, 97, 99, 103, 107, 108, 116–17, 118, 120, 122, 124
Amerihost Inn, 194–95
AmeriSuites, 194–95
Amtrak, 15, 156–58
Ansett Australian, 86, 87
Asia
airfares to, 202–208
airfares within, 208–09, 211
hotel discounts. *See* Foreign discount lodgings

rail passes, 256–61
Aston, 194–95
AT&T, 37, 110–11, 270, 271, 274
ATM cards, 263–64
Australia and the Pacific
airfares to, 202–208
airfares with, 209–10
hotel discounts. *See* Foreign discount lodgings
rail passes, 259–61
Austrian Airlines, 80, 87
Auto Europe, 230–38, 254
Automobile rentals. *See* Car rentals
Avis, 153, 230–38

Baggage, 5, 267–68
Balair, 57
Benelux Tourail Pass, 242–43, 250
Berkeley Arm Carefree, 278
Best Inns, 182–83, 186–87, 188–89
Best Inns & Suites, 194–95
Best Western, 182–83, 186–87, 188–89, 194–95
Bon Voyage by Car, 230–35, 237–38, 254
British Airways, 80, 86, 87–88, 91
British Midland, 88
Britrail Pass, 92, 242–43, 246–47
Budget car rental, 112, 153, 230–38, 254
Budgetel, 182–83, 186–87, 188–89, 190, 191

California Reservations, 175
Canadian International, 80, 86, 88, 94–95, 100, 101, 102, 104, 107, 116–17, 118, 120, 122, 123, 125
Canadian Pacific, 194–95
Candlewood, 194–95
Canrailpass, 155–56
Carnival Air Lines, 45, 52, 57, 80, 112
Car rentals, 2, 3–4, 14, 146–54
additional drivers, 147, 148
collision insurance, 5, 148–50
computer searches for best rates, 147
dangerous, 152
documentation, 150–51
driving record, check of your, 152–53
in Europe, 3–4, 225–44, 254
age limits, 242
airport surcharges, 239

booking and pickup, 240, 242, 244
combining rail and, 225, 246
currency for payment, 227–28
driving permit, 244
dual rates, 227
French leases, 229, 240
geographic limits, 240
highway fee, 239–40
insurance, 229, 239
model selection, 228–29
one-way rentals, 228
payment at end of rental, 227–28
prepaying in full, 227–28
rail versus, 225–26, 227
value added tax, 226–27
weekly touring rates, 226–27, 230–38
fuel tank, filling the, 151
geographic limits, 151
hidden extras, 147–50
insurance, 148–50
liability insurance, 150
mileage limits, 151
off-season, 15
one-way drop-off, 151–52
promotions, 146
redlining, 151
senior discounts, 147
toll-free reservation numbers, 304
upgrades, 148
weekend rates, 147
Carte Royale, 169, 172, 214, 215, 216, 219, 220, 223
Cathay Pacific, 80, 83, 88, 99
Cellular phone rentals overseas, 270–71
Center Reservation System (CRS), 176
Centers for Disease Control (CDC), 285, 292
Charge and credit cards, 263
CDW/LDW coverage, 39, 148–49, 227
discounters of airline tickets and, 62
frequent-flier credit earned with.
See Travel cards
Charter flights, 46–47, 73–75, 84
advantages of, 73
buying tickets for, 74–75
disadvantages of, 73–74
distinguishing characteristics of, 74

list of sellers, 75
premium seating on, 56–57
Children
airfares, 93–94
unaccompanied minors, air travel by, 96–97
See also Infants; Youth
China Airline, 80, 88
Cholera vaccine, 286
Citizens Emergency Center, 273–74
Clarion Hotels, 194–95
Climate, coping with, 294–95
ClubHouse Inn, 188–89, 190, 191
ClubHouse Inns & Suites, 194–95
Clubrooms, airport. See Airport lounge clubs
Clubs, travel, 12–15, 18–20, 48, 161
Cold weather tips, 294–95
Collision insurance, 5, 39, 148–50, 227
Colony Inns and Suites, 194–95
Compassionate airfares, 48–49, 94–95
Complaints, package tour, 23, 25
Condominium rentals, 10
Condor, 56, 57
Consolidators, 3, 47, 58–72, 207
Business and First Class tickets, 60
defined, 7, 59
disadvantages of tickets from, 60–61
overseas, 210–11
pricing of tickets by airlines to, 58
for travel agents only, 59, 70–72
Consular information sheets, 262–63
Consumer Reports Travel Letter (CRTL), 6, 76–77, 100, 128, 150, 155, 225, 274
Contact lenses, 285
Continental Airlines, 81, 86, 88, 91, 92, 94–95, 101, 103, 104, 107, 109, 111, 112, 116–17, 119, 121, 123, 125
Freedom Passport, 92–93
Council Travel, 92
Country Hearth Inns, 194–95
Country Inns & Suites, 194–95
Country Side Inn & Suites, 194–95
Courier travel, 51–52
Courtyard, 182–83, 186–87, 188–89, 190, 191, 194–95
Credit cards. See Charge and credit cards
Cross Country Inns, 182–83, 186–87, 188–189, 190, 191, 196–97

Crowne Plaza, 194–95
Cruise Lines International Association (CLIA), 27
Cruises, 25–28
    cabin selection, 26
    charge cards earning credits for, 33, 41
    club discounts, 14
    destinations, 25–26
    early booking, 25, 27
    extras, 28
    guidebooks, 26
    1997 outlook, 4–5
    singles travel, 17
    telephone service, 274
    tipping, 28
    toll-free reservation numbers, 302
    travel agencies selling, 26–27, 29–30
    upgrading your cabin, 27–28
CSA, 279, 283
CSA Czech, 81
Currency exchange, 267–68

Days Inn, 194–95
Delta Airlines, 81, 86, 88, 91, 95–96, 101, 104, 106, 107, 116–17, 119, 121
Dental visits, 284–85
DERCar, 230, 231, 232, 233, 234, 235, 236, 237, 238
Destination Europe, 270
Diarrhea, traveler's, 292
Diners Club, 32, 34, 100, 149, 150, 266
Dining discounts, clubs featuring, 14
Discounters of airline tickets, 58–72
    Business and First Class tickets, 60
    consolidators. *See* Consolidators
    directory of, 62–70
        for travel agents only, 70–72
    disadvantages of tickets from, 60–61
    discount fare defined, 61
    frequent-flier credit, 59
    making your deal, 61–62
    savings to expect, 59–60
Discover Card, 149, 150
Dollar Rent a Car, 154, 226
Doubletree, 194–95
Drury Inn, 182–83, 186–87, 188–89, 190, 194–95
Duty-free goods, 268–69

Eastwind, 45, 57
Econo Lodge, 194–95, 200
El Al, 53, 57, 81, 88, 91
Emergency medical evacuation (EME) insurance, 275–83, 289
Encore, 169, 172, 213, 216, 219, 220, 223
Enterprise car rental, 154
Entertainment Europe Hotel Directory, 213
Entertainment Publications, 169–71, 172, 213, 216, 217, 219, 220, 223
Eurail Guide, 229
Eurail Guide to World Train Travel, 258
Eurailpass, 92, 240–41, 246
EuroDollar, 226, 230, 231, 232, 233, 234, 235, 236, 237, 238, 254
EuroPass, 227, 240–41, 242–43
Europcar, 226, 230, 231, 232, 233, 234, 235, 236, 237, 238, 254
Europe
    air travel to, 202–209
    air travel within, 208–209
    car rentals in. *See* Car rentals, in Europe
    hotel discounts. *See* Foreign discount lodgings
    rail travel. *See* Rail travel in Europe
    visitor airfares, 207–11
European Car Reservations, 254
European East Pass, 242–43, 250
Europe by Car, 230, 231, 232, 233, 234, 235, 236, 237, 238, 254
EVA, 51–52, 57, 81, 83, 88
Exel Inn, 182–83, 186–87, 188–89, 190, 194–95
Express Reservations, 176
Eyeglasses, 285
Fairfield Inn, 182–83, 186–87, 188–89, 190, 191, 194–95
Family Inns, 194–95
Finnair, 81, 83, 88
Fodor's, 176
Food
    on package tours, 24
    safety of food supply, 291–92
Foreign discount lodgings, 212–24
    budget motels, 220–23
    half-price programs, 212–20
    list-price bargains, 218–20
    1997 outlook, 4

personal best buy, 220

France, discount lodgings in, 218, 219–20
  See also Foreign discount lodgings

Frequent-flier programs, 98–112
  advantages and disadvantages of, 106–107, 110–11
  blackouts and limits, 102, 104
  charge cards, earning miles with. *See* Travel cards
  consolidator tickets that earn mileage, 59
  credit required for free trips, 108–109
  destinations, 100–101
  earning credit, 100–106
  finding a seat, 106
  longevity of mileage, 102–105
  maximizing mileage benefits, 102
  nonairline partners, 99–100
  partner companies, 99, 100, 101
  payoff percentages, 181
  rating, 98–100
  on smaller lines, 112
  telephone companies, earning credit with, 37, 110–111
  upgrading your seat, 53–56, 104, 106
  very frequent flier, 3, 54–56
  upgrades, 54–56, 104, 106

Frequent-stay programs. *See* Hotels, frequent-stay programs

Frontier Airlines, 45, 57, 81, 112

Global Emergency Medical Services, 280, 283
Globaltel, 273
Going Solo, 18
Golf, 14, 41
Granada Inns, 220
Grand Heritage, 194–95
Great American Traveler, 171, 172, 215, 217, 219, 220, 223
Groupe Envergure, 222–23

Hawaii, 41
Hawaiian Airlines, 52–53, 57, 81, 112, 116–17, 119, 121
Hawaiian hotel chain, 182–83, 186–87, 188–89, 191
Health Care Abroad, 280, 283
Heartland Inns, 194–95

Heat, coping with the, 294
Hepatitis A vaccine, 286–87
Hepatitis B vaccine, 287, 293–294
Hertz, 112, 154, 230, 231, 232, 233, 234, 235, 236, 237, 238, 254
Hilton, 182–83, 186–87, 188–89
Holiday Autos, 230, 231, 232, 233, 234, 235, 236, 237, 238, 254
Holiday Inn, 182–83, 186–87, 188–189, 190, 191, 194–95
Hotel and Travel Index, 220
Hotel brokers, 4, 174–79
  arranging the discount, 174–75
  local, 177–78
  multicity specialists, 175–76
Hotel Reservations Network (HRN), 176
Hotels, 2, 159–201
  charge cards, 33
  corporate rates, 160
  decoding OHG ratings, 162–63
  direct discounts, forms of, 159–60
  foreign discount lodgings. *See* Foreign discount lodgings
  frequent-stay programs, 186–92
    awards and payoffs, 184–89
    earning credit, 184–89
    membership benefits, 188–90
    ratings, 190
    smaller companies with, 192
  half-price, 166–73
  money exchange, 266
  1997 outlook, 4, 5
  off-season rates, 15–16
  package tours, 24
  picking, 161–66
  preferred rates, 160–61
  private channels for room deals, 159
  public channels for room deals, 159
  senior discounts, 193–201
  toll-free reservation numbers, 302–304
Hotels & Compagnie, 222
Howard Johnson, 182–83, 186–87, 188–89, 190, 191, 194–95
Hubs, airline
  fare reductions, 47
  survival guide, 122, 124
Hyatt, 182–83, 186–87, 190, 196–97

Iberia, 801
Icelandair, 81, 202–203
Immunizations, 285–89, 298
Impulse, 172, 173
India, rail travel in, 257
Infants
    air travel by, 93–94
    vaccinations, 285
Infosys America Inc., 274
Innkeeper, 196–97
Inns of American, 196–97
InnSuites, 196–97
Insects, 292–93
Institute of Certified Travel Agents (ICTA), 8
Insurance
    car rental
        CDW/LDW coverage, 5, 148–50, 227, 239
        liability, 149–50
        theft, 227
    emergency medical evacuation (EME), 275–83, 289
    other travel policies, 277–78
    trip cancellation or interruption (TCI), 275–83
International Airline Passenger Association (IAPA), 161
International Driving Permit (IDP), 244
International SOS Assistance, 280, 281
International Telephone, 273
Interworld, 211
ITC-50, 172, 173, 213, 217, 219, 220, 223
ITS, 230, 231, 232, 233, 234, 235, 236, 237

Japan, rail travel in, 3, 257–58
Japan Airlines, 88
Japanese encephalitis, 287
Jet Express, 45, 57
Jettrain, 57

Kemwel, 230, 231, 232, 233, 234, 235, 236, 237, 288, 254
Kenning, 226, 234, 236, 238, 254
Kimpton, 196–97
Kiwi, 45, 51, 57, 81
KLM, 88
Knights Inns, 196–97
Korean Airlines, 81

Ladeco, 81, 83
LanChile, 81, 86
La Quinta, 182–83, 186–87, 188–89, 190, 196–97
Latin America
    airfares to, 204–205
    hotel discounts. See Foreign discount lodgings
Little Chef Lodges, 220–21
Lot Polish, 81
Lounge clubs. See Airport lounge clubs
LTU, 81, 91, 203–205
Lufthansa, 81, 86, 88, 91
Luggage, 267–68
    designer, 5

MainStay Suites, 196–97
Malaria, 287–88
Malaysia, rail travel in, 258–59
Marc Resorts, 196–97
Markair, 81
Marriott, 182–83, 186–87, 188–89, 190, 196–97
Martinair, 56, 57, 81, 89, 205–206
MasterCard, 149–50, 152
Master Hosts Inn, 196–97
Masters Economy Inns, 182–83, 186–87, 188–89, 191, 196–97
MCI, 37, 110, 111, 271, 274
Measles vaccine, 289
Medic Alert Foundation International, 289
Medical matters, 284–99
    common-sense guide while away, 290–96
    emergency medical evacuation insurance, 275–83, 289
    immunizations, 285–89
    medical care abroad, finding, 295–96
    medical kit, 289–90, 299
    medical records, 284, 289, 298
    on returning home, 296
    travel advisory service, 290
    trip cancellation or interruption insurance, 275–83
    before you go, 284–90
Meridien, 182–83, 186–87, 188–89, 190
Midway, 46, 57, 81, 92, 112
Midwest Express, 51, 57, 79, 81, 82, 92, 94–95, 101, 104, 107, 109

Money matters, 263–67, 274
Motels
    European budget, 220–23
    toll-free reservation numbers, 302–304
    U.S. budget, 4
Motel 6, 196–97
Mutual of Omaha, 282

National Association of Cruise-Only Agencies (NACOA), 27
National car rental, 154, 226
National Hotel & Dining Directory, 212
National Tour Association (NTA), 25, 28
Nationwide, 148
New Zealand, rail travel in, 260–61
Northwest Airlines, 40, 57, 81–82, 86, 89, 91, 94–96, 110, 101, 105, 109, 116–17, 119, 121, 125

OAG Electronic Edition Travel Service, 274
Official Airline Guide, 79, 83, 86, 122, 125
Official Hotel Guide (OHG), 161–64, 220
Off-season travel, 15–16
Omni, 182–83, 186–87, 188–89, 190, 191, 196–97
Outrigger, 196–97

Pacific, the. See Australia and the Pacific
Package tours, 21–25
    airline travel, 23
    basic, 21
    cancellations, 23
    choosing, 22
    club discounts, 14
    complaints, 23, 25
    consumer protection, 24–25
    documents, 23
    escorted, 21–22
    the fine print, 25–28
    food, 24
    hotels, 24
    inclusions and exclusions, 23–24
    independent travel, 22
    itineraries, 24
    itinerary changes, 23
    no-smoking, 24
    operators, 28

price changes, 22–23
    singles travel, 17
    toll-free reservation numbers, 300
Pakistan Airlines, 83
Pan Am, 112
Paris Airport Service, 208
Parker Company, 270–71
Payless Car Rental, 154, 200, 234, 254
Philippine Airlines, 82, 99
Physical examination, 284
Plague vaccine, 288
Players Express Vacations, 176
Polio vaccine, 288
Prestige Airways, 57
Prime Call, 273
Privilege Card, 172, 173, 214, 215, 216, 219, 220, 223
Public Health Service, US, 290
    Quarantine Station, 285

Qantas, 82, 86, 89, 99
Quality Inns & Suites, 196–97
Quest, 172, 173
Quikbook, 176

Radisson, 196–97
Rail travel in Europe, 3, 92, 240–55
    breakeven miles, 241–47, 249, 251, 253, 254
    combining car rental and, 225, 246
    companion passes, 246–47
    couple discounts, 252–54
    First Class versus Second Class, 239
    flexible passes, 246
    full time rail passes, 246
    guides, 229
    multinational, 240–45
    national passes, 246–53
    senior discounts, 248, 252–53
    timetable, 229
    youth/student discounts, 248, 252, 254
Rail travel in Japan, 3
Rail travel in U.S. and Canada, 155–58
    to airports, 129
    off-season, 15
Ramada, 182–83, 186–87, 188–89, 190, 191, 196–97
Rebel Tours, 57

Red Carpet Inn, 196–97
Red Lion, 182–83, 186–87, 188–89, 191, 196–97
Red Roof Inns, 198–99
Renaissance, 182–83, 186–87, 188–89, 191, 196–97
Renault Eurodrive, 254
Reno Air, 46, 57, 82, 92, 94–96, 112
RMC Travel, 176–77
Roadside services, clubs featuring, 14
Rodeway Inn, 196–97
Room Finders USA, 176
Royal Jordanian, 82
Ruesch International, 264, 265, 266, 274

Sabena, 82
SAS, 82
Scanrail Pass, 242–43, 250
Scottish Inns, 196–97
See America, 172, 173
Senior citizens
    car rental discounts, 147
    frail elderly, air travel by, 97
    hotel discounts, 193–201
    organizations offering travel benefits to, 16, 193, 201
    status airfares for, 48, 90–93, 94–95
Sexually transmitted diseases, 293–94
Sheraton, 182–83, 186–87, 188–89, 190, 196–97
Shilo Inns & Resorts, 196–97
Shoney's Inn, 196–97, 200
Shuttles, airport. *See* Airport shuttles
Sierra Suites, 196–97
Signature Inns, 196–97
Singapore Airlines, 82, 86, 89, 99
Singles travel, 17–18, 20
Sleep Inn, 196–97
Small Luxury Hotels of the World, 192
Sofitel, 182–83, 186–87, 188–89, 190
Southwest Airlines, 2, 61, 82, 92, 94–95 96, 112
Spinal meningitis vaccine, 288
Spirit Airlines, 46, 57, 82
Sprint, 37, 110, 111, 270, 271, 274
Standby airfares, 53, 55–56
Star Service, 220
State Department, U.S.
    consular information sheets, 262–63, 273–74
    travel warnings, 262, 290
State Farm, 148
Students
    low airfares for, 93, 94–95
    rail discounts in Europe, 246, 252–54
Summerfield Suites, 182–83, 186–87, 188–89, 196–97
Sumner Suites, 198–199
Sunair, 46, 57
Sun exposure and skin cancer, 294
Sunhitch, 55–56
Sunjet International, 46, 57
Super 8, 198–99
Susse Chalet, 182–83, 186–87, 188–89, 190, 191, 198–99
Swissair, 82, 86, 89

TAP Air Portugal, 82, 89
Teachers, low airfares for, 92
Telephone calls, 269–73
Tetanus-diphtheria shot, 289
Thai Airlines, 82, 89
Thailand, rail travel in, 259
Thomas Cook Currency Services, 265, 266, 274
"Thomas Cook European Timetable," 229
Thomas Cook Overseas Timetable, 258
Thrifty car rental, 154, 234, 235, 236, 237, 238, 254
Timeshares, 5, 164–65
TML Information Services, 153
Toll-free reservation numbers, directory of, 300–304
Top 10 travel deals for 1997, 2–5
Tower Air, 46, 52, 56, 57, 82, 206
Town and Country International, 226, 254
Travel agents and agencies
    consolidators selling only to, 59, 70–72
    as consultants, 8
    credentials, 8
    cruises sold through, 26–27
    fee-based, 8
    rebating, 8–12, 18, 48
    selecting, 7–8, 10–11
Travel Assure, 282
Travel cards, 31–42
    airline, 31, 35–36, 100
    bank, 31–32, 35–38, 48

dining cards, 39–42
fees and features, 34–39
recommendations, 42
special-interest, 41
travel and entertainment, 32–34, 37–38
Travelers, The, 279, 283
Traveler's checks, 264–65, 265–66
Travel Guard, 279, 283
Travel Guard Gold, 279, 282, 283
Travel Insurance Service, 283
Travelodge, 182–83, 186–87, 188–89, 190, 191, 198–99
Travelers Inns, 198–199
Travel warnings, State Department, 262, 290
Trip cancellation insurance (TCI), 275–83
Tristar, 46, 57
TWA, 51, 55, 57, 79, 83, 86, 89, 91–92, 93, 94–95, 99, 101, 105, 109, 112, 113, 116–17, 119, 121, 123, 125
Typhoid fever vaccine, 288–89

United Airlines, 57, 82, 83, 86, 89, 91, 94–95, 101, 105, 109, 116–17, 119, 121, 123, 125
United States Tour Operators Association (USTO), 24, 25
United States Tour Operators Association (USTOA), 28–29
USAir, 82, 89, 91, 94–95, 101, 105, 106, 109, 112, 113, 116–17, 119, 121

Vaccinations, 286–89, 298
Vagabond Inns, 182–83, 186–87, 188–89, 190, 198–99

Value-added tax (VAT)
    on European car rentals, 226–27
    refunds, 266–67
ValuJet, 3, 46, 57, 82
Vanguard Airlines, 46, 57, 82, 112
Varig, 89
VASP, 82
Very frequent flier programs. See Frequent-flier programs, very frequent flier
Virgin Atlantic, 52, 79, 82, 83, 86, 89, 207
Visa, 148, 150, 264, 265
Visitor airfares, 207–10

Wake-up calls, Weather Channel, 161
Walt Disney World Magic, 198–99
Water supplies, safe, 290–91
Weather Channel wake-up calls, 161
Wellesley Inns, 198–99
WestCoast, 198–99
Western Pacific Airlines, 46, 57
Westin, 182–83, 186–87, 188–189, 190
Wilson Inns, 198–99
Wingate Inns, 198–99
Woods Car Rental, 226, 238, 254
World Airways, 53, 57
Worldwide Assistance, 283
Worst travel deals for 1997, 5
Wyndham, 198–99

Yellow-fever vaccine, 289
Youth
    airfares, 93
    rail discounts in Europe, 246, 248, 252–54
    See also Children; Infants